FAMILIES, INDIVIDUALS, AND MARRIAGE

FAMILIES, INDIVIDUALS, AND MARRIAGE

SECOND EDITION

Michael J. Sporakowski

Virginia Polytechnic Institute and State University

Mary W. Hicks

Florida State University

KENDALL/HUNT PUBLISHING COMPANY
DUBUQUE, IOWA

Contents

Section IV Sex Is a Many Splendored Thing—Sometimes!

Section V Survival of the Fit

Introduction

This volume grew out of frustration with conventional text material in the "marriage area." It probably will ask more questions than it can possibly answer, but then we view that as growth. Although some research creeps in from time to time, most of what it contains is thought and humor—by our standards anyway. We see this book as a supplement to good teaching. Besides the readings, as you will see, there are "Rip Offs." These questions are meant to have our classes be ongoing research, an integral part of our teaching. Not only will the data be useful in the class you are in, but they will be useful to succeeding classes for comparative purposes. And, too, it will often be a good jumping off point for our discussions.

Since neither of us has tried a book of our own before, we have learned a lot in putting this one together. And to all who helped, thanks, even if we do not spell you out one by one.

PREFACE TO SECOND EDITION

Response to our first efforts with this text has been very favorable. In this second edition we have tried to eliminate out-of-date materials and bolster several areas that required some additional consideration. A significant addition is the appendix which contains early descriptive data from "rip offs" which, hopefully, will be useful in classroom comparisons and discussions.

Michael J. Sporakowski
Mary W. Hicks

Name: _____   Date: _____

Student #: _____   Sex: M or F

Curriculum: _____

Year: _____

Age: _____

Race: _____

1. Are you a member of a church or synagogue? Yes ____ No ____

2. What is your religious preference or affiliation?

    Specify _____

3. About how often do you attend Church services?

    ____ never

    ____ less than once a month

    ____ once or twice a month

    ____ three or four times a month

    ____ at least once a week

4. At what age did you have your first real date? _____

5. At what age did you start dating regularly? _____

6. Estimate the total number of people you have dated.

    ____ less than 10

    ____ between 10 and 20

    ____ between 21 and 40

    ____ more than 40

7. Estimate the proportion of time that you have gone steady since you began dating.

    ____ never

    ____ less than 1/4 of the time

    ____ 1/4 to 1/2 of the time

    ____ over 1/2 of the time

8. Where is your home?

    (Check one) ____ country, ____ small town, ____ city.

9. How would you rate your own sexual attitudes?

    ____ very liberal

    ____ somewhat liberal

    ____ moderate

    ____ somewhat conservative

    ____ very conservative

10. What is your marital status?

_____single

_____going steady

_____engaged

_____married

_____divorced, widowed, separated

_____remarried

11. What is your parent's marital status?

_____married

_____divorced

_____separated

_____widowed

_____remarried

12. How would you rate the happiness of your parent's marriage?

_____very happy

_____more happy than the average

_____average

_____more unhappy than the average

_____very unhappy

13. Mother's highest educational attainment: (circle one)

| 1 2 3 4 5 6 7 8 9 | 10 11 12 | 1 2 3 4 | Indicate advanced degrees |
| Grade School | High School | College | or years past college: _____ |

14. Father's highest educational attainment: (circle one)

| 1 2 3 4 5 6 7 8 9 | 10 11 12 | 1 2 3 4 | Indicate advanced degrees |
| Grade School | High School | College | or years past college: _____ |

15. Number of sisters you have: _____

16. Number of brothers you have: _____

Section I

FAMILIES IN THE U.S.: WHERE THEY'RE AT
Mary W. Hicks

In the 1970's, as in past decades, the same question is being raised. Will the family survive as the primary social system in the twenty-first century? Answers to this question vary with the source of facts about the immediate future of the family as an institution, and with the interpretation particular sociologists wish to make about these facts.

Pessimists, in answer to this question, quote the data of doom which consistently support the notion that the family is a disintegrating institution. They point to a key issue like divorce, for example, where the data show that one in four U.S. marriages eventually ends in divorce, and the rate is rising dramatically for marriages made in the past several years. Since 1967 the divorce rate has increased by 30%; and in some densely populated West Coast communities, according to the last census, is running as high as 75%. Further, the rate of divorce among those married under 18 is close to 50%. Data, such as these, support social science conclusions that the family is crumbling and will not survive in the twenty-first century.

Quite a different answer is given by the optimists who maintain that marriage continues to be the most popular voluntary institution in our society with only three or four percent of the population never marrying at least once. The U.S., they tell us, is probably the most marriage-and-home oriented nation in the modern world. In the 1960's the number of families grew at a greater rate than the population, and 87% of Americans live in families which include both parents. True, the divorce rate is rising, but so is the rate of remarriage among divorced people. There are, in other words, fewer people who never marry and more multiple marriages. Accordingly, the institution of marriage is as important as it ever was.

It seems likely that at the present time this controversy cannot be completely resolved—very probably neither side is right or wrong. It may well be, as Toffler has suggested, that the family will "neither vanish nor enter a new Golden Age."* It may be, as he suggests, that the family will break up only to come together in new structures quite different from those of the past. In this section, the first article deals with family strengths as seen by family members themselves; and the second delineates some of the novel forms the American family may have in the future.

Articles

1. Herbert A. Otto—What Is a Strong Family?
2. Alvin Toffler—The Fractured Family.

* Toffler, Alvin, *Future Shock,* New York, Bantam Books, 1971, p. 239.

3

Name: _____   Date:_____

Student #:_____   Sex: M or F

1. The following are what I consider to be the major strengths of the family in which I grew up.

2. The following are social forces which I believe will have major impact on the family of the future.

3. I believe the family of the future will be different from the family of the present in the following specific ways.

4. All persons should be encouraged to marry. Yes_____ No_____ If yes, why? If no, go to #5.

5. If your answer is "No," who should not be encouraged to marry? Why?

WHAT IS A STRONG FAMILY?

Herbert A. Otto

Very often, teachers, social workers and members of other helping professions, as well as lay persons, describe a family as being a "good" family—or a "strong" family. Their comments might lead to the assumption that they had some specific "good" qualities or "strengths" in mind. A closer examination, however, reveals considerable confusion and lack of clarity about the meaning of family strengths. Not only is there considerable confusion on this point on the part of those observing families, but it has been found that most families are not too clear about what may be their own strengths.

Currently in a series of research projects at the Graduate School of Social Work, University of Utah, we have been exploring this area. These projects are entitled "The Family Resource Development Project" and "The Personal Resource Development Project." The purpose of this research is to seek some answers to the following questions:

1. What are individual and family strengths?

2. How do we help individuals and families recognize and utilize their strengths and resources more fully?

3. How do we work with strengths?

In this article we will confine our discussion to the first of these questions.

As part of these research projects, a pilot study was conducted to find what families considered their strengths to be. A total of twenty-seven families filled in the Family Strength Questionnaire which asked them to respond to this open-ended item, "The following are what we consider to be major strengths in our family:_____." The blank lines were to be filled in. The questionnaire was filled in by both husband and wife in consultation with each other.

The following list indicates what the families considered to be their strengths and the number of times these strengths were mentioned:

a. Shared faith, religious and moral values . . 22

b. Love, consideration and understanding . . 17

c. Common interests, goals and purpose . . . 15

d. Love and happiness of children 13

e. Working and playing together 10

f. Sharing specific recreational activities . . . 10

g. Being in accord on discipline 5

h. Respect for individuality of family members 5

i. Shared sense of humor 4

j. Enjoying companionship 4

k. Good health 4

l. Desire for learning and education 4

m. Miscellaneous 34

Total 147

The twenty-seven families listed a total of only one hundred forty-seven strengths with an average of only five strengths for each family. The large number of families (twenty-two) listing "Shared faith, religious and moral values" as a strength is not surprising, as all families were church affiliated. The large number of "Miscellaneous" strengths indicates that families vary considerably as to what they consider strengths. Such items as "homemaking," "intelligence," "financial solvency," "acceptance of each other's limitations," and "trying new things" were some of the "Miscellaneous" strengths. Other "Miscellaneous" strengths were "agreement on expenditures," "trusting each other," "shared family traditions," and "liking people."

An outgrowth of the pilot study was the development of a framework of family strengths. It is presented in the hope that it will contribute toward a clarification of the concept of family strengths.

The dictionary defines strength as the "quality or state of being strong; ability to do or bear; solidity or toughness; that quality which tends to secure results."

The assumption can be made that "the quality of strength" is the end result of certain interacting components or factors which produce this quality. Family strength is, therefore, seen as the end product of a series of ever-changing factors or components. These components must be seen as fluid, interacting and related. They are not independent but interrelated, and variations in these abilities, capacities, or strengths occur throughout the life cycle of the family. The components are defined as "strengths" but with the recognition that, as an aggregate, they result in "Family Strength."

Reprinted from Herbert A. Otto, "What is a Strong Family," *Marriage and Family Living,* February, 1962, pp. 77-80. Reprinted by permission of The National Council on Family Relations.

What, then, were the components as indicated by these twenty-seven families? Eleven different ones were distinguished. Each will be noted and some brief comments made about it. Family strength may be composed of:

1. *The ability to provide for the physical, emotional, and spiritual needs of a family.*

Ability to provide for the family's physical needs implies not merely provision of food and shelter. There is the matter of management as well. For example, from the humblest home to the mansion, the way the physical space is used may be constructive and creative or restrictive. The living parlor or the out-of-bounds dining room for children comes to mind immediately.

Similarly, qualitative differences are distinguished in a family's preparation and use of food. Some families purchase, plan and prepare meals together and make this "fun" as well as educational. These seemingly mundane functions can represent both a strength, and a strengthening process. Finally, as a part of providing for the family's physical needs, health is included as a strength, and it is recognized that providing for family health is a strengthening process.

Providing for the emotional needs of the family includes the giving of affection or love, understanding, and trust. This is seen as a two-way process, with parents providing for the emotional needs of the children and the children also giving to the parents.

The ability to provide for the spiritual needs of the family includes the sharing of basic beliefs, and spiritual or religious values, as well as sharing the doubts and concerns about religious beliefs. Providing an environment of honesty and integrity is a family strength.

2. *The ability to be sensitive to the needs of family members.*

This includes sensitivity of the husband to the wife's needs. The children's sensitivity to the needs of parents is also seen as a strength.

Wives often seem to be more sensitive to the needs of husbands than husbands are to the needs of their wives. Frequently we hear wives make remarks such as this—"Darling, you have worked so hard lately. What you need is some quiet time—why not go fishing?"

More rarely husbands will comment—"I know this daily grind with children and housework is getting you down. What you need is more adult company. Let's do something about it."

3. *The ability to communicate.*

The ability to communicate in depth with each other—express both a wide range of emotions and feelings, as well as to communicate ideas, concepts, beliefs, and values, is a family strength. Communication is seen as including verbal expression as well as sensitive listening.

For example, if a family can communicate and share the depth of feeling and thought occasioned by a beautiful sunrise or sunset, this is a strength as well as a strengthening process. Also, children try out their "intellectual muscles" by communicating newly acquired ideas and beliefs to the family. Some parents will respond negatively. "Where did you pick up these *strange* ideas? That's a lot of nonsense!" Other parents will encourage their children to communicate and think independently by saying, "Isn't this an interesting idea! Now let's follow through and see where it leads us."

4. *The ability to provide support, security and encouragement.*

Giving family members a feeling of security, the sense that the family is "behind them" with moral and other support, providing them with encouragement in their various endeavors, is a source of family strength. Especially important is encouragement to seek new areas of growth, to develop creativity, imagination, and independent thinking.

One family held periodic "creativity sessions" during which family members were urged to think up new and better ways to improve family living. New ideas on furniture arrangement, interior decorations and food preparation were encouraged, and family problems were "brainstormed."

5. *The ability to establish and maintain growth-producing relationships within and without the family.*

The ability of family members to relate to each other and other persons so as to produce maximum growth and maturation is considered a family strength. Implicit is the concept that interpersonal relationships are the major media of personality growth, and that the apex of creativity in interpersonal relations is to stimulate and encourage other persons to grow and to make fuller use of their potential.

Examples of growth relationships can be found at all age levels. One six-year-old, for instance, told her mother, "Mommie, I talked and talked to Ruthie and told her animals hurt like we do, and she said she would stop hitting and hurting animals. Then we went and gave her dollie a good spanking."

6. *The capacity to maintain and create constuctive and responsible community relationships in the neighborhood and in the school, town, local and state governments.*

It is a family strength to assume responsibility and leadership in relation to local, social, cultural, and political organizations and activities. This implies involvement, membership, or active participation and interest, on a selective basis, in relation to these areas.

7. *The ability to grow with and through children.*

When parents can actively utilize their relationships with their children as a means of growth and maturation, this can be called a strength. For example, one mother, member of a P.T.A. group, said, "my child has taught me more about telling the truth and how we really feel, than anything ever has. She will come right out and tell you things that no adult would tell you. This is the type of honesty we need."

8. *An ability for self-help, and the ability to accept help when appropriate.*

Strength lies not only in the family's ability to help itself, but also in the capacity to accept and seek help when needed. Such help might be proffered or sought from agencies, organizations, individuals, or professional sources.

9. *An ability to perform family roles flexibly.*

It is strength when family members can "fill in" and assume each other's roles as needed. For example, a father can function as a "mother" and children can temporarily be "parents" to their father and mother.

10. *Mutual respect for the individuality of family members.*

When family members are recognized, respected and treated as individuals, rather than as stereotypes or categories, this is a strength. Parents are not only "daddies" and "mommies" or seen as providers and "doers for children," but are recognized as individuals and persons in their own right who need to be treated as such. Similarly, children are not only "the baby" or "the oldest." They have their own distinct individuality which, unfortunately, is often obscured by such categorization. One father illustrated this by saying, "We kept calling our youngest 'the baby' when he wasn't a baby any more. This kept him back. When we stopped this he really bloomed."

11. *A concern for family unity, loyalty, and interfamily cooperation.*

Although these qualities can be considered as outcomes of family strengths, the presence of these factors is also seen as a family strength.

In understanding a family, more than the total range of family strengths should be taken into consideration. It should be recognized that strength factors can, in certain situations and circumstances, become an impediment or detract from the effective functioning of the family. For example, a family which sees self-help as a major strength may, rather than call on outside help, wrestle with a problem for a long period of time with a consequent stultifying and discouraging effect on family members. This even though using such outside help would have led to a much more productive solution to the problem both in terms of effort, time, and overall effect on the family. Lack of flexibility in the use of a strength has, therefore, resulted in an impediment.

Finally, family strengths are not isolated variables, but form clusters or constellations which are dynamic, fluid, interrelated, and interacting. Current and past literature, with a few exceptions, reflects much emphasis and study of pathology of the family and pathological processes within the family. However, by extending our understanding and knowledge of what we mean by family strengths and resources, we are in a better position to help families in the development of their strengths, resources, and potentialities.

THE FRACTURED FAMILY

Alvin Toffler

The flood of novelty about to crash down upon us will spread from universities and research centers to factories and offices, from the marketplace and mass media into our social relationships, from the community into the home. Penetrating deep into our private lives, it will place absolutely unprecedented strains on the family itself.

The family has been called *"the giant shock absorber"* of society—the place to which the bruised and battered individual returns after doing battle with the world, the one stable point in an increasingly flux-filled environment. As the super-industrial revolution unfolds, this "shock absorber" will come in for some shock of its own.

Social critics have a field day speculating about the family. The *family is "near the point of complete extinction,"* says Ferdinand Lundberg, author of The Coming World Transformation. "The family is dead except for the first year or two of child raising," according to psychoanalyst *William Wolf.* "This will be its only function." Pessimists tell us the family is racing toward oblivion—but seldom tell us what will take its place.

Family optimists, in contrast, contend that the family, having existed all this time, will continue to exist. Some go so far as to argue that the family is in for a Golden Age. As leisure spreads, they theorize, families will spend more time together and will derive great satisfaction from joint activity. "The family that plays together, stays together," etc.

A more sophisticated view holds that the very turbulence of tomorrow will drive people deeper into their families. "People will marry for stable structure," says Dr. Irwin M. Greenberg, Professor of Psychiatry at the Albert Einstein College of Medicine. According to his view, *the family serves as one's "portable roots,"* anchoring against the storm of change. In short, the more transient and novel the environment, the more important the family will become.

It may be that both sides in this debate are wrong. For the future is more open than it might appear. The family may neither vanish nor enter upon a new Golden Age. It may—and this is far more likely—break up, shatter, only to come together again in weird and novel ways.

THE MYSTIQUE OF MOTHERHOOD

The most obviously upsetting force likely to strike the family in the decades immediately ahead will be the impact of the new birth technology. The ability to pre-set the sex of one's baby, or even to "program" its IQ, looks and personality traits, must now be regarded as a real possibility. Embryo implants, babies grown *in vitro,* the ability to swallow a pill and guarantee oneself twins or triplets or, even more, the ability to walk into a "babytorium" and actually purchase embryos—all this reaches so far beyond any previous human experience that one needs to look at the future through the eyes of the poet or painter, rather than those of the sociologist or conventional philosopher.

It is regarded as somehow unscholarly, even frivolous, to discuss these matters. Yet advances in science and technology, or in reproductive biology alone, could, within a short time, smash all orthodox ideas about the family and its responsibilities. When babies can be grown in a laboratory jar what happens to the very notion of maternity? And what happens to the self-image of the female in societies which, since the very beginnings of man, have taught her that her primary mission is the propagation of and nurture of the race?

Few social scientists have begun as yet to concern themselves with such questions. One who has is psychiatrist Hyman G. Weitzen, director of Neuropsychiatric Service at Polyclinic Hospital in New York. The cycle of birth, Dr. Weitzen suggests, "fulfills for most women a major creative need. . . Most women are proud of their ability to bear children. . . The special aura that glorifies the pregnant woman has figured largely in the art and literature of both East and West."

What happens to the cult of motherhood, Weitzen asks, if "her offspring might literally not be hers, but that of a genetically 'superior' ovum, implanted in her womb from another woman, or even grown in a Petri dish?" If women are to be important at all, he suggests, it will no longer be because they alone can bear children. If nothing else, we are about to kill off the mystique of motherhood.

Not merely motherhood, but the concept of parenthood itself may be in for radical revision. Indeed, the day may soon dawn when it is possible for a child to have more than two biological parents. Dr. Beatrice Mintz, a developmental biologist at the Institute for Cancer Research in Philadelphia, has grown what are coming to be known as "multi-mice"—baby mice each of which has more than the usual number of parents. Embryos are taken from each of two pregnant mice. These embryos are placed in a laboratory dish and nurtured until they form a single growing mass. This is then implanted in the womb of a third female mouse. A baby is born that clearly shares the genetic characteristics of both sets of donors. Thus a typical multi-mouse, born of two pairs of parents, has white fur and whiskers on one side of its face, dark fur and whiskers on the other, with alternating bands of white and dark hair covering the rest of the body. Some 700 multi-mice bred in this fashion have already produced more than 35,000 offspring themselves. If multi-mouse is here, can a "multi-man" be far behind?

Under such circumstances, what or who is a parent? When a woman bears in her uterus an embryo conceived in another woman's womb, who is the mother? And just exactly who is the father?

If a couple can actually purchase an embryo, then parenthood becomes a legal, not a biological matter. Unless such transactions are tightly controlled, one can imagine such grotesqueries as a couple buying an embryo, raising it *in vitro*, then buying another in the name of the first, as though for a trust fund. In that case, they might be regarded as legal "grandparents" before their first child is out of it's infancy. We shall need a whole new vocabulary to describe kinship ties.

Furthermore, if embryos are for sale, can a corporation buy one? Can it buy ten thousand? Can it resell them? And if not a corporation, how about a non-commercial research laboratory? If we buy and sell living embryos, are we back to a new form of slavery? Such are the nightmarish questions soon to be debated by us. To continue to think of the family, therefore, in purely conventional terms is to defy all reason.

Faced by rapid social change and the staggering implications of the scientific revolution, super-industrial man may be forced to experiment with novel family forms. Innovative minorities can be expected to try out a colorful variety of family arrangements. They will begin by tinkering with existing forms.

THE STREAMLINED FAMILY

One simple thing they will do is streamline the family. The typical pre-industrial family not only had a good many children, but numerous other dependents as well—grandparents, uncles, aunts, and cousins. Such "extended" families were well suited for survival in slow-paced agricultural societies. But such families are hard to transport or transplant. They are immobile.

Industrialism demanded masses of workers ready and able to move off the land in pursuit of jobs, and to move again whenever necessary. Thus the extended family gradually shed its excess weight and the so-called "nuclear" family emerged—a stripped-down, portable family unit consisting only of parents and a small set of children. This new style family, far more mobile than the traditional extended family, became the standard model in all the industrial countries.

Super-industrialism, however, the next stage of eco-technological development, requires even higher mobility. Thus we may expect many among the people of the future to carry the streamlining process a step further by remaining childless, cutting the family down to its most elemental compoents, a man and a woman. Two people, perhaps with matched careers, will prove more efficient at navigating through education and social shoals, through job changes and geographic relocations, than the ordinary child-cluttered family. Indeed, anthropologist Margaret Mead has pointed out that we may already be moving toward a system under which, as she puts it, "parenthood would be limited to a smaller number of families who principal functions would be childbearing," leaving the rest of the population "free to function for the first time in history—as individuals."

A compromise may be the postponement of children, rather than childlessness. Men and women today are often torn in conflict between a commitment to career and a commitment to children. In the future, many couples will sidestep this problem by deferring the entire task of raising children until after retirement.

This may strike people of the present as odd.

Yet once childbearing is broken away from its biological base, nothing more than tradition suggests having children at an early age. Why not wait, and buy your embryos later, after your work career is over? Thus childlessness is likely to spread among young and middleaged couples; sexagenarians who raise infants may be far more common. The post-retirement family could be a recognized social institution.

BIO-PARENTS AND PRO-PARENTS

If a smaller number of families raise children, however, why do the children have to be their own? Why not a system under which "professional parents" take on the childrearing function for others?

Raising children after all, requires skills that are by no means universal. We don't let "just anyone" perform brain surgery or, for that matter, sell stocks and bonds. Even the lowest ranking civil servant is required to pass tests proving competence. Yet we allow virtually anyone, almost without regard for mental or moral qualification to try his or her hand at raising young human beings, so long as these humans are biological offspring. Despite the increasing complexity of the task, parenthood remains the greatest single preserve of the amateur.

As the present system cracks and the super-industrial revolution rolls over us, as the armies of juvenile delinquents swell, as hundreds of thousands of students flee their homes, and students rampage at universities in all the techno-societies, we can expect vociferous demands for *an end to parental dilettantism.*

There are far better ways to cope with the problems of youth, but professional parenthood is certain to be proposed, if only because it fits so perfectly with the society's overall push toward specialization. Moreover, there is a powerful, pent-up demand for this social innovation. Even now millions of parents, given the opportunity, would happily relinquish their parental responsibilities—and not necessarily through irresponsibility or lack of love. Harried, frenzied, up against the wall, they have come to see themselves as inadequate to the tasks. Given affluence and the existence of specially-equipped and licensed professional parents, many of today's biological parents would not only gladly surrender their children to them, but would look upon it as an act of love, rather than rejection.

Parental professionals would not be therapists, but actual family units assigned to, and well paid for, rearing children. Such families might be multi-generational in design, offering children in them an opportunity to observe and learn from a variety of adult models, as was the case in the old farm homestead. With the adults paid to be professional parents, they would be freed of the occupational necessity to relocate repeatedly. Such families would take in new children as old ones "graduate" so that age-segregation would be minimized.

Thus newspapers of the future might well carry advertisements addressed to young married couples: "Why let parenthood tie you down? Let us raise your infant into a responsible, successful adult. Class A Pro-family offers: Father age 39, mother, 36, grandmother, 67. Uncle and aunt, age 30, live in, hold part-time local employment. Four-*child-unit* has opening for one, age 6-8. Regulated diet exceeds governmental standards. All adults certified in child development and management. Bio-parents permitted frequent visits. Telephone contact allowed. Child may spend summer vacation with bio-parents. Religion, art, music encouraged by special arrangement. Five year contract, minimum. Write for further details."

The "real" or "bio-parents" could, as the add suggests, fill the role presently played by interested godparents, namely that of friendly and helpful outsiders. In such a way, the society could continue to breed a wide diversity of genetic types, yet turn the care of children over to mother-father groups who are *equipped,* both intellectually and emotionally, for the task of caring for kids.

COMMUNES AND HOMOSEXUAL DADDIES

Quite a different alternative lies in the communal family. As transience increases the loneliness and alienation in society, we can anticipate increasing experimentation with various forms of group marriage. The banding together of several adults and children into a single "family" provides a kind of insurance against isolation. Even if one or two members of the household leave, the remaining members have one another. Communes are springing up modeled after those described by psychologist B.F. Skinner in *Walden Two* and by novelist Robert Rimmer in the *Harrad Experiment and Proposition 31.* In the latter work, Rimmer seriously proposes the legalization of a "corporate family" in which from three to six adults adopt a single name, live and raise children in common, and legally incorporate to obtain certain economic and tax advantages.

According to some observers, there are already hundreds of open or covert communes dotting the American map. Not all, by any means, are composed of young people or hippies. Some are organized around specific goals—like the group, quietly financed by three East Coast colleges—which has taken as its function the task of counseling college freshmen, helping to orient them to campus life. The goals may be social, religious, political, even recreational. Thus we shall before long begin to see communal families of surfers dotting the beaches of California and Southern France, if they don't already. We shall see the emergence of communes based on political doctrines and religious faiths. In Denmark, a bill to legalize group marriage has already been introduced in the Folketing (Parliament). While passage is not imminent, the act of introduction is itself a significant symbol of change.

In Chicago, 250 adults and children already live together in "family-style monasticism" under the auspices of a new, fast growing religious organization, the Ecumenical Institute. Members share the same quarters, cook and eat together, worship and tend children in common, and pool their incomes. At least 60,000 people have taken "EI" courses and similar communes have begun to spring up in Atlanta, Boston, Los Angeles and other cities. "A brand-new world is emerging," says Professor Joseph W. Mathews, leader of the Ecumenical Institute, "but people are still operating in terms of the old one. We seek to re-educate people and give them the tools to build a new social context."

Still another type of family unit likely to win adherents in the future might be called the "geriatric commune"—a group marriage of elderly people drawn together in a common search for companionship and assistance. Disengaged from the productive economy that makes mobility necessary, they will settle in a single place, band together, pool funds, collectively hire domestic or nursing help, and proceed—within limits—to have the "time of their lives."

Communalism runs counter to the pressure for ever greater geographical and social mobility generated by the thrust toward super-industrialism. It presupposes groups of people who "stay put." For this reason, communal experiments will first proliferate among those in the society who are free from the industrial discipline—the retired population, the young, the dropouts, the students, as well as among self-employed professional and technical people. Later, when advanced technology and information systems make it possible for much of the work of society to be done at home via computer-telecommunication hookups, communalism will become feasible for larger numbers.

We shall, however, also see many more "family" units consisting of a single unmarried adult and one or more children. Nor will all of these adults be women. It is already possible in some places for unmarried men to adopt children. In 1965 in Oregon, for example, a thirty-eight-year-old musician named Tony Piazza became the first unmarried man in that state, and perhaps in the United States, to be granted the right to adopt a baby. Courts are more readily granting custody to divorced fathers too. In London, photographer Michael Copper, married at twenty and divorced soon after, won the right to raise his infant son, and expressed an interest in adopting other children. Observing that he did not particularly wish to remarry, but that he liked children, Cooper mused aloud: "I wish you could just ask beautiful women to have babies for you. Or any woman you liked, or who had something you admired. Ideally, I'd like a big house full of children—all different colors, shapes and sizes." Romantic? Unmanly? Perhaps. Yet attitudes like these will be widely held by men in the future.

Two pressures are even now softening up the culture, preparing it for acceptance of the idea of childrearing by men. First, adoptable children are in oversupply in some places. Thus, in California, disc jockeys blare commercials: "We have many wonderful babies of all races and nationalities waiting to bring love and happiness to the right families...Call the Los Angeles County Bureau of Adoption." At the same time, the mass media, in a strange nonconspiratorial fashion, appear to have decided simultaneously that men who raise children hold special interest for the public. Extremely popular television shows in recent seasons have glamorized womanless households in which men scrub floors, cook, and, most significantly, raise children: *My Three Sons, The Rifleman, Bonanza* and *Bachelor Father* are four examples.

As homosexuality becomes more socially acceptable, we may even begin to find families based on homosexual "marriages" with the partners adopting children. Whether these children would be of the same or opposite sex remains to be seen. But the rapidity with which homosexuality is winning respectability in the techno-societies distinctly points in this direction. In Holland not long ago a Catholic priest "married" two homosexuals, explaining to critics that "they are among the faithful to be helped." England has rewritten its relevant legislation; homosexual relations between consenting adults are no longer considered a crime. And in the United States a meeting of Episcopal clergymen concluded publicly that homosexuality might, under certain circumstances, be judged "good." The day may also come when a court decides that a couple of stable, well educated homosexuals might make decent "parents."

We might also see the gradual relaxation of bars against polygamy. Polygamous families exist even now, more widely than generally believed, in the midst of "normal" society. Writer Ben Merson, after visiting several such families in Utah where polygamy is still regarded as essential by certain Mormon fundamentalists, estimated that there are some 30,000 people living in underground family units of this type in the United States. As sexual attitudes loosen up, as property rights become less important because of rising affluence, the social repression of polygamy may come to be regarded as irrational. This shift may be facilitated by the very mobility that compels men to spend considerable time away from their present homes. The old male fantasy of the Captain's Paradise may become a reality for some, although it is likely that, under such circumstances, the wives left behind will demand extramarital sexual rights. Yesterday's captain would hardly consider this possibility. Tomorrow's may feel quite differently about it.

Still another family form is even now springing up in our midst, a novel childrearing unit that I call the "aggregate family"—a family based on relationships between divorced and remarried couples, in which all the children become part of "one big family." Though sociologists have paid little attention as yet to this phenomenon, it is already so prevalent that it formed the basis for a hilarious scene in a recent American movie entitled Divorce American Style. We may expect aggregate families to take on increasing importance in the decades ahead.

Childless marriage, professional parenthood, post-retirement childrearing, corporate families, communes, geriatric group marriages, homosexual family units, polygamy—these, then, are a few of the family forms and practices with which innovative minorities will experiment in the decades ahead. Not all of us, however, will be willing to participate in such experimentation. What of the majority?

THE ODDS AGAINST LOVE

Minorities experiment; majorities cling to the forms of the past. It is safe to say that large numbers of people will refuse to jettison the conventional idea of marriage or the familiar family forms. They will, no doubt, continue searching for happiness within the orthodox format. Yet, even they will be forced to innovate in the end, for the odds against success may prove overwhelming.

The orthodox format presupposes that two young people will "find" one another and marry. It presupposes that the two will fulfill certain psychological needs in one another, and that the two personalities will develop over the years, more or less in tandem, so that they continue to fulfill each other's needs. It further presupposes that this process will last "until death do us part."

These expectations are built deeply into our culture. (It is no longer respectable, as it once was, to marry for anything but love.) *Love has changed from a peripheral* concern of the family into its primary justification. Indeed, the pursuit of love through family life has become, for many, the very purpose of life itself.

Love, however, is defined in terms of this notion of *shared growth*. It is seen as a beautiful mesh of complementary needs, flowing into and out of one another, fulfilling the loved ones, and producing feelings of warmth, tenderness and devotion. Unhappy husbands often complain that they have "left their wives behind" in terms of social, educational or intellectual growth. Partners in successful marriages are said to "grow together."

This "parallel development" theory of love carries endorsement from marriage counsellors, psychologists and sociologists. Thus, says sociologist Nelson Foote, a specialist on the family, the quality of the relationship between husband and wife is dependent upon "the degree of matching in their phases of distinct but comparable development."

If love is a product of shared growth, however, and we are to measure success in marriage by the degree to which matched development actually occurs, it becomes possible to make a strong and ominous prediction about the future.

It is possible to demonstrate that, even in a relatively stagnant society, the mathematical odds are heavily stacked against any couple achieving this ideal of parallel growth. The odds for success positively plummet, however, when the rate of change in society accelerates, as it now is doing. In a fast-moving society, in which many things change, not once, but repeatedly, in which the husband moves up and down a variety of economic and social scales, in which the family is again and again torn loose from home and community, in which individuals move further from their parents, further from the religion of origin, and further from traditional values, it is almost miraculous if two people develop at anything like comparable rates.

If, at the same time, average life expectancy rises from, say, fifty to seventy years, thereby lengthening the term during which this acrobatic feat of matched development is supposed to be maintained, the odds against success become absolutely astronomical. Thus, Nelson Foote writes with wry understatement: To expect a marriage to last indefinitely under modern conditions is to expect a lot." To ask love to last *indefinitely* is to expect even more. *Transience* and *novelty* are both in a league against it.

TEMPORARY MARRIAGE

It is this change in the statistical odds against love that accounts for the high divorce and separation rates in most of the techno-societies. The faster rate of change and the longer life span, the worse these odds grow. Something has to crack.

In point of fact, of course, something has already cracked—and it is the old insistence on permanence. Millions of men and women now adopt what appears to them to be a sensible and conservative strategy. Rather than opting for some off-beat variey of the family, they marry conventionally, they attempt to make it "work," and then, when the path of the partners diverge beyond an acceptable point, they divorce or depart. Most of them go on to search for a new partner whose developmental stage, at that moment, matches their own.

As human relationships grow more transient and modular, the *pursuit of love* becomes, if anything, more frenzied. But the temporal expectations change. As conventional marriage proves itself less and less capable of delivering on its promise of lifelong love, therefore, we can anticipate open public acceptance of temporary marriages. Instead of wedding "until death do us part," couples will enter into matrimony knowing from the first that the relationship is likely to be short-lived.

They will know, too, that when the paths of husband and wife diverge, when there is too great a discrepancy in developmental stages, they may call it quits—without shock or embarrassment, perhaps even without some of the pain that goes with divorce today. And when the opportunity presents itself, they will marry again...and again...and again.

Serial marriage—a pattern of successive temporary marriages—is cut to order for the *Age of Transience* in which all man's relationships, all his ties with the environment, shrink in duration. It is the natural, the inevitable outgrowth of a social order in which automobiles are rented, dolls traded in, and dresses discarded after one-time use. It is the mainstream marriage pattern of tomorrow.

In one sense, serial marriage is already the best kept family secret of the techno-societies. According to Professor Jessie Bernard, a world-prominent family sociologist, "Plural marriage is more extensive in our society today than it is in societies that permit polygamy—the chief difference being that we have institutionalized plural marriage serially or sequentially rather than contemporaneously." (Remarriage is already so prevalent a practice that nearly one out of every four bridegrooms in America has been to the altar before.) It is so prevalent that one IBM personnel man reports a poignant incident involving a divorced women, who, in filling out a job application, paused when she came to the question of marital status. She put her pencil in her mouth, pondered for a moment, then wrote: *"Unremarried."*

Transience necessarily affects the durational expectancies with which persons approach new situations. While they may yearn for a permanent relationship, something inside whispers to them that it is an increasingly improbable luxury.

Even young people who most passionately seek commitment, profound involvement with people and causes, recognize the power of the thrust toward transience. Listen, for example, to a young black American, civil-rights worker, as she describes her attitude toward time and marriage:

"In the white world, marriage is always billed as "the end"—like in a Hollywood movie. I don't go for that. I can't imagine myself promising my whole lifetime away. I might want to get married now, but how about next year? That's not disrespect for the institution (of marriage), but the deepest respect. In The (civil rights) Movement, you need to have a feeling for the temporary—of making something as good as you can, while it lasts. In conventional relationships, time is a prison."

Such attitudes will not be confined to the young, the few, or the politically active. They will whip acorss nations as novelty floods into the society and catch fire as the level of transience rises still higher. And along with them will come a sharp increase in the number of temporary—then serial—marriages.

The idea is summed up vividly by a Swedish magazine, Svensk Damtidning, which interviewed a number of leading Sedish sociologists, legal experts, and others about the future of man-woman relationships. It presented its findings in five photographs. They showed the same beautiful bride being carried across the threshold five times—*by five different bridegrooms.*

MARRIAGE TRAJECTORIES

As serial marriages become more common, we shall begin to characterize people not in terms of their present marital status, but in terms of their *marriage career or "trajectory."* This trajectory will be formed by the decisions they make at certain vital turning points in their lives.

For most people, the first such juncture will arrive in youth, when they enter into "trial marriage." Even now the young people of the United States and Europe are engaged in a mass experiment with probationary marriage, with or without benefit of ceremony. The staidest of United States universities are beginning to wink at the practice of co-ed housekeeping among their students. Acceptance of trial marriage is even growing among certain religious philosophers. Thus we hear the German theologian Siegfried Keil of Marburg Univeristy urge what he terms "recognized premarriage." In Canada, Father Jacques Lazure has publicly proposed "probationary marriages" of three to eighteen months.

In the past, social pressures and lack of money restricted experimentation with trial marriage to a relative handful. In the future, both these limiting forces will evaporate. Trial marriage will be the first step in the serial marriage "careers" that millions will pursue.

A second critical life juncture for the people of the future will occur when the trial marriage ends. At this point, couples may choose to formalize their relationhip and stay together into the next stage. Or they may terminate it and seek out new partners. In either case, they will then face several options. They may prefer to go childless. They may choose to have, adopt or "buy" one or more children. They may decide to raise these children themselves or to farm them out to professional parents. Such decisions will be made, by and large, in the early twenties—by which time many young adults will already be well into their second marriages.

A third significant turning point in the marital career will come, as it does today, when the children finally leave home. The end of parenthood proves excruciating for many, particularly women who, once the children are gone, find themselves without a *raison d'etre.* Even today divorces result from the failure of the couple to adapt to this traumatic break in continuity.

Among the more conventional couples of tomorrow who choose to raise their own children in the time-honored fashion, this will continue to be a particularly painful time. It will, however, strike earlier. (Young people today already leave home sooner than their counterparts a generation ago. They will probably depart even earlier tomorrow.) Masses of youngsters will move off, whether into trial marriage or not, in their mid-teens. Thus we may anticipate that the middle and late thirties will be another important breakpoint in the marital careers of millions. Many at that juncture will enter into their third marriage.

This third marriage will bring together two people for what could well turn out to be the longest uninterrupted stretch of matrimony in their lives—from, say, the late thirties until one of the partners dies. This may, in fact, turn out to be the only "real" marriage, the basis of the only truly durable marital relationship. During this time two mature people, presumably with well-matched interest and complementary psychological needs, and with a sense of being at comparable stages of personality development, will be able to look forward to a relationship with a decent statistical probability of enduring.

Not all these marriages will survive until death, however, for the family will still face a fourth crisis point. This will come, as it does now for many, when one or both of the parents retires from work. The abrupt change in daily routine brought about by this development places great strain on the couple. Some couples will go the path of the post-retirement family, choosing this moment to begin the task of raising children. This may overcome for them the vacuum that so many couples now face after reaching the end of their occupational lives. (Today many women go to work when they finish raising children; tomorrow many will reverse the pattern, working first and childrearing next.) Other couples will overcome the crisis of retirement in other ways, fashioning both together a new set of habits, interests and activities. Still others will find the transition too difficult, and will simply sever their ties and enter the pool of "in-betweens"—the floating reserve of temporarily unmarried persons.

Of course, there will be some who, through luck, interpersonal skill and high intelligence will find it possible to make long-lasting monogamous marriages work. Some will succeed, as they do today, in marrying for life and finding durable love and affection. But others will fail to make even sequential marriages endure for long. Thus some will try two or even three partners within, say, the final stage of marriage. Across the board, the average number of marriages per capita will rise—slowly but relentlessly.

Most people will probably move forward along this progression, engaging in one "conventional" temporary marriage after another. But with widespread familial experimentation in the society, the more daring or desperate will make side forays into less conventional arrangements as well, perhaps experimenting with communal life at some point, or going it alone with a child. The net result will be a rich variation in the types of marital trajectories that people will trace, a wider choice of life-patterns, an endless opportunity for novelty of experience. Certain patterns will be more common than others. But temporary marriage will be a standard feature, perhaps the dominant feature, of family life in the future.

THE DEMANDS OF FREEDOM

A world in which marriage is temporary rather than permanent, in which family arrangements are diverse and colorful, in which homosexuals may be acceptable parents and retirees start raising children—such a world is vastly different from our own. Today all boys and girls are expected to find life-long partners. In tomorrow's world, being single will be no crime. Nor will couples be forced to remain imprisoned, as so many still are today, in marriages that have turned rancid. Divorce will be easy to arrange, so long as responsible provision is made for children. In fact, the very introduction of professional parenthood could touch off a great liberating wave of divorces by making it easier for adults to discharge their parental responsibilities without necessarily remaining in the cage of a hateful marriage. With this powerful external pressure removed, those who stay together would be those who wish to stay together, those for whom marriage is actively fulfilling—those, in short, who are in love.

We are also likely to see, under this looser, more variegated family system, many more marriages involving partners of unequal age. Increasingly, older men will marry young girls or vice versa. What will count will not be chronological age, but complementary values and interests and, above all, the level of personal development. To put it another way, partners will be interested not in age, but in stage.

Children in this super-industrial society will grow up with an ever enlarging circle of what might be called "semi-siblings"—a whole clan of boys and girls brought into the world by their successive sets of parents. What becomes of such "aggregate" families will be fascinating to observe. Semi-Sibs may turn out to be like cousins, today. They may help one another professionally or in time of need. But they will also present the society with novel problems. Should semi-sibs marry, for example?

Surely, the whole relationship of the child to the family will be dramatically altered. Except perhaps in communal groupings, the family will lose what little remains of its power to transmit values to the younger generation. This will further accelerate the pace of change and intensify the problems that go with it.

Looming over all such changes, however, and even dwarfing them in significance is something far more subtle. Seldom discussed, there is a hidden rhythm in human affairs that until now has served as one of the key stabilizing forces in society: the family cycle.

We begin as children; we mature; we leave the parental nest; we give birth to children who, in turn grow up, leave and begin the process all over again. This cycle has been operating so long, so automatically, and with such implacable regularity, that men have taken it for granted. It is part of the human landscape. Long before they reach puberty, children learn the part they are expected to play in keeping this great cycle turning. This predictable succession of family events has provided all men, of whatever tribe or society, with a sense of continuity, a place in the temporal scheme of things. The family cycle has been one of the sanity-preserving constants in human existence.

Today this cycle is accelerating. We grow up sooner, leave home sooner, marry sooner, nave children sooner. We space them more closely together and complete the period of parenthood more quickly. In the words of Dr. Bernice Neugarten, a University of Chicago specialist on family development, "The trend is toward a more rapid rhythm of events through most of the family cycle."

But if industrialism, with its faster pace of life, has accelerated the family cycle, super-industrialism now threatens to smash it altogether. With the fantasies that the birth scientists are hammering into reality, with the colorful familial experimentation that innovative minorities will perform, with the likely development of such institutions as professional parenthood, with the increasing movement toward temporary and serial marriage, we shall not merely run the cycle more rapidly; we shall introduce irregularity, suspense, unpredictability—in a word, novelty—into what was once as regular and certain as the seasons.

When a "mother" can compress the process of birth into a brief visit to an *embryo emporium,* when by transferring embryos from womb to womb we can destroy even the ancient certainty that childbearing took nine months, children will grow up into a world in which the family cycle, once so smooth and sure, will be jerkily arhythmic. Another crucial stabilizer will have been removed from the wreckage of the old order, another pillar of sanity broken.

There is, of course, nothing inevitable about the developments traced in the preceding pages. We have it in our power to shape change. We may choose one future over another. We cannot, however, maintain the past. In our family forms, as in our economics, science, technology and social relationships, we shall be forced to deal with the new.

The Super-industrial Revolution will liberate men from many of the barbarisms that grew out of the restrictive, relatively choiceless family patterns of the past and present. It will offer to each a degree of freedom hitherto unknown. But it will exact a steep price for that freedom.

As we hurtle into tomorrow, millions of ordinary men and women will face emotion-packed options so unfamiliar, so untested, that past experience will offer little clue to wisdom. In their family ties, as in all other aspects of their lives, they will be compelled to cope not merely with transience, but with the added problem of novelty as well.

Thus, in matters both large and small, in the most public of conflicts and the most private of conditions, the balance between routine and nonroutine, predictable and nonpredictable, the known and the unknown, will be altered. The novelty ratio will rise.

In such an environment, fast-changing and unfamiliar, we shall be forced, as we wend our way through life, to make our personal choices from a diverse array of options. And it is to the third central characteristic of tomorrow, *diversity,* that we must now turn. For it is the final convergence of these three factors—transience, novelty and diversity—that sets the stage for the historic crisis of adaptation that is the subject of this book: future shock.

Section II

DEAR ABBY...
Mary W. Hicks

Available evidence points to some rather dramatic shifts in courtship behavior. Whether these shifts reflect current changes in the institution of marriage, or whether the institution of marriage is changing as a reflection of the shifts in courtship behavior is an important, though perhaps unanswerable, question. Contemporary courtship patterns do, though, point to a change in perspectives on the nature of the relationship between the sexes which must inevitably have some impact on the institution of marriage.

Disillusionment with the traditional marriage relationship seems rather common among college youth. In an attempt to improve this relationship, students are showing a growing interest in restructuring the mate selection process and the traditional monogamous conjugal marriage. They claim that there can be no justification for continued insistence on the forms of marriage and courtship they have inherited, at least not simply because they have inherited them. Thus, we see experimentation with nonpermanent, extra-legal, marriagelike liaisons among college youth as a prelude to marriage. Present data suggest, however, that there is only a small percentage of couples who actually attempt to develop and permanently maintain an unconventional relationship rather than the traditional conjugal one. Experimentation may delay marriage temporarily for some, yet the vast majority will adopt a more or less conventional marriage.

Although increasing numbers of young people are experimenting with alternative styles of relating as a substitute for the traditional dating game, research in this area is limited and there are few guidelines to assist the college student choose the behavior most likely to help him achieve the vital and fulfilling relationship he is seeking. Hence the title of this section: "Dear Abby." Perhaps only she has the answer!

The initial articles in this section revolve around the two dominant themes of courtship and marriage in our contemporary society: "man"-"woman" relationships, and love. "Man" still relates to "woman" and not to the individual behind the stereotype. Each gender is blinded by the sex image of the opposite gender, and the person behind the mask rarely emerges. The two images relate to each other—the persons remain strangers. So we are concerned with these images and have included one article pertinent to gender and gender identification.

Goethe has said "Love is an ideal thing, marriage a real thing, a confusion of the real with the ideal never goes unpunished." Since the "ideal" and the "real" continue to be confused in America today, we include three articles on love as it functions in courtship and marriage. The remaining articles in this section explore dating and some of the experimental forms of male-female relationships currently practiced on college campuses.

Articles
1. Jerome Kagan—Check One: ☐ Male ☐ Female.
2. John Alan Lee—Styles of Loving.
3. Snell and Gail Putney—Love or Marriage.
4. Sidney M. Greenfield—Love and Marriage in Modern America: A Functional Analysis.
5. Miriam E. Berger—Trial Marriage: Harnessing the Trend Constructively.
6. Robert N. Whitehurst—Living Together Unmarried on Campus.

Name: _____   Date: _____

Student #: _____   Sex: M or F

Which sex: (Circle the correct answer)

Male	Female	No Difference	
1. M	F	ND	is better at understanding people?
2. M	F	ND	is more gossipy?
3. M	F	ND	has the stronger sex drive?
4. M	F	ND	is more undependable?
5. M	F	ND	is more logical?
6. M	F	ND	is more emotional?
7. M	F	ND	is better at understanding children?
8. M	F	ND	is better in a crisis?
9. M	F	ND	is more likely to be concerned with what others think?
10. M	F	ND	is more romantic?
11. M	F	ND	is better at managing money?
12. M	F	ND	should have the final say in decisions?
13. M	F	ND	is better at driving a car?
14. M	F	ND	is more scheming and crafty?
15. M	F	ND	is more jealous?
16. M	F	ND	is more aggressive?
17. M	F	ND	is more dependent?
18. M	F	ND	is more punitive?
19. M	F	ND	can form deeper interpersonal relationships?
20. M	F	ND	is more intellectually curious?

21. Which of the above differences do you believe are the results of socialization?

22. Which are inherent?

23. What is your reaction to the following statements?

"In the sight of God there is equality between men and women but when it comes to governmental arrangements in the home the husband is the head. God says he cannot answer prayers which come from a woman who "doesn't take her Godgiven place in the home.""—Billy Graham.

24. If women would stay in the home, families in the U.S. would be happier.

In my associations with the other sex I have found that: (Circle the correct answer.)

25. Yes	No	I tend to be competitive with a person of the other sex.
26. Yes	No	I get along better when the male is definitely dominant and the female is submissive.
27. Yes	No	I am happier when I am submissive in the relationship.
28. Yes	No	I often feel pushed around by my date.
29. Yes	No	I like to date people who are as intelligent or more intelligent than I am.
30. Yes	No	I like to date people who let me make most of the decisions.

CHECK ONE: ☐MALE ☐FEMALE

Jerome Kagan

Every person wants to know how good, how talented and how masculine or feminine he or she is. Of the many attributes that go into the concept of self, sex-role identity is one of the most important.

It may seem odd that anyone should be unsure of his sex-role identity. A five-foot, 11-inch, 18-year-old human with X and Y chromosomes, testes, penis and body hair is, by definition, a male. It would seem that all such men should regard themselves as equally masculine. But the human mind, in its perversity, does not completely trust anatomical characteristics and insists upon including psychological factors in the final judgment. Man is as foolish as the cowardly lion who had to be reassured of his courage by the Wizard of Oz.

A sex-role identity is a person's belief about how well his biological and psychological characteristics correspond to his or her concept of the ideal male or female. The definition of the ideal—the sex-role standard—is influenced by the values of his particular culture. A Kyoto girl is taught that gentleness is the most important feminine quality; a Los Angeles girl learns that physical beauty is an essential quality.

A person is said to have a strong or firm sex-role identity when his subjective judgment of himself comes up to the standards of the ideal. If there are major discrepancies between the ideal and a person's view of himself, he has a weak or fragile sex-role identity.

To get at the dynamic significance of a person's sex-role identity, we must confront four questions: (1) How does a person initally learn sex-role standards? (2) Just what is the content of the standards? (3) Are some sex-role standards generalized across cultures? (4) What are the implications of a firm sex-role identity and a fragile one?

A child learns sex-role standards the way he learns many other concepts. He learns that an object that is round, made of rubber, and bounces is called a ball. He learns more about the definition of a ball by watching how it is used, by listening to people talk about it, and by playing with one himself. By the age of two he has learned that certain objects are called boys and men; others, girls and women. He learns the definition by noting what they do, how they look, and what they wear, and by listening and watching as others discuss the sexes. The categorization of human beings into the two sexes, usually in place by two and a half years, is one of the earliest conceptual classifications a child makes.

Sex roles are defined not only by physical attributes and behavior, but also by opinions, feelings and motives. Most American girls regard an attractive face, a hairless body, a small frame and moderate-sized breasts as ideal physical characteristics. American boys regard height, large muscles, and facial and body hair as ideal.

Some psychological traits that differentiate males from females are changing in American life. Aggression is one of the primary sex-typed behaviors. The traditional sex-role standard inhibits aggression in females, but licenses and encourages it in boys and men. It is difficult to find a psychological study of Americans that fails to note more aggressive behavior among males than among females.

Young children agree that males are more dangerous and punishing than females. This view also persists at a symbolic level: Six-year-olds believe that a tiger is a masculine animal, and that a rabbit is feminine. In one experiment, pairs of pictures were shown to young children. On the first run, the child selected from each pair the picture that was most like his father. The second time, the child selected the picture that was more like his mother. In the third run, he picked the one more like himself. Boys and girls alike classified the father as darker, larger, more dangerous and more angular than the mother. The boys classified themselves as darker, larger, more dangerous and more angular than the girls.

These perceptions are not limited to our culture. Charles Osgood of the University of Illinois showed similar pairs of abstract designs or pictures to adults from four different language groups: American, Japanese, Navajo and Mexican-Spanish. He asked each adult to indicate which picture of the pair best fitted the concept of man and which fitted the concept of woman. As the children had done, the adults from all four cultures classified men as large, angular and dark and women as small, round and light.

Dependency, passivity and conformity are also part of the traditional sex-role standard. Females in America and in most European countries are permitted these qualities; boys and men are pressured to *inhibit* them. Thus men experience greater conflict over being passive; females experience greater conflict over being aggressive.

These differences over aggressive and dependent behavior are reflected in a person's action, and in a reluctance to perceive these qualities in others. As part of an extensive personality assessment, 71 typical middle-class American adults watched while some pictures depicting aggression and some depicting dependency were flashed onto a screen at great speed. Each person was asked to describe each picture after it was flashed seven times. The women had greater difficulty than the men in recognizing the aggressive scenes; the men had greater difficulty in recognizing the dependency scenes.

Sex-role standards dictate that the female must feel needed and desired by a man. She must believe that she can arouse a male sexually, experience deep emotion and heal the psychological wounds of those she loves. The standards for males also stress the ability to arouse and to gratify a love object, but they also include a desire to be independent in action and to dominate others and to be able to control the expression of strong emotions, especially fear and helplessness.

The American male traditionally has been driven to prove that he was strong and powerful; the female to prove that she was capable of forming a deeply emotional relationship that brought satisfaction and growth to the partner—sweetheart or child.

These values are reflected in the behavior of young children from diverse cultures. John and Beatrice Whiting of Harvard University observed children from six cultures and found that the boys were more aggressive and dominant than the girls. The girls were more likely than boys to offer help and support to other children.

In one study, my colleagues and I observed two-year-old boys and girls in a large living room. The girls were more likely than boys to stay in close physical contact with their mothers during the first five minutes. Then a set of toys was brought into the room and the children were allowed to play for a half hour. Most children left their mothers immediately and began to play. However, after 15 or 20 minutes many became bored and restless. The girls tended to drift back to their mothers, while the boys preferred to wander around the room. Michael Lewis of Educational Testing Services has reported similar differences in children only one year old. Linda Shapiro of Harvard has studied pairs of two-year-olds (two boys or two girls) in a natural setting and found the girls more trusting, more cooperative, more nurturing and less fearful of each other than the boys.

It is interesting to note that the rhesus monkey and the baboon, who are not taught sex-role standards, display behavioral differences that resemble those observed in young children. Harry Harlow and his colleagues at the University of Wisconsin have found that threatening gestures and rough-and-tumble contact play are more frequent among young male than among female monkeys, whereas passivity in stress is more frequent among the females.

Some of the differences between males and females seem to stretch across cultures and species, suggesting that sex-role standards are neither arbitrary nor completely determined by the social groups. Each culture, in its wisdom, seems to promote those behaviors and values that are biologically easiest to establish in each of the two sexes.

The individual's sex-role identity, as noted, is his opinion of his maleness or femaleness, not a summary of his physical attributes. In one study, Edward Bennett and Larry Cohen of Tufts University asked American adults to select from a list of adjectives those that best described their personalities. The women described themselves as weak, fearful, capable of warmth and desirous of friendly and harmonious relationships with others. The men described themselves as competent, intelligent and motivated by power and personal accomplishment.

Sex-role identity differences among children arise from three sources:

First, a family-reared child is predisposed to assume that he or she is more like his or her parent of the same sex than like any other adult, and is inclined to imitate that parent. If a father is bold and athletic, his son is more likely to believe he possesses these masculine attributes than is a boy whose father is not athletic.

Second, the child is vulnerable to the special definition of sex roles shared by his peer group. A boy who is clumsy on the playing field is more likely to question his sex-role identity if he lives in a neighborhood devoted to athletics than he is if he lives in a community that values intellectual prowess.

Third, sex-role identity depends heavily on the quality of sexual interaction in adolescence. The sex-role identity has two important six-year periods of growth: one prior to puberty when acquisition of peer valued sex-role characteristics is primary, and one during adolescence, when success in heterosexual encounters is crucial. If the adolescent is unable to establish successful heterosexual relationships, he will begin to question his sex-role identity. To the adult, the potential for attracting the affection of another and entering into a satisfactory sexual union is the essence of the sex-role standard.

Let us consider the implications of a firm sex-role identity and a fragile one. Each of us tries all the time to match his traits to his notion of the ideal sex role. This is but one facet of the human desire to gain as much information about the self as possible. When one feels close to his ideal standard, his spirits are buoyed. He is confident he can come even closer, and he makes the attempt. If he feels he is far from his standard, he may turn away from it and accept the role of a feminine man (or a masculine woman). Acceptance of a culturally inappropriate role reduces the terrible anxiety that comes from recognizing in one's self a serious deviation from an ideal that cannot be obtained. The only possible defense is to redefine the ideal in attainable terms.

The continuing attempt to match one's attributes to the sex-role ideal allows men to display a more intense involvement than women in difficult intellectual problems. Males are supposed to be more competent in science and mathematics; as academic excellence is necessary for vocational success, it, therefore, is an essential component of a man's sex-role identity.

Adolescent girls view intellectual striving as a form of aggressive behavior because it involves competition with a peer. Since many females believe they should not be overly competitive, they inhibit intense intellectual striving. A visit to college dining halls often reveals males arguing so intensely that the air crackles with hostility. Intense debate in the female dining hall is less frequent because it threatens the girl's sex-role identity. Men seem to be better able to argue about an issue because they do not always take an attack on an opinion as an attack on the person.

Although intense intellectual striving is more characteristic of adult men than it is of women, this is not the case among young children. In the primary grades, girls outperform boys in all areas. The ratio of boys to girls with reading problems ranges as high as six to one. One reason for this difference is that the average American six- or seven-year-old boy sees school as a feminine place. On entering school he meets female teachers who monitor painting, coloring and singing, and put a premium on obedience, suppression of aggression and restlessness. These values are clearly more appropriate for girls than for boys. Studies of children affirm that they see school as feminine and seven-year-old boys naturally resist the complete submission it demands. If this is true, a community with a large proportion of male teachers should have a smaller proportion of boys with serious reading retardation. Some American communities, such as Akron, Ohio, are testing the hypothesis.

Depression and anxiety affect the sexes differently. Women are likely to suffer psychological stress when it is suggested that they are not attractive, loving or emotional. Some women experience serious depression after giving birth because they do not feel strong love for the infant and they question their femininity. Men become anxious at suggestions that they are impotent or not competent, successful or dominant. Depression is likely to follow a man's career failure.

The sex-role standards of a society are not static, and changes in the standards that surround sexuality and dependence are just becoming evident. The American woman has begun to assume a more active role in sexual behavior; her mother and grandmother assumed passive postures. This reach for independence has extensive social implications. Some college-educated women feel that dependence, especially on men, is an undesirable feminine trait. They want to prove that they can function as competently and autonomously as men and this pushes them to develop academic and career skills.

Why? The intense effort spent on getting into and staying in college has persuaded the young woman that she should use her hard-won intellectual skills in a job. And technology has made it less necessary for a woman to do routine housework and forced her to look outside the home for proof of her usefulness.

Most human beings seek the joy of accomplishment. A man tries to gratify this need in his job and he has something concrete with which to prove his effectiveness—an invention, a manuscript, a salary check. Woman once met her need to be useful by believing that her sweetheart, husband or children required her wisdom, skill and personal affection. Instant dinners, permissive sexual mores, and freedom for children have undermined this role. It is too early to predict the effect of this female unrest. It should lead to a more egalitarian relation between the sexes. It could make each partner so reluctant to submerge his individual autonomy and admit his need for the other, that each walks a lonely, and emotionally insulated path. Let us hope it does not.

Name: _____   Date: _____

Student #: _____   Sex: M or F

ATTITUDES TOWARD LOVE

Please read each statement carefully and circle the number which you believe most adequately represents your opinion.

1. Strongly agree (definitely yes)
2. Mildly agree (I believe so)
3. Undecided (not sure)

4. Mildly disagree (probably not)
5. Strongly disagree (definitely not)

	SA	MA	U	MD	SD
1. When you are really in love, you just aren't interested in anyone else.	1	2	3	4	5
2. Love doesn't make sense. It just is.	1	2	3	4	5
3. When you fall head-over-heels-in-love, it's sure to be the real thing.	1	2	3	4	5
4. Love isn't anything you can really study; it is too highly emotional to be subject to scientific observation.	1	2	3	4	5
5. To be in love with someone without marriage is a tragedy.	1	2	3	4	5
6. When love hits, you know it.	1	2	3	4	5
7. Common interests are really unimportant; as long as each of you is truly in love, you will adjust.	1	2	3	4	5
8. It doesn't matter if you marry after you have known your partner for only a short time as long as you know you are in love.	1	2	3	4	5
9. As long as two people love each other, the religious differences they have really do not matter.	1	2	3	4	5
10. You can love someone even though you do not like any of that person's friends.	1	2	3	4	5
11. When you are in love, you are usually in a daze.	1	2	3	4	5
12. Love at first sight is often the deepest and most enduring type of love.	1	2	3	4	5
13. Usually there are only one or two people in the world whom you could really love and could really be happy with.	1	2	3	4	5
14. Regardless of other factors, if you truly love another person, that is enough to marry that person.	1	2	3	4	5
15. It is necessary to be in love with the one you marry to be happy.	1	2	3	4	5
16. When you are separated from the love partner, the rest of the world seems dull and unsatisfying.	1	2	3	4	5
17. Parents should not advise their children whom to date; they have forgotten what it is like to be in love.	1	2	3	4	5
18. Love is regarded as a primary motive for marriage, which is good.	1	2	3	4	5
19. When you love a person, you think of marrying that person.	1	2	3	4	5
20. Somewhere there is an ideal mate for most people. The problem is just finding that one.	1	2	3	4	5

	SA	MA	U	MD	SD

21. Jealousy usually varies directly with love; that is, the more in love you are, the greater the tendency for you to become jealous.　1　2　3　4　5

22. Love is best described as an exciting thing rather than a calm thing.　1　2　3　4　5

23. There are probably only a few people that any one person can fall in love with.　1　2　3　4　5

24. When you are in love, your judgment is usually not too clear.　1　2　3　4　5

25. Love often comes but once in a lifetime.　1　2　3　4　5

26. You can't make yourself love someone; it just comes or it doesn't.　1　2　3　4　5

27. Differences in social class and religion are of small importance in selecting a marriage partner as compared with love.　1　2　3　4　5

28. Day dreaming usually comes along with being in love.　1　2　3　4　5

29. When you are in love, you don't have to ask yourself a bunch of questions about love; you will just know that you are in love.　1　2　3　4　5

30-32. Total of numbers 1-29: _____

Source: Knox, D. H. Jr. and M. J. Sporakowski. Attitudes of College Students toward Love. Article published in *Journal of Marriage and the Family.* November 1968. Inventory reprinted by permission of M. J. Sporakowski.

THE STYLES OF LOVING

John Alan Lee

We will accept variety in almost anything, from roses and religions to politics and poetry. But when it comes to love, each of us believes we know the real thing, and we are reluctant to accept other notions. We disparage other people's experiences by calling them infatuations, mere sexual flings, unrealistic affairs.

For thousands of years writers and philosophers have debated the nature of love. Many recognized that there are different kinds of love, but few accepted them all as legitimate. Instead, each writer argues that his own concept of love is the best. C.S. Lewis thought that true love must be unselfish and altruistic, as did sociologist Pitirim Sorokin. Stendhal, by contrast, took the view that love is passionate and ecstatic. Others think that "real" love must be wedded to the Protestant ethic, forging a relationship that is mutually beneficial and productive. Definitions of love range from sexual lust to an excess of friendship.

The ancient Greeks and Romans were more tolerant. They had a variety of words for different and, to them, equally valid types of love. But today the concept has rigidified; most of us believe that there is only one true kind of love. We measure each relationship against this ideal in terms of degree or quantity. Does Tom love me more than Tim does? Do you love me as much as I love you? Do I love you enough? Such comparisons also assume that love comes in fixed amounts—the more I give to you, the less I have for anyone else; if you don't give me everything, you don't love me enough.

"There is hardly any activity, any enterprise, which is started with such tremendous hopes and expectations, and yet which fails so regularly, as love," wrote Erich Fromm. I think that part of the reason for this failure rate is that too often people are speaking different languages when they speak of love. The problem is not *how much* love they feel, but *which kind*. The way to have a mutually satisfying love affair is not to find a partner who loves "in the right amount," but one who shares the same approach to loving, the same definition of love.

The Structure of Love

My research explored the literature of love and the experiences of ordinary lovers in order to distinguish these approaches. Color served me as a useful analogy in the process. There are three primary colors—red, yellow, and blue—from which all other hues are composed. And empirically I found three primary types of love, none of which could be reduced to the others, and a variety of secondary types that proved to be combinations of the basic three. In love, as in color, "primary" does not mean superior; it simply refers to basic structure. Orange is no more or less a color than red, and no less worthy. In love, as in color, one can draw as many distinctions as one wishes; I have stopped, somewhat arbitrarily, with nine types.

EROS

Stendhal called love a "sudden sensation of recognition and hope." He was describing the most typical symptom of eros: an immediate, powerful attraction to the physical appearance of the beloved. "The first time I saw him was several weeks before we met," a typical erotic lover said in an interview, "but I can still remember exactly the way he looked, which was just the way I dreamed my ideal lover would look." Erotic lovers typically felt a chemical or gut reaction on meeting each other; heightened heartbeat is not just a figment of fiction, it seems, but the erotic lover's physiological response to meeting the dream.

Most of my erotic respondents went to bed with their lovers soon after meeting. This was the first test of whether the affair would continue, since erotic love demands that the partner live up to the lover's concept of bodily perfection. They may try to overlook what they consider a flaw, only to find that it undermines the intensity of their attraction. There is no use trying to persuade such a lover that personal or intellectual qualities are more lasting or more important. To do so is to argue for another approach to love.

My erotic respondents all spoke with delight of the lover's skin, fragrance, hair, musculature, body proportions, and so on. Of course, the specific body type that each lover considered ideal varied, but all erotics had such an ideal, which they could identify easily from a series of photographs. Erotic lovers actively and imaginatively cultivate many sexual techniques to preserve delight in the part-

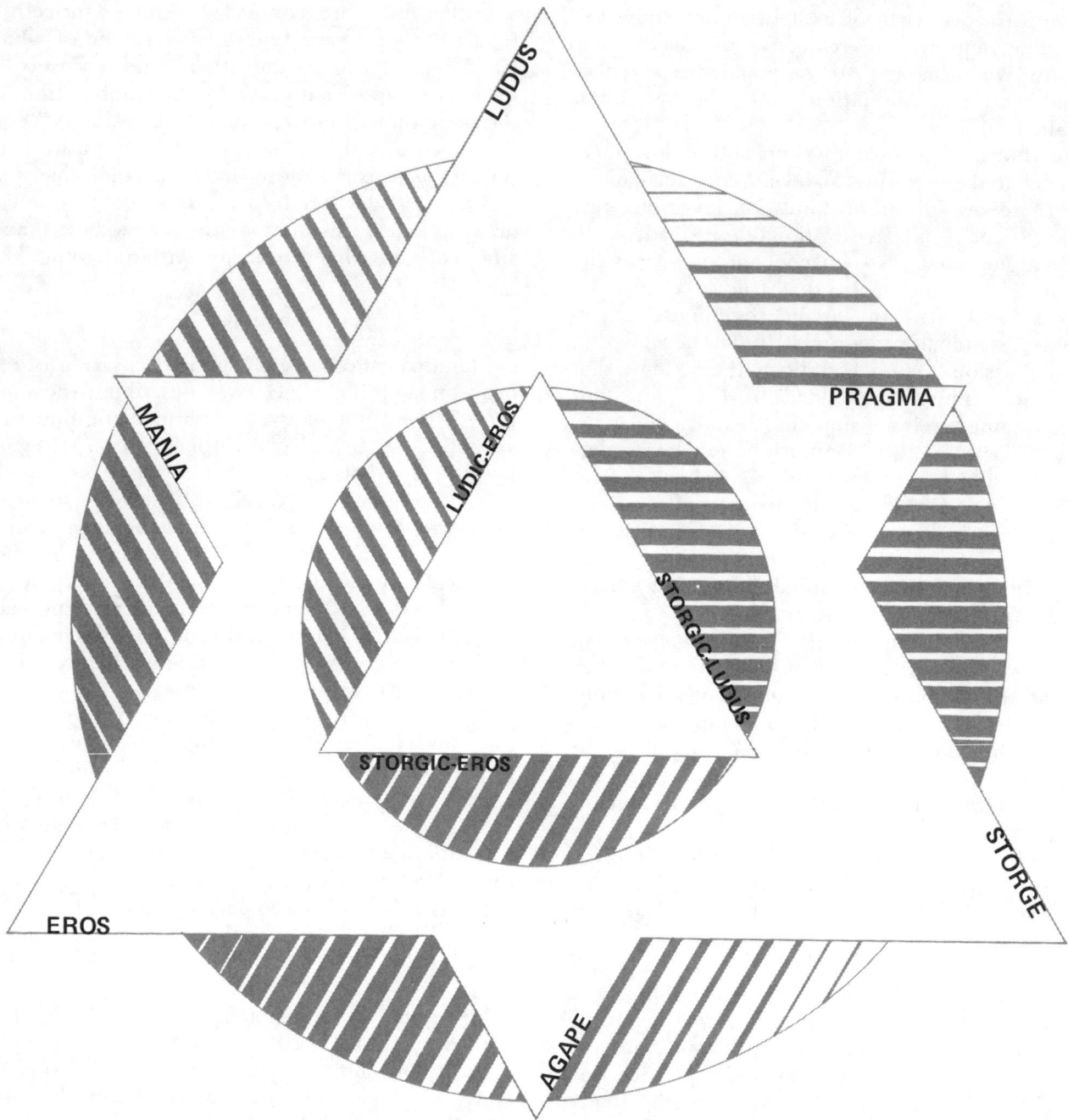

THE COLORS OF LOVE

ner's body. Nothing is more deadly for a serious erotic lover than to fall in love with a prudish partner.

Modern usage tends to define *erotic* as *sexual;* we equate erotic art with pornography. But eros is not mere sexual attraction; it is a demanding search for the lover's ideal of beauty, a concept that is as old as Pygmalion. Eros involves mental as well as sexual attraction, which is faithful to the Platonic concept. Most dictionaries define Platonic love as "devoid of sensual feeling," which is certainly not what Plato had in mind. On the contrary, it was sensual feeling for the beautiful body of another person that evoked eros as the Greeks understood it.

The Dream of the Ideal

The fascination with beauty that marks eros is the basis for personal and psychological intimacy between the lovers. The erotic lover wants to know everything about the beloved, to become part of him or her. If an erotic relationship surpasses the initial hurdles of expectation and physical ideals, this desire for intimacy can sustain the relationship for years. (And this knowledge must be first-hand. The playful lover may ask a friend what so-and-so is like in bed. No erotic lover would dream of relying on such vicarious evidence.)

An essential component of successful erotic love is self-assurance. It takes confidence to reveal oneself intensely to another. A lover who doubts himself, who falls into self-recriminations if his love is not reciprocated, cannot sustain eros.

The typical erotic lovers in my sample avoided wallowing in extremes of emotion, especially the self-pity and hysteria that characterize mania. They recalled happy and secure childhoods, and reported satisfaction with work, family, and close friends. They were ready for love when it came along, but were not anxiously searching. They consider love to be important, but they do not become obsessive about it; when separated from the beloved, they do not lose their balance, become sick with desire, or turn moody. They prefer exclusive relationships but do not demand them, and they are rarely possessive or afraid of rivals. Erotic lovers seek a deep, pervasive rapport with their partners and share development and control of the relationship.

But because the erotic lover depends on an ideal concept of beauty, he is often disappointed. The failure rate of eros has littered our fiction with bitter and cynical stories of love, and caused conventional wisdom to be deeply suspicious of ideal beauty as a basis for relationships. Indeed, I found

that the purer the erotic qualities of a respondent's love experience, the less his chances of a mutual, lasting relationship.

An erotic lover may eventually settle for less, but he or she never forgets the compromise, and rarely loses hope of realizing the dream. However, I found several cases of "love at first sight" in which initial rapture survived years of married life. The success of a few keeps the dream alive for many more.

LUDUS

About the year One A.D. the Roman poet Ovid came up with the term *amor ludens,* playful love, love as a game. Ovid advised lovers to enjoy love as a pleasant pasttime, but not to get too involved. The ludic lover refuses, then, to become dependent on any beloved, or to allow the partner to become overly attached to him or her, or too intimate.

Other types of lovers dismiss ludus as not a kind of love at all; erotic types disdain its lack of commitment, moralists condemn its promiscuity and hedonism. But to make a game of love does not diminish its value. No skilled player of bridge or tennis would excuse inept playing because "it's only a game," and ludus too has its rules, strategies, and points for skill. Ludus turns love into a series of challenges and puzzles to be solved.

Ludic Stategies

For example, ludus is most easily and most typically played with several partners at once, a guarantee against someone on either side getting too involved. "Love several persons," a 17-century manual advises, for three lovers are safer than two, and two much safer than one. A ludic lover will often invent another lover, even a spouse, to keep the partner from becoming too attached.

But most of my ludic respondents had other tactics. They were careful not to date a partner too often; they never hinted at including the partner in any long-range plans: they arranged encounters in a casual, even haphazard, way: "I'll give you a call"; "See you around sometime." Such indefiniteness is designed to keep the partner from building up expectations or from becoming preoccupied with the affair.

Of course, as in many games, one must be on guard against cheats. Cheats in ludic love are cynical players who don't care how deeply involved the partner becomes, who may even exploit such intensity. Such players scandalize ludic lovers who believe in fair play. Insincerity and lies may be part of the game, so long as both partners understand this.

The ludic lover notices differences between bodies, but thinks it is stupid to specialize. As the ludic man said in *Finian's Rainbow*, when he is not near the girl he loves, he loves the girl he's near. But ludus is not simply a series of sexual encounters. A lover could get sex without the rituals of conversation, candles and wine. In ludus, the pleasure comes from playing the game, not merely winning the prize.

Actually, sexual gratification is only a minor part of the time and effort involved in ludic love. Of any group, ludic respondents showed the least interest in the mutual improvement of sex techniques. Their attitude was that it is easier to find a new sex partner than to work out sexual problems and explore new sexual pleasures with the current one; this view contrasts sharply with that of erotic and storgic lovers. Ludic people want sex for fun, not emotional rapport.

Don Juans Aren't Always Doomed

Ludus has enjoyed recurring popularity through history. Montesquieu could write of 18th-century France: "A husband who wishes to be the only one to possess his wife would be regarded as a public killjoy." The first Don Juan emerged in Tirso de Molina's *The Trickster of Seville* in 1630, the diametric opposite of the erotic Tristan, the courtly ideal. Tirso's hero conquered only four women, but a century later Mozart's Don Giovanni won a thousand and three in España alone.

Of course the various fates of the legendary ludic lovers reflect society's ambivalence toward them. They usually go to hell, get old and impotent, or meet their match and surrender. Rarely is ludus tolerated, much less rewarded.

But I was struck by the fact that most of my ludic respondents neither suffered nor regretted their ways. Like successful erotics, they play from a base of self-confidence. They believe in their own assets so much that they convince themselves that they do not "need" other people like most mortals. These ludic lovers prefer to remain in perfect control of their feelings; they do not think that love is as important as work or other activities; they are thus never possessive or jealous (except as a teasing ploy in the game). They typically recall their childhoods as "average," and their current lives as "OK, but occasionally frustrating."

My ludic respondents seemed quite content with their detachment from intense feelings of love, but most failed the acid test of ludus: the ability to break off with a partner with whom they were through. Their intentions were ludic, but they had Victorian hangovers. They tended to prolong the relationship for the sake of the partner, until the inevitable break was painful. Ovid would not have approved. "Extinguish the fire of love gradually," he admonished, "not all at once . . . it is wicked to hate a girl you used to love."

The legendary ludic lovers, like Don Juan and Alfie, were generally men, and only in recent years—with the pill and penicillin—have women won entry into the game. Ludus is also frequently identified with male homosexual love; the term "gay" may have originated from the assumption that homosexuals adopt a noncommittal, playful approach to sex and love, which is not necessarily so.

There is a variant of this type of love that I call *manic ludus*, in which the lover alternates between a detached, devil-may-care attitude toward the partner, and a worried, lovesick desire for more attention. People in this conflicting state would like to be purely ludic, but they lack the vanity or self-sufficiency to remain aloof from intimacy. They both need and resent love, and they cannot control their emotions long enough to maintain a cool relationship.

STORGE

Storge (pronounced stor-gay) is, as Proudhon described it, "love without fever, tumult or folly, a peaceful and enchanting affection" such as one might have for a close sibling. It is the kind of love that sneaks up unnoticed; storgic lovers remember no special point when they fell in love. Since storgic lovers consider sex one of the most intimate forms of self-disclosure, sex occurs late in the relationship.

Storge is rarely the stuff of dramatic plays or romantic novels, except perhaps as a backdrop or point of comparison. In *Of Human Bondage,* the hero, Philip, follows a manic love affair with Mildred with a storgic marriage to Sally, whom he has known all along.

Storge superficially resembles ludus in its lack of great passion, but the origins of the two types are quite different. The ludic lover avoids intensity of feeling, consciously aware of its risks. The storgic lover is unaware of intense feeling. It simply doesn't occur to him that a lover should be dewy-eyed and sentimental about a beloved. Such behavior is as out of place in storgic love as it would be for most of us in relating to a close friend. Storgic love "just comes naturally" with the passage of time and the enjoyment of shared activities. You grow accustomed to her face.

In most modern cities people do not live near each other long enough to develop the unself-conscious affection that is typical of storgic love. I found some such cases among people who grew up in rural areas. However, among my urban respondents, who usually had few lasting contacts with their childhood friends, there were some storgic types who based their love on friendship and companionship. This characteristic distinguishes storge from other types of love, in which the partners may not treat each other at all like friends.

When a storgic lover gets involved with another type of lover, serious misunderstandings are likely to occur. The goals of storge, for instance, are marriage, home and children, avoiding all the silly conflicts and entanglements of passion. But to the erotic or ludic lover, storge is a bore. Storge implies a life that is reasonable and predictable; why make it more complicated by engaging in emotionally exhausting types of love? Erotic lovers would never understand that question.

The Strengths of Storge

Storge is a slowburning love, rarely hectic or urgent, though of course storgic lovers may disagree and fight. But they build up a reservoir of stability that will see them through difficulties that would kill a ludic relationship and greatly strain an erotic one. The physical absence of the beloved, for instance, is much less distressing to them than to other lovers; they can survive long separations (Ulysses and Penelope are a classic example of that ability).

Even if a break-up occurs, storgic lovers are likely to remain good friends. A typical storgic lover would find it inconceivable that two people who had once loved each other could become enemies, simply because they had ceased to be lovers.

In a ludic or erotic relationship, something is happening all the time. In eros, there is always some secret to share, a misunderstanding to mend, a separation to survive with letters and poems. In ludus, inactivity quickly leads to boredom, and a search for new amusement. In storge, there are fewer campaigns to fight and fewer wounds to heal. There is a lack of ecstasy, but also a lack of despair.

Eros, ludus, and storge are the three primary types of love, but few love affairs, and few colors, are pure examples of one type. Most reds have a little yellow or blue in them, and most cases of eros have a little storge or ludus.

The color analogy led me to distinguish mixtures from blends (compounds). You can mix two colors and be aware of both components. But it may happen that two primary colors are so evenly blended that an entirely new color emerges, unclassifiable as a hue of either, with unique properties. This is the case with mania, a fourth color of love.

MANIA

The Greeks called it *theia mania*, the madness from the gods. Both Sappho and Plato, along with legions of sufferers, recorded its symptoms: agitation, sleeplessness, fever, loss of appetite, heartache. The manic lover is consumed by thoughts of the beloved. The slightest lack of enthusiasm from the partner brings anxiety and pain; each tiny sign of warmth brings instant relief, but no lasting satisfaction. The manic lover's need for attention and affection from the beloved is insatiable. Cases of mania abound in literature, for its components— furious jealousy, helpless obsession, and tragic endings—are the stuff of human conflict. Goethe made his own unhappy bout with mania the subject of his novel, *The Sorrows of Young Werther*, and Somerset Maugham did the same in *Of Human Bondage*. The manic lover alternates between peaks of ecstasy when he feels loved in return, and depths of despair when the beloved is absent. He knows his possessiveness and jealousy are self-defeating, but he can't help himself.

From God's Curse to Popular Passion

Rational lovers throughout the ages, from Lucretius to Denis de Rougemont, have warned us to avoid mania like the plague. Fashions in love, of course, change. To the ancient Greeks, a person who fell head-over-heels, "madly" in love, had obviously been cursed by the gods. Many parents in the Middle Ages strongly disapproved of love matches, preferring their children to arrange "sensible marriages." But mania has gained popularity in the West since the 13th century; today many young people would consider it wrong to marry unless they loved "romantically."

So popular is mania in literature and love that I originally assumed it would be a primary type. But green, a color that occurs in nature more than any other, is not a primary, but a blend of yellow and blue. Similarly, the data from my interviews refused to reduce mania to one clear type. Instead, manic respondents derive their unique style of love from the primaries of eros and ludus.

These yearning, obsessed, often unhappy manic lovers are typical of frustrated eros. With eros, they share the same intensity of feeling, the same urgency to find the ideal beloved. But erotic lovers are not crushed by disappointment as manic lovers are; they keep their self-respect. Manic lovers, by contrast, are self-effacing, ambivalent, lacking in confidence. They don't have a clear idea of what they are looking for, as erotic lovers do, and they feel helpless, out of control of their emotions. "I know it was crazy, but I couldn't help myself," was a favorite explanation.

Oddly, manic lovers persist in falling in love with people they say they don't even like. "I hate and I love," wailed the Roman poet Catullus. "And if you ask me how, I do not know. I only feel it, and I'm torn in two." Aldous Huxley's hero in *Point Counterpoint* "wanted her against all reason, against all his ideals and principles, madly, against his wishes . . . for he didn't like Lucy, he really hated her."

For these reasons, some psychologists consider mania to be neurotic, unhealthy. Freud was most critical of obsessive love, and Theodor Reik, in *Of Love and Lust,* explains the obsessiveness of mania as a search for the qualities in a partner that the lover feels lacking in himself. The typical manic lover in my samples seemed to feel, as the song suggests, that he was nobody until somebody loved him.

Paradoxically, manic lovers also behave in ways similar to ludus. They try to hold back to manipulate the lover, to play it cool. But unlike successful ludic types, manic lovers never quite succeed at detachment. Their sense of timing is off. They try to be noncommittal, only to panic and surrender in ignominious defeat.

The Telephone Trauma

Consider this typical caper. The manic realizes that he has been taking the initiative too often in calling his beloved, so he asks her to call the next time. This is a consciously ludic ploy, since no erotic or storgic lover would keep count or care. But it is part of the game in ludus to keep things in balance.

The hour of the expected call arrives, and the phone sits silent. The true ludic lover would not be terribly bothered; he or she would quickly make a few calls and get busy with other lovers. The manic lover falls into a frenzy of anxiety. Either he

breaks down and calls the lover, or he is in such a state of emotional upset that he is incapable of ludic detachment when the lover does call: "Where were you? I was so *worried*!"

Manic lovers, in short, attempt to play by the rules of ludus with the passion of eros, and fail at both. They need to be loved so much that they do not let the relationship take its own course. They push things, and thereby tend to lose; mania rarely ends happily. Few lovers go to such extremes as violence or suicide, but most remain troubled by the experience for months, even years. Like malaria, it may return to seize the manic lover with bouts of nostalgia and unrest.

It is theoretically possible for mania to develop into lasting love, but the manic lover must find an unusual partner—one who can ride out the storms of emotion, return the intensity of feeling, and ultimately convince the manic lover that he or she is lovable. A ludic partner will never tolerate the emotional extremes, and a storgic lover will be unable to reciprocate the feelings. A strong-willed erotic partner might manage it.

Ludic Eros

Mania can be reduced by resolving the underlying conditions that create and sustain the lover's lack of self-esteem and his desperate need to be in love. Then the lover may move toward a more confident eros or, perhaps, a more playful ludus. This is the part of the color chart labeled *ludic eros,* the sector between the two primaries.

What enables one lover to mix ludus and eros in a pleasant compromise, while another finds them compounded into mania? Having previous experience in love and many good relationships is one factor. The manic lovers in my sample were discontented with life, but ludic-erotic lovers were basically content and knew what kind of partners they wanted. Ludic-erotic people resemble ludus in their pluralism, their desire for many relationships, but they resemble eros in their preference for clearly-defined types. They do not easily accept substitutes, as ludic types do.

Ludic-erotic love walks an exacting tightrope between intensity and detachment. Most people think this approach is too greedy, and therefore immoral. To the ludic-erotic lover, it is just good sense.

The Art of Passionate Caution

The tightrope isn't always easy. The lover may spend an evening in the most intense intimacy with his partner, but will always back off in a ludic direction at critical moments. Just when you, the beloved, are about to react to his passion with a murmur of confirmation, he leaps from the couch to make a cup of coffee. Or just when he is about to blurt out that he loves you, he bites his lips and says something less committal: "You really turn me on."

The successful combination of ludus and eros is rare, but it exists. The journals of Casanova are a classic example of the bittersweet taste of this type of love. Today many attempts at "open marriages" are in fact advocating a ludic-erotic approach to love: the spouses remain primarily involved with each other, yet may have intense involvements with others so long as these remain temporary.

PRAGMA

Pragma is love with a shopping list, a love that seeks compatibility on practical criteria. In traditional societies, marriages were arranged on similarities of race, social class, income, and so on. In modern society the pragmatic approach to love argues that lovers should choose each other on the basis of compatible personalities, like interests and education, similar backgrounds and religious views, and the like. Computer-match services take a pragmatic view.

The pragmatic lover uses social activities and programs as a means to an end, and will drop them if there is no payoff in partners. By contrast, a storgic lover goes out for the activities he enjoys, and thereby meets someone who shares those interests. The storgic lover never consciously chooses a partner.

Pragma is not a primary type of love but a compound of storge and ludus. The pragmatic lover chooses a partner as if she had grown up with him (storge) and will use conscious manipulation to find one (ludus). Pragma is rather like manufactured storge, a faster means of achieving the time-honored version. If a relationship does not work out, the pragmatic lover will move rationally on, ludic-fashion, to search for another.

The pragmatic approach is not as cold as it seems. Once a sensible choice is made, more intense feelings may develop; but one must begin with a solid match that is practically based. Oriental match-makers noted that in romantic love "the kettle is boiling when the young couple first starts out"—and cools with time, bringing disappointment. An arranged marriage, they say, is like a kettle that starts cold and slowly warms up. Pragmatic love grows over the years.

As pragma is the compound, so storge and ludus may combine as a mixture. The distinguishing features of a *storgic-ludic* affair are convenience and discretion. A typical example is that of a married boss and his secretary, in which the relationship is carefully managed so as to disrupt neither the boss's marriage nor the office routine. Of course, such affairs don't always stay in neat storgic-ludic boxes. In the film, *A Touch of Class,* the affair becomes too intense, threatening to interfere with the man's comfortably companionate marriage.

AGAPE

Agape (pronounced ah-ga-pay) is the classical Christian view of love: altruistic, universalistic love that is always kind and patient, never jealous, never demanding reciprocity. When St. Paul wrote to the Corinthians that love is a duty to care about others, whether the love is deserved or not, and that love must be deeply compassionate and utterly altruistic, he used the Greek word, *agape.* But all the great religions share this concept of love, a generous, unselfish, giving of oneself.

I found no saints in my sample. I have yet to interview an unqualified example of agape, although a few respondents had had brief agapic episodes in relationships that were otherwise tinged with selfishness. For instance, one of my subjects, seeing that his lover was torn between choosing him or another man, resolved to save her the pain of deciding; he bowed out gracefully. His action fell short of pure agape, however, because he continued to be interested in how well his beloved was doing, and was purely and selfishly delighted when she dropped the other man and returned to him.

Yet my initial sample of 112 people did contain eight case histories that came quite close to the sexual restraint, dutiful self-sacrifice, universality and altruism that characterize agape. These respondents mixed storge and eros; they had an almost religious attitude toward loving, but they fell short of the hypothetical ideal in loving the partner more than anyone else. They felt intense emotion, as erotic lovers do, along with the enduring patience and abiding affection of storge.

Storgic-erotic respondents felt an initial attraction to their partners, distinguishable from erotic attraction by the absence of physical symptoms of excitement. And unlike eros, these people felt little or no jealousy; they seemed to find enough pleasure in the act of loving another person so that the matter of reciprocity was almost irrelevant.

Testing One's Type of Love

Why construct a typology of love in the first place? Love is a delicate butterfly, runs a certain sentiment, that can be ruined with clumsy dissection. Who cares how many species it comes in, let it fly.

As far as I am concerned, any analysis that helps reduce misunderstandings is worthwhile, and there is no human endeavor more ripe for misunderstandings than love. Consider. A person who has just fallen in love is often tempted to test his sensations to prove it's "really" love. Usually such tests are based on a unidimensional concept of love, and therefore they are usually 180° wrong.

For example, the decision to test love by postponing sex would be disastrous for an erotic love affair, the equivalent of depriving a baby of food for a week to see if it is strong enough to live. A budding erotic love thrives on sexual intimacy. But delaying sex would be absolutely natural and right for a storgic lover, and it might be a positive incentive to a manic lover.

The advantage of my typology, preliminary as it is, is that it teases apart some very different definitions of love, and suggests which types of love are most compatible. Generally, the farther apart two types are on the color chart, the less likely that the lovers share a common language of love. One of my ludic respondents berated his storgic lover for trying to trap him into a commitment, while she accused him of playing games just to get her body. Different types, different languages. Eros insists on rapid intimacy, storge resents being rushed. Same feelings of "love," but opposite ways to express it.

Obviously, two lovers who represent unlike primaries will have trouble getting along unless they both bend toward a mixture or compromise. But it all depends on what each individual wants out of a relationship. Two storgic lovers have the best chance for a lasting relationship, and two ludic lovers have the worst chance—but they will have fun while it lasts.

The questionnaire at the beginning of this article will help you identify which of the primary types is most characteristic of you. It is only a general guide, and most useful to see how well matched in attitudes you and your lover are—which items you agree on, and on which you have serious disagreement. For a more precise way to locate yourself on the color chart, take the test on the next page. It lists 35 characteristics and the likelihood of their presence in eight types of love.

Remember to look for overall patterns in your experience. One swallow does not a summer make, and neither does one manic binge confirm you as an obsessive lover. One playful affair in a storgic marriage does not define you as ludus. While some people have enjoyed a variety of love experiences equally, most of us definitely prefer one type. We live with other kinds, as we live with many colors, but we still have our favorites.

THE METHOD FOR MEASURING LOVE
John Alan Lee

Literature helped me delimit the scope and varieties of love over the centuries. I began my research by collecting over 4,000 statements about love from hundreds of works of fiction and nonfiction, including Plato and the Bible, Doris Lessing and D.H. Lawrence, romantic Lord Byron and cynical La Rochefoucauld. I recorded each statement on a separate card, and then cross-classified them on topics such as jealousy, altruism, physical beauty.

Some preliminary clusters of ideas about love began to emerge. Some authors, such as St. Paul and Erich Fromm, spoke of love as a universal altruistic quality rather than as an attraction to one person. Others, such as Andreas Capellanus, were sure that true love includes jealousy and possessiveness. Out of the thousands of statements, I discovered six hypothetical types of love to test: love of beauty (eros), obsessive love (mania), playful love (ludus), companionate love (storge), altruistic love (agape), and realistic love (pragma).

A panel of professionals in literature, psychology, sociology and philosophy sorted through an edited number of the cards to select those that would best distinguish these types of love. I gave the resulting questionnaire of 30 statements to a variety of people, and found that they would agree with the most contradictory ideas in love. Almost

GRAPH YOUR OWN STYLE OF LOVING

Consider each characteristic as it applies to a current relationship that you define as love, or to a previous one if that is more applicable. For each, note whether the trait is *almost always* true (AA), *usually* true (U), *rarely* true (R), or *almost never* true (AN).

#	Characteristic	Eros	Ludus	Storge	Mania	Ludic Eros	Storgic Eros	Storgic Ludus	Pragma
1	You consider your childhood less happy than the average of peers	R		AN	U				
2	You were discontent with life (work, etc.) at time your encounter began	R		AN	U	R			
3	You have never been in love before this relationship				U	R	AN	R	
4	You want to be in love or have love as security	R	AN		AA		AN	AN	U
5	You have a clearly defined ideal image of your desired partner	AA	AN	AN	AN	U	AN	R	AA
6	You felt a strong gut attraction to your beloved on the first encounter	AA	R	AN	R		AN		
7	You are preoccupied with thoughts about the beloved	AA	AN	AN	AA			R	
8	You believe your partner's interest is at least as great as yours		U	R	AN			R	U
9	You are eager to see your beloved almost every day; this was true from the beginning	AA	AN	R	AA		R	AN	R
10	You soon believed this could become a permanent relationship	AA	AN	R	AN	R	AA	AN	U
11	You see "warning signs" of trouble but ignore them	R	R		AA		AN	R	R
12	You deliberately restrain frequency of contact with partner	AN	AA	R	R	R	R		U
13	You restrict discussion of your feelings with beloved	R	AA	U	U	R		U	U
14	You restrict display of your feelings with beloved	R	AA	R	U	R		U	U
15	You discuss future plans with beloved	AA	R	R				AN	AA
16	You discuss wide range of topics, experiences with partner	AA	R				U	R	AA
17	You try to control relationship, but feel you've lost control	AN	AN	AN	AA	AN	AN		
18	You lose ability to be first to terminate relationship	AN	AN		AA	R	U	R	R
19	You try to force beloved to show more feeling, commitment	AN	AN		AA		AN	R	
20	You analyze the relationship, weigh it in your mind			AN	U		R	R	AA
21	You believe in the sincerity of your partner	AA				U	R	U	AA
22	You blame partner for difficulties of your relationship	R	U	R	U	R	AN		
23	You are jealous and possessive but not to the point of angry conflict	U	AN	R			R	AN	
24	You are jealous to the point of conflict, scenes, threats, etc.	AN	AN	AN	AA	R	AN	AN	AN
25	Tactile, sensual contact is very important to you	AA		AN	U	AN			R
26	Sexual intimacy was achieved early, rapidly in the relationship	AA		AN	AN	U	R	U	
27	You take the quality of sexual rapport as a test of love	AA	U	AN		U	AN	U	R
28	You are willing to work out sex problems, improve technique	U	R		R	U		R	U
29	You have a continued high rate of sex, tactile contact throughout the relationship	U		R	R	U	R		R
30	You declare your love first, well ahead of partner			AN	R	AA	AA		
31	You consider love life your most important activity, even essential	AA	AN	R	AA		AA	R	R
32	You are prepared to "give all" for love once under way	U	AN	U	AA	R	AA	R	R
33	You are willing to suffer abuse, even ridicule from partner			AN	R	AA		R	AN
34	Your relationship is marked by frequent differences of opinion, anxiety	R	AA	R	AA	R	R		R
35	The relationship ends with lasting bitterness, trauma for you	AN	R	R	AA	R	AN	R	R

Column headers (rotated): Eros, Ludus, Storge, Mania, Ludic Eros, Storgic Eros, Storgic Ludus, Pragma

To diagnose your style of love, look for patterns across characteristics. If you consider your childhood less happy than that of your friends, were discontent with life when you fell in love, and very much want to be in love, you have "symptoms" that are rarely typical of eros and almost never true of storge, but which do suggest mania. Where a trait did not especially apply to a type of love, the space in that column is blank. Storge, for instance, is not the *presence* of many symptoms of love, but precisely their absence: it is cool, abiding affection rather than *Sturm und Drang*.

half of this pretest group, for example, agreed that *Two people can love each other truly, even when they know they have only a short time before they must part, never to meet again,* and also with *The test of time is the only sure way to know if love is real.* Some explained: "It depends on which kind of love."

Since the questionnaire asked only about a respondent's general attitude toward love, I constructed a method that would identify actual experiences in love. This was the love story card sort, in which a lover tells me, in an organized and precoded manner, what happened when he or she was in a relationship defined as love.

The card sort consists of 170 sets of questions, each dealing with steps in the love affair; the questions were the same for men and women except for appropriate pronouns. Each set consists of a green card with a question or incomplete sentence, followed by white cards that represent the range of answers ("other" is included). The respondent simply selects the white card that is his or her answer. For example, one green card asks the respondent for his reaction to the beloved on their first meeting. The answers range from "something seemed to draw us together, like a kind of magnetism" to "I ignored her for a while and we got together casually" to "I rather disliked her."

The questions cover a wide range of events in a person's life and in the love relationship. They begin with recollections of childhood, and move to feelings about work, family, close friends, self-esteem, and life in general at the start of the love affair. The card sort probes what one's expectations of love were like; the ideal lover, if any; how the lovers met; the respondent's thoughts and behavior while away from the lover; sexual intimacy and the nature of the sexual relationship; whether the partners felt jealousy; number and nature of arguments; break-ups and reunions. There is room for variations in love stories: love triangles, homosexuality, serial love affairs, simultaneous ones, and so on.

When I analyzed the individual card selections, three primary approaches to love emerged, which were independent of each other, along with six secondary approaches that were combinations of the primaries. The varied experiences of my respondents broke down to 35 factors that were best able to distinguish the nine types (see chart, page 37): for example, memories of childhood, initial frequency of contact, intensity of feeling.

I conducted my pilot study on 112 persons interviewed in four cities: Brighton and London in England, and Toronto and Peterborough in Canada. I simply approached people on the street, told them the purpose of my research, and scheduled an interview with those who agreed. The pilot sample was limited to white heterosexuals under the age of 35, since at the time I did the pilot I wanted only those who had been in love since the World War, an event that significantly changed mores and morals. This was hardly a random sample, but I was more interested in verifying my typology than in determining how many of each type there are. The 112 were approximately matched for age, sex, marital status, and social class.

When I compared the answers to questions according to nationality, sex, social class, and education, few differences emerged. Canadians were slightly more likely than the English to try to "cool off" the beloved's passion. Women were slightly more likely than men to describe their lovers as "holding back" on their emotions, a finding that fits cultural expectations. Younger respondents tended to be slightly more manic than older ones. But the types of love did not vary with education or class. While working-class men reported more sexual difficulties than professional men, they had felt every nuance of passion and imagination that middle-class men did.

Since the pilot study, I have tested the typology on respondents up to age 65, on Americans, and on 60 homosexual males. It remains to study people from other cultures and countries, and nonwhites in Western societies. So far, the typology has held up.

LOVE OR MARRIAGE
Snell and Gail Putney

Why, you would not make a man your lawyer or your family doctor on so slight an acquaintance as you would fall in love with and marry him! George Bernard Shaw

The typical American really believes that it is impossible to understand why he falls in love. He does, however, have a clear idea of how to tell *when* he is in love: he expects to be at once ecstatic and miserable, to behave erratically, to experience a floating sensation, and to lose his appetite. Sophisticated Americans discount these notions, but not as much as they think they do. They smile at romantic love but expound earnestly on "real love" or "mature love." They debate the merits of different forms of love, but never seem to question the idea of love itself.

The American divorce rate has been variously attributed to teenage marriage, delayed marriage, premarital sexual experience, lack of sexual experience, decline of religious influence, residual Puritanism, glamorization of divorce, and even the automobile. But our analysis suggests a different, perhaps a shocking answer: American marriages are unstable because Americans marry for love.

Let it be understood at the outset that we are not confining our discussion to the romantic notions of adolescents, suggesting that all would be well if only they achieved "mature love." It is love itself, mature or immature, real or illusory, which we are challenging.

Because the myth of love is deeply imbedded in American culture, such an assertion may seem absurd, even threatening. The American fears that his life (and especially his marriage) would be flat and joyless without love. Moreover, he thinks that without someone to love him he could never accept himself.

Yet the questioning of any widely accepted myth seems initially unsettling. It was once feared that if people lost faith in the proposition that kings ruled by Divine Right, no authority would be tolerated and anarchy would engulf society. And once a myth is dead, it seems incredible that anyone ever took it seriously.

By no means do all peoples take love seriously. There are societies in which love is regarded as a rare form of insanity. There are other societies which have no word for love except as a euphemism for sexual desire. There are still other societies which speak simply of sexual desire, and have no word for love in their language.

When the adjusted American learns that love is not universal, he is likely to express pity (if not contempt) for people who are so backward or so cold that they do not fall in love. He has been imbued with the notion that love is of supreme importance in life and he considers any adult who has never been in love to be emotionally stunted.

This belief in the power of love to transform and to mature the individual is curiously parallel to the aboriginal American Indian belief in the power of trance experience. It was the custom in many tribes to send adolescent boys into the hills in search of a vision. To some a vision came easily and soon; to others it came only after days of fasting. But, until it came, a boy could not become a man. His vision endowed him with power for life, and determined whether he would become a hunter, warrior, shaman, or transvestite.

The American would be amused at the suggestion that he choose his career while in a trance, as the Indian boy did. Yet he finds nothing odd in the practice of choosing a wife according to the vagaries of the ecstatic trance he calls love. Ethnocentrism aside, the one practice is as illogical as the other.

But the American takes for granted the view of love which is inculcated by his culture. The only question he is prepared to raise about love regards its authenticity: is his feeling infatuation or is it the Real Thing? Circumstances which might lead an objective observer to have grave doubts about a marriage seem insignificant to the American in love. It is an article of faith with him that love conquers all. *His question is not whether the marriage would be sound, but whether his love is real.*

If concern about the authenticity of an ecstatic experience has a medieval ring, it might be recalled that romantic love is an invention of the Middle Ages. The troubadours built the myth of love and fashioned such ideas as love at first sight, the existence of an Ideal lover for each person, and the power of True Love to conquer all. One glimpse of the fair maiden leaning over the parapet and the knight was supposed to be smitten. He might pine away if his love was not returned, but let his lady encourage him by some token and his strength was increased tenfold. Possessed by love, he had the

Reprinted from *Normal Neurosis: The Adjusted American* by Snell Putney and Gail J. Putney. Copyright © 1964 by G.J. Putney and Snell Putney. By permission of Harper and Row, Inc. Publisher.

power to conquer all obstacles in his path, including any dragons guarding the maiden.

But in the Middle Ages love was not the basis for marriage. Family connections, land ownership, political convenience, and at times even military alliance were the foundations of aristocratic marriage. And peasant marriages were contracted on similarly pragmatic bases. Romantic love was an aristocratic diversion, but the nobility that amused itself with love explicitly assumed that love and marriage were incompatible. The daily familiarities of marriage could only erode romance. So it was not his bride that the medieval prince expected to love, modern fairy tales to the contrary notwithstanding; when knighthood was in flower, one knight's love was another knight's lady.

At the end of the Middle Ages, the emerging middle class adopted the aristocratic ideology of love. But the middle class was uncomfortable about the extramarital setting, so they made love fit their moral code. Keeping the medieval idea of love nearly intact, they wrapped it into a neat middle-class package by making love the basis for marriage. As individual choice gradually superseded family dictates, marriage for love became part of Western tradition.

And so Americans marry for love—a culturally defined emotion which was considered incompatible with marriage by those who shaped it. Americans regard as a supreme experience an emotional seizure which some people consider akin to running amuck. They deliberately place love beyond comprehension and control, and thereby surrender in advance any hope of autonomous choice when love affects their lives. And then—wondrous irony—they demand to know what has gone wrong with their marriages.

Love can be fun, and the autonomous individual might choose to experience it—but hardly as a basis for marriage. Choosing a spouse while under the influence of an emotion which the individual himself insists is unpredictable, incomprehensible, and irresistible is incompatible with autonomy. One could as well marry while drunk. But fortunately love *is* comprehensible and (to a surprising degree) predictable. And, once understood, love need not be a compulsive emotion.

This Thing Called Love

A love affair may involve many of the mechanisms found in friendship: a mutual admiration society, a nonaggression pact, unrecognized self-discovery, reciprocal rationalization, habits of mutual need satisfaction—all of these, or none. But the unique quality of love itself derives from yet a different psychological mechanism. Love *is* more than friendship.

Men love much as they hate; the mechanism of the one emotion is an inversion of the other. When a person alienates from himself some quality or potential which he despises, he projects it onto someone else, where he hates it. Conversely, when he alienates some quality or potential which he would like to experience in himself but does not, he projects it onto someone else, where he loves it. The people he loves, like those he hates, are merely convenient targets for his projections.

It may seem curious that anyone would alienate potentialities he longs to experience in himself, but there are several reasons why people do so. Often, the individual alienates qualities that seem contradictory to his fundamental self-image. He may regard these characteristics as desirable in abstract, but as inappropriate for himself. Thus he may not permit himself reckless bravado, impulsiveness, impracticality, whimsey, or bounding optimism, but he may project his potential for such behaviors onto someone else and adore it in them. Here lies the reason for the attraction of opposites (although lovers may not seem so opposite to outsiders as they seem to each other).

Many of the characteristics which are alienated from the self and loved in others are those which the culture has assigned to the opposite sex. Most societies designate some behaviors and qualities as "masculine" and others as "feminine". But this does not mean that men are devoid of potential normally attributed to women, or vice versa. On the contrary, what is normal masculine behavior in one culture may be normal feminine behavior in another. Margaret Mead reports that among the Tchambuli of New Guinea the women are expected to be practical, comradely, and sexually aggressive, whereas the men are expected to be passive and artistic, to gossip and primp.* For what matter, not far back in Western history the dashing cavalier wore long curls and perfume; with the rapier and stallion went powder and lace and soft leather boots that displayed a well-turned calf. Whatever is defined as "manly" at a given time and place determines to a large degree which of his potentialities a boy will try to realize and which he will alienate.

In modern America, boys past the age of four or five learn that it is not manly to cry, to want to be cuddled, to be fearful, too clean, or too pretty. Although the boy may enjoy indulging some of

* See Margaret Mead, *Sex and Temperament in Three Primitive Societies.* William Morrow and Co., New York, 1935, Chapter 15.

these characteristics (such as his desire to be cuddled), he comes to disown them as he seeks to become an acceptable man. As his self-image is directed toward the cultural image of masculinity, he alienates his potential for responding in "feminine" ways.

This alienation does not rid him either of his capacity for responding in these ways, or of his potential enjoyment of such responses. He would still like to be cuddled and fussed over, to be comforted when hurt, to adorn himself. But the stronger side of his ambivalence is the desire to be a little reserved, rugged, and "masculine" in appearance and demeanor, to shrug aside offers of condolence. A man coming out of anesthesia once summarized the ambivalence by growling at his wife "Go away and stop leaving me alone!"

Having alienated those aspects of himself which he has learned to regard as incompatible with his manhood, the male projects them onto the women around him. In his mother, his daughter, his wife, and particularly his sweetheart, he sees and loves his own desires to be dependent, vain, impractical, demonstrative, and all the other things he has learned to consider unsuitable in himself. Indeed, he often demands that his women display such characteristics.

In a parallel but reverse manner, the little girl in America is encouraged to seek comfort when she scrapes a knee, to be openly affectionate, to be proud of her curls and ruffles—and is scolded for a dirty face or a bold manner. She learns to alienate her potential for being aggressive, self-assertive, proficient in sports and mechanics. She is likely to adore masterful men.

It would be oversimplification to view the cultural ideal for men and for women as direct opposites, corresponding like a photographic print to its negative. But there are many qualities which one sex is encouraged to display and the other to alienate and project. These customary projections on the opposite sex lead to a general attraction of men to women and vice versa—over and above the biological interest in the opposite sex.

Another reason for alienating and projecting valued facets of the self is that a person may become falsely convinced that he lacks some quality which he considers desirable. As a child he may have been reminded of his inability to do something so often that the deficiency became an established part of his self-image. As his parents dwelt on the capacity, they underscored its desirability at the same time that they convinced the child that he lacked it. However great or small his potential in this area might have been, the child came to cherish it at the same time that he alienated it. His capacity may remain inaccessible to him throughout his life. If so, he will experience it only via projection on others—to whom he feels strongly attracted.

Having always been told, say, that he has no talent for making friends (but like anyone else having some ability to do so) he alienates his potential and projects it onto someone who displays an outgoing, gregarious nature. He will then find himself drawn to this person, perhaps (if other projections follow the first) "falling in love." But the love is for lost facets of himself. Almost everyone has a minimal capacity to do almost anything humanly possible—and the person who is in fact totally deficient in some quality is not likely to value it in others. He may be aware of qualities which he lacks, but he will not adore them: the color-blind man is not enamored of the artist's color sense. The qualities he adores in others are his own displaced potentialities.

Thus each individual makes idiosyncratic alienations which fill in details on the cultural image of the opposite sex, and out of these he creates his own specific "Ideal." The subsequent search for the Ideal mate is in reality a quest for the alienated but desired facets of the self which have been shaped into the idealized image. When a man first falls in love he simply hangs this image on some woman and loves it. If the fit is extremely poor, he may soon withdraw his projections—and believe that he was only "infatuated." But if the ready-made image fits her reasonably well (with a few alterations in minor details) and if other positive projections supplement those of the original ideal image, he is soon a man in love.

Bystanders (who are not making comparable projections) may wonder what he sees in her, or shrug and say that love is blind. In a sense it is, for the lover peers through a haze of projections. Even if the projections are a good fit, it does not alter the fact that it is his own alienated potential that he loves. The compelling power of love derives from the desire to reunite with the alienated and loved capacities of the self.

The adolescent girl who sighs and screams over a singer she has never seen off the stage is ridiculed by her elders, but she is correct in insisting that she is in love. Her emotion is love in its purest form; that is, it is not an admixture of romance and friendship. Her love is, moreover, in the best medieval tradition; inaccessibility of the beloved was originally a vital element in romantic love. Distance enables the lover to see his beloved purely in terms of the projections he hangs on her.

The demonstration that love is not caused by unique qualities of the beloved is as simple as noting that a constant cannot explain a variable. John may not love Mary, may come to love Mary, and may cease to love Mary—all while Mary remains unchanged. Clearly it is something within the lover which causes him to love and that something is the desire to recapture alienated self-potential. Beauty is in the eye of the beholder, as the saying goes, and so is love.

The True Love of John and Mary

John has definite ideas about what he wants in a wife. To the cultural expectation that she must be exciting, warm, pretty, dainty, and in need of his love and protection, he has added various other potentialities which through circumstance he has alienated from his self-image. All he needs is a target on which he can project this idealized image—and Mary dances by. He hears her laugh, and feels a sudden "irresistible attraction." He flings after his impression of a girl the image that he is prepared to love, and is drawn to it. The basic mechanism would have been the same had he fallen gradually in love with the girl next door, but John happen to fall in love at first sight. He maneuvers an introduction, and the romance begins.

A romance is a prime situation in which to enjoy many aspects of the self. It offers an opportunity for being loving and lovable, excited and exciting. It puts John in a mood to enjoy himself, even under circumstances (such as waiting for a bus in the rain) that he would normally have thought miserable. He surprises himself with the ingenuity he uses to find places to take Mary, and things to do. By tradition (and because parties to a romance are usually at a stage in life when other responsibilities are not too burdensome) many pleasant activities are virtually set aside for those in love. In the context of the romance, John seizes the opportunity to enjoy aspects of himself that he has rarely experienced. Unrecognized self-discovery is a sizable component in the thrill of any romance. Being American, however, he assumes that it is the girl who thrills him.

Among the activities traditionally reserved for romance is the exploration of sexual capacity. Whether the couple copulate or not, there is a sexual focus in romance. John is not a complete novice to sex, but he expects to find it more rewarding with someone he loves; moreover, Mary corresponds to his particularized conception of a desirable sexual partner.

Like most Americans, John also sexualizes his desire to repossess the alienated qualities which he has projected onto his beloved. The lover wants to make these characteristics a part of himself, to reunite with his alienated potential. But, because he thinks of these things as aspects of his sweetheart, he assumes that his desire is to unite with her—a phrase which in America is a euphemism for sexual relations. Following his culture's definitions and interpretations, John develops a *sexualized* interest in Mary which is quite independent of his biological urgings.

John has projected so much of himself onto Mary that he is miserable without her. He is jealous of anyone else who is close to her, for he wants exclusive and constant possession of the potential he projects onto her.

Mary is in a similar state. She finds and loves in John many qualities which she has alienated from her self-image: poise, wit, forcefulness, self-assurance. She, too, has an Ideal, composed of conventional as well as idiosyncratic projections, of many things she would like to be but is sure she is not. She hangs this image on John and finds that he is wonderful.

Moreover, finding someone who thinks that *she* is wonderful is a balm to ease her self-doubts. As an adjusted American girl, Mary has learned to seek self-acceptance indirectly, through winning approval, admiration, and love from others. John's love for her seems the epitome of acceptance and Mary clings to it.

Because each wants to be loved, each agrees to love the other (not that the bargain is explicit, of course, but it is understood all the same). Like most lovers, these two form a mutual admiration society, dedicated to indirect self-acceptance. No romance is ever open and candid, for both parties are intent on making and maintaining a good impression. Mary seems a faultless angel to John because he is seeing what he has projected onto her—a view she encourages by seeking to conceal less flattering characteristics and by trying to fit his picture of her. Anything he praises, she seeks to emphasize, and because he complements her on what he expects to see (independently of reality) she finds herself cultivating new and exciting self-potential.

All of this could lead to self-discovery on Mary's part. As realists have long noted, the appearance and disposition of an unattractive, shrewish girl can be remarkably improved by daily assertions that she is beautiful and sweet tempered. Mary would like to believe the image of herself that she sees reflected in John's eyes. But she knows that she is concealing other facets of herself (perhaps ill-tempered or slovenly proclivities) and, moreover, she finds it hard to believe that the charms John attributes to her are real. Any changes which she does perceive in herself she believes are elicited by John and she fears that if she lost him she *might* turn into a pumpkin. So she clings to him as a prop for a masquerade she hopes will never end. Her self-discovery remains unrecognized.

Mary has yet another reason for wanting to believe that she is in love. Having learned a contradictory set of ideas about sex, she is ambivalent about the sexual nature of the romance. She is uneasy about being sexually aroused and thinks that, if her feeling for John is only infatuation, her awakening sexual interests are dangerous and wrong. But she believes that if her feeling is Love she ought to desire him. Since she does find herself desiring him, she feels she had better be in love, and any questions about the suitability of marriage with John are pushed out of her mind.

John and Mary are in love, and they believe it is neither possible nor desirable to know why. But, as adjusted Americans, they are confident that love and marriage go together, and so they are wed.

The Marriage of John and Mary

Although evidence is abundant, it is seldom remarked that the degree to which people are in love when they marry is not correlated to the amount of pleasure they derive from marriage. Some who were wildly in love find disappointment, and some who were never in love find happiness—but the reverse can also be true. The fact is that marital bliss depends on other variables than love, although love may complicate marital adjustment.

John and Mary have been married several years. The excitement of engagement and marriage rituals and the thrill of setting up housekeeping are forgotten and both of them would admit that the honeymoon is over. More precisely, the nature of their relationship has changed. Self-discovery has atrophied, largely because they no longer exercise initiative in enjoying themselves as they did during their romance. The unflattering light of continual association makes it difficult for either to maintain an idealized image of the other, and each is well aware that the other no longer thinks he is perfect. Moreover, they have begun to hang negative

projections on each other. Unlike a True Love, a spouse is a convenient depository for undesired aspects of the self. For example, John feels trapped by mounting expenses. His own desire to spend recklessly seems threatening, so he projects it onto Mary and finds her demanding and extravagant.

Mary is still caught up in her ambivalence about sex. She projects onto her husband her desire to experiment sexually, then complains that he is intent on pressuring her into sexual variations. This is a traditional middle-class pattern, and it is probable that her mother and her grandmother made similar projections and complaints.

But, because Mary is a modern wife, her sex life is complicated further by her belief (acquired from marriage manuals) that her adequacy as a woman is measured by her sexual competence and the degree to which she enjoys intercourse. Her natural desire to enjoy sex is obscured by the feeling that she *ought* to enjoy it. She alternates between avoiding sexual relations and concentrating so intently on achieving orgasm that there is little pleasure in the process.

In these sexual complications, John is no help. The same marriage manuals have informed him that he has a choice between being a selfish, brutal male, and being a sympathetic, competent lover who makes sure that he gives full satisfaction to his partner. Wanting to be a sympathetic, competent lover, he becomes hyper-conscious of her response. He watches her to see how much pleasure he is able to give her, and Mary watches him watching her. Proving his competence by giving her pleasure becomes so important to him that his own enjoyment is greatly reduced. Moreover, his preoccupation with her response encourages her idea that sexual excitement is something she ought to feel in order not to disappoint John. (She sometimes finds herself thinking that life and sex might be simpler if her husband were a selfish, brutal male who allowed her to respond or not as she pleased.)

Finally, as their positive projections on each other have dimmed, so has the sexualized desire to repossess them. With sexualization gone, they are left with only the sexual urge itself, a fact which they manage to regard as a sign of sexual incompatibility.

Yet, during this same period, they are achieving a general adaptation to each other, a growing acceptance of each other's quirks, even (in spite of their confusions) some sexual competence. They no longer feel the need for pretense with each other, or at least they have largely abandoned efforts to maintain it. The way is opening for a candid intimacy. Moreover, they are building ties of mutual need satisfaction. Any advance either of them could make in understanding himself and his needs would be richly rewarded in their enjoyment of each other.

But John and Mary are more aware of the dissolution of old ties based on love than of the emergence of new ones founded on mutual need satisfaction. Mary feels threatened by the changing nature of her relation to her husband and (projecting her doubts onto him) asks at odd moments, "Do you still love me?" John has his own doubts about his feelings and the question serves to magnify them. Preoccupied with what they believe are interpersonal failures, they do not perceive the intrapersonal origin of their difficulties.

The specific quarrels that John and Mary have are largely irrelevant; even if by fortuitous amnesia they were able to forget and begin their marriage anew, their love would not last. The simple fact is that the adulterous aristocrats of the Middle Ages were right: marriage is corrosive to love.

And love is an impediment to marital happiness. Founded on projection, abetting the quest for indirect self-acceptance, love can contribute neither to candid intimacy nor to self-acceptance. But, like most of their adjusted compatriots, this couple believe that love is the only basis for marriage. As they feel love evaporating, they begin to wonder if their marriage was a mistake. In their concern for love, they blind themselves to the possible success of their marriage.

The True Love of John and Sue

It has become apparent that John's Ideal image was not a good fit on Mary (he would say that Mary has changed) and, without letting himself recognize what he is doing, he has been looking for someone else on whom he can project it. Sue happens to be handy, and although familiarity may erode love, propinquity helps initiate it. So the time comes when John transfers to Sue the sides of himself which he once had projected onto Mary. He interprets the transfer as the discovery that Sue is his Ideal, and he feels drawn to her.

John wants to repossess alienated sides of himself which he has not enjoyed even vicariously since his troubles with his wife began. As before, he interprets this feeling as a desire to possess the girl on whom he projects the beloved but alienated sides of himself—and thus he sexualizes the attraction. John's sexual needs are easily and conveniently satisfied with his spouse (or at least could be if he would quit worrying about being a sympathetic, competent lover). But, having projected onto Sue qualities that he wants to make part of himself, he thinks he wants to "make" Sue.

This desire is disturbing to John, for part of his self-image involves being an ethical man. During his marriage he has experienced fleeting desires for other women, but nothing like the intense desire produced by the sexualization of his projections on Sue. Not comprehending the nature of his attraction, he has trouble reconciling it with his desire to be a faithful husband. The myth of love resolves his dilemma with a comforting rationalization: having learned to regard love as unpredictable, irresistible, and involuntary, he can argue that if he is in love with the girl he is noble for hiding his feelings, rather than guilty for having them. Quite predictably, he falls in love with Sue.

This is the mechanism of the Great Romance. The married individual projects desired potential onto someone other than his spouse, is drawn to it, sexualizes the attraction, then rationalizes the resulting adulterous desire by claiming it to be the flowering of True Love. This is the Great Romance of his life, and how can he deny himself and his beloved? This pattern is common among adjusted Americans, and John falls into it and into his first affair.

In his romance with Sue, he recaptures many of the pleasures he had once known with Mary. He experiences again the flattering role of the lover, to which tabu adds relish. And he enjoys the positive projections that Sue hangs on him. Even if he discounts her view of him, it is a joy to find again someone who thinks he is wonderful. Gratefully, he reciprocates.

But in spite of the excitement of his new romance, John is confused and unhappy. He feels that he has a right to his Great Romance, and he feels that he is a heel. His thoughts of how unfair his unfaithfulness is to Mary are countered by thoughts of how unfair it is to remain with her when he and Sue really love each other. In the end, he runs from the conflict by projecting onto his wife his own desire to remain with her, and experiencing it as if it were possessiveness on her part. He becomes convinced that all *he* wants to do is divorce Mary and marry Sue. He laments the fact that he did not meet Sue first—never dreaming that, if he had, the partner in his Great Romance might well have been Mary.

The True Love of Mary and Bill

As Mary first suspects and then discovers her husband's extramarital adventure she finds in it proof of her own inadequacy. Her self-doubts seem confirmed and her need to find herself acceptable mounts. She becomes increasingly tense, a feeling which she interprets as anger. Following the line of cultural expectation, she turns her tension into tearful denunciation of her unfaithful spouse.

Were Mary capable of direct self-acceptance, the situation might develop quite differently. It might still be difficult for Mary to avoid some emotional entanglement in John's confusion, but if she were self-accepting she could ease him over his Great Romance. With time, John would discover that his projections fit Sue no better than Mary. He is accustomed to satisfying many needs with his wife, and in the long run would probably recognize that the ties to Mary are stronger than the attraction to Sue.

But feeling threatened and wronged, Mary pulls away from her husband. She refuses to satisfy needs with John as a means of punishing him, and the result is that she deprives herself and becomes more needful, tense, and angry. At the same time, she is breaking the ties of mutual need satisfaction that could have held John.

Many an indignant wife has consulted a lawyer at this point, but Mary is as anxious to ease her feelings of inadequacy as she is to punish John. In some societies the children she has borne would be proof of her adequacy as a woman, but Mary is an American and believes that the proof of her femininity is her ability to appeal and to respond to men sexually. After several years of washing diapers, scrubbing sinks, and scolding children, Mary feels more like a bedraggled housemaid than an enticing female.

In an effort to prove to herself that she can still be attractive, Mary splurges on a startling dress and a new hair style, and goes to a party alone (John had declined the invitation, pleading that he had to work late). It is not surprising that men should begin paying Mary compliments, although she would not want to admit that she had invited their advances. An acquaintance named Bill soon monopolizes her, and for the moment, at least, her self-doubts are eased. She slips out of the party with Bill and sets out to do the town. She has not experienced the "orchids and champagne" Mary in years, but she expects to recapture this feeling with Bill—and so she does.

Part of her self-image involves being a faithful wife in spite of what John may do, and she has never thought that she would become involved in an affair. Like John, she is ambivalent. But she alienates her disapproval, and her scruples then seem an unreasonable demand by "society" that she be faithful when her husband is not. Bill assures her that the double standard went out with bloomers and Mary is ready to agree.

In the abandon of an affair, Mary ceases to regard sex as something she *ought* to enjoy and begins to think of it as something she *wants* to enjoy. The result is that she makes some startling discoveries about her own capacity for sexual enjoyment. However, she fails to perceive that her enjoyment is the result of her own attitude and behavior, and assumes that it is a consequence of having changed partners. It distresses her to feel guilty about her new-found pleasure in sex. She is soon able to rationalize it by discovering that her affair with Bill is the Great Romance of *her* life.

The rebellious affair helps Mary to experiment sexually, but it inhibits any self-understanding. Even during periods when she thinks she would like to make her marriage work, she finds it difficult to admit that her Great Romance could be motivated by hostile retaliation. Besides, the positive projections she now hangs on Bill convince her that she really loves him. Before long, Mary is too far out on the limb of loving Bill to get back.

John is jealous, but at the time he finds his wife's affair a convenient justification for his own behavior. He can assure himself that he and Mary were incompatible after all, and that both of them will surely be happier married to their new loves. So the marriage of John and Mary ends, but (barring unlikely insight) their future may be more predictable than either of them realizes.

On whom will John hang his idealized projections after he becomes disillusioned with Sue? Recoiling from a second divorce, he may settle down in resignation. Or he may pursue his idealized projections and marry again and again. But the person agonizing over the decision of divorcing his spouse to marry his love is likely to miss the crux of the problem, which is the unsuitability of love as a foundation for marriage. Those who long to stay in love forever seldom stay married for long.

Beyond Love

Some people would object that the concept of love we have employed is too narrow, that love is more than this. Certainly the attraction between two people may involve any one or a combination of different mechanisms: mutual admiration, reciprocal rationalization, unrecognized self-discovery, localized self-acceptance, or mutual need satisfaction, as well as the projection of alienated but desired characteristics. It would be possible to define love as involving some combination of these, or to designate the forms of attraction as love$_1$, love$_2$, love$_3$, etc. This would not alter the analysis, only the terminology.

For the sake of clarity, we have restricted the word *love* to that attraction which is based on the projection of alienated but desired characteristics. Such projection leads to an intense desire to be with the person on whom the projections are hung, to exhilaration when he is present, to depression when he is absent, to possessive jealousy. Our usage is thus consistent with the kind of feeling an American usually has in mind when he says, "I love you."

Love thus defined is a major factor in the American's choice of spouse, but if those who marry for love find happiness, it is more in spite of love than because of it. Without comprehending what they are doing, they must overcome the projections of love which lead away from self-knowledge and blur their perceptions of each other. They must make a transition from this to the candor and understanding of at least a localized self-acceptance.

But most couples assume that happiness will come to them if only they marry the one they love, and thus they are more concerned with clinging to love than with building a rewarding marriage. The assumption that the spouse is the source of pleasure in marriage leads the individual to blame his spouse when he fails to find the pleasure he had expected. As long as he makes this assumption, he is likely to look for another spouse instead of altering the behaviors through which he seeks marital satisfaction.

The parties to a successful marriage learns to *expect to enjoy the self in marriage rather than to expect to enjoy the spouse.* Because the expectation is different, the interaction is different. As each partner seeks to maximize his own enjoyment of the marriage, he assists his spouse in doing the same. Each is seeking candor and warmth, and the exploration of self-potential (sexual capacities and many others), all of which is facilitated by the co-operation of someone else engaged in a similar development. Such persons are not preoccupied with being loved or with maintaining romantic illusions. They are trying to enjoy life—together.

It may be that the phrase "mature love" is sometimes intended to convey the idea of this kind of relationship, but if so the usage is misleading, for it implies that the so-called "mature love" is a natural outgrowth of romantic love. This is hardly the case, for love leads in the opposite direction. It is no accident that the greatest tales of love end with the death of the lovers: there is simply no other plausible ending that would not conflict with the myth of love. Love may form the basis for a charming weekend, but it is an unstable foundation for a marriage.

The American has difficulty imagining how he would choose a mate apart from the compulsion of love. Actually, the specific person he marries is less important to his happiness than he believes—the attitudes with which he approaches marriage are far more significant. The person who sees marriage as an opportunity for experiencing the warm, demonstrative potential in himself, and for satisfying needs in a candid and stable association, usually finds what he seeks. The general rule is that people who enjoy life enjoy marriage. Some people would be unhappy with any spouse, for they do not allow themselves happiness. A few other people would be happy almost regardless of whom they married. The large middle group, however, is most likely to find marital happiness if they seek a spouse who has an unusual degree of self-understanding and self-acceptance.

The idea of moving beyond love is initially frightening to most Americans, once they grasp that love itself is being challenged, and not just romantic illusion. Many people fear that analysis of their loves would undermine the sense of being loved that seems so essential in their pursuit of indirect self-acceptance. Others regret the effect of insight on the poetic aura which surrounds love. Yet love is at best a temporary euphoria, and the individual who pursues it finds it impossible to seize and hold. The quest for love, like the quest for indirect self-acceptance, is a neurotic pattern—an impediment to the fulfillment it falsely promises.

LOVE AND MARRIAGE IN MODERN AMERICA: A FUNCTIONAL ANALYSIS

Sidney M. Greenfield

Love and Marriage in Modern America: A Functional Analysis

'Voi, che cose e amor?' asked Cherubino in Mozart's *Marriage of Figaro.* "Tell me, you know, what is this thing, love?" Cherubino was still a beardless adolescent and did not know the answer, but he took it for granted that there was one. So have most other people, and many of them have tried to give it, but the most noteworthy feature about all their answers is how thoroughly they disagree. Sometimes, it seems, they cannot be referring to the same phenomenon, or even to related ones. After a while one wonders whether there is something wrong with the question itself, or whether perhaps it employs a word of no fixed meaning and can have no answer.[1]

Love, wrote Theodor Reik, "is one of the most overworked words in our vocabulary. There is hardly a field of human activity in which the word is not worked to death."[2] The literature on the subject, to say the least, is voluminous. However, "if it is true that science is the topography of ignorance, as Oliver Wendell Holmes once said, then the region of love is a vast white spot.[3]

Most of what we know of love comes from the pens of poets, dramatists, novelists, and philosophers. What they have to say, however, is so variable, idiosyncratic, and full of contradictions that, in sum, it adds relatively little to our understanding of the subject.

Psychologists also have written about love. Most of what they have to say, however, is an elaboration upon, or modification of, Freud's notion that love is "aim inhibited sex."[4] Furthermore, most of their attention has been focused on therapy and counseling, and here they tend to be at one with the numerous sociologists and marriage counselors who have done work on the subject. The vast majority of these students and therapists, as Goode has recently stated, have "commented on the importance of romantic love in America and its lesser importance in other societies, and have disparaged it as a poor basis for marriage, or as immaturity."[5] Although they have helped us to specify and describe what love in the United States is—in the ethnographic sense—they have done very little in the way of analyzing their observations and contributing to our understanding of love. Instead, they have devoted their efforts to exposing the evils of romantic love and preaching against its practice.

The present paper is an attempt to apply modern sociological thinking to the analysis of the descriptive materials that have been accumulated on the subject of romantic love. In this sense then it is offered as a partial contribution to the understanding of the general phenomenon of love. More specifically, however, it is offered as an analysis of the place of love in modern American society. Following the lead of the family sociologists and marriage counselors, love will be treated not in the philosopher's or poet's sense of a "sweeping experience," not in the psychologist's sense of a universal physical power, and not in the sociologist's sense of a universal attribute of man. Instead, love shall be looked upon as a part of society, as a distinctive pattern of social behavior—as a specific culture trait. Thus we shall take the word to mean a given behavioral complex that exists in a specifiable social context. In this sense, our approach is ethnographic and synchronic. In this paper, therefore, the term love will be used to refer to a specific culture trait that has been described in modern American society. Whether or not it exists in other societies—or in all human societies—in the same or a modified form is a matter to be demonstrated ethnographically and not assumed *a priori.*

The most abundant descriptive material available on the behavioral pattern called love comes from observations made in the contemporary United States—but restricted primarily to members of the middle class. Thus we shall limit our analysis to this segment of our own society and leave comparisons for another time.

Love, or romantic love, as it is called in the literature, is a behavioral complex composed of a series of specific features or elements. In the first place, it is a pattern that characterizes the behavior of adolescent and adult members of the middle class engaged in the quest of a mate.[6] Such individuals generally act in a distinctive way—distinctive with respect to the way in which individuals not in quest of a mate behave in the same society. In general, middle-class Americans are extremely sober and rational. These same people, however, when they are "in love" tend to be anything but.

Emotion, as opposed to reason, may be taken as characteristic of the thoughts and acts of a person in love; reason is believed to dominate at all other times. The quality of the emotions may be characterized best by a word such as "flighty." Phrases such as "walking on air," "floating on cloud nine," and so forth, are used to describe both the feelings

Reprinted from *Sociological Quarterly*, 6 (Autumn, 1965), pp. 361-377. Reprinted by permission of the *Sociological Quarterly*.

and the behavior of someone in love. The theatrical extreme, for example, has been stated by the heroine of a once popular musical comedy when she sang: "I'm as corny as Kansas in August, as high as a kite on the fourth of July. If you'll excuse an expression I use, I'm in love. . ."

The song writer obviously overstated the case as dramatists often do to emphasize what is commonplace to their audience. Most Americans do not go around singing of their love as one might imagine after watching their movies and theater. However, they do tend to behave in a manner that by their normal standards may be considered flighty and irrational.

In the more exceptional cases, ungovernable impulses are overtly indulged. At times, the person in love can scarcely think of anything but his beloved. A great tenderness is experienced by the lover along with extreme delusions as to the nature of the loved person. On rare occasions all else but love seems to cease to matter to the lover; the emotion of the experience is all-consuming. As a French author once put it, one ceases to live when the loved person is absent, and begins again only when he or she is present once more.

Another aspect of the pattern is that one falls in love not by design and conscious choice, but according to some accident of fate over which the victim has no control. Of course it is a well known fact that individuals are taught to fall in love. Whether or not the pattern is learned, however, the significant factor is that individuals come to believe that love can and does strike at almost any time and in any place, and that when it does, the parties involved are helpless victims: they lose control, so to speak, over themselves, their actions and their reason, and they tend to behave emotionally and irrationally.

Directly related to this is the idea that there is one person, or lover for each man and woman in the society. Thus, if and when the paths of these two "right for each other" parties cross, they are helpless and must succumb to the "forces of the Universe."

The recent increase in the incidence of divorce has in no way challenged this belief. At most the pattern has been altered slightly so that there is now one "right one" at a time.

That the entire syndrome is atypical for the society may be seen in the inability of the individual to help falling in love. The general American belief is that man is able to master and control his environment. But in the realm of love, he is the victim of forces even stronger than himself.

Along with the idea of a "right one," goes the over idealization of the loved one. Once he or she is found, and the lovers succumb to their destiny, the real features of the loved one's character become lost in the emotional irrationality that dominates behavior. Love is said to be blind and the lovers are blinded to the faults of their new found mates.

Overriding everything is the belief that love is a panacea. Love is believed to "conquer all" and once it is experienced everything is expected to be better than it was before. One consequence of this is that it is both good and desirable to fall in love.

For middle-class Americans the expected climax of a love affair is marriage. "The sentiment of love," write Waller and Hill, "is the heart of . . .the family. In our culture, people customarily get married because they are in love: indeed it seems preposterous to us that anyone should marry for any other reason."[7]

The syndrome of features that constitutes the pattern, or culture trait, that has come to be called romantic love in American society then may be summarized as follows:

1. Two diligent, hard working, rational adolescents or adults of the opposite sex meet, most probably by accident, and find each other to be personally and physically attractive.

2. They soon come to realize that they are "right for each other."

3. They then fall victims to forces beyond their control, and fall in love.

4. They then begin—at least for a short time—to behave in a flighty, irrational manner that is at variance with the way in which they formerly conducted themselves.

5. Finally, believing that love is a panacea and that the future holds only goodness for them, they marry and form a new nuclear family.

At this point we may note that sexual behavior in middle-class America, in general, is directly related to the romantic love complex. Sex, in the ideal, is restricted to people who are in love and then its practice is generally postponed until after marriage. Thus sexual gratification is linked to and becomes the culmination of the syndrome just described. In terms of ideal patterns we may state that sexual activity is to be engaged in only by people who are married to each other. We know, however, that the incidence of premarital and extramarital sexual behavior is relatively high, and is on the increase. It appears that in spite of this sex is still linked to the romantic love complex in that, by and large, middle-class couples who engage in premarital or extramarital sexual activity invariably believe—at the time—and behave as if they are in love with their illicit partners. Thus it appears that the tie between sex and love is strong though the restriction of sex to marriage is weakening.

Though the pattern is quite clear, most middle-class Americans as Hunt reminds us, "are firmly of two minds about it all—simultaneously hardheaded and idealistic, uncouth and tender, libidinous and puritanical; they believe implicitly in every tenet of romantic love, and yet know perfectly well that things don't really work out that way."[8] As with other culture traits, however, individuals, to a greater or lesser degree, do tend to approximate the ideal presented above.

The behavior and sentiments associated with romantic love appear to be at odds with what may be taken to be the general characteristics of American society. People in love are flighty and irrational in contrast with the sober rationality that generally prevails.

Students of non-Western societies tend to agree that the pattern just described for the United States is nonexistent, or at best very rare in the non-Western world.[9] The most quoted statement, probably because it is extreme, was made by Linton:

> All societies recognize that there are occasional violent emotional attachments between persons of opposite sex, but our present American culture is practically the only one which has attempted to capitalize these and make them the basis for marriage. Most groups regard them as unfortunate and point out the victims of such attachments as horrible examples. Their rarity in most societies suggest that they are psychological abnormalities to which our own culture has attached an extraordinary value just as other cultures have attached extreme values to other abnormalities. The hero of the modern American movie is always a romantic lover just as the hero of the old Arab epic is always an epileptic. A cynic might suspect that in any ordinary population the percentage of individuals with a capacity for romantic love of the Hollywood type was about as large as that of persons able to throw genuine epileptic fits. However, given a little social encouragement, either one can be adequately imitated without the performer admitting even to himself that the performance is not genuine.[10]

In addition to being both cross-culturally infrequent and atypical in comparision with the general range of behavior in American society—and possibly abnormal—the trait also has been considered pathological. As Truxal and Merrill put it: "The state of being romantically in love exhibits many characteristics of certain pathological conditions known as trance or dissociation phenomena."[11]

But to middle-class Americans, falling in love is not only the right thing to do, it is a panacea, and right and good for its own sake. As Hunt indicates: "At no time in history has so large a proportion of humanity rated love so highly, thought about it so much, or displayed such an insatiable appetite for word about it."[12] As a sympathetic observer (de Sales) once remarked, this "appears to be the only country in the world where love is a national problem."[13] In no other country do people devote so much of their time and energy to a conscious attempt to experience love—atypical, abnormal, and pathological though it may be.

It is at this point that sociologists and marriage counselors generally begin to point out that this is not a good way to begin a relationship as important as marriage. They warn that the euphoria of love generally begins to wane after the first few months. Then the parties gradually return to their more normal way of thinking, feeling, and behaving. With the return of their more rational and sober perspective, however, the promised best of all worlds often begins to crumble as the actual characteristics of the chosen mate are noticed for the first time. Then, in an increasing number of cases, the newly formed family moves along the road of strife, conflict and eventual separation and divorce.

True as this may be, romantic love has persisted in American society and, as we have already indicated, is as strong, or stronger today than it ever has been. Why this is so is the problem to which the remainder of this paper is devoted, our task is to account for, or to explain both the existence and strength of the romantic love complex in contemporary American society.

The type of explanation to be employed will be the one most used in modern sociological analysis. Functionalism, according to Kingsley Davis—who sees it as synonymous with sociological analysis— "is commonly said to *do* two things; to relate the parts of society to the whole, and to relate one part to another."[14] Four decades ago Radcliffe-Brown elaborated upon this as follows:

> It is a mistake to suppose that we can understand the institutions of society by studying them in isolation without regard to other institutions with which they coexist and with which they may be correlated,. . .no explanation of one part of the system is satisfactory unless it fits in with an analysis of the system as a whole.[15]

To employ functional analysis as an explanatory mechanism, however, requires the addition of something more. Carl Hempel provides this for us with the logical rigor of the philosopher of science:

> The kind of phenomenon that a functional analysis is invoked to explain is typically some recurrent activity or some behavior pattern in an individual or a group; it may be a physiological mechanism, a neurotic trait, a culture pattern, or a social institution, for example. And the principal objective of the analysis is to exhibit the contribution which the behavioral pattern makes to the preservation or the development of the individual or the group in which it occurs. Thus, functional analysis seeks to understand a behavior pattern or a sociocultural institution in terms of the role it plays in keeping the given system in proper working order and thus maintaining it as a going concern.[16]

To provide a functional explanation of romantic love then, we must examine next the relationships that exist between this trait, or complex of institutionalized behavior, and the other social patterns with which it coexists, and then demonstrate the contributions that it makes towards "keeping the system in proper working order and thus maintaining it as a going concern."

American Society as the Social Context of Romantic Love. We may begin this brief examination of the institutions with which romantic love is functionally interrelated in American culture by noting, as most of the numerous observers of our society already have done, that materialism ranks high in our value system. The ever increasing accumulation of material goods and services—the economists commodities—may be taken as one of the primary goals towards which socialized adult members of the system consciously strive. Consequently, the production, distribution, and consumption of material goods and services—loosely called economic behavior—tends to take precedence over almost all other activities engaged in by the members of the society.

Correlated with, or perhaps underlying, this desire for goods and services is the existence of a highly complex industrial technology that helps to make available the valued commodities. Large and efficient factories rationally mass produce goods and are constantly being improved by the incorporation of new technological innovations. The result is that the United States has been able to produce more goods and services, cumulatively and per capita, than any other society in human history.

The complex and elaborate machines that are the core of the rationally organized technology require highly specialized and intensive human skills. The social system that has emerged to implement the technology has been successful in training and utilizing the members of the society in such a way that their material aspirations are met—though, almost by definition, they can never be satisfied.

The social groups that produce and distribute the valued commodities are voluntary associations, or organizations—universalistic instrumental achievement structures, in Parsons' terms[17] The use of the association, or organization as the means of ordering human social relations lead to certain distinctive problems, however. All social organizations, for purposes of analysis, may be viewed as a series of social positions that have associated with them complexes or normative behavior — roles — that are performed by individuals when they occupy any specific one of the positions. For social systems to work—i.e., things to get done—the positions must be filled by persons able to perform the expected roles. The analytic problem then is: How are the positions filled?

In most of the societies reported on in the ethnographic record, individuals are assigned to specific social positions by means of kinship, age, sex, and so forth. The term "ascription" is conventionally used to refer to those ethnographically more prevalent cases in which individuals are placed in positions without reference to either specific talents, or their wishes. In contrast with this, the term "achievement" is used to refer to the instances in which persons come to hold positions as the result of desire and successful competition based upon their possessing special talents, skills, or abilities.

The voluntary association is a form of social organization that uses the achievement mechanism to fill its ranks. Associations are created to accomplish specific objectives. To obtain their goals a series of positions with specific roles are established. When persons able to perform the roles are recruited to fill the positions, the desired result, or goal, of the organization is achieved. The question remains: How are the positions within the association filled after they are created? That is, how are the proper individuals, those with the necessary talents and abilities, induced to fill the positions and to perform the designated tasks, or roles? In achievement-oriented societies there is a need for some mechanism or force sufficient to motivate individuals to want to fill the positions and perform the expected roles. Rewards are needed that will successfully motivate enough individuals with the right combination of skills to "get the job done." In the contemporary United States, money in the form of wages or income is the primary inducement offered to fill most social positions.

Within this market-oriented society, money functions as a medium of exchange. That is, it stands for the valued commodities in that it can be exchanged in the market for goods and services. In a sense, however, it has come to be valued in its own right as the symbol of goods and services. It "is the universal agency for satisfying any desires that can be met by purchasable goods."[18] But there is more than this to the social function of money in American society. "It is the symbol and measure," as Santayana has pointed out, the American "has at hand for success, intelligence, and power. . ."[19]

Robin Williams has elaborated upon the implications of this insight as follows:

> In a society of relatively high social mobility, in which position in the scale of social stratification basically depends upon occupational achievement, wealth is one of the few obvious signs of one's place in the hierarchy. Achievement is difficult to index, in a highly complex society of diverse occupations, because of the great differences in abilities and effort required for success in various fields. At the time, the central type of achievement is in business, manufacturing, commerce, finance; and since traditionalized social hierarchies, fixed estates, and established symbols of hereditary rank have had only a rudimentary development, there is a strong tendency to use money as a symbol of success. Money comes to be valued not only for itself and for the goods it will buy, but as symbolic evidence of success and, thereby, of personal worth.[20]

Money, then, along with the material goods and services that it can purchase, is itself an important value in the society.

The valued commodities then are produced in the United States by special purpose organizations. The positions in each organization are filled by offering rewards—generally income, or wages—sufficient to induce individuals to join the organization and to perform the tasks that have been laid out by the rational planners of industry. Membership in the organizations, as we have noted, is voluntary. One consequence of this is that there tends to be a competition both by persons for positions and by organizations for individuals with specific recognized skills.

Since all positions are not equal in importance, however, nor equally demanding, the income offered is not the same for all jobs. Those positions considered to be most important by the members of the society generally pay the highest income. For the multitude of other jobs there is a gradual decrease in rewards offered, with the least income going to those positions taken to be least important.[21]

In theory, anyone with the appropriate skills can achieve any position in the system—i.e., it is open. Since the primary reward, money, both stands for success and is convertible directly into the valued goods and services, the achieving of positions that offer more and more rewards is also desirable. Mobility thus is another dominant theme in the culture, as is an aggressive competition for positions that offer high salaries and other rewards.

Filling social positions by means of achievement, however, appears to be working so well in what is generally referred to as the industrial sector that it has been carried over as the dominant means of filling positions in other parts of the social system. Also, the organization, or voluntary association, tends to be the form taken by the vast majority of American social groups.

The material goods and services, so highly valued by the members of the society, can be obtained only in the market where these commodities are bought and sold for money. Money, however, can be obtained in theory—and in most cases in fact—only as the result of achieving a position in an organization that produces goods and services, and performing, or executing its prescribed role.

The positions in the industrial sector, however, are restricted generally to the adult male members of the society—and, in an increasing but still small number of cases, to adult females.[22] All other persons—the majority of women and all children—do not have access to the income needed to obtain both subsistence and prestige goods and services.

For the system to work, then, there must be a means by which women and children are provided with the necessary and highly valued goods and services—both in terms of absolute survival requirements and culturally defined prestige wants. Another way of phrasing this is to ask: How are women and children articulated with the industrial sector that produces and distributes the material items in the culture? In the United States, the family, in addition to its other activities, serves as the needed link.

The American family is a small, nuclear kinship unit composed of parents and children. Each group ideally occupies its own dwelling unit, and in general, is structurally and functionally isolated from other kinship units in that contacts with related kin groups are generally kept to a minimum.

Within the family—which is the society's unit of consumption for economic goods—the position husband-father calls for its occupant to provide support for the entire group in the form of money with which to purchase goods and services. The money, as we have seen, is obtained by the occupant of the position husband-father holding a job in the industrial sector. Adult males, therefore, are expected to occupy a position in an industrial or occupational organization and a position in a family simultaneously. The role wife-mother, meanwhile, calls for its occupant to take the money earned by its specific male counterpart into the market to purchase the goods and services needed by the entire family.

Individuals are articulated with the culturally dominant economic system, and the highly valued goods and services are distributed to, and consumed by, all members of the society as long as all adult males hold both a position in an occupational group and the position husband-father in a nuclear family and adult females occupy the position wife-mother *vis a vis* a gainfully employed male.

The associations, or organizations in the industrial sector can and do produce and distribute the highly valued goods and services. Without the family, however, organized as it is, the socially desired commodities cannot be distributed to all of the members of the society without drastically modifying the total sociocultural system. Also, they would not be consumed were it not for the family.

A general requirement for the continued operation of the American system of producing, distributing, and consuming the valued goods and services then, is that nuclear families be formed and that the role expectations of the positions husband-father and wife-mother be discharged. This activity or function of the family is in addition to its contribution in the area of reproduction and socialization. Our intent here is not to slight the importance of these contributions but rather to point up the role of the family in maintaining our distinctive economic arrangements. In this respect we may say that the reproductive and socialization activities of the American family are self-evident. It is commonly argued, however, that the modern family no longer performs economic functions. To us this appears to be a restricted view. The reason may be that the economic and, for that matter, stratification functions of the family are not very evident and in this era of sociological specialization they tend to be neglected. Furthermore, by emphasizing the economic tasks performed by the family the contribution of romantic love to maintaining the larger social system is made more apparent.

With respect to the distribution and consumption of goods and services then, once families are formed—the positions husband-father and wife-mother are filled, there are numerous legal and social mechanisms that can be employed to insure role performance in the event that the socialization process does not train people adequately. Before these sanctions can be involved, however, individuals in this achievement-oriented society must be induced to fill the aforementioned positions. In the United States the positions husband-father and wife-mother are filled—nuclear families are formed—by the marriage of two adolescents or adults of the opposite sex. Our next problem, therefore, is to inquire as to why and how people get married.

We have already seen that achievement is the general mechanism used to fill social positions. Individuals learn to compete with each other for the rewards—generally money—that are associated with most positions. What rewards, we may ask, are offered to induce people to marry? Negatively we may note that the rewards used to fill the broad range of social statuses are not offered as inducements to fill the positions husband-father and wife-mother. In fact, it is generally considered improper to offer money, or other material items as inducements for marriage; most Americans would be shocked at the idea and such behavior probably would be regarded as indecent.

In the United States, however, there are no prescribed marriage patterns. Cousin marriage, the sororate, the levirate, etc., are not practiced. There are no extended kinship groups to pressure individuals into getting married.[23] Also, there are no institutionalized matchmakers. Moreover, in this affluent, market-oriented society all basic needs can be satisfied in the market. That is, there is no fundamental sexual division of labor that leads men and women to marry because they cannot survive without the service of a mate. Everything from food and clothing to sexual gratification can be purchased in the market.

One consequence of the combination of the materialistic values—specifically the desire of individuals, when presented with choices, to select the alternatives that maximize their material rewards—and the requirements of the husband-father and wife-mother roles within the family, which actually deprive the individuals of goods and services that they otherwise might have been able to obtain, is that, other things being equal, individuals would be negatively motivated toward marriage. In fact, in terms of the logic or rationale of the culture of the contemporary United States, in many instances getting married might well be considered an irrational choice of action.

If individuals do not marry, however, nuclear families would not be formed; and without them the mechanism for distributing and consuming the valued goods and services, reproducing and socializing the population, and maintaining the stratification system, among other things, would cease to operate. In brief, the social system, as it is presently constituted, would cease to operate.

What appears to be necessary for the maintenance of American culture in its present form then, is a special mechanism that would induce these generally rational, ambitious, and calculating individuals—in the sense of striving to maximize their personal achievement—to do what in the logic of their culture is not in their own personal interest. Somehow they must be induced—we might almost say in spite of themselves—to behave emotionally and irrationally and to desire and to occupy the positions husband-father and wife-mother. In conformity with the emphasis on achievement, it appears that something valued, to serve as a reward, is needed to motivate otherwise reluctant individuals to want to compete and to achieve these particular positions.

The negative aspects of the roles often require their occupants to dissipate rather than accumulate commodities, and to do so in a manner that does not bring prestige to the consumer (such as paying doctor and hospital bills for the birth of a child, or purchasing the host of specialized artifacts that we have come to believe are needed for the adequate care and rearing of children), indicates, however, that it is necessary to establish a special reward in that individuals are being motivated to perform what in other circumstances would be considered irrational acts. Only by the institutionalization of a separate pattern of both rewards and behaviors, appropriate only in this special setting it appears, can the positions be filled. But, we may ask, how can an entire population, at a specific point in the life cycle of the individual—i.e., when searching for a mate—be induced to behave in a manner that can be considered abnormal and irrational within the context of their culture, and like it?

What we are suggesting is that the romantic love complex in middle-class America serves as the reward-motive that induces individuals to occupy the structurally essential positions of husband-father and wife-mother. As the pattern was described above, it provides what may be considered institutionalized irrationality that can be compartmentalized and separated conceptually and behaviorally so that it is not dysfunctional with respect to the operation of the rest of the culture.

Individuals may behave strangely and not in accord with their own material interests, but they do so for only a short time. Soon they recover and get back to work. But while in this separable realm of cultural reality they respond to rewards, both real and symbolic, that motivate them to do what must be done, and thus the incidence of marriage is at an all time high.

The careful control of sex noted earlier, so that sexual gratification, ideally at least, is restricted to people in love and generally postponed until after marriage, serves to make sexual gratification a very real reward for those who marry.[24] In addition, marriage, as the culmination of the love affair, offers affection, companionship, emotional security, and general happiness to those who enter into matrimony. As a reward to be achieved, this is significant in terms of what may be considered a counter trend in the value system. It is generally held that there should be something more to life than the accumulation of material goods. The content of this "more than" category, however, invariably is left unspecified. The romantic love complex subsumes many of the possibilites. Though at times it may imply an actual negation of material values, it is often interpreted as providing the unspecified other values. Culminating the love affair with marriage thus promises the values (or rewards) of affection, companionship, care, emotional security—in a society in which most activities are highly anxiety-provoking—and general happiness. This appears to be more than enough to motivate the members of the society. And though, as we have noted earlier, middle-class Americans are realistic enough to know that life does not always work out this way, they do give it a try hoping for the best. Thus romantic love may be considered as an almost separate realm of reality in which modern Americans are permitted (or permit themselves) to behave in response to a higher set of values than the material ones that motivate them in the ordinary work-a-day world.

With respect to the individual, love has thus come to be a thing that is a value in itself—its own reward. And it serves to motivate individuals to do what must be done so that the total social system can maintain itself as a going concern. In short, romantic love induces Americans to fill positions—in conformity with the general achievement orientations—that, though they are essential to the operation to the society, they would not otherwise be motivated to fill. Furthermore, the very atypical, abnormal irrationality of romantic love is the very thing that enables it to work.

With respect to the individual, a person who falls in love and marries comes to believe that he or she is "doing the right thing" and takes understandable pride in doing so. If one is in love in contemporary middle-class America and then gets married it is considered good and proper. The individuals involved may come to have a feeling of satisfaction that goes with doing the right thing. This feeling is then given group support and validation by friends and relatives. The sentiments involved thus may be compared with those of the person in a kin oriented society who has made a "proper marriage"—a person, for example, who marries a cross-cousin in a society with a pattern of prescriptive cross-cousin marriage. This is the right thing and both the involved parties and those around them know it and rejoice in the feeling that goes with doing what is right.[25]

To conclude, then, the function of romantic love in American society appears to be to motivate individuals—where there is no other means of motivating them—to occupy the positions husband-father and wife-mother and form nuclear families that are essential not only for reproduction and socialization but also to maintain the existing arrangements for distributing and consuming goods and services and, in general, to keep the social system in proper working order and thus maintaining it as a going concern.

NOTES

1. Morton M. Hunt, *The Natural History of Love* (New York: Alfred A. Knopf, 1959), p. 3.

2. Theodor Reik, *A Psychologist Looks at Love* (New York: Reinhart, 1944), p. 3.

3. *Ibid.*, p. 4.

4. Sigmund Freud, *Group Psychology and the Analysis of the Ego* (London: Hogarth, 1922), p. 72.

5. William J. Goode, "The Theoretical Importance of Love," American Sociological Review, 24:38 (1959).

6. This is to differentiate from other behavioral complexes to which the same work is applied: love of art, money, God, and so forth.

7. Willard Waller and Reuben Hill, *The Family* (New York: The Dryden Press, 1951), p. 101.

8. Hunt, *op. cit.*, p. 363.

9. For an opposing position, see Goode, *op. cit.*

10. Ralph Linton, *The Study of Man* (New York: D. Appleton-Century, 1936), p. 175.

11. Andrew Truxal and Frances Merrill, *The Family in American Cultures.* (New York: Prentice-Hall, 1947), p. 139.

12. Hunt, *op. cit.*, p. 341.

13. Raoul deSales, "Love in America," *The Atlantic Monthly*, 161:645-51 (1938).

14. Kingsley Davis, "The Myth of Functional Analysis," *American Sociological Review*, 24:758 (1959). Though this form of analysis and the kind of explanation it results in restricts of our understanding to a delimited period of time, it does add insights that cannot be gained, at least in the present stage of development of anthropology, by historical and evolutionary orientations. Thus we are not attempting to provide all the answers. However, within the range of its limitations, functional analysis has added and still can add to and enrich our comprehension of human behavior.

15. A.R. Radcliffe-Brown, *Structure and Function in Primitive Society* (Glencoe, Ill.: Free Press, 1952), p. 17.

16. Carl Hempel, "The Logic of Functional Analysis," in *Symposium on Sociological Theory*, ed. by L. Gross (Evanston, Ill.: Row, Peterson, 1959), p. 278.

17. Talcott Parsons, *The Scoial System* (Glencoe, Ill.: Free Press, 1951), pp. 182-91.

18. Cooley, quoted in Robin M. Williams, Jr., *American Society* (New York: Alfred A. Knopf, 1960), p. 420.

19. George Santayana, *Character and Opinion in the United States* (New York: 1920), p. 185.

20. Williams, *op. cit.*, pp. 420-21.

21. Kingsley Davis and Wilbert E. Moore, "Some Principles of Stratification," *American Sociological Review*, 10:242-49 (1945).

22. Though many women are now in the labor force, and the percentage of females to males is increasing, it is still true that, for the population as a whole, the adult male (husband-father) is still the primary source of support. By and large, the contribution of women to the household income is in the form of extras or prestige items that would not otherwise be available. The crucial aspect of the adult male role as provider, however, is to be found by turning to the stratification system. Nuclear families are the units. They are distributed into a series of social classes. The primary determinant of any given family's place in the system is based upon the occupational achievement of its adult male. The rewards earned at a job, therefore, in addition to providing the group's material necessities, also determine its place in the prestige system. Though women may add to the material and social-psychological well being of the family, the task of placing it in the stratification system—determining its prestige—accrues to the occupant of the position husband-father; and this is based primarily upon his achieved position in the industrial sector.

23. An exception, however, may be found in the behavior of women toward their mature, unmarried daughters.

24. Sexual gratification may be available in the market place, but if, as is the belief amongst middle-class Americans, love must accompany it to make it truly enjoyable, prostitution ceases to be a fully satisfying outlet. That is, it can never provide complete satisfaction.

25. Before concluding we may note that in American society there are actual restrictions in the general pattern of romantic love. In theory anyone is permitted to fall in love with anyone else. In fact, however, as Goode *(op. cit.)* has pointed out, falling in love has been structured so that lovers actually select each other not at random but from within specific cultural categories that have been defined as structural isolates. That is, not only is it right to fall in love, but it is "more right" to fall in love with and to marry someone who is a member of the same ethnic, racial, religious, educational, age, socioeconomic, etc. category as you are. This structuring of love not only gets people to marry and to occupy the positions husband-father and wife-mother, but also helps to maintain the structure of the society in accord with the categories.

Name:_____   Date:_____

Student #:_____   Sex: M or F

1. T   F   Drinking is quite a problem on this campus.

2. T   F   Petting and sexual relationships receive considerable emphasis on this campus.

3. T   F   Finding dates is difficult on this campus.

4. T   F   Activities for dating couples are too few on this campus.

5. T   F   Dating costs on this campus make dating prohibitive.

6. T   F   Generally speaking, students on this campus are opposed to engaging in premarital intercourse.

7. T   F   Some unmarried couples are living together.

8. T   F   The old, formal dating patterns are about gone.

9. T   F   Co-ed dorm living has altered dating patterns a great deal.

10. T   F   There is a great difference between the "Establishment" and "hippy student" when it comes to dating or socializing in any way.

11. T   F   Physical beauty, campus prestige, and social status are over emphasized.

12. I think dating would be better if men (women) would:

Name: _____   Date: _____

Student #: _____   Sex: M or F

1. Given the "right conditions" (the right person, etc.) do you think you will ever live with a person of the opposite sex in a "marital relationship" without being married? Yes_____ No_____ Undecided _____

2. Do you think the phenomenon of couples living together in a marital type relationship without being married will become more common, less common, stay the same? More_____ Less _____ Same _____

3. Do you think our country would do well in the future to adopt and accept patterns of unmarried but marital-type relationship? Yes_____ No_____ Undecided _____

4. Do you think our country would do well in the future to adopt patterns of legalized trial marriage, to be followed by a permanent marriage, if the couple so chooses. Yes_____ No_____ Undecided _____

5. Do you think you would be willing to live in a communal relationship with other adults, men and women (sexual relationships being unrestricted)? Yes_____ No _____ Undecided _____

The following are 4 types of "living together" relationships.

Type 1: Cohabitation: shared a bedroom (or a bed) with someone of the opposite sex for *4 or more nights a week* for *three or more consecutive months.*

Type 2: Long-term "weekender" relationships: shared a bedroom (or a bed) with someone of the opposite sex for *three or more months,* but were generally together *less than 4 nights a week.*

Type 3: Short-Term intense relationships: shared a bedroom (or a bed) with someone of the opposite sex for *4 or more nights a week,* but *not for as long as three months.* (Note: relationship could still be continuing and, in time, go beyond 3 months)

Type 4: Periodic overnight relationships: shared a bedroom (or a bed) with someone of the opposite sex for *less than 4 nights a week* and for *less than 3 months duration.*

I have experienced the following type of relationships:

6.   Type 1 _____ How many _____
7.   Type 2 _____ How many _____
8.   Type 3 _____ How many _____
9.   Type 4 _____ How many _____

TRIAL MARRIAGE: HARNESSING THE TREND CONSTRUCTIVELY

Miriam E. Berger

The concept of trial marriage is traced historically and anthropologically. Highlights of a recent NCFR Workshop are reported. To harness the trend constructively the author recommends that young people who have had a living-together experience, evaluate it with a counselor in order to gain insight about their potentialities as mates. Research is recommended to determine whether trial marriage is a valid preparation for marriage.

Anthropological and Historical Survey

Trial marriage has been practiced among the Peruvian Indians of Vicos in the Andes for more than four centuries. (Price, 1965; MacLean, 1941) Arranged by the parents in the earlier form, the purpose was to test the girl's work abilities and the couple's general compatibility. In modern Vicos there is a free choice of marriage partners with romantic love playing an important role, but men will seek responsible, hardworking girls who have mastered household skills and can help in the fields. Study of couples who entered a trial marriage for the first time indicated that the average duration of such trials was less than fifteen months and that 83 per cent of the relationships were finalized with marriage. There was no stigma if the couple had children, but did not marry. Permanent separations after marriage were rare, occurring in two to three per cent of the cases. One of the advantages of these trial marriages noted by Price was the ease of transition from adolescence to adulthood. The couple acquired certain social and sexual advantages of adulthood without assuming full responsibility.

The Trobrianders had a "bachelor's house" in which courting couples slept together and had exclusive sex prior to marriage. In contrast to Western civilization, before marriage Trobriand couples were not permitted to eat together or share any interests, except sex. (Malinowski, 1929)

In the eighteenth century, Maurice of Saxony, illegitimate son of the Elector Augustus the Strong and Countess Aurora of Konigsmark, sought a solution to the marriage problem. He recommended temporary marriages, contracted for a limited time. If the partners agreed, the contract could be prolonged, but marriage for life was a "betrayal of the self, an unnatural compulsion." (Lewinsohn, 1956)

"Bundling" originated in Europe and was brought to the New World in the eighteenth century. In New England, where it was too cold to sit up late, courting couples were permitted, with parental approval, to get into bed with their clothes on. Some bundling experiences were probably innocent, especially when they included a center-board for the bed (Marriage Museum), but "certainly many got sexually involved and married when conception occurred." (Scott, 1960; Fielding, 1961)

"Trial nights," an old Teutonic custom, (Marriage Museum) is still practiced today in Staphorst, Holland, an insular, inbred town whose customs have for centuries sealed them off from contemporary life. The swain spends three nights a week with his girl friend, with the knowledge of her parents who hope she will prove fertile. Until she becomes pregnant, there can be no marriage. If she is barren, the community regards her with primitive suspicion and contempt. Once she is pregnant, however, the marriage must take place. (Gibney, 1948)

Twentieth Century America

The first American to propose trial marriage as a concept was Judge Ben B. Lindsay. (1927) Bertrand Russell who was then teaching in New York, approved of Lindsay's Companionate Marriage, but felt it did not go far enough. Russell favored trial marriage for university students and believed that work and sex were more easily combined "in a quasi-permanent relationship, than in the scramble and excitement of parties and drunken orgies" that were prevalent during the Prohibition Era. Russell felt that if a man and woman chose to live together without having children, it was no one's business but their own. He believed it undesirable for a couple to marry for the purpose of raising a family without first having had sexual experience. (Russell, 1929)

Lindsay and Russell were ostracized, and the concept of trial marriage lay dormant until an evolving sexual morality led anthropologist Margaret Mead to revive it. (Mead, 1966) Building on Lindsay's Companionate Marriage, she recommended a two-step marriage: *individual,* in which there would be a simple ceremony, limited economic responsibilities, easy divorce, if desired, and no children; and *parental marriage,* which would be entered into as a second step by couples who were ready to undertake the lifetime obligations of parenthood, would be more difficult to enter into and

Reprinted from *The Family Coordinator,* Vol. 20, No. 1, January, 1971. By permission of The National Council on Family Relations.

break off, and would entail mutual continuing responsibility for any children. Her rationale was that sex, now considered a normal need in youth, often drove them into premature and early marriage, frequently leading to unhappiness and divorce. She made the plea that divorce be granted before children are conceived, so that only wanted children of stable marriages are brought into the world. Responses to Dr. Mead's proposal, (Mead, 1968) ranged from disapproval for tampering with tradition (instead of helping couples adjust to traditional marriage) to complaints from students for setting up too much structure. A typical student response was: "Why get married? Why can't we live together, with a full sex life, with no pregnancy, until we're ready to get married and have children?"

Margaret Mead's two-step marriage was elaborated on by Michael Scriven, a philosophy professor, who proposed a three-step plan:

> We try to make one institution achieve three aims, which all too often lie in perpendicular dimensions. The aims are sexual satisfaction, social security and sensible spawning. The solution would be to create three types of marriage arranged so that any combination is possible: preliminary, personal and parental marriage. The first would simply be legitimized cohabitation, contractually insulated against escalation into "de facto" commitment. It would be a prerequisite for other kinds and would impose a period of a year's trial relationships before the possibility of conversion to personal marriage . . . (Scriven, 1967)

In *The Sexual Wilderness*, Vance Packard (1968) concluded that the first two years of marriage are the most difficult. He recommended a two-year confirmation period, after which the marriage would become final or would be dissolved. Packard felt that this proposal differed from trial marriage because the couple would marry in earnest and with the hope that the marriage would be permanent. He saw trial marriage as highly tentative and little more than unstructured cohabitation. Packard's concept is based on his conviction that the expectation of permanency contributes to success in that it motivates a couple to work hard to adapting, and is, in fact, a strong stabilizing and reinforcing factor.

In "Marriage as a Statutory Five Year Renewable Contract," Virginia Satir, family therapist, said:

> Maybe there needs to be something like an apprentice period. . .in which potential partners have a chance to explore deeply and experiment with their relationship, experience the other and find out whether his fantasy matched the reality. Was it really possible through daily living to have a process in which each was able to enhance the growth of the other, while at the same time enhancing his own? What is it like to have to undertake joint ventures and to be with each other every day? It would seem that in this socially approved context, the chances of greater realness and authenticity continuing would be increased, and the relationship would deepen, since it started on a reality base. (1967)

Another variation of the renewable contract concept was proposed by Mervyn Cadwallader, a sociology professor, in "Marriage as a Wretched Institution:"

> Marriage was not designed to bear the burdens now being asked of it by the urban American middle class. It was an institution that evolved over centuries to meet some very specific needs of a nonindustrial society. . . Marriage was not designed as a mechanism for providing friendship, erotic experience, romantic love, personal fulfillment, continuous lay psychotherapy, or recreation. Its purpose . . . has changed radically, yet we cling desperately to the outmoded structures of the past. . . The basic structure of Western marriage is never questioned, alternatives are not proposed or discussed. . . Why not permit a flexible contract, for one or more years, with periodic options to renew? If a couple grew disenchanted with their life together, they would not feel trapped for life. . . They would not have to go through the destructive agonies of divorce, and carry about the stigma of marital failure, like the mark of Cain on their foreheads. Instead of a declaration of war, they could simply let their contracts lapse and while still friendly, be free to continue their romantic quest. . . What of the children in a society that is moving inexorably toward consecutive, plural marriages?. . If the bitter and poisonous denouement of divorce could be avoided by a frank acceptance of short-term marriages, both adults and children would benefit. Any time spouses treat each other decently, generously, and respectfully, their children will benefit. (Cadwallader, 1966)*

Today many young people have carried the concept of trial marriage a step further, as Bertrand Russell advocated, by living with a roommate of the opposite sex. Sociologist Robert N. Whitehurst coined a word to describe them, "unmalias," a condensation of unmarried liaisons. (1969) Whitehurst mentions some of the problems encountered by students who have an "experimental semester" of living together, such as when a male senior must leave the campus for graduate school, job, or military service. (1969)

The Harrad Experiment (Rimmer, 1966) incorporated some of the above mentioned ideas on trial marriage and added some new dimensions. In Rimmer's novel, college students lived with computer-selected roommates of the opposite sex. Unlike the informal arrangements now made by college students on their own, (Karlen, 1969; Life, 1968) the Harrad Experiment was controlled and guided by the Tenhausens, a husband-and-wife team of sociologist and marriage counselor. The novel focused on several couples who married after four years of living together. The students attended various neighboring colleges, but roomed at Harrad during the four years, and were required to take a course in human values at Harrad taught by the Tenhausens and to do required reading in the subjects of marriage, love, sex, contraception, moral values, philosophy, etc. Whenever the students were troubled about their relationships, the Tenhausens were available for consultation. There was also considerable peer support through endless discussions of common problems. Rimmer favored a structured, socially approved form of premarital experimentation that would give the male and female an opportunity to realize themselves fully, without guilt, and to adjust to their new marital roles without legal entanglement, recognizing marriage as the commitment a couple makes to society when they decide to have children. Accused of trying to undermine America's family structure, Rimmer asserted that, on the contrary, he believed a strong family to be a *sine qua non* of social existence and that his proposals would strengthen and preserve that structure.

In an article in *The Humanist* (1970) Rustum and Della Roy discussed alternatives to traditional marriage in view of the increasing divorce rate:

> By one simple swish of tradition, we can incorporate all the recent suggestions for trial marriage,. . . and cover them all under the decent rug of the "engagement" —engagements with minor differences—that in today's society they entitle a couple to live together, but not to have children. . . By no means need this become the universal norm.

NCFR Workshop

A workshop led by the author was conducted at the annual meeting of the National Council on Family Relations in 1969. The participants were primarily college instructors of marriage and family courses, but included a social worker, a clergyman, a sociologist, and a college counselor of students. The following is a summary of the highlights of the workshop:

It was agreed that there ought to be alternative methods of courtship, approved by society, that would serve as a better preparation for marriage than dating. Those opposed to trial marriage as one such alternative felt it was not the same as a real marriage and therefore not a valid preparation for

marriage. It was also subject to exploitation and abuse, as was any method of courtship, and was more to the interest of the male than the female, who is likely to be more concerned about security. Opponents also pointed out that it takes a great deal of maturity to make a relationship work, and if a couple are not mature enough to marry, they may not be mature enough to end a relationship when indicated, nor to cope with the attendant rejection, not to mention accidental pregnancy, or a partner who flits from one relationship to another.

Those who favored trial marriage felt it should be morally sanctioned by society as an optional alternative.

Clerical Attitudes

Although many clergymen disapprove of trial marriage, there have been some notable exceptions. Typical of the negative opinion is that of Dean John Coburn of the Episcopal Theological School, Massachusetts:

> How can two people trust one another on a temporary basis? Marriage is a total commitment, and trial marriage is a contradiction in terms. (Eddy, 1968)

On the other hand, a Unitarian minister, Robert M. Eddy (1968), regarding the casual promiscuity and resulting unwanted children as tragic developments of the "new morality," offered the following alternatives:

> (1) that parents continue the financial support of their college-attending children who are having companionate marriages
>
> (2) that it be illegal for youngsters under the age of seventeen to conceive; that seventeen to nineteen year olds, after obtaining parental consent, might live together with the privileges and responsibilities of the relationship defined by a contract as detailed or loose as the parents would desire. Such a relationship could be solemnized by a rite similar to the wedding ceremony and could be ended by mutual consent, as long as the couple did not have children. The next type of cohabitation agreement essentially would be identical to the present marriage relationship, but under the new system, would be limited to adults and would be, in effect, a license to raise children.

Harnessing the Trend Constructively

Whether one's professional or religious beliefs lead to a view of trial marriage as conservative or radical, acceptable or sinful, a valid or nonvalid preparation for marriage, there may be a need to recognize that trial marriage and its variations are being practiced by some young people. (Eddy,

1968; Karlen, 1969; Life, 1969; Whitehurst, 1969) As a marriage counselor and emotional health consultant, the author proposes a service that would guide and serve young people who do venture into trial marriage, legal or otherwise, so that they learn from their experiences, rather than stumble blindly from one relationship to another. It is recommended that they assess the experience with a consultant, exploring, individually or in a group, some of the following:

What did I learn about myself from this experience? How did I adjust to living with a peer, as distinguished from living with parents and siblings, or alone? What have the problems of adjustment been? Would I have the same problems with another roommate or spouse? How much did I contribute to these problems and how much was the responsibility of the partner? What neurotic games did we play? What hangups did I bring to the relationship that were reinforced by our interaction? What kind of person do I need to live with, dominate, submissive, detached, involved, affectionate, etc? What was our style of communication, constructive, (Gordon, 1968) silent treatment, hitting below the belt? (Bach, 1968) How effectively do I communicate my needs and feelings? How did our communication problems affect our sexual adjustment? On the assumption that personal happiness is achieved through satisfying closeness to another human being, what problems did I have in achieving and maintaining that closeness?

The author would like to see colleges take the leadership by providing emotional health consultants for the preventive service described above, in addition to the usual counseling services. To encourage college students to avail themselves of the service, its use is recommended as a preventive mental health measure, e.g., at the end of each year when living arrangements are likely to be changed, when students finish that first year in a dormitory, whether single-sex or co-ed dorm, the second and third years with a roommate of the same sex, and whatever the arrangement is for the fourth year. Once accustomed to using the service and finding the consultant understanding, nonjudgmental, and helpful in developing insight, the student is more likely to use the service to discuss any relationships with the opposite sex. Periodic check-ups would give the consultant a chance to know a student and to provide direction and guidance. When a student is ready to marry his current partner or someone else, his selection of a mate will have greater sophistication and insight, or he may be motivated if he had repeated adjustment problems with successive roommates, to obtain counseling. (Kardiner,

1970) If colleges initiated such a preventive service, it would, in time, become acceptable for noncollegians. In urban centers where many young people live away from their families, the service is available through the facilities of "Check-Up" for Emotional Health; it could also be available in community settings, such as family agencies, premarital counseling services, Y's, community mental health centers, and religious organizations.

Research Indications

One critical issue is whether trial marriage is a valid test and preparation for marriage. Some probably know of couples for whom trial marriage culminated in a satisfactory legal marriage. Nevertheless, the following case studies raise questions about the validity of trial marriage as a test:

Sue, age 24, was referred for psychotherapy because of severe anxiety symptoms that had their onset immediately after marriage. She had lived with her husband six months prior to marriage, during which phase she had been relaxed, her real self, and not unduly concerned over the success of the relationship. Exploration revealed that Sue was so anxious for the marriage to succeed that she was repressing all negative feelings, and denying her identity in an effort to fulfill her image of a good wife. Now she was afraid of becoming as aggressive, argumentative, and opinionated as she had been as a teenager.

Ada, age 22, came for psychotherapy because of severe obsessional symptoms. Since her marriage two years earlier, she had been frigid. She had lived with her husband weekends for one year prior to marriage, during which phase she had experienced orgasm. The source of conflict revealed in the exploration was that after marriage she felt her husband was too demanding sexually, that he valued her only for sex, which made it demeaning to her and that she found it difficult to limit him. She had transferred her excessive need to have her parents' approval to having her husband's approval, resolving the conflict by denying her resentment and thereby becoming frigid and obsessional.

Sue's and Ada's trial marriages were not deliberate tests; both had drifted into their living-together experiences. Perhaps, when the trial marriage is deliberate, similar anxieties would occur before, rather than after the permanent marriage. Was it just that trial marriage was not a valid test for these women with neurotic personalities? It is only the troubled who come to the attention of the professional. Study of the marriages of a large sample of couples who first had trial marriages might provide more reliable information upon which to base a conclusion. In planning the research design, it would be necessary: (1) to distinguish between deliberate trials and unstructured cohabitation that happened to result in permanency; and (2) to explore whether motivation to adapt (Packard, 1968; Lederer and Jackson, 1968) differed during the trial and in permanency.

References

Bach, George and Peter Wyden. *Intimate Enemy.* New York: W. Morrow and Company, 1968.

Cadwallader, Mervyn. "Marriage as a Wretched Institution," *Atlantic Monthly*, 1966, 218 (5), 62—66.

Eddy, Robert M. "Should We Change Our Sex Laws?," *The Register-Leader*, March 1966, Detroit, Michigan.

Eddy, Robert M. "Why We Must Allow Sexual Freedom for Teens," *Pageant*, September, 1968, 118—129.

Fielding, Wm. J. *Strange Customs of Courtship and Marriage*, London: Souvenir Press. 1961.

Gibney, Frank. "The Strange Ways of Staphorst," *Life*, September 27, 1949, 2—8.

Gordon, Thomas. *Parent Effectiveness Training.* 110 South Euclid Avenue, Pasadena, California.

Kardiner, Sheldon H. "Convergent Internal Security Systems—A Rationale for Marital Therapy," *Family Process*, 1970, 9(1), 83—91.

Karlen, Arno. "The Unmarried Marrieds on Campus," *New York Times Magazine*, January 26, 1969, 29—30.

Lederer, Wm. J. and Don D. Jackson. *The Mirages of Marriage.* New York: W. W. Norton and Company, 1968, Ch. 21—23.

Lindsey, Ben B. "The Companionate Marriage," *Redbook*, October 1926: March 1927.

Lewinsohn, Richard. *The History of Sexual Customs*, New York: Harper Brothers, 1958. Original edition in German, 1956, translated by Alexander Mayce.

MacLean, R. "Trial Marriage Among the Peruvian Aborigines," *Mexican Sociology*, 1941, 1, 25—33, in Spanish.

Malinowski, Bronislaw. *The Sexual Life of Savages.* London: Geo. Routledge and Sons, 1929.

Marriage Museum, formerly located at 1991 Broadway, New York, N. Y.

Mead, Margaret. "Marriage in Two Steps.." *Redbook*, 1966, 127, 48—49.

Mead, Margaret. "A Continuing Dialogue on Marriage," *Redbook*, 1968, 130, 44.

Packard, Vance. *The Sexual Wilderness.* New York: David McKay Company, 1968, 466—468.

Price, Richard. "Trial Marriage in the Andes," *Ethnology*, 1965, 4, 310—322.

Rimmer, Robert H. *The Harrad Experiment.* Los Angeles: Sherbourne Press. 1966.

Rimmer, Robert H. *The Harrad Letters.* New York: New American Library, Signet Book No. 4037.

Rustum, Roy and Della Rustum. "Is Monogomy Outdated?" *The Humanist*, 1970, 30 (2), 24.

Russell, Bertrand. *Marriage and Morals.* New York: Liveright Publishing Company, 1929.

Satir, Virginia. "Marriage as a Statutory Five Year Renewable Contract," Paper presented at the American Psychological Association 75th Annual Convention Washington, D.C., September 1, 1967. Copy available from author, P.O. Box 15248, San Francisco, Calif. 94115.

Scott, George Ryley. *Marriage—An Inquiry Relating to all Races and Nations from Antiquity to Present Day.* New York: Key Publishing Company, 1960.

Scriven, Michael. "Putting the Sex Back into Sex Education," *Phi Delta* 1968, 49 (9), based on a paper given at a Notre Dame University Conference on "The Role of Women," Fall, 1967.

Whitehurst, Robert. "The Unmalias on Campus," presented at NCFR Annual Meeting, 1969. Copy available from author, University of Windsor, Ontario, Canada.

Whitehurst, Robert. "The Double Standard and Male Dominance in Non-Marital Living Arrangements: A Preliminary Statement," paper presented at the American Orthopsychiatric Association Meeting, New York, 1969. Copy available from author, University of Windsor, Ontario, Canada.

LIVING TOGETHER UNMARRIED ON CAMPUS

Robert N. Whitehurst

The tendency for campus youth to practice varied forms of trial marriage has caught the fancy of the mass media and some concerned social scientists and practitioners.[1] Although the habit of living together unmarried (LTU) is certainly not new, the numbers currently involved appear to be much increased and possibly the meanings today are altered. This paper is an attempt to discuss in sociological perspective the natural history of the developing ideology that allows and permits LTU behaviour. The six topics, in order of their historical flow to be discussed are: disruption in the conventional institutions and sources of social control, alienation from traditional ways of behaving, opening of new opportunity structures to indulge in deviance*, the development of new social forms, reference group support for the new behaviour, and finally, emerging ideologies to solidify the social forms.

Institutional Disruption

The problem of causes and correlates of social change occupy a significant place in contemporary sociological literature. In reviewing most of the literature on family sociology, one is led to the conclusion that on the whole, stable family forms are only slowly changing, and that those who deviate from the norm are only a small and unimportant minority. The question of institutional disruption is a very thorny empirical problem because bits of data must be drawn together and interpreted—from a necessarily incomplete picture of the facts. Depending on the source of "facts" and the interpretation one wishes to make, different conclusions may be drawn about the immediate future of the family as an institution. Aside from the visible evidence which is incomplete, there is to be considered a less visible underground level of deviant activity. Thus, the intensity, meaning and level of activity associated with this behaviour is essentially an unknown quantity. Its importance can be denied, but the evidence for its impact can be gleaned from diverse sources.

One source of support for understanding the trend in institutional disruption might be seen in the recent CBS report on the generations in which data from a national sample of youth were discussed and reviewed.[2] This report suggests that "There is no reliable way to state that the rebel-

lious minorities are larger in size than they have ever been in the past. But they are large, and they *are* concentrated in the 'youth leadership' communities—the college campuses—where indeed on some issues they actually become majorities."[3] The report goes on to say that in the sections of the survey dealing with political and institutional values by which adult America lives (or presumes to do so), there is revealed a "deep-seated sense of disaffection on the part of the young with these values and institutions".[4] Large minorities and on campuses sometimes majorities of youth are "sharply critical of our economic and political systems and the 'Establishment' and authorities who run them."[5] As an example of this type of response, 24 per cent of the youth agreed with a statement regarding the obsolescence of the present institution of marriage.[6] This single item is difficult to interpret since no one knows how large a minority would be needed to involve itself in alternatives to marriage to be a threat to society. Of course there are other considerations, and no one knows how many who agree with this type of statement would in reality follow up his values with action in terms of violation of institutional norms. This is, I would suggest, a large and growing minority that expresses dissatisfaction with the status quo. In the same report, 51 per cent of college youth "strongly agreed" with the statement that "sexual behaviour should be bound by mutual feelings, not by formal ties." When those who "paritally agree" are added to this, college youth totalled 84 per cent.[7] This is indeed an indicator of great importance when we view on the one hand the formal codes governing sexual relations and on the other the great number of youth who are in colleges and tend to become the forefront of social change.

Alienation

An item on alienation was also suggestive of the problems faced by youth. In response to the question, "The individual in today's society is isolated

Robert N. Whitehurst, Associate Professor of Sociology, University of Windsor, Windsor, Ontario, Canada.

* It should be noted that the author's use of the term "deviance" to describe LTU behaviour does not convey a valuable judgment, but rather departure from established norms governing sex behaviour.

62

and cut off from meaningful relationships with others," 59 per cent of the college youth sample either strongly or partially agreed. A slightly smaller portion of the total youth responded the same (56 per cent).[8] Whether this reflects a folk-norm of college life (that is to talk about one's alienation experiences) or whether it is a real phenomenon, the fact that this sample responds so heavily in this direction gives us cause to wonder about the failure of meaning and belonging, tasks usually associated with our major institutions.

Another recent study by the author showed college youth much more alienated than an older sample they were compared with, especially on certain items such as social isolation and work alienation.[9] Such conditions are interpreted by some sociologists of the mass society variety to mean that radicalization of minorities can occur much more easily now than under conditions of institutional stability. Another indicator of alienation from standard values is seen in one of the few replicative studies done over a ten year period on a college population. Christensen has found in a repeat study of college attitudes toward premarital sex a trend toward liberalization.[10] Changes most dramatically are shown in the female attitudes in this time period (from 1958 to 1968). In 1958, Christensen's data showed in his midwest sample that 20 per cent of the females said they had actually experienced premarital sex, whereas in 1968, 34 per cent made this claim. At the same time, the proportion claiming that premarital sex "never should be approved under any circumstance" dropped from 49 per cent in 1958 to 27 per cent in 1968 (data for females). All the findings seem to indicate a general loosening of attitudes and probably behaviour, making probable the seeking of other kinds of relationships considered before as seriously deviant.

One more indicator of increasing looseness of the institutional hold marriage as an institution maintains over the young can be seen in data from a study involving a comparison of marriage attitudes and alienation.[11] In a college sample polled in the summer of 1969, 39 per cent said they believed that it is possible to be in love with more than one person at a time while 72 per cent agreed with a statement suggesting that "good marriage adjustment is either difficult to impossible because of current social conditions." These bits of information point up again that we are living in a period of rapid change in which old ways are being re-evaluated and the result is often levels of alienation from established ways.

New Opportunity Structures

Given a certain amount of institutional looseness and a sense of alienation, we must account for new opportunities for deviance in order to anticipate an increase in the behaviour. Opportunity to live in a nonmarital living arrangement can be seen as arising basically out of two facets of social change: breakdown of old sources of social control in the community, family and in the religious institutions and vastly changed economic base affecting youth in qualitatively new ways. These two factors, coupled with high rates of mobility away from home and families of orientation in late adolescence, make for an increased probability of involvement with a socially permissive milieu. No previous generation has been placed so much on its own with such adequate financial support as has the current college population*. It should be noted that most of the youth who tend to indulge in LTU appear to be serious in their search for meaning. Adult projections often see it simply as sexual; this idea is more of an adult fantasy than youthful reality as the norms governing their behaviour often stress the relationship aspect of the pairing rather than only the hedonistic elements. Search for self and search for meaning are validated by this type of paired relationship according to the participants.

Thus, opportunity is made possible by a loose web of social control and supported by the economic forces at work which so differentially affect our affluent youth as compared to previous generations.

New Social Forms

College is a period in the lives of older adolescents in which old values are examined, new ideas tried out in the relatively free arena of academic give and take. Historically, social change that has occurred through academic institutions has involved working with and altering the institutions prevailing. Some of the major social movements have been created out of the stuff of persecuted minorities, not in colleges. Given the social context described above, however, this may now be in the process of change—universities may in some ways be creating a radical intelligentsia which focuses on social forms not seriously considered before as within the realm of possibility. A renewed interest in variant social forms of community has been given stimulus by recent changes. Within the past few years professional work in sociology has included some comment on these problems of community.[12] The recent habit of college youth to attempt to develop communes has also attracted much attention. Since the current crop of American youth have been reared in homes of a reasonably privatized variety (and probably with more privacy given to the individual family member than ever before in history—especially since World War II), it seems a plausible hypothesis to suggest that most youth will have great difficulty living in communes because of their early socialization and individualistic tendencies. The same factor that makes communal living difficult may make the paired relationships in LTU behaviour seem all the more desirable and likely as an outcome. Thus, contemporary youth may be in a transitional stage—freed essentially from the old mores about sex, but unprepared to do anything but try a slightly deviant form of interaction—the LTU adaptation. This does not mean that there will not be a continued trend toward communal development, for this is likely—but it will take a still-different generation to make these work as it appears now. The essential point to note here is that there is no shortage of experiments and possibilities under examination and in various stages of exploration. This in itself as a social fact tends to loosen up further exploration, experimentation, and discussion about real life adaptations in a society youth feel no longer provides vital answers to their lives in terms they can accept. The functionality of this type of new adaptation has only been marginally discussed by sociologists; such work can lead to an assessment of the meaning of the emerging values in terms of economic and political institutions in a society characterized by surplus and cybernetically controlled production. In other words, the transitional organizations under discussion today may be functional for some future poorly understood at the moment—but that is indeed another problem.

Group Support

No new social form such as LTU can survive without normative and comparative reference group support. What are the sources of these? Normative change, supported by close reference groups was long ago noted by Newcomb in his Bennington college study.[13] As students, we are taught to almost revere the idea of higher education. Although the old image is rapidly changing and giving way to a more questioning and doubting ethos, a still—large number of students can be categorized as "serious." This means in effect that college is a kind of serious business replete with meanings not always conveyed to professors by their students who do listen intently and assimilate new-found bits of information. As a group, teachers are quite often taken more seriously than we understand and we do become positive integers in reference terms for some youth. If we look at the themes in sociology as an example, we find much that can be potentially disruptive to old ways of seeing the world and in responding to it.[14] These can have social change implications even if the change is not seen as radical.

Basically, there are three potential sources of group support for the deviant behaviour as reflected in the LTU adaptations: teachers, especially college teachers in disciplines involving the social sciences and humanities, peers—and this may be the most single significant source of support for LTU behaviour in terms of positive referents; finally, other adults, including parents (who generally serve as a positive model for some aspects of behaviour, but increasingly less frequently as models for what a marriage or male-female relationship should be). The level of rejection of the conventional model for marriage as related to parents is highly variable as would be expected, but it is probably safe to say that unconventional youth see their parents from a tolerant and bemused (almost smug) sense of their own convictions that a relationship could and ought to do more and be better. They thus become anti-models for their own relationships. The bogey of the "Establishment" lumps in all of the remaining institutions and their representatives that form a kind of nucleus to act as a negative reference group (one to disidentify with or that one wishes to be unlike). This does not mean that any of the above-named groups (teachers, peers, or establishment—others) consciously try to structure the LTU adaptation into or out of the lives of youth; it simply means that there is now an enhanced probability more frequently occurring because of the way these forces act on college youth of today.

Alterations to Ideology

When we examine some of the dominant themes, values, and sometimes, the basic stuff of ideologies, we find a number of good American values that can be seen as contributory to the LTU adaptation. Individualism, resourcefulness and self-reliance are all involved in making the decision to defy the conventional authority in this type of relationship. Democracy as a value can be seen to foster the participation of youth in LTU behaviour since they feel conventional marriage involves the double-standards and discrimination. Freedom and truth-seeking can also play a role in this, and the test of the truth of an institution may to many youth lie in demonstrating its ineffectiveness in meeting human needs as they practice the new way.

Seeking of humanitarian goals may also be involved as the institution of marriage is sometimes seen as stultifying rather than building of personalities and character to the fullest. Rationality, involving an examination of the means in relation to the ends sought (often involving science) is also implicated in the process of a developing ideology of acceptance of LTU behaviour. It is a well-developed American practice to take a pragmatic approach to problems, to refuse to take things on blind faith or tradition. Youth who want to know for themselves (and are encouraged to use this approach in other spheres) are likely to transfer this learning—even though society at large does not like this kind of spill-over effect. American norms and values are organized to support a straightforward and honest approach to problem-solving. We must recognize that no human society has so elongated the period between puberty and preferred marriage age while at the same time unloading via the mass media on youth an unprecedented amount of sexual stimuli—all the while holding the line (formally at least) for chastity before marriage. It seems a forthright and honest approach to a matter of human need, not only sexually but socially to the participants, already alienated and suffering in some degree from the rigers of mass life. A related theme invōlves a quite old and respectable norm of essentially grappling with one's problems, making decisions, living and learning from them and not belabouring errors. We are told to learn by involvement, doing, participating, and living. Possibly no other single American theme creates as positive a sense of ideological support for LTU behaviour. In many respects, then, living together is simply an extension of North American values that are held in esteem when used in other spheres of life. It should not be so much a matter of disapproval and surprise when our youth see opportunities to apply values and learning in one sphere when thoroughly internalized in others.

Summary and Conclusions

Evidence points to a developing set of circumstances supportive of the increased tendency of youth to live together in what has been described as LTU relationships. Although no apparent major-ity of youth have experienced or possibly anticipate the idea of engaging in LTU, an ever larger and poorly understood minority seem to be indulging. The more conventional society seems to have at least partly gone beyond simple castigation because of the illicit sexual activity (this social fact may be attributed to hippies, since they most clearly got us used to the idea that possibly all sex outside marriage may not be as bad, sinful, etc., as we seemed to believe before). Most parents still are shocked, especially when daughters are involved, but adjust they usually do. It is less rare for parents now to "understand" and possibly be helpful when these relationships occur, but it is still usual that when parents arrive on the scene, the "stage" is reset for them so they do not find out the truth (another existential problem for the truth-seekers!)

Some of the factors contributing to the potential increase in LTU adaptations have been discussed. In part, there are historic precedents that set the stage for LTU as well as common American values involved, so the behaviour is not really so strange when we look at the history of its generation and the social context today which makes it so easy. In another place the problem of the relationships involved is discussed in more detail.[15] There are no doubt some repercussions and implications for the future that can now be seen only in dim outline. The further decline in the double standard seems inevitable. The fairly new trend of openness in male-female relationships seems likely to be extended. A possible outcome may be the future institutionalization of trial marriage of some sort—or of several sorts if the primitive trends in organizing a truly pluralistic society continue.

It is extremely difficult to predict either the magnitude or ultimate social meanings of a trend as the contemporary one involving LTU. Even if it would turn out to be a major social habit in North America, it may ultimately have little impact on marriage other than possibly making mate-selection as a process a bit more rational. There is no evidence as yet in the trend that people are going to refuse to marry at all because LTU is a viable option or a true alternative to marriage. It clearly is not as long as the ubiquitous landlord and tax-collector still maintain the sanctioning powers they have. Although parental influence can be often bypassed or set aside as a problem for varying lengths of time, the problems of getting housing and the economic advantages accruing to the legally married with respect to landlords, employers and others in the community cannot be ignored. What results with increasing frequency is the tendency of people who experience LTU for some time, to get married in essence with their fingers crossed. It is not uncommon to encounter young people, newly married, who apologize for or otherwise try to 'explain away' their reasons for getting married. They are pragmatic and rational, and have little to do with supporting the basic institutions related to it, at least in its older forms. One hypothesis that may prove interesting to test in the near future involves the outcome of marriage styles that emanate from these marriages which are contracted more out of convenience than out of a lifetime commitment. Since the advent of books such as the O'Neill's THE OPEN MARRIAGE,[16] it is probable that the guidelines therein provided will serve as major cues to many. As a book on the best-seller list, it will likely have a continuing impact on struggling marriages. It seems a logical extension of the freedoms sought in LTU behaviour to suppose that the rules of open marriage might be at least attempted. How many will succeed in making their marriages truly open ended, nonpossessive, and essentially without jealousy and a concept of ownership of spouse is one of the problems for future research.

It is unclear that the expectations of youth regarding long-term inspiriting relationships can be realized. There is little reason to believe that even though more rational mate-selection is practiced in the process of LTU, that this per se will produce better or more vital marriages. Perhaps the monogamous ideal is simply a gross overstatement of the probable and that new information may lead to a slightly tempered and more reality-based expectation. Western man, however, does not give up easily in his search for a better way. Perhaps it will yet be found; in the meantime, an open mind and a researcher's eye on the future may produce information that will aid the adjustment of those now enmeshed in a system that leaves much to be improved.

NOTES

1. CBS Playhouse, Feb. 25, 1969, "The Experiment," Arno Karlen, "The Unmarried Marrieds on Campus," *New York Times Magazine,* Jan. 26, 1969, pp. 29-30.
2. Daniel Yankelovich, "Generations Apart," television special presented on CBS, May 20, 27 and June 3, 1969.
3,4. *Generations Apart,* a research report in which the CBS survey findings are published, CBS, 1969, pp. 3-4.
5. Ibid., pp.3-4.
6. Ibid., p. 18.
7. Ibid., p. 23.
8. Ibid., p. 24.
9. Robert N. Whitehurst and Marene M. Olson, "Alienation and the Generations: A Comparative Study of Perceptions and Attitudes," paper read at the Ohio Valley Sociological Society, May 1, 1969, Indianapolis, Indiana.
10. Harold T. Christensen and Christina Gregg, "Changing Sex Norms in America and Scandinavia," *Journal of Marriage and the Family,* November 1970, pp. 616-627.
11. Robert N. Whitehurst and Barbara Plant, "A Comparison of Canadian and American Reference Groups, Alienation, and Attitudes toward Marriage," *International Journal of Sociology of the Family,* Vol. 1, No. 1, March 1971, pp. 1-8.
12. As an example of the range of sociological interest, two sources might be cited: Robert A. Nesbet, *The Quest for Community,* New York, Oxford, 1953, and: Carolyn Symonds, *Sexual Mate-Swapping: Violation of Norms and Reconciliation of Guilt,*—A study of ideology of swinging. The Symonds paper is an outgrowth of her MA thesis studying the differences in ideologically or communally oriented swingers and recreational swingers, Department of Sociology, University of California, Riverside, 1968.
13. Theodore M. Newcomb, "Attitude Development as a Function of Reference Groups," in Eleanor E. Maccoby, Newcomb and E.L. Hartley, *Readings in Social Psychology,* 3rd ed. New York: Holt, Rinehart & Winston, 1958, pp. 265-275.
14. Peter Berger, *Invitation to Sociology,* Anchor—Doubleday, New York: 1963, p. 52.
15. Robert N. Whitehurst, "The Double-Standard and Male Dominance in Non-Marital Living Arrangements: A Preliminary Statement," paper presented as the American Orthopsychiatric Association Meeting, New York, March 29, 1969.
16. N. & G. O'Neill, *The Open Marriage,* M. Evans Co., New York: 1972.

Section III

FUN AND GAMES WITH MARTHA AND GEORGE
Michael J. Sporakowski

Adjustment to living with someone else, especially someone of the opposite sex, in a marriage relationship offers many great expectations. William Stephens* found that the research literature seems to give the best chance for positive marital adjustment as follows:

Girls: Marry a Rotarian who is active in his church, who gets on well with his parents, who has never been divorced, who is about your age, whom you have known for years. Don't get pregnant first. Don't marry without your parent's blessings. Don't marry until you are out of school. Marry of your own kind vis a vis religion and social class position. And stay out of big cities.

Conventionality seems to be the key for marriages lasting. Another example of this might be found in a recent comment in *Changing Times*:**

Recipe for a solid marriage: A family income over $15,000 and a union in which both parties are college grads. These couples, says the Census Bureau, generally have the best prospects of weathering marital storms. The lower the income and the educational level, the greater the risks of breakup. A more worrisome revelation is that an increasing percentage of married women are divorced by their early thirties. In 1955 this had happened to about one out of ten wives. The figure currently is about one out of six. It's not all grim, however. Of the 49,000,000 married couples, 1,200,000 last year could triumphantly boast they had passed their fiftieth wedding anniversary.

The intent of this section is to examine factors involved in adjusting to the marital relationship. We begin with a humorous look at "Pairing Patterns," then move to the state of marriage legally, including a rather unique proposal before the Maryland legislature and some ideas on marriage contracts. Types of marriages are then commented on, including the childless. Articles viewing various aspects of marital stress and breakup complete this section.

Articles

1. Carlfred Broderick—Man + Woman: A Consumer's Guide to Contemporary Pairing Patterns Including Marriage.
2. Kathryn Young—Legal Aspects of Marriage.
3. Virginia Satir—Marriage as a Statutory Five Year Renewable Contract.
4. Delegate Lee—Marriage-Contractual Renewal.
5. Marsha Harshbarger—Marriage Contracts.
6. William Lederer and Don Jackson—Types of Relationships.
7. Mary W. Hicks—A Resumé of Marital Types I, II, and III.
8. Nena O'Neill and George O'Neill—Open Marriage.
9. Vivian Cadden—The Most Unexpected Threat to a Good Marriage.
10. Angus Campbell—Marriage Sí, Children Only Maybe.
11. Jack Harrison Pollack—Why Marriages Break Up After 40.
12. Pauline Bart—Portnoy's Mother's Complaint.

* Stephens, W. *Reflections on Marriage*. N.Y.: T.Y. Crowell, 1968, p. 128.
** *Changing Times—The Kiplinger Magazine*, December, 1972, p. 5.

Name: _____ Date: _____

Student #: _____ Sex: M or F

1. (a) Many types of marital adjustment exist in fact and fancy. Briefly list and discuss what you expect from, and to give to, a marriage.

   (b) What would your expectations be of your marriage partner?

2. (a) Would you consider a marriage contract which specified that it had to be renewed every "X" number of years?

   Yes _____   No _____
      Go to b.   Go to c.

   (b) If yes, what would you feel should be the number of years between renewals?_____Why? Why would such a contract interest you?

   (c) If no, why would you not think it to be a good idea?

3. (a) What would be the advantages of a renewable marriage contract?

   (b) What would be the disadvantages?

4. Describe, as you see them, what you consider to be the five most essential elements in a successful marriage.

5. Discuss briefly the following words as they relate to marriage:

(a) happiness

(b) success

(c) adjustment

(d) satisfaction

(e) sacrifice

(f) tradition

(g) conventionality

(h) harmony

Name:_____   Date:_____

Student #:_____   Sex: M or F

A MARRIAGE CONTRACT*

Suppose your state legislature was considering a bill that would change the current marriage and divorce laws in such a way as to allow individuals and couples greater freedom of choice in determining the contents of the marriage contract. A marriage contract form would be available to you when you applied for a marriage license or, if you were already married, you and your spouse could apply for such a contract at your county court house. The contract would have many options, or clauses. You could choose *any, all,* or *none* of the options, tailoring the contract to fit your own needs. The state would provide legal counsel (a lawyer) and a marriage counselor at each court house, to assist you in the drawing up and completion of your own marriage contract. Review and revision of the contract would be possible at intervals you specified: for example, you might decide to review/renew your contract every three years.

The marriage contract might contain any of the following options or clauses. Remember, each couple would be free to choose any of the clauses it wanted so that the conditions of the marriage would suit its own needs.

1. *Marriage termination/renewable clause.* This clause would let the couple be married for specified periods of time. At the end of each time period, the marriage would automatically be renewed, or terminated or reviewed, at the specific request of the couple. The couple could decide how often it wanted the marriage renewed (every 3 years, every 5 years, etc.)

2. *Choice of name clause.* The wife could choose to keep her own last name, take her husband's name, combine last names (Rowan and Martin could become Romart), or hyphenate last names (Smith-Jones). The names to be used if and when the marriage ended could be stated. The names of children could be decided upon. For example: If a son were born, whether or not he would use his father's whole name could be decided.

3. *Family Planning Clause.* The couple could state:
   a. Whether or not to have children.
   b. The number of children planned and the spacing of these children.
   c. Who would be responsible for birth control and methods of birth control that would be acceptable.
   d. If and when, and under what conditions, adoption would be acceptable.

4. *Place of residence clause.* The couple could agree upon:
   a. Their immediate place of residence.
   b. What to do if the wife's circumstances (perhaps her job) seemed to be reason for moving.
   c. What to do if the husband's circumstances seemed to be reason for moving.
   d. When, if ever, it would be acceptable to have separate homes.
   e. Within a given home, what would be considered acceptable sleeping arrangements (twin or double beds), what special needs of either partner in the forms of work or recreational space would be necessary (sewing room, home office, tool room, etc.)

5. *Use of human resources clause.* The couple could state:
   a. Who will work for money, and how much responsibility each will have for supplying income to the family.

*Based on a framework developed by Harshbarger and Bogdanoff (1972).

b. Whether the wife will be expected to work when there are small children.

c. How the nonincome producing labor will be divided: who cleans the house, shops for groceries, cooks, mows the lawn, etc.

6. *Use of nonhuman resources clause.* The couple could decide:
a. Who will be responsible for writing checks and paying bills.
b. If separate or combined checking accounts will be maintained.
c. How credit will be used.
d. Priorities for acquiring goods. (Will two cars be more important than owning a house? Will buying a washer and dryer be more important than a lawn mower?)
e. Responsibility for purchasing decisions. (Who will choose the cars: the husband, the wife, or both?)

7. *Child care clause.* This clause might not be used until a decision to have children is made, or even after children are present in the home. Items that could be included:
a. Physical responsibility for children. (Who gives the baths, feeds the children in the evening?) This could be important if both mother and father work.
b. Time to be spent with children by each parent.
c. Spiritual education of children.
d. Types of other-than-parental care that would be acceptable: Day care centers, nurseries, babysitters, other family members, etc.

8. *Individual rights and freedoms clause.* The couple might choose to set up sexual, social, and intellectual freedoms within and out of the marriage that have not traditionally been acceptable. Adultery, as ground for divorce, might or might not be seen as acceptable. Specifying the acceptable behaviors of each might include the acceptability or unacceptability of communal marriage, mate swapping, swinging, etc., and the conditions for these behaviors (whether they be public or private).

9. *Religious practices clause.* The couple could choose to retain or not retain their own beliefs and practices as part of each person's individuality. (This could be very important when the marriage is an interfaith one.) Considerations might be:
a. How involved each will be in his/her religious practice.
b. How much time and money each expects to give to his/her religious institution.
c. Religion for children: attendance, choice of church, etc.

10. *Dealing with other people clause.* This clause deals with relationships with third parties: in-laws, friends, business associates, social and professional groups. The couple might reach agreements about family visits (where to spend certain holidays), living with in-laws or having in-laws live with the couple, or having lodgers in the home, the amount and time spent with others (Will the husband have a night out every week with the boys? Will the wife belong to a bowling league?)

a. Based on the above information, please answer *yes* or *no* to the following:

Yes No

( ) ( )   1. Would you use this type marriage contract if it were easily available and legal?

( ) ( )   2. Would you like to see this type marriage contract available to others, even though you might not use it yourself?

( ) ( )   3. Do you think your fiance/spouse would use this contract?

b. Assuming you were in a position to use all the clauses in this contract, check the column at the left that best describes how you might use each clause:

Definitely Use	Probably Use	Probably Not Use	Definitely Not Use	Clauses
( )	( )	( )	( )	1. Marriage renewable/termination
( )	( )	( )	( )	2. Choice of names
( )	( )	( )	( )	3. Family planning
( )	( )	( )	( )	4. Place of residence
( )	( )	( )	( )	5. Use of human resources
( )	( )	( )	( )	6. Use of nonhuman resources
( )	( )	( )	( )	7. Child care
( )	( )	( )	( )	8. Individual rights and freedoms
( )	( )	( )	( )	9. Religious practices
( )	( )	( )	( )	10. Dealing with other people

MAN + WOMAN
Carlfred B. Broderick

A Consumer's Guide to Contemporary Pairing Patterns Including Marriage

Now! At last! The new fall lineup of the very latest plans and styles for satisfactory living together. The list includes a dazzling variety of sizes and shapes, options and accessories, never before made available to the general public, and the cost is surprisingly low. You pay your money and take your choice, and may you live happily ever after. Or at least until next Tuesday.

Dr. Broderick is Executive Director of the Marriage and Family Counseling Center at the University of Southern California.

The man-woman relationship has always been a popular but variegated commodity and the behavioral sciences have never been loath to set up guidelines for consumers. Until recently the "rational" guidelines for choosing a suitable partner and developing a fulfilling relationship were pretty much agreed upon by the large body of "experts" with only an occasional dissenting voice to add color and provide a straw man for the main position. Today all that has changed. The tide of books and articles advocating the widest variety of styles of pairing has reached flood proportions. As if this were not enough there is a seemingly infinite choice of lectures, classes, workshops, marathons and training sessions available to help the couple enrich their relationship (each according to its own rights).

Even the most enrichment oriented couple might get confused as to whether it was best to strive toward an Open Marriage, Mini-Marriage, Multilateral Marriage or Trial Marriage, or perhaps simply Honest Sex, Total Sex, or Desensitized Intimacy (in the latter case they get to watch several hours of filmed heterosexual and homosexual intercourse, masturbation, and fun and games in living color). Clearly there is a need for a Consumers' Guide so that you can see at a glance just what the basic issues are that differentiate one approach from another.

After considerable sifting it is possible to reduce the number of key issues to five. The anatomy of most of the New Visions and also of most of the Traditional Wisdoms can be clearly viewed when their positions on each of these five issues are determined. To plot the profile of each movement would be too great a task for one brief article. Instead we will lay out each of the five issues and some of the most frequently discussed positions on each issue. The reader can then analyze the features of completing pairing patterns or even develop his own model, tailored to his own position on all five issues.

Issue # 1
Freedom from Parenthood vs. Fulfillment through Parenthood

Position A: anti-natal (utopian or brave new world variety). In the best of all possible worlds children would be the wards of the state freeing all adults to pursue careers, fulfillment, etc., without encumbrance. Whether in the Huxlean fantasy where children are conceived in a test tube, developed in a bottle and decanted to a state nursery or in the more pragmatic mode advocated by Plato and Marx and Engles where the children are born to mothers but are immediately turned over to professional caretakers, this position holds that both children and adults profit from the elimination of the parent role in society. Freed from family ties the couple is free to be infinitely flexible in its arrangements, sex is free, commitments are open, etc.

Position B: anti-natal (elitist or jet-set variety). This is not a societal philosophy but a personal preference to live an unencumbered life. Research shows that children compete with pair intimacy. These couples opt for an adult-centered life style of dual careers, travel, cultural enrichment, and exciting shared experiences. Moreover, with two incomes they can afford it.

Position C: time-limited parenting. These couples commit 20 to 25 years of their marriage to childbearing but before and especially after attempt to achieve the life style of the jet-set group in Position B. Often the parenting years themselves are characterized by a conscious determination not to let the children stifle the growth of the romance or of the career goals of the wife-mother.

Position D: parenthood as career. These couples have parenthood as a central focus of their pair relationship. The mother only works outside the home if she can justify it as "best for the family." Much of the father's spare time is spent with the family as a whole. Family rituals and traditions develop. After the children are officially launched important ties are maintained between the families.

Reprinted from *Human Behavior,* Vol. 1, No. 4 (July/August, 1972) by permission of the author and publisher.

The relationship changes as the children raise families of their own, but the older couple never fully vacate their parental role while adding the grandparental role.

Issue #2
Pair as a Setting for Self Actualization and Individual Growth vs. Pair as a Mutual Aid Society with Division of Labor and Interdependency

Position A: whole-soul (utopian orientation). The "whole soul" point of view is that the man-woman relationship (or any other relationship, for that matter) only reaches its full potential when it facilitates its members' reaching their full human potentials. There are many versions of what constitutes "full human potential" and the vocabulary of each is, to some degree, unique.

Nevertheless there are several points common to nearly all versions of the movement. Everything is focused in the here and now. The past is dead, the future may never be; it is what you are experiencing at the very moment which is real and getting in touch with it is your prime imperative if you would be whole. This has two aspects. First, it emphasizes keeping your current options open by not mortgaging your future with long range commitments. In this way you avoid getting "boxed in" or "closed minded." Secondly, *awareness* is all; for example, the couple must be absolutely honest with each other about their feelings and especially their most unacceptable feelings—anger, lust, fear, pain. The standard treatment for hung-up couples is sensitivity training or group confrontation—often on a marathon basis where barriers to emotional honesty erode under the stimulus of group pressure and physical exhaustion. Equally important is the development of sensory awareness, becoming intensely in touch with your own body and your senses of touch and taste and sight and smell. One branch of the movement is especially sensitive to the symbolic and actual defense against openness which clothes afford. For this group, at least, "letting it all hang out" is not just a vivid phrase.

One step further in the same direction is the ecstatic experience or the altered state of consciousness. This takes many forms both as to means and ends with each school defending its own mark of grace against all comers. Within the movement you may seek *satori* (the state of sublime detachment from all desire) through Eastern religious disciplines, *rebirth* through accepting Jesus, *astrotravel* through occult meditation, *grooving* through psychedelic drugs, *tranquility* through

training your alpha waves with an electronic brain wave monitor and many, many more. Currently in fashion is pain as a royal road to the exalted state. Two of the most chic versions are Primal Scream therapy (based on sensory deprivation and re-experiencing all pains back to the pain of birth) and Rolfing (where each part of your body is painfully massaged until you have worked through all of the meaning attached to each pain).

But whatever the approach, the key to this position is that the pair is only valuable if it facilitates the growth of the one. Constricting relationships should be exchanged for those in which the partners are helping each other to find their full Human Potential.

Position B: mutual enrichment. Midway between the thoroughgoing (and often expensive) personal renovations of the whole soul movement and the more traditional "strengthening marriage" position discussed below are a variety of mutual enrichment programs. Some are aimed impartially at both partners, laying out programs of improved communication, more effective arguing, better sex or whatever. Others are aimed primarily at the woman, urging her to develop in ways that will enrich both. Prescriptions vary from recipes for becoming a "fascinating" woman (mix equal parts canny Victorian matron and behavioral mod shaping technique) to brews designed to convert any housewife into a "sensuous" woman (add Masters and Johnson to a basic blend of grandpa's racier fantasies and then lace generously with women's lib).

Position C: strengthening marriage. Rather than personal enrichment (let alone achieving the "full human potential") this position focuses on the institution of marriage itself. It emphasizes sacrifice, mutual support, and the traditional values of stability exclusivity, and the fulfillment of conventional role expectations. The husband should be a good provider (steady pay check, provides the "advantages" to his family), a good father (spends time with the children, firm but understanding, backs up mother) and good husband (good leadership ability but emotionally supportive and personally gentle). The wife should be a good housekeeper (attractive home—neither too messy nor too compulsively neat, good manager), a good mother (warm, interested in children, informed on child development and applied psychology) and a good wife (warm, sexy, supportive). Books and articles on this view are less eye catching but nearly all of the mass media supply persuasive material supporting this "middle American" position.

Issue #3
Inclusivity vs. Exclusivity

Position A: multilateral marriage. Marriage among three or more persons is held by many to be the ultimate expression of interpersonal maturity and openness. Everyone in the group is not married to everyone else but each person is married to at least two other persons.

This arrangement provides a broader base of intimate companionship within the marriage. In particular it includes unusual opportunity for closeness with adult members of one's own sex. Sexual life is enriched with variety in the context of commitment. Children receive the benefits of multiple parenting. And finally the whole group can become a continual encounter session with a unique combination of group support and group pressure for change.

The trouble with group marriage is that it makes heavier demands on individuals' discipline and selflessness than many can bear. Out of 20 that were followed in a study for two years only six survived that time period. Apparently pleasing two or three husbands or wives when compounded with trying to get along with two or three co-husbands or co-wives is not exactly a piece of cake.

Position B: the commune. Although communes take many forms, all are an attempt to establish face to face intimacy with a larger circle of close associates. Most communes are more conventional in their sexual arrangements than multilateral marriages, but a few are based on open sexual patterns. Close association is always demanding and the communes that survive best are those based on common religions or ideological commitment and discipline.

Another stable form described by James Ramsey (he calls them "evolutionary" communes to distinguish them from the more radical "revolutionary" variety) is based on formal social contract (including legal incorporation more often than not). These groups band together to enable members to succeed better in the competitive American system through pooling their resources, living arrangements, etc. The least stable are the revolutionary or utopian communes which tend to resist organization and structure and thus fail to sustain themselves or their boundaries.

Position C: swingers. These couples are traditionally exclusive with respect to most things (living arrangements, care of children, holding of property, etc.) but involve themselves with other couples in sexual exchange or in group sex. Since they swing as a couple and by mutual consent they do not view this lack of sexual exclusivity as a threat to their own relationship. Many claim their marriages have been strengthened by this style of life although others do not survive. Studies indicate that most swingers return to a more traditional marital format after two or three years simply because it is such an emotionally taxing style of life.

Position D: open marriage. Couples committed to the human potential philosophy (see Issue #2 above) may maintain conventional living arrangements and yet be open to intimate friendships with other couples or individuals which may include sex. This differs from swinging in that swingers typically avoid close emotional ties with their partners, and tend to view sex recreationally. Proponents of the Open Marriage (or Honest Sex, or whatever name various authors chose to give it), on the other hand, exalt sexual intimacy as an ultimate sacrament of togetherness between persons who are already in deep communion in other dimensions.

Position E: traditional monogamy. "Forsaking all others, till death do us part." Still popular although on the defensive as a moral position in view of the enthusiasm of the advocates of alternative positions.

Issue #4
Permanent Commitment vs. Permanent Availability

Position A: universal total availability. Outside of the writings of a few Utopians (and also a few anti-Utopians such as Aldous Huxley, who were scared to death by the future they foresaw) the condition of universal total availability has never existed. There are individuals in our society committed to this principle, however.

Position B: tentative commitment—options open. The position that in the best of all possible worlds one could enjoy mutual love, trust and sexual satisfaction while avoiding marriage has been popular from ancient times. Formerly it was usually identified with the traditional male aversion to the "ball and chain," but in recent years it has become popular with both sexes and especially among college students. The rationale has both pragmatic and philosophical components. On the practical side these young people feel that their futures are too uncertain to make long range commitments. Moreover they are in a period of rapid personal development and they don't want to settle permanently on someone who may not "keep up" with their own growth. Finally, until they are settled in a job they may feel in no position to take on the commitments of home and family. From a philosophical viewpoint also they find this open ended relationship more attractive than marriage. For one thing, it is more sincere since there is no constraint against either person leaving if they tire of the arrangement. Moreover, it avoids the distasteful necessity of involving representatives of the establishment (clergy, magistrates, county registrars, etc.).

Research on this form of pairing is being done at several universities but the results are not all in yet. Early returns suggest that it seldom survives graduation and job placement. Couples either break up and go their separate ways or get married.

Position C: time-limited commitments. The concept of a three or five year renewable marriage contract has been seriously suggested, although, so far as we know, it has never been put into practice anywhere. The notion is that the emotional and financial costliness of divorce could be avoided in this way along with the equally costly experience of a long term empty or destructive marriage. Certainly such an idea would necessitate a complete restructuring of modern romantic thought (try substituting "for three years" in place of "forever" in the standard romantic exchange). Also it would seem that bringing a child into the world with so tenuous a guarantee of partnership might be particularly taxing. Another variation would have a time-limited trial marriage contract to be followed (if the option were exercised) by a regular life-time commitment.

Position D: open-ended marriage with serial polygamy. This is, in effect, our present system. California is the first state to grant divorce on a no fault, no contest basis. Either partner may end the marriage by filing for divorce. The judge's only job is to preside over the equal division of property and the assignment of custody of the children. Other states will follow. An increasing number of people will promise to "love, honor, and cherish till death do us part" more than once.

Position E: life long (or even eternal) commitment. This traditional model is still the ideal of most Americans, even those who get divorced. Most people wouldn't believe it but despite the excitement about rising divorce rates, over two-thirds of us die married to the only spouse we have ever had. Surveys show that many believe (contrary to the doctrines of their own denomination) that their marriage will survive in after-life, as well. Curiously those who expect the most from marriage (in terms of personal growth and satisfaction) are often those most disappointed by it; marriages based on division of labor with mutual support appear to be the most enduring.

Issue #5
Equality vs. Complementarity

Position A: radical women's liberation. This position would settle for nothing less than the universal elimination of all social and economic distinction based on sex. Most feminists do not reject what might be called stylistic differences as long as they do not connote inferiority/superiority but they would insist that responsibility for housework, child care, and income belong to each sex equally. Moreover, each would have equal access to the full range of economic, social and political activities available to the other. In order to achieve this, many, but not all, adopt an anti-marriage or anti-natal position.

Position B: cake eaters (or moderation in all things). These people want a world in which women can compete successfully with men in any field and be rewarded equally for equal performance in any field, but are committed also to the woman's right not to compete with men at all. They would like traditional sex roles to be an available option for women and men who prefer that pattern.

Position C: complementarity. This point of view is that men and women are fundamentally different in their makeup and in their relationship to society. Men are naturally more aggressive, sexual, cerebral, mechanical, etc. Women are naturally more gentle, nuturant, expressive, manually dextrous, etc. It does women and men and society at large a disservice to attempt to suppress these differences in the name of equality. Men and women are most fulfilled when teamed in a complementary coalition with each supplying strengths the other lacks.

Well—there you are. Choose your pairing profile and may you find what you seek.

As a parting service here is my own choice for Best Buy.

Although some customers may be happy to pay a little extra for some of the special models available, years of laboratory testing indicate that the model with the lowest maintenance costs and the sturdiest performance record is the ever-popular, traditional marriage (permanent, monogamous, mutual support oriented, featuring parenthood as career and optional cake-eating or complementary stance in sex roles). In fact, I've had one for twenty years myself and it's running better today than when it was new. I recommend it. Your Best Buy.

Well, there you have it. The up-to-date rundown of pairing patterns. Being nosey, we'd like to hear about your choice. Ready to trade the old one in for something snappier? Or do you agree with the author's choice for best buy? Fill out the convenient, self-addressed, postpaid card next to page 80 and mail it in. We can't guarantee anything, of course, except that we'll share the statistical results with you (no names, addresses or phone numbers) naturally in an upcoming issue.

LEGAL ASPECTS OF MARRIAGE
Kathryn Young

Marriage is a civil status and is often defined as the foundation of our present social structure; it is a contract in that there are certain obligations and responsibilities assumed by the partners in exchange for certain rights which accrue to each. With the increase in luxury and leisure available within our society, many have come to look upon happiness and companionship as realistic expectations of marriage. Recreation and pleasure are considered the individual's just due, and love between the spouses is recognized as a supreme goal.

The husband-wife relationship becomes the most important outlet for affection as well as society's only sanctioned outlet for the sex drive. Many aspects of life have become competitive so that much of our social interaction is frustrating and marriage is expected to help both the male and the female meet the need for status and recognition. People look to the marital relationship for much of their ego satisfaction.

In this reading we will examine how the present legal requirements for marriage meet (or fail to meet) the needs of individuals in their attempt to fulfill the responsibilities inherent in that institution. The procedural legalities and restraints on marriage will be reviewed as will the assumptions underlying the legal requirements. Questions will be posed as to the relevancy of some of these assumptions in today's society. The advantages of premarital and marital counseling, and the utility of conciliation courts will be explored along with how greater equality for the husband and wife will create an atmosphere in which mutually satisfying and actualizing relationships can be cultivated.

STATE REGULATION OF MARRIAGE

Because of the essential role that marriage plays in our society the state has always had an interest in its regulation. Weitzman (1974) has broadly categorized these interests as those which are served through the licensing process and those which depend on the family to ensure more general societal goals. The licensing process serves the functions of maintaining vital statistics, promoting public health, and protecting children too young to consent to marriage. The interests which are concerned with the preservation of the family system include promoting public morality, ensuring family stability, assuring support obligations, and assigning responsibility for the care of the children.

The regulation of marriage in our country has been left to the individual states by the Federal Government; each state has passed its own laws on marriage and some of these differ considerably from those of the other states.[1] However, the typical marriage is the one which conforms to statutory requirements and restrictions such as those discussed in the following section.

PROCEDURAL LEGALITIES RELATING TO MARRIAGE

The primary concern of the state in regulating the process of getting married is to make the marriage a matter of public record. The minimum requirements include the issuance of a marriage license and a certificate by the person solemnizing the marriage, or an affidavit of witnesses, to show that the parties did indeed become husband and wife. (Florida Family Law, 1.4) The following is a brief summary of the steps to be taken to fulfill the legal requirements to become married in the state of Florida.

Based on a paper written for the Florida Conference on Marriage and the Family Unit, held in Tallahassee, Florida in October, 1975.

A. Application to County Judge

Application in the form of an affidavit signed by both parties is made to the county judge of the residence of the bride.

B. Blood Test

Applicants must file with the county judge a certificate from a duly licensed physician which states that the applicant has had a serological test not more than thirty days prior to the date of application for the marriage license, and that the applicant is not infected with syphilis.

C. Waiting Period

The applicants must wait for three days after application, during which time the county judge is required to post a true copy of the application at the front door of the courthouse in the county where application was made. The license is valid for a period of thirty days.

D. Solemnization of Marriage

No particular form of ceremony is prescribed. All regularly ordained ministers, elders in communion with some church, persons connected with the Society of Friends who perform marriage ceremonies and all judicial officers and notaries public of Florida are authorized to perform the marriage ceremony.

E. Recording of Marriage

The officiating person is required to make a certificate of the marriage on the license itself and transmit it to the office of the county judge who issued it. The original license is sent by the county judge to the Bureau of Vital Statistics. The county judge is required to keep a record of all licenses issued.[2]

RESTRAINTS ON MARRIAGE

There have always been restraints on marriage which, if violated, render the attempt to enter the institution of marriage either void or voidable. For example, all states have statutes disallowing a marriage which involves incest. Below are the primary statutes regarding restraints on marriage in the state of Florida.[3]

A. Age

Florida law requires consent of parents or guardian, prior to issuance of a marriage license, only for persons under the age of 18. Marriage can be contracted with parental consent if the male is 18 and the female is 16. Procedure is established whereby younger parties may obtain a license in case of pregnancy or birth of a child.

B. Kinship of parties

No one may marry another to whom he or she is related by lineal consanguinity nor may one marry one's brother, sister, uncle, aunt, niece or nephew. Marriage with any of these persons constitutes the felony of incest.

C. Existing Prior Marriage

A purported marriage is void when one of the parties has a spouse from an undissolved prior marriage.

D. Mental Capacity

The possession by the parties of sufficient mental capacity to consent to the creation of the marital status is essential to a valid marriage. The Florida Statutes further state that if one is intoxicated to the degree that he does not know what he is doing the marriage is invalid. In addition to these restrictions no one is permitted to marry a lunatic or an idiot.

E. Physical Capacity

Capacity for consummation is a term implied in every marriage contract. Impotency existing at the time the marriage was executed unknown to the other spouse will render it voidable. However, impotency under the amended F.S. 61 adopted in 1971 does not constitute an express ground for the dissolution of a marriage.

F. Miscegenation

Effective July 1, 1969 the miscegenation statutes were declared invalid.

ASSUMPTIONS UNDERLYING CURRENT MARRIAGE PRACTICES

1. *Assumption: No specific education is necessary to meet the demand of marriage.*

Although the contract assumes that marriage is for a lifetime, it also assumes that by the time human beings reach marriageable age they will have attained adequate knowledge regarding communication, family economics, human sexuality, interpersonal relationships, parenting, and many other areas pertaining to performing successfully as a married person for as many as 50 years or more. We assume that our children grow up with the ability to create meaningful relationships and with the knowledge of how to develop social and sexual intimacy. In reality many people go through life without learning how to express their affectional needs; without becoming cognizant of their own value system in relation to that of their spouse; without realizing the degree of responsibility inherent in parenthood; and without attaining knowledge of the social and psychological aspects of sex.

The rising rate of divorce and the recent trend toward alternate marriage forms and experimental lifestyles indicate that the majority of people are not properly prepared for what is no doubt one of the most significant decisions in their lives—that of getting married. Few guidelines are offered to young people who often enter marriage with unrealistic expectations and the beliefs which lead them toward disillusionment, discontent, and ultimately to the divorce courts.

2. *Assumption: Counseling for couples is to be utilized primarily as a means of patching up troubled marriages.*

There are a number of different kinds of counseling or therapy available to couples either before, during, after, or between marriages. Among these services are premarital, marital, postmarital, family, and divorce therapy.[4] Various approaches to these different modes of treatment include marital groups, conjoint therapy, marital enrichment groups, concurrent and collaborative treatment, communication therapy, and crisis intervention.

It is evident that divorce counseling is only one of several types of treatment which could be utilized by couples if they were aware of the availability and of the value of the different modalities. Both premarital and marital enrichment counseling have educative value and growth potential for the individuals concerned. Marital enrichment counseling is carried out either with a single couple or with couples in groups and is often educative in areas such as parent-child relationships, communication, financial problems, and human sexuality. These groups are often sponsored by churches for couples within their membership or by private practitioners for the general public.

Premarital counseling has a great deal of potential for reaching those young couples who have had no training, who often have little conception of the meaning of marriage, or who bring unrealistic expectations into the partnership. In 1970 California empowered the Superior Courts of that state to require premarital counseling of marriage license applicants if either of them is under the age of eighteen and if the Court deemed such counseling necessary. The legislature passed the law because it believed that counseling would increase the likelihood of marital success among teen-agers who have accounted for 40 percent of the divorces in the state. Divorce is difficult for any family, but it is believed it is particularly so among teen-age couples because so many children are involved. It is felt that the counseling service offered through the Conciliation Court will reduce the likelihood of marital and family difficulties in the future. Although the couples are seen for only three sessions they explore social, economic, and personal responsibility inherent in the traditional marriage and review plans for work and school, patterns of communication, feelings for each other, as well as other areas involved in the intimate marital relationship.

Premarital counseling offers a preventive measure and opens the door to professional assistance if and when the couple need it at a later time. Perhaps with this type of introduction to therapy, couples will not wait until it is too late to reach out for professional help.

Another type of preventive therapy for married couples which is merely beginning to be recognized by the public is the concept of periodic marital check-ups with a competent marriage counselor done on a voluntary basis similar to the annual physical check-up. Both periodic marital check-ups and premarital counseling focus on the preventive approach rather than the remedial and place the emphasis on improving the marriage rather than on attempting to glue it together after it has begun to fall apart.

It is probable that as people become aware of the dynamic quality possible in marriage—that marriage does not have to become static, and that marriage is an institution which can be nurtured and encouraged to grow—they will seek out these preventive services. Mace and Mace (1975) write of the hands-off policy of government agencies regarding the institution of marriage; they point out that not one agency in the United States exists specifically for the purpose of improving marriages. If there were such an agency, programs could be developed to offer the training, support, counseling, and guidance that are needed to assist people in their efforts to build good marriages.

3. *Assumption: There is one acceptable contractual form for all marriages.*

Marriages today often become dysfunctional; approximately one of three end in divorce. Traditional monogamous marriage has been faltering under the burden of adapting to the more unconventional trends such as the decision of many couples to cohabit without legalizing the relationship; the counter-culture's plea for individualization of marriage contracts; the move toward egalitarianism in the division of labor; and the increasing number of couples who prefer to remain childless.

Our ancestors relied upon traditional marriage contracts in the stable society in which they were born, lived, and died. The dynamic and rapidly changing society of today, in which life expectancy has been extended and in which individuals are seeking emotional and psychological support in addition to physical survival, challenges the adequacy of one marriage contract for all couples.

Contractual agreements regarding property division, support obligations, retirement benefits, child custody, or life insurance are not enforceable if made before the couple has decided to separate because of the states' contention that such agreements tend to encourage divorce. However, the higher divorce rates, the more liberal divorce laws, and the greater acceptance of divorce are indications of the increased normality of divorce today. It certainly seems that it would be more realistic if our legal system would allow couples to plan for the possibility that their marriage may end in divorce. To prohibit forethought and planning for the needs of those who dissolve their marriages before death prevents individuals from preparing for the future events which very well may occur.

Although most states still do not enforce antenuptial contracts between partners, some courts have recently upheld contracts made between spouses regarding property and support in case of divorce and there is some movement toward recognizing the legality of such contracts which concern essential elements of the marital relationship.[5]

Since the failure of communication is present in nearly all marriages which are dissolved through divorce, it is suggested that anything which improves the partners' communication system will also help them develop better marital relationships. If two people struggle to work out a contract stipulating the means of dealing with possible problem areas *before* marriage, they are likely to become aware of ideas, philosophies, feelings, and concerns of their spouse which often are not communicated nor recognized until after existing differences begin to create feelings of antagonism. Being aware of these differences before entering marriage allows the individuals to bring more realistic expectancies into the relationship.

Since new problems arise throughout the marriage and unforeseen events give new direction to the relationship, renewal of the marriage contract on an annual basis may provide a built-in safety valve. Both the original contract and the renewal may be worked out by the couple alone or with the assistance of an attorney or a marriage counselor. Renewing the contract with the counselor could become part of the periodic marital check-up mentioned earlier. When couples rely on annual check-ups and annual renewal of contracts, they are much less likely to deny existing differences; dealing with those differences as they arise does not allow the relationship to get bogged down in past recriminations and dilutes the hurt feelings experienced by the spouses.

If, in addition to having the opportunity to write individual contracts, couples also were allowed to carry marriage insurance which would take care of alimony and/or child support in the event such was awarded either spouse in a divorce, both members of the dyad would experience less stress over financial burdens at the time when stress levels are high even under the best circumstances. If the financial burden following divorce can be reduced through an insurance plan, both partners will be free to use more of their energies toward establishing a new home, giving psychological support to children involved, and re-establishing equilibrium in their own emotional and social lives.

One of the obstacles which prevents such an insurance plan from being instigated is the prevalent feeling that it offers couples an easy way out if the marriage gets rough. Another way of looking at that same phenomenon is that the divorce rate is already high and by withholding the financial security which insurance would provide, we are placing additional burdens on the adults and children involved when they are least able to handle it. It seems doubtful that marriage insurance would encourage divorce any more than carrying automobile insurance encourages automobile accidents. Divorce is almost always traumatic; insurance which assures the participants financial security would not make it pleasant, but might relieve some of the hurt.

If the spouse who has to pay alimony or child support was covered through insurance and if the spouse who is to receive the payments was thus assured it would be forthcoming, each would be less likely to feel animosity toward the other. And if divorce can be made more amiable, all members of the disintegrating family as well as members of the new families which will be formed will be the benefactors.[6]

4. *Assumption: Economic and social equality for partners is not a necessary component of marriage.*

Historically the husband has been recognized as the head of the household and as the breadwinner for the family; the wife has had the single role of homemaker with its attendant child-care responsibilities. Women have been economically dependent on their husbands and socially indistinguishable from them; women's social status has been dependent on that of their husbands—they have assumed their husband's name and acquired his legal domicile as that of their own.

Equality for the husband and wife is not possible as long as the two roles are radically different in the family and occupational systems. The belief that women ought to be economically supported by their husbands must be effectively refuted. This concept is a direct obstacle to the economic independence of women and their ability to compete on equal terms in the labor market. Similarly, the husband's traditional obligation to support his wife must be modified to constitute a responsibility which is shared with the wife for the support of the children.

There needs to be more sharing of the nurturant, homemaking role and of the family provider role. Until these two roles are shared on a more equal basis, there cannot be an equal economic partnership between husband and wife. A woman cannot be equal to a man on whom she feels dependent; a man cannot be equal to a woman for whom he feels economically responsible. The person who feels controlled will be resentful and the person who does the controlling will feel guilty; this situation presents a superior-inferior relationship instead of the more viable relationship between two equals with its mutual responsibility, security, reciprocity, and respect.[7]

Each of the partners should be given the role for which he or she feels best suited and which can be worked out to complement the spouse's preferences. If one of the partners chooses to do all of the housework and child-care while the other takes on the role of provider, there should be an agreement that the homemaker is to be paid according to the earning power of the provider. The homemaker will cease to be economically dependent on the one in the provider role and the marital relationship will move toward becoming an equal economic partnership.

The acceptance of housework as a paid job would eliminate the powerlessness of the homemaker and would allow the homemaking spouse to accumulate equity and to receive economic benefits such as retirement, unemployment, and health insurance. It would create a more equal economic partnership within the marriage, giving both partners an opportunity for economic security.

Within an equal partnership neither of the partners should experience the loss of legal and social identity through having to assume the other's name or domicile. There should be equal opportunity for the male and the female to retain their original surnames when the marital partnership is formed; many women will choose to assume their husband's surname upon marriage as has been traditional.[8]

In the same vein many women will be willing to accept their husband's domicile as their legal domicile, but all women should be free to choose their legal domicile as are unmarried women and married or unmarried men. The implications of the domicile rule on the psychological and sociological aspects of a woman's life are far-reaching in that it affects a broad range of legal rights and duties. In a society in which 60 percent of the working women are married and approximately 34 percent of the nonwhite and 20 percent of the white households have a woman as head of the household it seems appropriate that the wife share an equal interest in the location of the family's domicile.

SUMMARY

Marriage is still the most popular voluntary institution in our society, but concurrent with rising marriage rates are rising divorce rates.[9] Marriage is seldom the fulfilling and growth producing relationship which couples entering the institution expect and desire. Increasingly individuals are entering marriage with the expectations of creating a meaningful and mutually actualizing partnership. Husband and wife are beginning to realize that they need to structure their own role relationships according to their individual needs rather than to simply accept the traditional roles as handed down from the past.

The changing expectations of marriage are creating a situation in which growing dissatisfaction will result unless couples are allowed more freedom to define individual needs through legal marriage contracts and unless the state supports its citizens in their attempt to adjust to the transition from an inferior-superior type of marriage to the equal economic partnership which will provide the individuals and the relationship which they have formed a means of attaining their creative and productive potential and reaching emotional and psychological fulfillment.

References

DeCrow, K. *Sexist Justice*. New York: Random House, 1974.

Mace, D.R. & V.C. Marriage enrichment—Wave of the future? *The Family Coordinator*, Vol. 24, 1975, pp. 131-135.

Weitzman, L.J. Legal regulation of marriage: tradition and change. *California Law Review*, Vol. 62, 1975, pp. 1169-1288.

NOTES

1. For variations of marriage laws in the different states see 52 Am Jur 2d Marriage, Doc. No. 124.

2. For further details regarding statutory requirements see Florida Family Law: 1.3 through 1.9.

3. For variations see footnote 1.

4. The terms therapy and counseling are used interchangeably in this paper although therapy usually denotes more in-depth treatment than does counseling.

5. See Weitzman (1266-70) for details on the cases in Florida (1970), Illinois (1972) and Oregon (1973) in which courts enforced antenuptial agreements providing stipulations for alimony or lump sum settlements in the event of divorce.

6. See Weitzman, (1180-7) for a discussion of how "spousal support obligations of the husband are rarely enforced in an on-going marriage. . . .women fare just as poorly, if not more so, in enforcing this obligation after separation or divorce." Karen DeCrow supports the contention that women are put in a precarious position if they blithely assume they will be protected in their economically dependent role which they are encouraged to assume as a full time homemaker. She states that "Perhaps the proper way to look at alimony is not as a way of sustaining the wife who is unable to support herself, but rather as back pay." (DeCrow, 1975:163)

7. The traditional marriage contract in which the husband is solely responsible for the economic support of the family generates this unhealthy and dysfunctional relationship. In case of divorce it places hardship on both parties—on the woman who has not developed economic competence and on the man who is often in a financial bind in his responsibilities for the economic support of (often) two families. The law creates the dichotomy of the responsible man and the dependent woman, but "women who rely on the law's promise of spousal support are likely to find their expectations thwarted." (Weitzman:1181)

8. However, those who choose to retain their maiden name in order to retain their identity throughout life should be allowed to do so. Assuming a new name can be a real loss to a business or professional woman; she needs the legal recognition of the state if she chooses to retain her maiden name. Weitzman states "A woman who tries to use her maiden name may have difficulty voting, obtaining a driver's license, running for office, and securing credit." (Weitzman:1174) She reports a case in 1971 in which the court "held that it was constitutional for the Alabama Supreme Court to adopt the common law rule which requires a woman upon marriage to take her husband's surname." The United States Supreme Court subsequently affirmed this decision.

9. According to Vital Statistics (Vol. 19, 1971) the rate of marriages in 1970 was 10.7 per 1000 individuals which was the highest it had been in twenty years; the number of divorces had almost doubled from 1950 to 1970. However, remarriage rates are also increasing—nearly one of four brides and grooms today are persons marrying for at least the second time. There is a great deal of social pressure placed on the divorced and widowed individual to remarry; approximately seven out of ten divorced persons eventually remarry.

MARRIAGE AS A STATUTORY FIVE YEAR RENEWABLE CONTRACT
Virginia Satir

When I was asked to write this paper, the idea excited me. I have many thoughts about this subject. As I sit down now to write, I am overwhelmed at the enormity of their implications. My power of imagination fails me in visualizing how all these changes could be accomplished, given this world as it is today with its vast numbers of people and the prevailing low image of a human being as it exists today, where love and trust are rarities and suspicion and hate are expected.

Person-peson, male-female, and adult-child relations, generally speaking as they exist today, seem pretty inhuman and many times even anti-human. The current surrounding legal and social structure frequently acts to aid and abet these inhuman relations. Given the state of human relations today, it

Presented at the American Psychological Association—75th Annual Convention, Washington, D.C., September 1, 1967. Printed here for the first time.

is not hard to understand current human behavior in marriage, the family and other non-familial human transactions.

The effect of these inhuman and anti-human relations seems abundantly obvious in the widespread presence of mistrust and fear between human beings. If relationships are experienced as mistrust and fear, how can love and trust come about? Statistics on alcoholism, drug addiction, suicide, murder, mental illness, crimes against other persons and property, and family crimes are more specific indications of inhuman and anti-human treatment. Continuing wars between nations, racial strife, and poverty are more global evidences of these same practices.

While these statistics do not include every person in our population, enough are included to make it more than just a random or accidental occurrence. This raises a very basic question. Is this how man really is inherently or is this the result of how he has been taught? I would have to stop this paper right now if I believed that man's present behavior is the result of what he is, inherently. I believe man's behavior reflects what he learned. I take hope in the fact that anything that has been learned can be unlearned and new learning can be introduced.

This of course raises another basic question. What are these new learnings? To talk about a change in the marriage relationship without talking about making changes in the human beings who are making the marriage is in my opinion, putting the cart before the horse.

I would like to present some ideas, that if they were implemented might go a long way to getting us all a notch forward in our whole human existence. What Would Happen If:

1. Children were conceived only by mature adults. That they felt prepared and knew beyond few questions of doubt that they had the skills to be wise, patient, and joyful, creative, productive, loving, curious, real adults. Further, that this conception was an active mutual choice which represented a welcome addition, instead of a potential deprivation or a substitute for a marital disappointment.

2. Parenting were seen as probably the most crucial and important, challenging and interesting job for each adult when adults are engaged in it.

   a. Business and the working world would manage in such a way that young fathers would not be asked to be gone from Monday to Friday. Men are essential and their nonpresence hands child rearing almost exclusively over to the woman. This skews the kind of parenting a child gets, which is reflected in his image of himself and others. An integrated person needs to have an intimate familiarity in reality with both sexes. For many children, their fathers are ghosts, benign or malevolent. If they are males, this leaves them with a hazy and incomplete model for themselves. If they are females, their relations and expectations of men evolve more from fantasy than reality. It seems to me that this is a large factor in satisfaction in married life. Furthermore, male absence overdraws on the woman's resources, paving the way for all kinds of destructive results for herself, her children and her husband. However we slice it, we come into the world with life equipment, but it remains for our experiences to teach the uses of it. After all, the husbands and fathers, and wives and mothers of today are the boys and girls of yesterday.

   b. Women who are mothers and men who are fathers could have auxiliary help without stigma in their parenting. Parenting for the first five years is a 24 hour a day job. This gets pretty confining, if there is no relief. This might go some way toward breaking the possession aspect of adults and their children and move it more toward real responsibility of developing the child's humanity.

   c. There were family financial allowances to people who needed it, not on the basis of being poor and making just survival possible, but because it was needed to facilitate optimum growth.

   d. Preparation for parenting was seen as something to be actively learned instead of assuming that the experience of conception and birth automatically provided all the know-how one needed. Nobody calling himself an engineer would even be considered for an engineering job if all the preparation he had consisted of his wish to be one, and the knowledge he gained by watching his father who was one.

3. The idea of developing human beings was considered so important and vital that each neighborhood had within walking distance a Family Growth Center, which was a center for learning about being human from birth to death. Further, to assist others to learn what it means to be human. These might well replace the current public welfare offices among other things. In my opinion, this process about learning how to be human will never end because I believe the human potential is infinite. We have barely scratched the surface.

4. The literal context surrounding the birth event included full awareness to the woman giving birth, the active witnessing of the birth process by the father of the child, and the rooming-in of all of them for at least the first two weeks. Everyone would get a chance to be in on the getting acquainted process that necessarily takes place. In a first birth, the female meets her husband in his father role for the first time, the male meets his wife in her mother role also for the first time and each meets the new person for the first time. Many women and men feel like strangers to each other when they meet as father and mother despite the fact that they have been husbands and wives to each other.

The subsequent celebration following the birth be considered not only a birth of a new human being, but a birth of new roles for the adults as well. The way some celebrations have gone would suggest Immaculate Conception. Men must often feel like a useless appendage at this time. No wonder there are fears of replacement on their part.

I wonder whether it would be as possible for men who are fathers to leave their families as readily as they now can, if they were part of the literal birth proceedings, and openly hailed and honored as having been and being essential, as is clear with the woman. I wonder too, if this were done, whether it would be as easy for the birth of a baby to create as much estrangement between the husbands and wives as it often does.

5. Child rearing practices were changed.
   a. The emphasis on child rearing was on helping the child find out crystal clearly how he looked and sounded, how to tune in on how he felt and thought, how to find out how he experienced others, and how he affected others, instead of only the admonishment to be good and find out how to please others.
   b. That from the moment of birth, he was treated as a person who had the capacity to hear, to see, to feel, to sense and to think, different from the adult only in body development and initially in putting his sensory experiences into words.
   c. That he had a predictable place in time and space.
   d. That he had real and openly welcomed opportunities to feel his power and his uniqueness, his sexuality and his competence as soon as his resources permitted it.
   e. That he was surrounded by people who openly and clearly enjoyed each other and him, and were straight and real with one another and him, thus giving him a model for his own delight in interacting with people. Thus, the joy in relationships might overcome the grim responsibility outlook for becoming an adult that many children must have.
   f. That "yes" and "no" were clear, reliable, appropriate and implemented.
   g. That realness was valued over approval when there had to be a choice.
   h. That at every point in time, regardless of age or label, he was always treated as a whole person. He is never regarded as too young to or too old to be a person.
   i. Every child's feelings were always regarded with dignity and respect, meaning being listened to and understood and if those around him did the same with each other.
   j. Every child's actions were considered separately from his expression, instead of linking expressions of feeling with an automatic specific act. Further, he was taught that actions had to be subject to the time, place, situation, other persons and purpose, instead of attempting to give a stereotyped "should" that applies universally.
   k. That differentness from others was clearly an opportunity for learning; it

holds an important key to interest in living and real contact with others, instead of seeing it primarily as something to be tolerated, to be destroyed, or to avoid.

l. Every child had continuing experience matched by his models that human life is to be revered, his and that of all others.

m. Every child received openly continuing knowledge of how he and all his parts work—his body, his mind and his senses. That he receive encouragement for expressing, clarifying and experimenting with his thoughts, his feelings, his words, his actions and his body, in all its parts.

n. To look forward to each new step in growth as an opportunity for discovery encompassing pain, pleasure, knowledge and adventure. And that each phase of growth had special learnings that were particularly planned for, and that the evidence showing that a new growth step had been achieved would be openly and obviously validated, like celebrating with a party the onset of menstruation for girls and maybe a change of voice party for boys at the time of puberty. Further examples would be: parties for the first step, first tooth, first day at school, the first overnight visit with nonfamilial members, the first date, first sexual intercourse, and the first obvious and costly mistake.

o. To see males and females as different, yet interesting and essential to each other, and free to be separate instead of being implicit enemies of feeding on each other.

p. To get training in male-female relations—preparing openly for a mate and for parenting in turn, which is held to be desirable and demonstrated as such.

q. To be openly let in on the experiences of adults in parenting, maritalling, and selfing.

6. One would have the awareness of freely experiencing in an openly welcoming way the sexual self emerge. This requires the cover of secrecy on the genitals and all that entails.

7. The goal of being human was how to be real, loving, intimate, authentic and alive as well as competent, productive and responsible.

We have never had people reared anything like this on a large enough scale to know how this would affect marriage, family, and in general people to people relationships. What impetus to a really better world, socially more evolved people, and what new horizons might open up to what now seems the insurmountable problems of suicide, murder, alcoholism, illegitimacy, irresponsibility, incompetence, war, racial and national conflicts could be envisaged if we had. I think it is worth trying for.

In our society, marriage is the social and legal context in which the new humans originate and are expected to grow into fully developed human beings. The very life of our society depends upon what happens as a result of marriage. Looking at the institution of marriage as it exists today raises real questions about its effectiveness.

The marriage contract in the Western Christian world has no provision for periodic review or socially acceptable means of termination. I would offer that this contract as it stands, is potentially inhuman and anti-human and works against developing love, trust, and connectedness with other human beings. It is made with the apparent assumption that the conditions present at its inception will continue without change for eternity. This asks people to be wiser than they can possibly be. It is made at a time in the lives of the respective parties when they have the least preparation in fact with which to make this contract.

This contract exacts an explicit agreement that other intimate relationships with the same and other sex shall cease and each partner shall be the sole resource of total comfort and gratification for the other. Implicitly, the marriage contract abolishes individual autonomy and makes togetherness mandatory. Independent wishes and acts, contradictory opinions are seen as threats to marriage.

If marriage partners hold on to their integrity and their individuality, their independent wishes and acts, and contradictory opinions, they may retain their integrity but lose the relationship. So, to preserve the marriage one has to lose one's integrity if to manifest the integrity loses the marriage.

Almost any study of sexual practices of married people done today report that many marital partners do not live completely monogamously. Marital partners report from a few to many extramarital sexual relationships, which are largely secret. Frequently married persons practice a kind of consecutive spousing which is sort of polygamy done in parts. Mate swapping, which is polygamy in the open, in beginning to be more frequent. The myth is monogamy. The fact is frequently polygamy. Evidently, the expectation that each mate should completely suffice the other is failing, and maybe by its failure, demonstrates its unreality of this expectation.

Maybe with these facts we have to consider the possibility that human beings are not naturally monogamous, and that any agreement to treat people as if they were courts trouble.

Maybe monogamy is a more efficient and economic way to organize heterosexual relations to permit child raising. If so, could monogamy as well as being efficient and economic also be creative, enjoyable, growth producing as well? Maybe this hinges on making it possible to have individual autonomy as well as togetherness. Right now it looks as though monogamy is experienced after a relatively short time as grim, lifeless, boring, depressing, disillusioning and potential contexts for murder, suicide, mental illness and human decay. Perhaps persons who had rearing of the kind I described would make marriage an exciting and alive experience.

The marriage contract with its implicit social expectations of chastity is based on the assumption that the expectation of an experience is the same as the actual experience. Our courtship expectations are such that in the main they are based on hunting and advertising principles. "Catch against your will and put the best side out."

The current marriage contract is derived from a chattel economic base, which stresses possessing. This gets translated into duty and becomes emotional and sometimes literal blackmail. The quality of joy is lost in the game of scoreboard. "Who loses, who wins, and who is on top?" The result is the grimness I referred to earlier.

Obviously only mature people can make workable contracts with some hope of achievement, not because they can predict the events, but because they have a reliable, workable growth producing coping process to meet whatever comes along. Few people have open access to information and experience that prepares them for how to be a person, let alone be a marriage partner.

From the time of puberty the underlying message is be careful of the other sex—the other sex is dangerous. The symbol of this is genital contact, namely intercourse. Many marriages are made by persons who secretly fear that the other sex is dangerous. Out of this is supposed to come intimacy, tenderness, and joining of efforts. How do potential enemies easily translate their relationship into one of intimacy and tenderness?

Maybe there needs to be something like an apprentice period which is socially approved that preceeds an actual marriage, in which potential partners have a chance to explore deeply and experiment with their relationship.

In a period of living together, which was socially approved and considered desirable, each could experience the other and find out whether his fantasy matched the reality. Was it really possible through daily living to have a process in which each was able to enhance the growth of the other while at the same time enhancing his own? What is it like to have to undertake joint ventures and being with each other every day? It would seem that in this socially approved context, the chances of greater realness and authenticity continuing would be increased, and the relationship would deepen since it started on a reality base.

Right now such important learning is denied in an effort to preserve the fiction of chastity. It seems to me that this puts undue weight on something that is peripheral to the big goal—healthy relationships.

We have to have a socially accepted and desirable way to terminate a marriage when it appears that it no longer works. What if it could happen just by mutual consent and the only problem was how to plan for the continuing parenting of children. I doubt whether that between people who were authentic and real that this would be either so destructive or so frequent. Human beings with the best intentions and integrity make errors. There needs to be an honorable way to treat this most important error.

If we could truly see that the act of sexual intercourse has more to do with enabling self esteem in the partners and can represent the highest and most satisfying form of male-female contact, we would be more discriminating. Further, we could openly teach ways to make this possible. For this we must lift the cover of secrecy and ignorance. At the present time sexual contact is frequently seen as degrading, a form of war, merchandise, lust, a means of scalp hunting and a scoreboard. In these circumstances, when the outcome is conception, the child is potentially doomed to the "psychiatric couch", to prison, to poverty, to premature death, or maybe worse yet, to conformity and boredom. How can one degrade or be destructive toward that which he considers openly, truly beautiful and part of his joy in existence?

If we were all to see the sexual act as the renewal value of the other and the increase of self esteem in the self, and that the decision to procreate was a voluntary mutually shared one that was entered into after the intimate, satisfying, renewing experience had been achieved by a male and female pair, what magnitude of revolution might we stimulate in a new model for person-person relations.

Anyone who has studied family process at all can see with one eye, how (1) the sexual relationship is symbolic of the heterosexual interrelationship and this carries the significance of the person-person relationship, and (2) that the fate of the child hangs on this interrelationship.

Intercourse is a fact, not a symbol. Conception, pregnancy and birth, are also facts not symbols. The child is a result of these facts, but his maturing is guided by the feelings that surround these facts.

I am implying three changes:

1. The cover of secrecy be removed from the sexual part of the human being. With this cover off, ignorance can be removed.
2. There be as much attention, care, interest and implementation, openly, creatively and confidently given to the care, maintenance and use of the genitals as there is, for instance, to one's teeth.
3. That a couple have a means to know when they have achieved intimacy in their relationship which is based on their experience with, and awareness of, each other as real persons whom they value, enjoy, and feel connected with.

If we were taught from childhood on that our most important goal as a human being was to be real and in continuing touch with ourselves, which in turn would ensure a real connection with others, and that creativity, authenticity, health, aliveness, lovingness and productivity were desirable goals, we would have a much greater sense of when this was achieved. We would also find it much easier to do.

With the expectation of the age of marriage being around 20 and life expectancy being around 70, close to 50 years of a person's life can be expected to be lived under the aegus of a marriage contract.

If the contract does not permit an alive, dynamic experience with growth possible for both, the result is outrage, submission, destructiveness, withdrawal, premature death or destructive termination. Maybe this is impossible. If it is, then perhaps what we need to do is to find a way to conceive and bring up children that does not depend on a relatively permanent relationship between the parents. The act of conception and birth could be entirely separated from the process of raising children. We could have child manufacturers and child raisers. We have much of this now except that it is socially stigmatizing. We work awfully hard to make adoption successful. "He is not my real child," or "She is not my real mother." Actually most of us know that the significance of the blood tie is mostly in our heads.

Maybe the most important thing is that new humans get born, and then they are raised. Who does either or both may not be as important as that it is done and how it is done. Maybe if this were done, the energies of all the adults of the world would be more available for the work and joy in the world, and less tied up with what they "should" be.

Procreation coming about as it does with little evidence that it will change much in the near future—guarantees that there will be males and females around, that they will be attracted to one another in or out of marriage. Maybe this could be openly acknowledged and we could find ways to use it for our mutual benefit.

As for me, I think a relationship of trust, worth and love between people is the highest and most satisfying way of experiencing one's humanity. I think this is where real spirituality takes place. Without it, humans become shrivelled, destructive and desolate.

Right now, our current forms of human interaction, our fears, our suspicions, and our past are working against us. We have all the resources for the needed change, but we do not yet know how to use them. Our survival as a society may well depend upon finding these uses.

MARRIAGE-CONTRACTUAL RENEWAL

Delegate Lee—Judiciary

General Assembly—HB3
No. 3, Pre-Filing Series—1973 Session LR3
Filed April 10, 1972

A BILL ENTITLED

1 AN ACT to add new Section 32 to Article 16
2 of the Annotated Code of Maryland (1966
3 Replacement Volume), title "Chancery,"
4 to follow immediately after Section 31
5 thereof and to be under the new subtitle
6 "Marriage-Contractual Renewal," to pro-
7 vide that any marriage may be considered a
8 contract for three years with an option to
9 renew for three years, renewable for succes-
10 sive periods, upon mutual consent thereto;
11 to provide for the event that either one or
12 both of the parties wish to terminate the
13 contract at any time; and generally relating
14 thereto.

15 SECTION 1. BE IT ENACTED BY THE
16 GENERAL ASSEMBLY OF MARYLAND,
17 That new Section 32 be and it is hereby
18 added to Article 16 of the Annotated Code of
19 Maryland (1966 Replacement Volume), title
20 "Chancery," to follow immediately after Sec-
21 tion 31 thereof and to be under the new sub-
22 title "Marriage-Contractual Renewal," and to
23 read as follows:
24 MARRIAGE-CONTRACTUAL RENEWAL
25 32.

26 (A) THE PROVISIONS OF THIS SEC-
27 TION ARE IN ADDITION TO THE PRO-
28 VISIONS OF LAW OF THIS STATE RELAT-
29 ING TO DIVORCE AND ANNULMENT
30 AND SHALL BE CONSTRUED AS IN-
31 CREASING, BUT NOT LIMITING, THE
32 LAW PRESENTLY EXISTING IN THIS
33 STATE.

34 (B) ANY MARRIAGE PERFORMED IN
35 THIS STATE FROM AND AFTER JULY 1,
36 1973, MAY BE A CONTRACT OF MAR-
37 RIAGE FOR THE TERM OF THREE (3)
38 YEARS. THE CONTRACT AT THE END OF
39 THAT PERIOD OF TIME SHALL BE SUB-
40 JECT TO RENEWAL FOR AN ADDI-
41 TIONAL THREE (3) YEAR PERIOD UPON
42 THE MUTUAL AGREEMENT OF BOTH
43 PARTIES THERETO. THE RENEWAL OP-
44 TION SHALL BE AVAILABLE AT THE
45 END OF THE ORIGINAL THREE (3) YEAR

46 PERIOD AND EACH AND EVERY THREE
47 (3) YEAR PERIOD THEREAFTER. IF
48 EITHER PARTY TO THE ORIGINAL
49 MARRIAGE CONTRACT AT THE END OF
50 THE ORIGINAL TERM OF ANY EXTEN-
51 SION THEREOF DOES NOT AGREE TO
52 AN ADDITIONAL THREE (3) YEAR OP-
53 TIONAL EXTENSION TO RENEW, AND IF
54 THE OTHER AGREEABLE PARTY SO RE-
55 QUESTS, THE CIRCUIT COURT OF THE
56 COUNTY OR BALTIMORE CITY, AS THE
57 CASE MAY BE, WHETHER EITHER OF
58 THE PARTIES RESIDES OR WORKS OR
59 MAINTAINS A PRINCIPAL PLACE OF
60 BUSINESS, HAS JURISDICTION TO DE-
61 TERMINE:
62 (1) ALIMONY OR MAINTENANCE,
63 OTHER SUPPORT, IF ANY, WHETHER
64 PENDENTE LITE OR PERMANENT, PAY-
65 ABLE BY THE SPOUSE NOT RENEWING
66 THE MARRIAGE CONTRACT TO THE
67 PERSON WISHING TO CONTINUE THE
68 MARRIAGE;
69 (2) CHILD SUPPORT, IF ANY, FOR
70 ISSUE BORN AS A RESULT OF THE
71 INITIAL MARRIAGE CONTRACT OR ANY
72 RENEWAL THEREOF OR ADOPTED BY
73 THE PARTIES THERETO DURING THE
1 ORIGINAL TERM OR ANY RENEWAL
2 THEREOF;
3 (3) PROPERTY SETTLEMENT BE-
4 TWEEN THE PARTIES TO THE INITIAL
5 MARRIAGE CONTRACT OR ANY RE-
6 NEWAL THEREOF;
7 (4) ANY AND ALL OTHER QUES-
8 TIONS WHICH WOULD BE WITHIN THE
9 JURISDICTION OF THE APPROPRIATE
10 COURT UNDER THE EXISTING DIVORCE
11 AND/OR ANNULMENT LAWS OF THE
12 STATE; AND
13 (5) ATTORNEY'S FEES OF THE
14 PARTY APPLYING FOR RELIEF HERE-
15 UNDER.
16 (C) THE COURT HAS THE SAME
17 POWERS UNDER THIS SECTION AS IT
18 WOULD HAVE UNDER THE LAWS OF

19 THIS STATE CONCERNING DIVORCE
20 AND ANNULMENT IN REGARD TO EN-
21 FORCEMENT OF COURT ORDERS
22 ISSUED UNDER ANY APPLICATION FOR
23 RELIEF BROUGHT HEREUNDER OR BY
24 RIGHT UNDER THE DIVORCE AND AN-
25 NULMENT LAWS OF THIS STATE.
26   (D) IF THE PARTIES TO THE CON-
27 TRACT, OR EITHER OF THEM, DO NOT
28 WISH TO CONTINUE THE MARRIAGE
29 FOR THE ORIGINAL THREE YEAR PERI-
30 OD, OR ANY EXTENSION THEREOF, THE
31 PARTY SEEKING RELIEF OR THE OTHER
32 PARTY TO THE CONTRACT MAY RE-
33 QUEST THE CIRCUIT COURT OF THE
34 COUNTY OR OF BALTIMORE CITY, AS
35 THE CASE MAY BE, TO PROCEED UNDER
36 THE TERMS OF THE CONTRACT OR UN-

37 DER THE EXISTING LAWS PERTAINING
38 TO DIVORCE.
39   (E) ANY AGREEMENT SIGNED BY
40 THE PARTIES TO THE ORIGINAL MAR-
41 RIAGE CONTRACT, WITH REGARD TO
42 ALIMONY, MAINTENANCE AND SUP-
43 PORT, PERMANENT OR PENDENTE LITE,
44 OR ANY OF THEM, AND CHILD SUP-
45 PORT, PROPERTY SETTLEMENT, ATTOR-
46 NEY FEES, AND OTHER QUESTIONS
47 PROPERLY BEFORE THE COURT OR
48 WITHIN ITS JURISDICTION, OR ANY OF
49 THEM, SHALL BE INCORPORATED IN A
50 DECREE OR ORDER OF THE COURT.
51   SECTION 2. AND BE IT FURTHER EN-
52 ACTED, That this Act shall take effect on
53 July 1, 1973.

MARRIAGE CONTRACTS: WHAT WAS, WHAT IS, AND WHAT COULD BE

Marsha Harshbarger

MARRIAGE CONTRACTS: A BIT OF HISTORY

The concept of marriage contracts is not new. They have been part of marital arrangements stretching back to biblical times. They were both legal and binding, and could be entered into either before or after marriage. They differed, however, from the more recently proposed marriage contracts, in that they tended to deal exclusively with property issues.

As the use of property-oriented marriage contracts has waned, relationship-oriented contracts have begun to appear. As early as 1792, Mary Wollstonecraft and William Godwin submitted to marriage only after they agreed upon their own terms. There were separate quarters and they each retained the right to separate friends. In 1855, Lucy Stone and Harry Blackwell wrote their own marriage contract protesting the inequities of American marriage at the time (Edmiston, 1972). Lucy Stone retained her maiden name and publicly repudiated the marriage laws of the time, which suspended the legal existence of the wife during marriage (Edmiston, 1972; Andreas, 1971).

More recently, contracts such as the one that follows appeared. (Names and places have been changed to assure confidentiality.)

J.F Smith
To
Lavinia Davis

March the 11th 1947, Washington County, Virginia
Memorandum of an agreement of contract between J.F. Smith of the one part and Lavinia Davis of the other part.

WITNESSETH: That the said J.F. Smith hereinafter called the party of the first part, and the said Lavinia Davis hereinafter called the party of the second part. This is to forever bear witness that in case the said J.F. Smith of the first part and the said Lavinia Davis party of the second part may marry, this is to witness that there is a full and complete understanding that the said J.F. Smith party of the first part shall have full, free and unmolested control of the home premises, farm, property both real and personal including all the belongings of both the party of the first part and the party of the second part, and he shall in no way be hindered from his duties as a Minister, surveyer, "Lodge man," or anything else he may desire to be employed in or by, to go and come at his will and pleasure unmolested and not to be spoken against by the party of the second part and have all the belongings of the house, or houses, on all lands, owning all lands and all household goods as well as all other property both real and personal and shall have full and complete authority to control all such properties and shall say who shall come, and who shall go, who shall stay, and who shall be dismissed, sent away, and have full control unmolested of all persons and belongings, as to who to go, and who to stay, and whether any one shall be allowed to "live with" them any time after marriage and to hire such hands as he, the party of the first part may select whether male or female, young or old, and the said Lavinia Davis hereby agrees that she will after becoming the wife of the party of the first part sign any other paper, deed, contract, or other writings her husband may direct her to sign, and he the party of the first part shall not be bound by an obligation to furnish anything to go on, or to live on, or to support his wife on, except as he may desire to do, or not to do, and the said Lavinia Davis party of the second part agrees not to allow any ruff words, or bad language, or fussing, or love songs, or no music except sacred music, or nothing else about the house except such as right talk, prayer, preaching, right singing or sacred songs and the said J.F. Smith shall not be sued for anything and she further agrees that in all things to take the advice of the said J.F. Smith and work in harmony with his plans, and advice, as witnesseth the following signatures.

J.F. Smith   (Seal)
Lavinia Davis (Seal)

Washington County Court Clerk's Office

This instrument was this day presented to me in my office, and thereupon, together with the certificate thereto annexed, is admitted to record.

Teste: O.J. Simpson, Clerk
DeAnne Lucy, Deputy

Unacknowledged Writings Book 1 at page 210.

Obviously, Mr. Smith had some liberal ideas about what was O.K. for him, and some conservative thoughts as to what was O.K. for "his wife." Interestingly enough, both parties agreed to the contract and signed it.

MARRIAGES CONTRACTS NOW

Today, marriage contracts written by individual couples are of interest to many people. Popular magazines, such as *Redbook* (Shulman 1971; 1972) and *Ms.* (Edmiston, 1971; Cody and Sadis, 1973) have carried articles that outline strategies for developing one's own marriage contract, describe well-known persons' marriage contracts,

or report on their readers' reactions to marriage contracts. Some persons have rejected them on religious or moral grounds, others because they see marriage contracts as lacking the flexibility to grow with the marital relationship. Proponents of marriage contracts view them as frameworks for helping people establish relationships in which each person's expectations are laid out and examined before a legal commitment is made to a relationship.

Regardless of how the public views the new breed of marriage contracts, they are usually not, at this point in time, legal and binding. On the other hand, they are not illegal, i.e., a couple can certainly choose to adopt the strategy of drawing up a document that states explicitly what is or is not wanted in marriage before—or after—the wedding without any legal repercussions.

Increasing public interest in marriage contracts suggests the following:

—There are major issues of concern within the marital dyad—both traditional and innovative—that may well need a framework within which to be resolved. Such a framework may become even more necessary as role models become less well defined than they are today, and as the expectations of society and of the particular persons entering into a dyadic relationship become more open to change.

—People may no longer be satisfied with marriage laws under which they are now operating as they have been in the past. They may be seeing other alternatives to the traditional monogamous marriage and all that implies and may—while recognizing that alternatives are becoming more and more acceptable within their social worlds—also recognize that these alternatives are not at all acceptable within the legal world. Interest in marriage contracts may be an indication of the need, then, for domestic law to keep abreast of the times through reform and through supplying society with the necessary tools for making innovation legal and respectable.

HOW DO YOU COMPARE?

Two other groups, one similar to yourself, i.e. college students, and one quite different,* responded to the questionnaire included as Rip Off #7b. Their answers are summarized in following:

* This group was composed of persons (N=110) who filled out the same questionnaire after reading a newspaper article that described the marriage contract. Ages ranged from 11-81. Seventy-six per cent were female, 70% were married. Educational attainment ranged from below eighth grade to doctoral degrees. The occupations were so diverse that they defied classification.

TABLE I
General Use of a Marriage Contract: College Students Compared to
Newspaper Poll Respondents

Question	Yes		No	
	Students[1]	Poll[2]	Students	Poll
1. Would you use this type marriage contract if it were easily available and legal?	39.8%	50.9%	60.2%	49.1%
2. Would you like to see this type marriage contract available to others, even though you might not use it yourself?	79.6%	67.0%	20.4%	33.0%
3. Do you think your fiancee/spouse would use this contract?	30.1%	31.8%	69.9%	68.2%

[1] N = 93
[2] N = 110 except for question 2 where N = 109

TABLE II
Use of Clauses: College Students Compared to Newspaper Poll Respondents

Clause	Definitely Use		Probably Use		Probably Not Use		Definitely Not Use	
	C.S.*	N.P.**	C.S.	N.P.	C.S.	N.P.	C.S.	N.P.
1. Marriage renewable/ termination	15.1%	35.5%	25.8%	12.7%	24.7%	10.0%	34.4%	41.8%
2. Choice of names	9.7%	20.9%	24.7%	15.5%	33.3%	20.9%	32.3%	42.7%
3. Family planning	29.0%	56.4%	45.2%	19.1%	11.8%	2.7%	14.0%	21.8%
4. Place of residence	9.7%	28.2%	32.2%	27.3%	35.5%	15.4%	22.6%	29.1%
5. Use of human resources	19.4%	34.5%	43.0%	30.9%	21.5%	8.2%	16.1%	26.4%
6. Use of nonhuman resources	22.6%	37.3%	35.5%	33.6%	24.7%	6.4%	17.2%	22.7%
7. Child care	20.4%	30.9%	31.2%	28.2%	28.0%	14.5%	20.4%	26.4%
8. Individual rights and freedoms	9.7%	31.8%	33.3%	15.5%	28.0%	13.6%	29.0%	39.1%
9. Religious practices	10.8%	39.1%	41.9%	30.0%	30.1%	7.3%	17.2%	23.6%
10. Dealing with other people	12.9%	42.7%	28.0%	26.4%	34.4%	11.8%	24.7%	19.1%

*C.S. = College Students
**N.P. = Newspaper Poll Respondents

As you can see, both groups were more accepting of the use of a marriage contract for others than they were for themselves; however, both groups felt that their spouses or fiancees would be less likely to use a marriage contract than they, themselves, would. Why? One can only speculate, but it may be that the subjects of both groups were exhibiting a more general acceptance of liberal behavior for others (not spouses or fiancees) than for themselves, similar to that found by Ehrmann (1959) when he studied premarital sexual behavior. A possible explanation for the subjects' perceptions of their spouses' or fiancees' likely nonuse of the marriage contract would be that they saw their spouses or fiancees as being more conservative than they saw themselves to be.

POPULARITY OF CLAUSES
IN THE MARRIAGE CONTRACT

For both groups, the clauses fell into two distinct categories: Those that would be more likely used, and those that would be less likely used. Those clauses that make up the first category (#3,4,5,6,7,9,10) were entitled "Traditional Tasks," since all the issues addressed within these clauses are issues that are typically pursued in any marital relationship. The second category (#1,2,8) consists of those clauses that were less likely to be used by these subjects, and was entitled "Innovative Tasks." The issues addressed in these clauses are not those about which people typically find themselves making unique decisions; i.e., the behaviors have been prescribed by society and individual freedom is thus limited. For example, there are strong legal sanctions against extramarital sexuality (Individual rights and freedoms), and most persons assume that the wife will take her husband's name (Choice of name), even though there is no state that has a law that specifies she do so (Center for Woman's Own Name, 1974). In the same vein, people are expected to marry for life, and the concept of marriage for a specified period of time is a relatively new proposal, even though at least one state has tried to legislate a marriage contract that would allow for five-year marriages (Maryland, 1972).

SIGNIFICANCE OF CATEGORIES

If there is any significance in the fact that there were clauses which were much more likely to be used than others, it may be that it suggests if marriage contracts such as the one that has been described, were to become legal and easily available, their use would not significantly alter the tasks nor the structure of the marital dyad for the majority of the subjects who stated they would use a marriage contract. These persons seemed more interested in clarifying issues with which they either anticipated or were already dealing than with interjecting innovative issues into their relationships.

References

Andreas, Carol. *Sex and Caste in America.* Englewood Cliffs: Prentice Hall, 1971.

Center for a Woman's Own Name. Booklet for Women Who Wish to Determine Their Own Names After Marriage. Barrington, Illinois: Center for a Woman's Own Name, 1974.

Cody, Harriett M. and Harvey J. Sadis. "To Love, Honor, and . . . Share: A Marriage Contract for the Seventies." Ms. 1 (June, 1973):62-64.

Edmiston, Susan. "How to Write Your Own Marriage Contract." Ms. 1 (Spring, 1972): as introduced in the center of New York Magazine 4 (December, 1971):66-72.

Ehrmann, Winston. *Premarital Dating Behavior.* New York: Bantam Books, 1959.

Harshbarger, Marsha L. Acceptance or Rejection of a Marriage Contract. Unpublished thesis. Virginia Polytechnic Institute and State University, Blacksburg, Virginia, 1974.

Harshbarger, Marsha L. and Katherine Bogdanoff. "Marriage Contract—a Possibility." Unpublished paper presented November 20, 1972, Virginia Polytechnic Institute and State University, Blacksburg, Virginia.

Maryland, State of. General Assembly. Marriage Bill: "Marriage—Contractual Renewal," 1972, (H. No. 42. 31A).

Shulman, Alix. "A Challenge to Every Marriage." *Redbook* (August, 1971):57.

———. "A Challenge to Every Marriage." *Redbook* (September, 1972):89.

THE MARITAL SPECTRUM
William J. Lederer and Don D. Jackson

The Different Types of Marriage

Spouses who can identify their marriage as belonging to a certain type find it easier to hold discussions concerning marital problems. Once they agreed on the general category of their marriage, the perspective in which they see particular marital processes and ways of behaving seems to become clearer. We shall therefore attempt to describe the "spectrum of marriage"—a broad classification of marriages from the "best" down to the "worst." This spectrum is not a scientific classification, but merely a way of thinking about marriage which we hope will be helpful.

Throughout this book, there are frequent references to the functional, or workable marriage. The concept of the functional marriage is especially important in this chapter. Such a marriage is not necessarily "happy," and cannot be described in terms of its specific goals. A functional marital system is one which is functioning or operating without debilitating blockage or impasses, despite the variety of both positive and negative elements it contains.

One cannot accurately categorize a particular marriage as "happy" or "violent." The outside appearance of a marriage is often social camouflage; the packaging often fails to indicate the contents of the box. Homicides have occurred among spouses who were never known to quarrel. Many discordant marriages appear happy, and sometimes, on the other hand, spouses who quarrel in public have achieved a functional union, occasionally even a joyous one. The analysis-in-depth of a marriage must go far beyond the apparent mood or appearance of the partners. Marriage is a process and a relationship between two people. Therefore, to analyze the marriage it is necessary to examine the process and the relationship interactions.

Three avenues must be explored in order to define marital categories:

First, *functionality*. How functional is the relationship? How well can the spouses work together in complementary fashion? How wide a range of behavior can they achieve, or have they brought into the marriage? How appropriately does their behavior fulfill the needs and expectations of both parties? How suitable is their behavior for achieving the various common goals of the relationship, with impasses and blockages kept to a minimum?

Second, *temporal compatibility*. How are the two spouses oriented temporally? That is in terms of time what are their views, their desires, their ambitions? Are the short-term and long-range goals of each compatible with those of the other?

And third, *vector relations*. In what direction and at what speed is the marriage changing? Are the spouses developing a collaborative relationship, or are they headed toward irreversible discord because they agree less and less on the direction and rate of change of the relationship?

In seeking answers to these questions, the reader must understand that the human being is a goal-oriented animal, and that the attempt to achieve goals involves a complicated and sometimes incompatible or antithetical use of time and energy. *Homo sapiens* is often a perverse creature who may desire one thing, and yet, paradoxically, behave in a manner which makes the realization of his desire impossible.

As yet no scientist has come up with a *wholly* reliable classificatory description of marriage. In the social sciences there are bound to be some hazy areas. But this is no reason for not presenting the principles of a system. Therefore, in the following pages we sketch—in broad strokes—a spectrum of marriage. We feel it is important to do this. Most people require a landmark, a frame of reference, with which to orient themselves with respect to any philosophical or behavioral system which involves them deeply and objectively.

Classification of Marriages

The following classification is based on the concept that at any one moment in time a marriage can be regarded as belonging *more or less* in one of the listed categories. The categories are arranged in order of desirability and functionality. The one at the top is the "best," and the one at the bottom is the "worst." Each category has two subcategories.

I. The Stable-Satisfactory Marriage
   1. The Heavenly Twins
   2. The Collaborative Geniuses

II. The Unstable-Satisfactory Marriage
   1. The Spare-Time Battlers
   2. The Pawnbrokers

Reprinted from *The Mirages of Marriage* by William J. Lederer and Don D. Jackson. By permission of W.W. Norton and Co., Inc. Copyright ©1968, by W.W. Norton and Co., Inc.

III. The Unstable-Unsatisfactory Marriage
    1. The Weary Wranglers
    2. The Psychosomatic Avoiders
IV. The Stable-Unsatisfactory Marriage
    1. The Gruesome Twosome
    2. The Paranoid Predators

It is easy to place a marriage in one of these categories. But as one does so, it is important to remember that they represent segments of a *continuum*. Marriage is a continuous process, involving constant growth and metamorphosis. As the partners change, or their relationship changes, or the status of one partner changes, or the external pressures or environment changes, the marital state may move from one category into another. One of the purposes of this book is to assist the reader to recognize the trends of his own marriage, to halt those which are destructive, and to stimulate and nourish those which promise functionality and satisfaction.

A particular marriage may wobble from one category to another and then back again. No category is absolute. The "best" category, the Stable-Satisfactory, marks the upper limit of the continuum and represents a marital state probably never achieved in its pure form. This perfect, harmonious relationship, this absolute compatibility, is extremely rare because no two spouses are ever completely alike, nor do they have total congruity of backgrounds, nor absolute similarity of tastes and interests. Minor tensions based on conflicting interests, requiring some degree of change and compromise, occur at some time in all marriages. Differing periods of a marriage require different modes of adjustment.

Likewise, marriages classified as belonging to the "worst" category, the Stable-Unsatisfactory, hardly ever reach complete implosion. A totally destructive relationship is impossible. The husband and wife in a miserable marriage are certain to enjoy at least a few pleasant moments and small triumphs, even if their pleasure consists of hurting each other.

The position of marriages along the continuum is determined by their relative success, with most falling in a cluster somewhere in the middle two categories. The extreme marital types which approach the two ends probably constitute only from 5 to 10 per cent of all marriages.

The Stable-Unsatisfactory Marriage

Though marriages in this category are stable, they are the "worst" of the lot. In a quiet, socially respectable manner the people in this group suffer more pain, hate more profoundly, and cause more discomfort to others than do the members of the other three groups. *Yet the spouses appear to be unaware of their behavior.* There is a deadly virulent glue of hate that is only visible to the keen eye of the behavioral scientist or the brilliant novelist.

One of the most obvious types is the Gruesome Twosome. This consists of individuals who are growing old together in an unsatisfactory marriage which is quite stable because neither is able nor willing to acknowledge his dissatisfaction. Indeed, very often both will claim they have a wonderful marriage. They do not recognize their inability to live either with or without each other.

Such couples consult marital counselors or other therapists usually because of problems with their children. The spouses themselves would not seek help because they are not conscious of the nature of their marital relationship; but they force themselves, or are forced by their physician, to seek help for the children.

One of the common ways in which such spouses attempt to minimize their pain is by becoming cultists of some sort. The wife in a Gruesome Twosome we know attends church twice every day. She seeks the counsel of the minister on everyday matters "so that my wonderful family can live in a way that is a glory to God." In the meanwhile, she has bullied her husband to the point of tragic passivity. She identifies her bullying as "looking after poor Tom." The husband has developed into a helpless person—unable to fry an egg, to initiate even the simplest activities, to manage his finances—and often says "My wife is the dearest person in the world, the most wonderful wife a man could be blessed with."

Both assert as loudly as possible, at every opportunity, how much they love each other and how happy they are. But observe an incident from their life together:

Their only daughter was being married on July 4, in Buenos Aires. This event was of intense interest to the parents. On the afternoon of July 4, the husband, who was fond of baseball, went to a neighbor's house to watch a game on television. During his absence, the daughter telephoned from South America to tell her father and mother about her marriage and to have her husband say hello.

When the father returned, the mother said, "Tom, if you hadn't cared more about baseball than about the welfare of your daughter, you would have been here when Betsy and her husband telephoned from Buenos Aires."

A look of shock came over the husband. Neither of them had known the daughter would telephone, and he was extremely disappointed to have missed her; now he was startled by his wife's cruel and untrue accusation.

After a few moments he put his arms around his wife, wiped his tears off on her shoulder and said, "What would I do without you, darling? You take care of everything for me. Thank God, you were here for the call."

"You must be tired," said the wife. "I'll fix you some tea and then I'll tell you what Betsy and her husband said *to me* in their long-distance call from South America."

Holding each other's hands, they walked into the kitchen.

This Gruesome Twosome constantly repeats the game just described, regardless of the issue. But they tell everyone how happy they are. She is disappointed in her husband's failures both as a man and as a businessman. He is disappointed in his wife's performance as a supportive person. Yet they never admit this situation to the world, to each other, or even consciously, to themselves. As is to be expected, their three children all have miserable marriages.

Another man and woman we met became human vegetables in the course of maintaining their union. Before marriage, the woman was aggressive and competent, and she had done very well in high school. She was unhappy at home, however, and married a muscular young marine private who was a high-school dropout and a fearful underachiever. She hoped to help him "realize his potential." After five years of marriage, the wife weighed close to three hundred pounds and was so afraid to meet people that she locked herself in the house, with the heat up to 90 degrees and all the shades down. She spent her time watching television and knitting endlessly. Her husband remained in the Marine Corps, with a menial base job; he was always the last man in his speciality to progress in rank; but he eventually advanced enough to remain in service because he was dependable and gave no reason to be expelled.

The couple had no sexual life or outside interests. They had no children. Although their behavior *appeared* to be saccharine and supportive most of the time, it was punctuated on the wife's part by occasional outbursts of anger followed by guilt and remorse. The dull, passive husband was awkward and inadequate when in his wife's company; he would go to bed when he came home from work, sleep until supper, watch two television

shows, and then return to bed. *Once*, in a semi-drunken state, the wife revealed to one of us that she was afraid that if she lost weight, went to work, and met other people, she would leave her husband. Except for this one moment of truth, the couple always assured everyone that they were happy. The wife's hermitlike, fearful behavior produced such uncertainty and lack of self-confidence in the husband that he felt helpless without her, and made it difficult or impossible for him to fully utilize his minimal drive and obtain advancement. In turn his inability to achieve and progress in his employment made his wife feel a need to protect him and appear more inferior by contrast, and so each pulled the other downward. The wife succeeded, at great personal expense, in appearing more helpless than he did; he, at least was able to hold a job.

Environmental factors played a part here too, for the wife's lack of formal education limited her ability to achieve in accordance with her own expectations. Also, the husband had a job which provided security and permanent employment, even though he was not doing particularly well. Had one of these or of a number of other factors changed, the balance of this relationship would have had to undergo change also if the marriage was to stay intact. At the time of our contact with this couple, the husband and wife were twenty-five years old. If they could achieve such a condition in six years of marriage, the chances of any dramatic improvement occurring in the future—barring death—are very slim.

The members of a Gruesome Twosome live in accordance with the old proverb "People who live in glass houses shouldn't throw stones." Neither spouse dares to comment on the other's behavior or on the nature of their marriage except to forgive and offer unrequested succor. Each is afraid of what the other may do or say in response to a critical or openly attacking remark. The children are taught not to mention unpleasant matters or even notice the nature of their parents' relationship. For by doing so they might bring distasteful or uncontrollable material to their parents' attention, and then the children would feel the repercussions. These couples form a rigid coalition on one point only—that they will not admit the condition of their marriage or of their true feelings—but that point they defend against all intruders. The children often grow up to be cautious and reserved, and unable to judge the quality of any relationship. They justify their denials and lies by insisting that "it is better to tell a small falsehood than hurt someone's feelings." When a child gets into difficulties (the couple whose daughter was married in Buenos Aires, also had one son who drank excessively and another who was expelled from college for spending the night in a girl's room), the parents form their usual coalition of denial and insist that nothing can be wrong with their baby. The school system is at fault, the police department is incompetent, or perhaps there is something wrong with the child's health. A child of theirs who manifests emotional problems must, they are sure, have suffered a brain injury during childhood.

In the second subcategory of Stable-Unsatisfactory marriages are husbands and wives who exist by avoiding each other, without its being evident that they do so. Thus, in a different way from the Gruesome Twosome, they are able to dissemble a miserable relationship. The husband may be zealously involved in this business and the wife in civic activities, the church and so forth, but their activity possesses a quality which marks them as different from the busy Unstable-Unsatisfactory couples. We call these men and women the Paranoid Predators, for they both take a stand against a world perceived as hostile and form a team to fight it. The man may practice ruthless business methods because he is obsessed by the notion that "in our society today everyone hates a poor man. To survive you have to have dough and screw the other guy before he screws you." The wife supports this attitude. The wife may work ten hours a day for militant anti-Communist organizations "because it is our duty as good Americans to stop the Communists from destroying freedom and Christianity." The husband agrees with her and carries this attitude also into his own activities.

The intense activity of the Paranoid Predators is motivated by their need to avoid each other by focusing on something outside themselves, which can unite them in a common goal or attitude, and thereby keep the marriage intact. They accomplish this by seeing little of each other and by being mutually disdainful and suspicious of others. Together they may criticize other individuals or groups, support extremist organizations, and so on. In doing so they deny the misery and emptiness of their own relationship.

Paranoid Predators employ extremely destructive behavior. Their two-against-the-world approach to life enables them to maintain the marriage, but only at tremendous cost to themselves, their children, and society as a whole.

In one such case, the husband was an alcoholic merchant seaman who was promiscuous in every port. After some years, a severe case of syphilis brought his Southern Baptist conscience to the fore, and he left the sea, returned to his wife and two children, and became a part-time minister and carpenter.

The family lived in mortal terror of offending the Lord, and spent their days working together to ferret out possible enemies of Christianity. They succeeded in organizing their small community to avoid one sixteen-year-old out-of-wedlock mother, who later committed suicide! The husband and wife had renounced sex as sinful since they had already procreated (and the husband wasn't sure whether syphilis had rendered him sterile). Finally, the odd behavior of their oldest boy brought the parents to the school's attention. The parents refused to cooperate and moved to a different community. We do not know what befell them, but hazard a guess that the son went to a mental hospital and the marriage survived.

This material has been included so that spouses may identify their own marital type in general terms, so that they may have some frame of reference of which to locate themselves—simply to aid them in their own discussions. There is no undeviating classificatory description of marriage, and the categories are given in broad stokes only.

In reviewing the various categories into which marriages can be divided, it is important to remember that no one knows for sure what a normal marriage is. Surveys do reveal those qualities that seem to be related to workable marriages, but there have been no in-depth studies—let alone longitudinal studies—of marriages which are actually happy and collaborative, or the opposite.

Therefore, a person who becomes envious when a friend or neighbor describes how ecstatic his marriage is, or feels depressed after reading about the joys of certain wedded Hollywood stars, is probably trying to apply to his own marriage some sort of standard or gauge which does not really exist. Most of us have some kind of fairy-story image of the ideal marriage because our parents weren't frank with us about their own marital problems and because our culture is so loaded with movies, television programs, magazine articles, and books about marital bliss.

We have attempted to offer a kind of classification of marriage, based not on ideals of "happiness" or "perfection" (which everyone defines differently), but on the exchange of behavior between spouses which result in a more or less workable relationship. A marriage is regarded as "workable" when it is sustained without a great personal loss of mental or physical health by either spouse.

The categories we have presented in semi-anecdotal form could also be distinguished in terms of the *clarity of communication* between spouses. Communication is clear when the amount of explicit information exchanged is great compared to the amount of noise (or meaningless communication, as when a code is heard that cannot be deciphered).

Defined in terms of communication, the Stable-Unsatisfactory marriage is one in which virtually no relationship information is exchanged between the spouses. Their lives together are usually quiet, separate, and distant, and the manifold problems in the marriage are represented nonverbally by the emotionally sick children, who are usually regarded by their parents as having organic disorders rather than severe emotional problems.

The Unstable-Unsatisfactory marriage does include some exchange of information between the spouses, but it is limited, frequently inappropriate or out of context, and new information introduced into the system (often by the children) causes upheaval. The spouses have difficulty exchanging information without precipatating serious battling or psychosomatic flareups, but they may nevertheless actually be able to exchange information during times of upheaval. The children often suffer from being scapegoated or from getting caught in the middle and becoming wise old diplomats before their time. This quality often separates them from their peers leaving them feeling lonely, "different," and vaguely inadequate.

The partners in an Unstable-Satisfactory marriage can exchange some information and can occasionally collaborate. New information, new

problems or challenges, initially may cause dissension, but this will usually quiet down, be denied, or be handled by edict. Thereafter, it seems to be forgotten; but it is filed away in the unconscious and the reason that many of these marriages slowly become Unstable-Unsatisfactory is often that what was supposed to be forgiven and forgotten has accumulated underground, until one spouse suddenly finds that he is "out of love" and can't live the rest of his life that way. He abruptly walks out, to the amazement of the other, who wails that "there was so much good in our marriage!" The mental health of the children of such couples can be relatively good despite a considerable amount of disagreement between the parents because the conflict is overt often enough for the children to see what is really going on. Frequently the best communication between the Unstable-Satisfactory married spouses occurs after an upheaval, when they are in the process of making up and are willing to listen to each other.

The Stable-Satisfactory spouses are able to exchange information easily, often in part because of similarities in their backgrounds. They know each other so well that long dissertations or lengthy harangues are unnecessary; a smile, a nod of the head, or a disapproving glance is sufficient. Such husbands and wives are able to collaborate, but they are also clearly to distinguish the circumstances in which it is important to them to be autonomous. The children of such marriages are fortunate and look forward to getting married themselves. Because the parents are able to collaborate, they do not fear intervention by the children (i.e., they do not fear that their coalition will be split apart) and thus the children can be taken seriously and their opinions can be given whatever consideration is suitable. The most important single element observable in such marriages is the operation of trust.

A RESUMÉ OF MARITAL TYPES I, II, AND III
Mary W. Hicks

I. *The Stable-Satisfactory Marriage.* According to Lederer and Jackson[1] this relationship is almost hypothetical. It represents the ultimate in collaboration; and when it occurs, it is made possible by the hand-in-glove fit of the two spouses. Their backgrounds must be so similiar that each partner

clearly reads the other's signals, and responds with unambiguous messages. This effective communication makes possible the establishment of trust which leads to the acceptance of each other's differences. Differences are regarded as indications of varying tastes or values, not as symbols of a hostile relationship. In a collaborative relationship the man and woman may not always agree, but when they do not, they accept the disagreement comfortably and seek a team solution permitting recognition of both parties. Their noncompetitive relationship makes possible close interaction with almost all people and situations. The *Heavenly Twins* are spouses who appear to have been "born for each other." Such couples are extremely rare and most often come from similar backgrounds. They are likely to share the same values concerning almost everything from food to religion. The *Collaborative Geniuses* are spouses who did not have extremely similar backgrounds, yet still developed a Stable-Satisfactory union early in the marriage. These couples probably begin marriage with a greater-than-average similarity in basic tastes, values, and background, and an unusual degree of flexibility.

The cards are probably stacked against people who dream of getting married and being *Heavenly Twins* or *Collaborative Geniuses*. In the contemporary world of big cities, fast transport, and instant communication, almost everyone has more to do with strangers than with the boy or girl next door. In almost all contemporary marriages the partners begin with foundations of dissimilar experiences, backgrounds, values, and tastes. These differences eliminate the possibility of easy communications and shared assumptions.

II. *The Unstable-Satisfactory Marriage.* Jackson and Lederer claim that most marriages which last more than five or ten years are in this category. In many marriages of this sort, though the spouses believe they have a comfortable relationship, their disappointment with each other on occasion is obvious. In times of stress, hostility and buried resentment emerge. There are periodic outbursts of subtle or open aggression. The spouses attack each other emotionally and inflict fresh wounds. Some of the wounds heal; and even though scabbing and scarring occur the marriage remains basically sound. These people are the *Spare-Time Battlers.*[2]

The Spare-Time Battlers may get into a limited status struggle, which frequently has overtones of the battle of the sexes. They may show hostile competitiveness with each other at the bridge table or in budgeting, or may try to outshine each other conversationally. However, there is an underlying network of agreement about what each is willing to do, reciprocally, for the other. Therefore, the unpleasant skirmishes usually are seen within the context of a total marriage. In the spouses' eyes, the importance of the marriage outweighs the periodic hostilities or disappointments. The assets are remembered even during the battles over liabilities. They expect marriage to have its ups and downs, and meanwhile, their attention is focused upon children, money, security and status.

Another type, nearly stable, is classified as the *Pawnbrokers.* They know they are not in love. They have exchanged something very much desired (money, social status, security, companionship, sex, assistance to a coveted goal, an unusual professional situation, and so forth) for a spouse who is "not ideal." One or both spouses believe the limited satisfaction gained by staying married is preferable to the uncertain rewards which may or may not be found by looking further for another mate or by returning to the single state. Since people cannot not communicate, the message "I'm not really in love with you" gets across, and the marriages of the *Pawnbrokers* are consequently unstable. Many *Pawnbroker* marriages today occur between spouses who have been married before, and seek a second relationship permitting greater freedom-with-comaraderie than the first marriage (based on romance and "falling in love") allowed. Such marriages are often very satisfactory for the people involved.

III. *The Unstable-Unsatisfactory Marriage.* The *Weary Wranglers* and the *Psychosomatic Avoiders*—and their situations are as unattractive as these names suggest—form a considerable proportion of the American married population. These couples make up the majority of couples as seen by counselors, psychologists, or psychiatrists.[3]

These spouses recognize that they have a wretched marriage, but usually are unwilling or unable to do anything about it. Frequently the *Weary Wranglers* are angry people who are not prone to introspection or self-accusation so they need the combat which their marriage provides. Directing hostility outward is one of the ways in which an individual relieves the discomfort of anxiety and frustration. The *Weary Wranglers* find a degree of comfort in being hostile to each other, for the situation enables each to shift the responsibility for his unhappiness to the other.

One reason the *Weary Wranglers* have such a shaky future is that the spouses do not know how to stop their argumentative games and begin to form coalitions. In any discussion or activity each is more interested in winning than in dealing effectively with the matter at hand. They tend to blame each other explicitly for the failures and disappointments in their relationship; and, often, they involve the children in their conflict. Many couples in the *Unstable-Unsatisfactory* category begin as *Weary Wranglers*, but after a few years they grow tired of arguing and become *Psychosomatic Avoiders*. Some who are unable to express anger openly never try to fight it out and are Psychosomatic Avoiders from the beginning of the relationship. The primary characteristic of such couples is that they wage their battle covertly, expressing their anger and disappointment primarily through subtle sarcasm, double-edged humor, tangentialization, or nonverbal means. A few of the more common nonverbal methods of expressing their frustration are illness, alcoholism, and frigidity. Both parties unconsciously recognize that the disturbed spouse is expressing discontent with the marriage, but our health-oriented culture allows them to focus on doctors, pills, and heating pads.

These couples often give the impression of togetherness when in fact they live in quite separate emotional, and perhaps also physical worlds. In most couples this deception takes one of two forms. The first form is typified by the man and wife who individually maintain active, absorbing lives, each having professions and social roles so demanding that he sees little of the other, yet preserve a facade of an integrated marriage through such accouterments as a large house, several children, and a dog. The other form is typified by those who have developed common interests strong causes to which they can devote enormous amounts of time and energy. An intimate examination of their marital situation often reveals that they are virtually never alone with each other. Although a husband and wife may appear to be sharing, if their goals in life or their ways of behaving are based on the wishes of one spouse rather than both, they are not actually sharing. Many of these couples stick together physically despite the lack of emotional closeness and amount of consequent general misery is great.

NOTES

1. Lederer, William J. and Jackson, Don D., *The Mirages of Marriage,* New York, W.W. Norton & Company, Inc., 1968.
2. Lederer and Jackson, *op. cit.,* p. 135.
3. Lederer and Jackson, *op. cit.,* p. 141.

OPEN MARRIAGE: THE HAPPY SOLUTION
Nena O'Neill and George O'Neill

The old concept of marriage is much too limiting and restrictive. It is in a word, *closed.* We propose replacing it with a new type of marriage that is *open.* Open marriage is not an abstract ideal, but a concrete way for partners to develop a workable life-style according to their individual needs. Open marriage encourages growth for both husband and wife; it thrives on change and new experiences.

Open marriage is an honest relationship between two people, based on equal freedom and identity for both partners. It is a non-manipulative relationship between man and woman—a relationship of peers in which there is no need for dominance and submission, no arbitrary restrictions or stifling possessiveness. Neither partner is locked into a role. The domestic chores of marriage are shared according to real convenience, not predetermined rules. Each partner has interests and friends that the other may or may not share—which enables both to enrich the marriage by the contribution of their separate experiences.

Instead of describing open marriage in the abstract, however, let us show you three contemporary couples on a typical evening. See if you can spot the open marriage.

Couple 1

Elsa, an attractive blond in her early thirties earns a good salary as a buyer for a large department store. For the past six years she has lived with Stewart, a lawyer, in an unofficial relationship. They consider themselves married, and so do all their friends.

This evening, Elsa gets home a little before six, straightens the living room, makes the salad and prepares the steak. Then she bathes, changes into a long skirt, and is ready to greet Stewart when he comes in a few minutes later. "Golly, I'm tired!" he says pitching his briefcase on the hall chair. Elsa

Reprinted from *Woman's Day,* January, 1972. By permission of the authors.

101

kisses him, makes him a drink, sets cigarettes and an ashtray on the table beside his chair, and goes to put the finishing touches on the meal.

Couple 2

Laura and Paul, married eight years, met while in art school together. Their apartment is attractive and comfortable, but neither luxurious nor in apple-pie order. Laura is busy in the small kitchen trying to get dinner on the table so that she and Paul, a successful executive in a design firm, can sit down to eat as soon as he gets home. He comes in and gives her a hug. "I'm starving." he says, taking off his coat. "Come make yourself a drink while I finish dinner," she answers. Paul comes into the kitchen and they talk about their respective days while Laura fries pork chops. Then they sit down to a hasty dinner, since she has to make an eight o'clock class and Paul is going to a friend's opening at an art gallery.

Couple 3

In a small suburban house, Bill, an assistant English professor at a nearby university has just received a call from his wife, Cathy, telling him she will be late getting home from the city. She still works in the publishing job she had when she and Bill were married five years ago. Bill likes having her work, enjoys having a literate companion in his own field. He willingly starts to prepare dinner. Since his last class was at three, he's been home for hours. By the time Cathy gets home the table is set and dinner almost ready to serve.

Have you guessed which of these three couples has an open marriage? Don't judge from the obvious. Before you draw final conclusions, let's see how the couples spend the rest of the evening.

Couple 1

After a candlelight dinner, Elsa puts the dishes in the dishwasher while Stewart throws himself on the couch to watch television. When Elsa is finished in the kitchen, she joins him, cuddling beside him while they talk disjointedly over the sound of the television. Then he goes off to his study to work and Elsa continues to watch television. The phone rings and she answers, talking enthusiastically for several minutes. Stewart comes out of the study and hangs over her; she reaches out and caresses his arm as if to reassure him. When she hangs up, Elsa explains that it was a man from work calling about some new designs, but Stewart

sulks, only half believing her. "I can't see why that job always has to follow you home!"

"But, darling," Elsa answers, "things have to be settled when they come up—why, you're actually jealous!" Stewart snorts and goes back to his study, slamming the door. In ten minutes he is out again, in the mood for sex. Elsa obliges.

Couple 2

While Laura goes off to class (she's working for her master's degree in art history), Paul does the dishes and then takes off for the gallery opening. He arrives a bit late, spends half an hour there, then goes on to a party he and Laura have been invited to—arriving long before Laura, who doesn't get there until ten-thirty. He introduces her to some new people he has met and they stay for another hour. Home by midnight, they sit over the dessert they skipped earlier and compare notes on their hours apart. It's late and Paul has to get an early start in the morning, but they still make love before going to sleep.

Couple 3

Cathy and Bill have a leisurely dinner while Cathy unwinds from her day's tensions. She appreciates what Bill has cooked and they do the dishes together. But she is exhausted and sprawls on the sofa when they are through. Bill reminds her that they have been invited to a party. He would like to go, but Cathy says she's too tired. "Well, what about a movie then?" But she is too tired even for that. In fact, she falls asleep on the sofa while Bill prepares for next week's classes.

Which couple has the open marriage? If you guessed couple #1, you're wrong. In spite of Elsa's career and the fact that she lives with Stewart without marriage, their relationship operates in all ways like a closed marriage (despite the fact that they're *not* married). She waits on Stewart hand and foot while he combines the authority of the patriarch with the petulance of a little boy. His jealousy over Elsa's phone call triggered their lovemaking. In spite of her financial independence, she is emotionally dependent on him and uses her household services to keep *him* dependent on her. Their intimacy is based on this mutual leaning. In fact, they have the most completely closed relationship of any of the three couples.

Couple #3 doesn't have an open marriage, either. Though they switch the traditional marital roles—taking the tasks according to common sense—they are still tied into the kind of knot of exclusive togetherness. Bill has granted Cathy the freedom to achieve identity through her work, but Cathy deprives him of similar freedoms. Because she works with people all day, her relaxation is being alone with Bill and resting. But for Bill, who spends much of the day alone or giving formal lectures, relaxation means socializing, getting involved in give-and-take with other people. In short, Laura and Bill have kept the part of the traditional marriage contract that insists couples must do everything together. Since that contract doesn't allow for differences in mood, need or interest, it means one partner usually sacrifices.

Laura and Paul, Couple #2, have the true open marriage. On nights when Laura has a class at six o'clock and doesn't get home until eight-thirty, Paul prepares dinner for himself if he is hungry, or has it ready so they can eat together when Laura gets home. But they are not only flexible about their roles at home; they are also flexible about their social life. It is more important for Laura to go to class than to a gallery opening, but that does not mean Paul has to stay home. If he wants to go, she wants him to go. If anyone at the gallery were to assume there was trouble between them because Paul was alone, both would feel such a person's opinions are of little value anyway. When they are finally alone together later in the evening, they have far more to talk about than couples who do everything together. Also, since they trust each other when they are apart, they can share their separate experiences when they're together.

Open marriages are custom-made and highly individual; there are no set rules for establishing such a relationship. We have, however, devised a set of guidelines to help you write your own open contract—whether it is new or one you are "renegotiating" in an ongoing marriage. The eight guidelines, which we'll discuss in turn, are: (1) living for now; (2) privacy; (3) open and honest communication; (4) flexibility in roles; (5) open companionship; (6) equality; (7) identity; and (8) trust. Where do love, sex and fidelity fit in? They are basic components of marriage, but not guidelines. Many of the problems in closed marriage stem from a false concept of the part that love, sex and fidelity play in the relationship between a man and a woman. The guidelines for open marriage form the basis in which love, sex and fidelity achieve their meaning.

1. Living for now

An overriding obsession with the future is a hallmark of the closed marriage. If you're always planning and saving for the future—for new furniture, a new car, a down payment on a house, a trip to Europe, a first child, a summer cottage, a second child—your present life becomes merely a time to pass through on your way to the future, and that's a mistake. You can lose your personal selves in striving to attain such goals.

Of course, there is nothing wrong with knowing what you want out of life, but if material goals are allowed to become the central focus of your life instead of personal growth, by the time you have that house by the sea you may not have the same mate you planned it with. A couple's commitment should be to one another rather than to goals that may or may not be achievable. In an open marriage, the partners know that *they* are the most important ingredients of the marriage. They don't tie themselves down to a subscription on the future.

2. Privacy

If husbands and wives understand the normal human need for privacy, there should be no hurt feelings or fear of rejection on either side when one or the other closets himself away for a while. Most couples with young families recognize their need for time away from their children, but the same people are often reluctant to admit that they need time off from each other as well. This doesn't mean they have to separate for a weekend or a vacation. In most cases, a few hours or even a few minutes will do it—and the separation may be psychic rather than physical.

One prominent psychologist and teacher worked out a signal system with his wife to indicate their need for psychic privacy to each other. If the professor was thinking through a difficult problem and the interruption of his train of thought would be disturbing, he put on his favorite golf hat. To his wife, the hat said: "Leave me alone now; I'm thinking." His wife's signal to him was a particular bandanna. Sometimes the golf hat or bandanna would be worn for very short periods, sometimes for much longer. But each respected the other's need for privacy and left the one wearing the privacy signal strictly alone.

Learning to be alone together is particularly important to couples living in small, cramped quarters where it is difficult to be physically alone. But even couples with room for retreat will find that being alone together offers special pleasures—it means being private in a way that simultaneously enhances their sense of sharing. This is why privacy actually promotes the shared growth of open marriage in a way that the enforced togetherness of closed marriage cannot.

3. Open communication

Much of what passes for communication in the everyday world is in fact ritual. If someone asks you how you are, you will probably answer, "I'm fine"—even though your father's in the hospital, your ten-year-old lost two front teeth in a fight and you have a sinus headache. And that's all right, since asking how you are is usually just an expression of general friendliness anyway. The trouble is that over the years these shallow ritualistic responses become so ingrained that we find it difficult to communciate openly and honestly even when we want to. We must find ways to break through the wall of self-defense and get back in touch with our mates.

Research has established that approximately 70 per cent of our communication is nonverbal. The way your mate walks, stands, holds his head, drums his fingers, smiles or frowns can often tell you far more than words. Unfortunately, we become so used to our mate's nonverbal signs that they cease to affect us consciously. Sometimes we deliberately screen them out—either from impatience or from refusal to recognize the message being sent.

Confused messages occur when our verbal and nonverbal forms of communication contradict one another. Bill may say to his wife, "I'm listening, I'm listening!" but if his body is hunched attentively over the television set, she has good cause to doubt it. It's the nonverbal message that usually tells the truth. A verbal lie is all too easy to tell, but controlling your body to back up your lie is more difficult. Couples developing new openness in their marriages may find that pinpointing contradictory messages is a useful method of improving communication; it can uncover unrecognized needs, feelings and desires.

In an open marriage there is no need to say things you don't mean. Bill shouldn't have to say, "I'm listening," when he isn't. If he is intently watching television, that is not the time for Mary to start a conversation on unimportant matters. If her message is urgent, however, she should be able to say so—and Bill should be able to turn off the television and listen.

Sensuality—actual touching—is another important means of nonverbal communication. Couples need to relearn the full use of physical expression as a means of intimate communication. Sex should not be our only outlet for sensual communication; touching and embracing to express tenderness and caring fulfill a human need that is just as important as the need for sexual climax.

This does not mean that verbal communication is unimportant. It's still the bridge that makes it possible for partners to know and love each other in intimacy, and to sustain a relationship in depth over a period of time. Good sex, for instance, has never, by *itself,* settled a real difference between marital partners nor preserved a marriage that wasn't working on other levels. Unless you *tell* your husband how you feel, he'll be forced to guess—and the guess will probably be at least part wrong. Before you can talk openly and honestly with your mate, however, you have to be honest with yourself. You must take time to find out who you are and to clarify your own thoughts and feelings.

Next, you need the courage to reveal to your partner what you have found out about yourself. This thought makes us hesitate, for we fear exposing our vulnerabilities. We may claim that we hold back our true feelings out of concern for our mates, but generally that concern is also for ourselves. We are afraid we will appear less "good" or "strong" than our mates expect us to be, or that our feelings will be unacceptable.

Telling the truth does not mean telling vicious truths that will wound, or confessing past misdeeds that need never have been dug up. What open marriage *does* require is honesty about how you feel now in relation to the life you are making with your mate. Without such honesty you will find it impossible to rewrite your marriage contract according to your own specific needs. Self-knowledge, self-disclosure and honesty are the basis of good communication between marriage partners.

4. Role flexibility

A marriage ceremony is what anthropologists call a crisis rite, marking the passage from one status to another. One couple who got along very well when they lived together without being married started having problems the minute they legalized their union. As the husband explained it, "Before we married, everything was free and easy and really great. So okay, we marry, and right away she begins to take me for granted. Now I'm a husband and should empty the garbage. Instead of working it out like we did before, suddenly I'm *supposed* to do this or *supposed* to do that." His wife had similar complaints. What happened was they stopped being *people* and started to play the *roles* of husband and wife.

As the women's liberationists are fond of pointing out, this role-playing reduces the woman to inferior status and undermines the marital relationship. Recognition of this fact has prompted many couples to try to reassess their roles and responsibilities in terms of personal convenience and common sense, rather than stereotyped traditions of gender: Interestingly enough, men have as much to gain as women from this loosening of conventional bonds. Our concepts of masculinity are far more restrictive than those of femininity and women may "cross the line" from feminine to masculine traits with far greater ease than men can do the reverse. If husbands and wives could learn to see both male and female as embracing the total range of human emotional expression and intellectual capacity, the outdated cultural hangups that bind us to restrictive roles could be cast aside.

How can we achieve this mutual liberation of male and female? One useful technique is role reversal. Henry can do the dishes and mop the floor while Jane repairs the screen door and balances the bank account. Exchanging chores for a day, a week, or on a regular rotating schedule refreshes both partners who are sick of routine. It also helps you to understand each other's problems and feelings. In addition, you might try mental reversals, with each partner expressing what he thinks is the other's viewpoint on a particular subject. You'll not only learn to empathize with each other, you'll also open to correction any misunderstandings about how you really do feel.

5. Open companionship

Each of us is a unique combination of memories, characteristics and potentials. Although we all have certain hook-up points that can reach out and connect with other human beings, these, too, fall into unique patterns. Your mate's pattern of hook-up points is not the same as yours. Although you probably got together because you found a great many of these points matched, you each have other hook-up points you do not share.

In a closed marriage, only those hook-up points that match our mate's are allowed to be fulfilled. The closed marriage contract demands that all friends must be acceptable to both partners, and that all social functions must be attended jointly. While two people can be many or even most things to each other for a limited time—as with newly married couples who are learning to know each other—exclusivity eventually limits the couple's marital intimacy in range and depth. Opening a marriage to a wider spectrum of interests and friendships, on the other hand, can enrich life for both partners while improving their relationship.

Frank, a mathematician, and Janet, a musician, have achieved open companionship in their marriage. Frank explained it this way: "For our marriage to stay together," he said, "we both have to be living, functioning human beings. We have shared interests, but we also have different individual interests. So how can we live our whole lives attached to one another? Is Janet going to get all her humor from me, all her sympathy, all her intellectual interest? I can't fill that role. If she meets another man who is a musician, say, I think it's all right for her to go to dinner or a ballet or a concert with him. Sometimes she and I go to the ballet together, too, but I can't supply the same sort of stimulus and companionship she can get with another musician."

"Nor can I be everything to *him*," Janet said. "Frank has some interests—like discussing philosophy and working out mathematical puzzles—that bore me. He has a new woman friend who is just as fascinated by these things as he is, and they have a running competition about solving puzzles."

All very well, you may think, but don't they ever get jealous of one another? "This freedom means a lot to both of us," said Janet.

"And inherent in this freedom," added Frank, "is the risk that Janet or I may meet someone handsomer, smarter, richer, or more intellectually stimulating than the other, and that could be the end of the marriage. But life offers no guarantees, and I'm not afraid of competition."

Added Janet: "Many people are afraid of their own relationship. We've built a secure and honest one. Our honesty and freedom is really a bond that holds us together."

This last point of Janet's is important. The bond of honesty and freedom is positive; the bond of jealousy and possessiveness is negative. The positive bond is invariably more durable. Open marriage is about belonging *with* another person instead of to him; the openness that permits relationships outside marriage—and dares their risks—brings enrichment to both partners who trustingly permit it.

6. Equality

The basic premise of open marriage is that you take into consideration the individual differences of each mate. Equality in such a marriage does *not* mean sameness; no one person can ever be exactly equal to another in terms of capacities, abilities, talents, needs, or desires. It refers to *equality of personhood* for both wife and husband, equality of responsibility for the self, and equality of consideration, concern and love for the other.

Marriage as a 50—50 deal—half for you and half for me—is a false equation. It substitutes trading for sharing. Closed marriage expects partners to "compromise" to reach equality—to *give up* rather than to *give*. Wives may have to give up their careers, husbands their friends.

Equality, as we see it in an open marriage is a 100—100 equation between two peers of equal stature. If it were put into words it might go something like this: "I am going to consider you, and treat you, and relate to you as an equal. When you complain about something, I am not going to treat you like a child; I am going to give you my attention, and try to provide you with a helpful response. I am going to try to give you equal privileges, equal rights, equal access to my time and feelings—what I expect you to give me when the situation is reversed."

This kind of equality entails giving rather than giving up. The couple who achieve it work and play and grow together.

7. Identity

The concept of identity has been a part of all the previous guidelines. Privacy, honest communication, open companionship, freedom from rigid roles and equal sharing, all serve the search for identity. Isolating identity is difficult, but it is *not* being a wife and mother, or being a breadwinner and father. These may or may not be aspects of total identity, but identity can never be just one thing. Having identity means knowing who you are and liking that person: It means you believe in yourself and are responsible for your actions. You have your own opinions and let others have theirs.

You are confident of your abilities and respect those of others. Unlike partners in a closed marriage—who come to lean on each other like the sides of an A—frame house—those with a strong sense of identity are able to stand alone.

This emphasis on the individual and self-developmemt may sound like an endorsement of selfishness, but nothing is further from the truth. Selfishness usually arises out of fear that if you give too much, you won't have enough left for yourself. The creation of a strong identity combats such fears and makes it easier to give. Giving and identity are intimately related to each other. The development of strong identity leads to increased openness—not increased selfishness.

8. Trust

Let us examine the degree of trust that exists in three marital relationships:

(1) Mary and Roger have been married for twenty years. Mary often says, "I wouldn't trust Roger any further than I could throw him."

(2) Dorothy and Gene have been married twelve years. "My husband has a lot of female friends at work," she says. "We trust each other so it doesn't matter if he has lunch with them to talk shop. If he went to bed with one of them, though, it would be the end of our marriage. Even if he were tight at a convention and it was just a fling—no way. It couldn't happen unless something was wrong with our relationship. He feels the same way."

(3) Robert and Glenda have been married four years. Robert says, "Trust takes time. Once, at a party, I thought Glenda was playing up to another man and I got very jealous. As it happened, she wasn't but I interpreted it that way because I was changing jobs and feeling insecure at the time. It was something inside *me* more than anything she was doing, I realized later. Trust is really faith. We have faith in the fact that what we have together is more than any relationships with other people."

Of these three marriages, the first wife, Mary, has no trust at all. Such mistrust often indicates a deep insecurity. The second couple has what we call *static trust*—it applies only in particular areas. Dorothy's belief that she can be everything to Gene is unrealistic, and her vehemence on the subject of possible infidelity make it clear that the balance of trust could be tipped by even the appearance of infidelity on his part. Robert and Glenda are working toward what we call *open trust*, which is built on honesty. Robert can say to Glenda, "I think Jane has a sexy figure," without harming the trust he shares with her. In fact, that honest admission will increase the trust between them.

It takes time to develop true open trust between even the most loving partners. We've all learned by painful experience that trust cannot be given indiscriminately; in developing trust in intimate relationships we are struggling against justifiable cautions. Thus, it must be carried out at a slow pace and with caution. Spouses can start by being open and honest about small things. A wife can tell her husband the real price of a purchase instead of saying, "I bought it at a sale." A husband can tell his wife he doesn't want to spend another evening at the Joneses, or that he feels silly going to her garden-club tea. As they learn that small honesties hurt less than they thought, they build mutual trust in each other so that they can move on to more sensitive areas.

Honesty is essential to the growth of intimacy—indeed to all growth—and growth is essential to the concept of open marriage. It is the absence of room to grow that makes closed marriages become increasingly painful and ultimately impossible. In open marriage the union develops constantly in an upward spiral. Each partner grows through freedom toward selfhood—adding new experiences from the outside while receiving the benefit of his mate's outside experience.

Closed marriage is the kind of marriage that is dying today. It offers a certain phantom security and a measure of static contentment, but it leads to an inevitable stunting of growth. Open marriage offers the opportunity to go on forever expanding our horizons together.

Name: _____ Date: _____

Student #: _____ Sex: M or F

Rank from most important (1) to least important (12) the following aspects of marital adjustment as *you* view them:

	Rank			Rank
1. Money	_____	7. Conventionality		_____
2. Sex	_____	8. Spouses jobs		_____
3. In-laws	_____	9. Children		_____
4. Recreation	_____	10. Communications		_____
5. Friends	_____	11. Religion		_____
6. Demonstration of affection	_____	12. "Doing things together"		_____

13. What five factors do *you* think are the biggest, most frequent contributors to marital upset or conflict?

Divorces occur most frequently at three basic time periods in married life. List several reasons why you think divorce would be most likely to occur at the following times in a marriage:

14. The first three years of marriage

15. Around seven years into the marriage

16. Twenty to twenty-five years into the marriage

Parenthood is often looked on as being a positive force in marriage—"children *cement* a marriage." But cement, though frequently a stabilizing factor, can sometimes be dead weight.

17. List the five most positive influences children have on a marriage.

18. List the five most negative influences children have on a marriage.

19. As children grow and move out of the nuclear family, parents sometimes experience role crisis. Whom do you think experiences more crisis as they grow out of the parenthood role:

mothers_____ fathers _____

20. Why do you believe this to be?

21. How does this fit into their overall life style? (In other words, are there other factors leading up to this crisis?)

THE MOST UNEXPECTED THREAT TO A GOOD MARRIAGE

Vivian Cadden

Every young couple expects children to enrich and strengthen their marriage. But there is growing evidence that the result, in even the best of marriages, is quite different.

Among the memorable if minor characters of American humorous literature is a man by the name of Mr. Arbuthnot, defined by his creator, the late Frank Sullivan, as a "cliché expert." Mr. Arbuthnot could always be counted on to give the absolutely right, absolutely trite answer to any question. If you asked him how the bride looked, he would assure you that she looked "radiant." If you asked him what a daughter is to her aging mother, he would say, unhesitatingly, "A comfort." There is not the slightest doubt that if anyone had asked Mr. Arbuthnot what children do to a marriage, he would have replied promptly that "children *cement* a marriage."

Mr. Arbuthnot's cliché may cause some indulgent smiles; but on the whole, most people would agree with the spirit, if not the exact wording, of his proposition. Children may not be the only reason for marriage; we no longer believe that children can be counted on to patch up a poor marriage; and a childless marriage is not necessarily a disaster. We assume, however, that children represent the fulfillment of the nuptial relationship, the enhancement and enrichment of a marriage.

But do they?

Over the past ten years, among the people who study family relations, there has been a growing suspicion that far from cementing a marriage, children may actually drive a wedge right down the middle of it. This suspicion, documented by some hard facts, has burgeoned so quickly in the past few years that in April the Groves Conference, an important annual assemblage of the country's leading family-life experts and sociologists, devoted its three-day meeting to a discussion of the effect of parenthood on marriage. And a keynote to the disquiet and perplexity of family-life experts was sounded by Reuben Hill, professor of sociology at the University of Minnesota.

"There was a time when children were thought to be the fulfillment of marriage," Dr. Hill said. "But we must face up to the disturbing fact that more and more of our research suggests that the advent of a child is not necessarily the fulfillment of marriage but possibly the first point of cleavage that separates husband and wife—and that this cleavage widens with each additional child, disrupting the marriage relationship to such an extent that when the children are adolescent, the parents are so far apart that instead of being bereft at their leaving, they are, in fact, reunited, happy to pick up where they left off in the wonderful days before they had children."

That's quite a statement. How can he say such a thing? What is he talking about?

As is often the case, the ending of the myth, the cliche and the folklore came with the asking of an irreverent question: What do children do to marriage?

For more years than one cares to remember, the questions about family life have centered around what parents do to children. Parents rear children, for better or for worse (and in recent years we've been given to think for worse). We do things to children that make them grow up this way or that way. If they're good, it's to our credit. If they're bad, it's our fault. In any event, the important question is what we do to them. Simply to ask what they do to us is almost heresy. And yet, gradually, cautiously, almost guiltily, the irreverent question has been asked. What do children do to us? What do they do to a marriage? As Dr. James Lieberman, psychiatrist at the National Institute of Mental Health, remarked, the question has the puzzling sound of a "familiar tune played backward."

One of the first studies to suggest that children might be a divisive rather than a cohesive factor in marriage was a report on "Parenthood as Crisis" by Dr. E. E. LeMasters, published in *Marriage and Family Living* just ten years ago. Dr. LeMasters reasoned that the arrival of the first child forces a drastic reorganization of the family and thus might constitute a crisis for the couple whose lives were being so basically changed by the event. To test this hypothesis, Dr. LeMasters interviewed forty-six young couples about their reactions to the arrival of their first child. They were a fairly typical middle-class group of parents—among them a minister, a bank teller, a social worker, a high school teacher, an accountant, a college professor, an athletic coach and a small-business owner.

Thirty-eight of the forty-six couples reported "extensive" or "severe" crisis in adjusting to the new baby; the remaining eight couples reported

Reprinted from *McCall's* July 1967, by permission of publisher and author.

relatively milder reactions. There was strong evidence in the study that severe crisis reactions had nothing to do with the baby's being unwanted or unplanned—thirty-four of the thirty-eight who found the adjustment very difficult had wanted their babies. The same proportion of couples had, by their own account and the evaluation of their close friends, a good marriage. Nor were husbands and wives who suffered most any more neurotic than those who took parenthood more calmly.

The conclusion seemed to be that the arrival of the first child constituted a "normal" crisis that was to be expected by any normal couple—a kind of necessary hurdle in the transition to parenthood. Dr. LeMasters' findings caught on fast in the professional and popular literature, to a point where a young couple that doesn't have a "crisis of the first baby" seems a trifle backward.

But crises presumably go away after a while. By definition, they are short-range. As Dr. LeMasters himself observed. "In all fairness, it should be reported that all but a few of the couples eventually made what seems to be a successful adjustment to parenthood." Dr. LeMasters' study did not really refute Mr. Arbuthnot's cement theory; it merely showed that the cement might take a while to set.

Nevertheless, once the idea had caught hold that children, or at least the first child, may adversely affect a marriage, at least in one of its stages, the suspicious nature of social scientists was aroused. Another "first-baby" study, confirming Dr. LeMasters', and a study of some 900 wives by a University of Michigan team, which turned up considerable evidence of the baleful influence of children on marriage, added fuel to the fire.

In 1964, Harold Feldman, professor of child development at Cornell University and chairman of this year's Groves Conference, launched an ambitious research project, not designed principally to study what children do to marriage but rather to take a broad look at the nature of the husband-wife relationship as it develops over the life cycle of the pair. Dr. Feldman wanted to follow the marriage relationship from its inception through the various stages of childbearing and child rearing and on to the phase when the children have left home. He had no particular hypothesis in mind and was not out to prove anything, except perhaps the general concept that sociologists have been evolving of marriage as a developing rather than a static institution. It was, however, the findings about children and marriage that leaped from the study, astonishing even Dr. Feldman, who, like most sociologists,

family-life experts and just plain parents, would prefer to believe that children enhance a marriage.

Dr. Feldman and his colleagues interviewed a total of 852 couples in various stages of the marriage cycle: recently married, with preschool children, with schoolchildren, with the children beginning to be launched, with the children all launched, and in the later post-child-rearing years. For each of these major groups—the childbearing, the child-rearing and the post-child-rearing—Dr. Feldman had a control group of childless couples of matching age.

The husbands and wives were asked some point-blank questions about their children and their marriage: To what extent did they agree or disagree, for example, that "our baby's demands are somewhat of a strain on the husband-wife relationship" or that "having a baby has made our marriage even better"? They were also given an entire battery of questions relating to every aspect of their relationship. Husbands were asked the extent to which statements such as the following applied to their marriage: "I wish my wife would spend more of her leisure time doing things that interest us both," or "The sexual aspects of our marriage are not fully satisfactory at present," or "I would like to tell my wife more about my work than I do now." Both husband and wife were asked to note, along an "always" to "never" scale, how often they felt "blue," "satisfied with myself," "pleased with the way the house looks," "nervous," "tired" and how often they had "free time to use as I liked." They were asked about the topics they talked about and the amount of talk and laughter they shared. A whole series of questions probed the matter of how they solved disagreements now as compared with past periods. Did quarrels end with door slamming, with self-criticism, with a caress? All in all, the couples answered sixteen pages of questions about themselves, each other, their children and their attitudes toward child rearing.

The net results, as Dr. Feldman reported them to the Groves Conference, were: "Something odd is going on here. It doesn't have to do with the length of the marriage, and it doesn't have to do with the age of the husband and wife. It has to do with children."

The odd something was that perplexing U curve to which Dr. Hill had referred. Marital satisfaction was at its highest among the newly married couples who had no children and among the older couples whose children had been completely launched. The groups in which marital satisfaction was at its lowest were those whose youngest child had just entered school, the parents of teen-agers and those whose oldest child had just entered school. Relatively more satisfied than, but not as euphoric as, the still-childless and the again-childless were those in the process of launching their children and those whose children had recently been launched. Apparently, the real thing that cements a marriage is the absence of children!

The clear verdict of this first Cornell study made Dr. Feldman want to look even more closely at the transition to parenthood—the coming of the first baby, which signaled the onset of the decline in marital satisfaction. For this purpose, the Cornell team interviewed 500 couples at three intervals—when the wife was in her fifth month of a first pregnancy, when the baby was about five weeks old, when the baby was about five months old. And because he wanted to isolate the "first-baby effect," Dr. Feldman had a control group of childless couples and followed another group through the pregnancy and birth of a second child. This study has yielded a wealth of material on the marriage relationship during a wife's pregnancy and confirmed the disruptive effect of the first child—although there is evidence of a short "honeymoon" period right after the arrival of the baby, when everything seems quite rosy. But perhaps the most striking finding of the study is the news that the arrival of a first child is a picnic compared with the arrival of the second.

The comparatively widespread acceptance of the Cornell studies can be attributed, first, to the thoroughness of the studies themselves and, second, to the fact that other studies confirm Dr. Feldman's conclusions. Sociologist Peter C. Pineo had material on approximately a thousand couples from the famous Burgess-Wallin study, which followed couples from the time of their engagement until twenty years after their marriage. Disregarding the engagement material, Dr. Pineo compared the couples from a point approximately three years after their marriage to a point twenty years after their marriage. He came up with the unmistakable conclusion that these seventeen years of married life are characterized by what he called "disenchantment." There is, he found, "a general drop in marital satisfaction and adjustment. . . there is a loss of a certain intimacy. Confiding and kissing and reciprocal settlement of disagreements become less frequent; more individuals report loneliness." This was not the disenchantment that springs from an overly romantic notion of one's partner or an overidealized view of what marriage is like—*that* kind of disenchantment and

disillusion comes very soon after marriage, as the reality of it unfolds. The kind of disenchantment Dr. Pineo observed seemed to be a gradual process that typified the marriage relationship.

Dr. Pineo's study made hardly any reference to children. It had no hypothesis about the effect of children and was not concerned at all with the question. Some of the couples among the thousand must have been childless—Dr. Pineo doesn't say. But when his study is taken in conjunction with the Cornell studies, one must suspiciously note that the seventeen years of marriage Dr. Pineo reviews are precisely those years during which children are born and reared—but not yet launched. One suspects that if Dr. Pineo had interviewed these same couples five or ten years later, he might have found a reversal of the disenchantment.

That there is such a reversal has been documented by Dr. Irwin Deutscher, now of the Syracuse Youth Development Center. Dr. Deutscher interviewed a group of lower-and upper-middle-class husbands and wives in Kansas City, Missouri, all between the ages of forty and sixty-five, with from one to four children, all of whom had been launched. He tape-recorded lengthy interviews with them, designed to explore their feelings about their present phase of life as compared with past ones. He asked such questions as: "If you could divide your life into parts, which part would you say was the best time?" and "Which part was the worst time?," "How is your life different now from what it was when the children were home?," "Now that the children have left, do you notice any difference in your wife (or husband)?"

Twenty-two husbands and wives felt that the postparental phase was "better" than preceding phases, while only three felt it was "worse." Fifteen found it at least as good, while two found it "as bad" as any other part of their married lives.

Again, from a very different method of work, there is confirmation for the Cornell studies.

What are we to make of these studies and their unsettling implications? How can we explain this troubling picture of so significant a portion of our married lives? What does it all mean?

First it would be sensible to clear up what it *doesn't* mean. No one is suggesting or has proved that American parents are, on the whole, a miserable, dissatisfied lot, gloomily plowing through their childbearing and childrearing years and hopefully awaiting the departure of the children. A moment's reflection—without any massive studies—assures us that there are a great many different kinds of satisfaction in life. At the same time that parents may be experiencing some impoverishment in their own relationship, they are probably getting anywhere from some to a great deal of satisfaction from their children. There are satisfactions, too, in work—in a man's job, in a woman's homemaking and child rearing. There is satisfaction in a competence gained, a crisis met, a growth achieved. There are, for some, unparalleled satisfactions in intellectual and creative achievement. Anyone who measures life by marital satisfaction alone is surely diminishing the scope of human experience.

So much for that. But when we have put marital satisfaction in its place and assured ourselves that it is not the be-all and end-all of life, something stubborn within us still says, "That's all very well, but does one satisfaction have to come at the expense of another—and, in particular, does the satisfaction we get from children have to come at the expense of the satisfaction we get from our marriage?" Is the children-marriage satisfaction a kind of pie—if one slice is bigger, must the other slice be slimmer? Something in us says, "Dammit, it shouldn't be so." Children should make for a bigger pie.

Most of us can understand, if not necessarily accept, the same-size-pie aspect of children and marriage when the children are very young. The day is twenty-four hours long, we know, and a woman's and a man's energies are finite. If the baby needs time—and what baby doesn't?—there is less time for a husband and wife to spend together; if a mother is often exhausted, surely when a sociologist comes around and inquires about her sex life, she will have to admit it's not exactly flourishing. Certainly some of the spontaneity goes out of a marriage when it is regulated by a clock in a baby's stomach.

Fair enough—or, if not fair enough, at least understandable. But how long does this need to go on, and is it *all* a question of time and energy and baby-sitters, and, if so, how does one explain the continued disenchantment when there are teen-age children—children who, far from taking up their parents' time, are not even likely to give their parents the time of day? Something seems to be at work here besides time and energy.

Sociologists have worked out some fairly complex theories about relationships—between two, among three and four and more. But it doesn't take a complex theory to make us aware that the addition of a third person to a relationship can change its character altogether. Possibly there are several ways in which three people can relate to one another; but in the most familiar type of relationship among three, one is, in a sense, left out. The primary relationship in a family can be between husband and wife, or between mother and child, or, as in some cultures, between father and son.

Dr. Feldman remarked at the Groves Conference that we recognize three stereotypes of behavior in couples with young babies. The baby starts crying. In one instance, the mother jumps up and takes care of the baby's needs while the father continues to read his newspaper. In another tableau, the father gets up and tends to the baby, while the mother looks on fondly. In a third version of family life, the father gets up to help, and the mother snatches the baby from him. It's *her* baby. It was the third way that was most characteristic of the couples in the Cornell survey. Fathers typically wanted to help more than mothers permitted them to. This was particularly true with the first baby. With the second baby, it was true to a lesser extent. The fathers had apparently given up.

No one will claim that this finding can explain or substantiate something like two decades of declining marital satisfaction, which seems to characterize the American family-life cycle. Yet one can say quite simply that the studies show that the central axis of the family—the husband-wife relationship—is bent or broken by the presence of children and that this is both a description and a cause of marital dissatisfaction.

It may be that the cleavage is inevitable, that it is the cost of having children and raising them, the price of the satisfaction they bring. If this were so, most of us would go on having children anyway, presumably swapping some of one kind of satisfaction for some of another, enriching our lives by the differing qualities of the two experiences—marriage and parenthood. But it is also possible that the cleavage is *not* necessary—that we have fallen into this way of family life because children demand it of us, or women prefer it, or child-care theory advocates it, or men allow it, or because we accord the marriage relationship no conscious priority. When there are children, the marriage becomes expendable; we let it slip from us without fighting for it. We have heard a great deal about neglected children. It is clear that there are a great many neglected marriages.

Dr. Alice S. Rossi, of the National Opinion Research Center of the University of Chicago, in a thoughtful paper, "The Transition to Parenthood," delivered at the American Orthopsychiatric Association in Washington, this March, notes the findings of a British writer who detects a tendency among young parents today "to establish some barriers between themselves and their children, a marital defense against the institution of parenthood. . . .

This may eventually replace the typical coalition in more traditional families of mother and children against husband-father."

No one is advocating anything as simple and as silly as "Parents come first" or a "Let's be selfish" campaign for adults. No one wants to equate the needs of a hungry baby with those of a hungry husband. But there is a *quality* to family relationships that transcends the everyday details of living. One knows there are families with children in which the husband-wife relationship is the central one from which all others stem, the relationship that is guarded and cherished with something akin to jealousy. In this kind of family, there are a *primacy* and a *privacy* to marriage that exclude all others—even children.

The sociologists have done us a great service by raising the irreverent question. For once we ask what children do to a marriage, we add another dimension to our view of family life.

Dr. Harold Christensen, professor of sociology at Purdue University, gave an example of this at the Groves Conference. Speaking about the spacing of children in the family, he remarked that obstetricians were concerned with child spacing from the point of view of the mother's health; psychologists and pediatricians were concerned about the problem from the point of view of sibling rivalry and the relationships between children in the family. No one asked or studied how the spacing of children affected the marriage.

Or, to take another example: The other day, there came across my desk a pamphlet on sexual curiosity in children. One very cogent section of it was devoted to a discussion of the psychological damage that accrues to young children if they are allowed to finish the night in their parents' bed when they awake with a nightmare or need comfort. It was a familiar Freudian argument, and I had read it and agreed with it before. But this time I found my attention wandering from the point in hand and found myself thinking: Never mind what children's scampering into their parents' bed does to the children! Think what it does to parents. Think what it does to a marriage.

Once the question had been raised, it refuses to go away. And perhaps all that we need is an awareness of the question. But if the National Institute for Mental Health has some spare research funds, one might suggest the following projects:

1. A detailed study of the minority of families in the Cornell and other studies whose experience was contrary to the trend. There are families, apparently, who find an increase in marital satisfaction over the family cycle or whose peaks and troughs are at different points from the majority. Why? What's different about them?

2. To what extent is it competition for time and energy that cleaves parents apart, not only after the first but after successive babies? If you compare couples who have no help, couples who have the help of relatives and couples who have help and/or nannies, what kinds of difference do you find in marital satisfaction?

3. Someone ought to take a good, hard look at that period when the youngest child enters school. One would have thought that this would be a good time for parents. To find it ranking among the lowest period of marital satisfaction is puzzling. Is this the *real* crisis of the empty nest—without the compensations of freedom and financial ease that come years later, when the children have actually left home? Is this the time when women should go back to school or work?

4. It would be fascinating to know the extent to which satisfaction or dissatisfaction with the development of children nurtures or poisons a marriage. The striking loss in marital satisfaction of parents with teenage children makes one wonder. Teenagers don't often impinge on privacy, hog time or demand much attention, but they are probably the greatest cause of parental worry today. Is it difference of opinion about how to handle them, concern about them, fear of having failed or *what* that makes this a particularly hard time for a husband and wife?

It seems probable, from what we know about swings of the pendulum, that if several years of research and concern are devoted to the question of what children do to marriage, we then will return to the old question—what parents do to children. And in a new version of this old question, we might then want to ask, "What do parents who put a very high priority on their marriage do to children?"

THE AMERICAN WAY OF MATING: MARRIAGE SÍ, CHILDREN ONLY MAYBE

Angus Campbell

"And so they married, and lived happily ever after." This classic fairy-tale ending, which has raised the eyebrows and occasionally the hackles of many adult readers, may not be as far off the mark as skeptics suppose. We find that married Americans are far happier and more satisfied with their lives than singles are, in spite of national mumblings and grumblings about the tired institution of matrimony.

However, most marriages are followed by children, and having children, it turns out, is a mixed experience. The patter of little feet aggravates as well as delights. The positive effect of marriage and the stress-producing impact of children on the quality of life in America are two striking results from our recent national survey. Philip Converse, William Rodgers, and I studied a random sample of 2,164 adults in order to get a sense of how people feel subjectively about the quality of their lives, and how their feelings change with experiences over the life cycle. Previous quality-of-life studies have concentrated on objective indicators—the money a person earns, health statistics, education, the amount of pollution one has to endure, and so on. We were less interested in how people's lives look from the outside than in how they feel to those who are living them.

We asked our interviewees, first, to give us a judgment of their satisfaction with their lives in general. Then we tapped more emotional dimensions, to find out whether they were in high spirits, jolly and optimistic, or discouraged, lonely, or bored. We gave them eight pairs of adjectives (such as "interesting/boring") and asked them to check, on each pair, the point that best represented their current mood about their lives. And finally, as a third measure of the emotional quality of life, we developed a scale of six questions that probed their feelings of pressure or stress.

Overall, men and women evaluate their lives in very similar terms; we did not find, as some might have expected, that more women than men are unhappy or dissatisfied. On the contrary, Americans of both sexes seem to be a contented crowd, in spite of their various problems. Fewer than 10 percent described their lives in sour terms—boring, miserable, lonely, empty, useless—and far more than half think their lives are worthwhile, full, hopeful, interesting, and other happy positives. They admit to some stress—about one fourth feel

rushed all the time and often worry about bills—but overall they are stubbornly cheerful.

Dissatisfactions and sex differences show up, however, when we compare people at nine various phases of the life cycle. Six of these categories represent the typical life-patterns, from young adulthood before marriage, through marriage and parenthood, to the death of one's spouse. The last three categories cover people who diverge from the typical pattern: the four percent who never marry, the five percent who are married but never have children, and the 10 percent who, at any moment in time, are divorced.

"The world has grown suspicious of anything that looks like a happy married life," wrote Oscar Wilde, but if marriages aren't happy today, at least married people are. All of the married groups—men and women, over 30 and under, with children and without—reported higher feelings of satisfaction and general good feelings about their lives than all of the unmarried groups—the single, divorced, or widowed. (Remember, though, that I am talking about group averages—there are plenty of miserable married people and satisfied singles.) The link between marriage and satisfaction is striking and consistent, whichever the cause or effect: marriage may make people happy, or perhaps happy people are more likely to marry.

Good feelings about the emotional quality of one's life, oddly enough, are not necessarily related to the absence of stress. A person who feels many pressures may be less satisfied with his or her life overall; but a person under little stress is not automatically more satisfied with life. Widowed men and women, whose feelings about their lives are generally depressed, nonetheless report the lowest amount of stress and pressure. And married couples with small children, who are happier than singles, report the greatest amount of stress.

Carefree Spinsters, Anxious Bachelors

Unmarried women are healthier, physically and psychologically, than married women, according to many studies; but they aren't happier. Apparently most young women in America still believe that marriage is essential for fulfillment, for they consider their lives less worthwhile without it.

For women, age 30 is still the Great Divide. Most under 30 will eventually marry; those over 30 are much less likely to. Whether she doesn't marry by choice or circumstance, the older single woman is not as negative in her feelings about life and does not feel nearly as much stress as her younger counterpart. Perhaps this is because the longer a woman remains single, the more she likes it, or at least adjusts to it; and because she is more likely to hold a satisfying, better-paying job, and to have a well-defined career.

Women get along without men better than men get along without women, contrary to what John Wayne and Sam Peckinpah would have us believe. Single women of all ages are happier and more satisfied with their lives than single men. So much for the stereotype of the carefree bachelor and the anxious spinster; the truth is that there are more carefree spinsters and anxious bachelors.

Euphoric Brides, Nervous Grooms

The best of all possible worlds, for most Americans, is to be newly married and not have children. If single people in their 20s feel that something is lacking in their lives, married couples of that age are the happiest of all groups—especially young wives, who are more satisfied than anyone else, anywhere, any age. They are positively euphoric; they are the most likely group to enjoy doing housework, which single women consider drudgery. It appears that marriage is still considered a woman's greatest achievement, and when she marries, the sigh of relief is almost audible.

Young men get happier with their lives when they marry too—though they don't reach the glowing level of their wives—but the two sexes' feelings of pressure change in opposite ways. The women report much *less* stress after marriage than before, but their husbands now feel *more* stress. This cannot be explained by any storybook scenario that pictures the carefree young wife spending her day getting ready to welcome her husband home from the office. Three out of four of these young wives are themselves employed, almost as high a proportion as that of their husbands. Despite whatever trends there may be toward equal roles among young married couples these days, the man still appears to feel more burdened by the responsibilities of marriage than the woman. In our study, only 20 percent of the young wives said that they worry at least some of the time about paying the household bills, but twice as many of their husbands (38 percent) do. Eighteen percent of these

wives describe their lives as "hard" rather than "easy"; 34 percent of the husbands see their lives as hard. These differences disappear, however, when the first child arrives and this phase of the life cycle ends.

The Stress of Parenthood

"Familiarity breeds contempt," wrote Mark Twain, "and children." Almost as soon as a couple has kids, their happy bubble bursts. For both men and women, reports of happiness and satisfaction drop to average, not to rise again significantly until their children are grown and about to leave the nest (age 18).

Couples with young children also report feeling more stress and pressure than any other group. The mothers, most of whom are between the ages of 25 and 34, carry the burden of childrearing, and the pressures are most acute for them. They are the most likely of any other group of wives or husbands to describe themselves as feeling tied down, to express doubts about their marriages and to wish occasionally to be free of responsibilities of parenthood. The husbands feel less satisfied with children too; but they don't show the great swing that their wives do, partly because they were less euphoric about marriage to begin with.

For most couples, the arrival of a child is a happy event, but one that puts unanticipated strains on the marriage. Part of the strain is economic, part is psychological; inevitably, husbands and wives have less time for each other after a baby is born, and adjusting to the loss of companionship can be difficult.

There is hope for the disgruntled or disappointed parent, however. Wait 17 years or so until you are alone with your spouse again. Your satisfaction with life and your all-around good mood will return to where it was before you had kids. Indeed, parents of older children were among the happiest groups in the study, and this was true for both sexes. Couples settled back in the "empty nest" reported feelings of companionship and mutual understanding even higher than they felt as newlyweds. Raising a family seems to be one of those tasks, like losing weight or waxing the car, that is less fun to be doing than to have done.

Children and marriage still go together and always will, but children are becoming less popular. The continuing, substantial decline in the birth rate in this country indicates that many people no longer regard having children as an inevitable process. The childfree marriage, once pitied or disparaged, is now increasingly recognized as a fulfilling lifestyle and many young couples simply admit, without embarrassment or apology, that they do not intend to have children. Sociologist Jessie Bernard marshalls evidence that they may have happier marriages as a result.

The decision not to have children does not doom a couple to loneliness, despair, and misery as the prochildren forces have assumed for years. Childless husbands over 30 reported the highest satisfaction with life, and they feel less pressure than most men. Altogether, the quality of their lives is higher than that of any other group of males, with the possible exception of fathers of children over 17 (which makes them childfree too, in a sense). Freedom from the economic worries that parents have is part of the reason. Childfree couples over 30 do not have particularly high incomes, but they are the most likely group to be satisfied with their savings and the least likely to worry about bills.

Childless wives over 30 also describe their lives in generally positive terms. They aren't quite as rosy about life as their husbands, but they aren't *less* satisfied than women their age who do have children. Childlessness offers women a different but not unsatisfying life—much less stress, somewhat fewer emotional rewards, but overall the same level of satisfaction. In view of the strong cultural pressures for women to have children, we were surprised that childfree wives find the grass on their own side of the fence green enough. Perhaps having children is no longer as essential to woman's role as it once was.

Possibly these couples will feel different about not having children when they are old, or when one spouse dies. When wife or husband is left alone, without the psychological support that the other provided, she or he may feel more keenly the absence of children. Still, grown children do not always pay much attention to their aging and sometimes lonely parents, perhaps a widowed person is better off with no expectations about children than with shattered ones.

Stress Dies With the Spouse

We tend to think that the quality of life for most widowed people is bleak, but this perception misses the mark. In terms of general life satisfaction, widows and widowers dip to slightly below average; even so, they are quite a bit more content than single or divorced people of any age. And they report the least amount of stress and pressure of any other group, even though their family incomes are the lowest. They don't, after all, have to worry about work—the great majority are of retirement age—or young children, and many feel free of the pressures to marry that the single and divorced experience. On the other hand, widows and widowers did describe the emotional quality of their lives in negative terms, about as negatively as single and divorced people. The difference between the two groups is that the widowed are more satisfied with their lives than singles are, which may simply reflect the willingness or resignation of older people to accept the conditions of their lives.

Divorce: Anxious Women, Carefree Men

In spite of all the cheerful books on creative divorce, no-fault divorce, and better living through divorce, people whose marriages fail are miserable. Most of them, men more than women, marry again, but while divorced they face problems that their single and married friends do not.

Divorce hits women hardest. Most of them have to work (71 percent) and care for children (84 percent), without moral, economic, or psychological support from a husband or partner. They earn less than single women their age, certainly less than divorced men, and less than married women who can rely on family incomes. Only four percent of all divorced women can afford to hire someone to help with the housework, so they have that to do too. And they lack the opportunities that divorced men have to date and remarry. For all these reasons, divorced women feel the greatest pressure and stress of any group, report the greatest dissatisfaction with their lives, and describe the emotional quality of their lives in gloomy terms. Indeed, one fourth of these women admit to worrying that they might have a nervous breakdown, compared to only eight percent of the divorced men.

Divorced men aren't so happy with their lives either, but they feel less pressure than almost any other group of males. It is as if divorce was an instant relief; over half, 58 percent, say they never worry about meeting their bills, compared to 30 percent of the divorced women who report being that confident. Only 12 percent of the divorced men say they always feel rushed, but nearly three times as many divorced women (34 percent) see themselves as always rushed. Twenty-five percent of these men, but 42 percent of the women, describe their lives as difficult.

Then too, divorced men who find their newfound single status intolerable remarry more easily

118

than their former wives, while those who enjoy the single life may choose to keep it. Divorced women have less freedom of choice, economically or socially, which contributes to their dissatisfactions. Of course, we do not know how the attitudes or feelings of divorced people change in the years after the marriage ends; we have only the sketch they paint as a group.

Life Stages and Satisfaction

When we compared all of the women in our study with all of the men, we found few differences. There were some reasons to expect, overall, that women would be more dissatisfied than men, but it turned out that it was necessary to specify *which* women and *which* men. There are some groups of women, such as those divorced, who describe their lives as more frustrating and less rewarding than men do. But there are also some groups of males who are less happy than their female peers, such as unmarried men. To understand how people feel about their lives, it is less important to know whether a person is a woman than to know whether she is a young, childless wife or a single career woman or married with grown children. We can't assume that all men view their lives as rich and fulfilling, either; we must know first whether the man is an aging bachelor or an empty-nest father.

Several recent reviews of community-mental-health surveys found that women are in worse shape than men. Women consistently have higher rates of mental illness—both psychosis and neurosis, including depression, anxiety, suicidal tendencies—regardless of whether they come voluntarily for treatment, are committed, or take part in a random survey. Such symptoms of pathology would suggest that women's lives are less satisfying than men's but women overall did not report this.

The reason may be that a person's evaluation of her life is based partly on the fit, or lack of it, between her objective circumstances, and her hopes and expectations. The black community in this country has raised its sights dramatically in the last 10 years, and women are beginning to do so also. The dissatisfactions reported by college-educated and divorced women in our study, for example, indicate that changes are occurring in the traditional values and roles for women. More women are going to college, working, and having fewer children. That's bound to make some changes eventually in the institution of marriage, which is currently the rock on which both sexes base much of their happiness and satisfaction with life. We can be sure that pressures for change will be met by resistance to change, and whether the irresistible force or the immovable object gives way, we'll be part of an interesting transition.

WHY MARRIAGES BREAK UP AFTER 40
Jack Harrison Pollack

Two of every five divorces are between couples married 10 years to 25 years or more, and experts predict the rate will soar in coming years. But for couples who want to stay together, there are still ways to fulfill that "lifetime contract."

Divorce hearings are ordinarily routine. But in California recently, an impatient judge interrupted the legalistic recital of a lawyer and demanded of his client, a well-dressed woman in her early forties: "Now tell me, madam, in your own words, exactly what are these 'irreconcilable differences' with your husband?"

"Our son is in the Army, our daughter has gone off to college, and. . ."

"You have nothing left but each other, and that isn't enough?"

"No," said the woman unhappily. "We stayed together all these years only because of the children."

The reason for her marital discord was not unusual—nor, as a matter of fact, was the divorce itself. Indeed, during the past 20 years the breakup of longtime marriages has become relatively commonplace and divorces have reached record-breaking proportions. Moreover, the problem is growing.

According to the latest U.S. Department of Health, Education, and Welfare statistics, two of five of this nation's half-million annual divorces terminated marriages of 10 years or more. One in four of the unions ended had lasted 15 years. And one in six—as opposed to one in 25 before World War II—canceled out marriages of 25 years or more.

Over the years, the public has become accustomed to divorces, separations, and remarriages of long-wed public figures—Louisiana Sen Russell B. Long (30 years), former Minnesota Sen. Eugene McCarthy (24 years), former Detroit Mayor Jerome P. Cavanagh (17 years), New York Gov. Nelson Rockefeller (31 years), auto magnate Henry Ford II (23 years), and sex researcher William H. Masters (28 years).

Even those "happy" Hollywood marriages sour with age—among the divorces are Loretta Young (29 years), Robert Cummings (25 years), Burt Lancaster (22 years), and Dean Martin (20 years). Reflecting the temper of the times, actress Jean Peters, in filing for divorce from billionaire Howard Hughes, explained defensively: "Our marriage lasted thirteen years, which is long by present standards."

But divorce and quick remarriage are not the exclusive provinces of the "not-so-young" celebrity set. They are increasingly common among the middle-aged middle class. And whatever the prospects for success, most of these late remarriages do not face what experts consider one of the prime stumbling blocks of more youthful unions—our child-centered society.

In a four-year study of the dissolution of longtime marriages, Dr. Alfred A. Messer, Professor of Psychiatry of Emory University's School of Medicine in Atlanta, reported in *Mental Health*: "Communication between parents is through their children—who are the nucleus around which most activities flow. There are endless energy-draining car pools for school, music, art lesson, athletic activities, cookouts, and campouts which the parents must oversee. Many women cook and dress for their children more than for their husbands. Many men often feel more comfortable going off with their youngsters than with their wives for a weekend or holiday. What happens when their children grow up and leave home? A void ensues." What she neglected to mention was that the children so dominated the household that both she and her husband had always turned to them for "understanding," thus aggravating the noncommunication problem which the experts find is common.

However, in Canada, where the situation parallels that in the United States, P.A. Royal of the Edmonton Family Service Association feels that children are only part of the problem. The basic fault, he believes, is the emotional immaturity of the marriage partners. During their years together, he says, "Many of these couples have entered into silent conspiracies to avoid real giving and emotional growth. They pretend that their marriages are a success and base this pretense upon a mutual interest in their children, home, and business. While living in this camouflaged conflict, they do not intrude into each other's domain—until finally deciding that their marriages are empty relationships."

Studies show that better health and increased longevity are also major factors in middle-age divorce. With their children no longer acting as buffers, couples feeling unloved or no longer useful have more opportunity for mutual resentment and more time for boredom. Divorce and a possible new life through remarriage seem like a happy escape.

From a longevity standpoint, says Dr. Richard A. Kalish, of the School of Public Health at the University of California, Los Angeles, many couples in their fifties can anticipate at least 15 more years of an active life. Moreover, it is not uncommon for people of this age to be sexually vigorous. "Thus," according to Dr. Kalish, "if a wife with whom he has lived twenty-five years is no longer attractive to a man, he has compelling motivation to leave. Five years of a new relationship may not be worth a divorce, but the prospect of fifteen years makes it seem worthwhile."

As a consequence of the better health of our population, says Dr. Kalish, the divorce rate for older people will probably rise substantially by 1990. He also envisions a rise in the marriage rate of men in their sixties and women in their forties, as well as marriages in which the bride may be a considerable number of years older than the groom.

Nationwide studies also reveal that the economic independence of a large segment of the middle-aged population is another leading divorce factor. In greater numbers than ever before, women return to work after their children are grown. And men generally reach the heights of their business success in their forties and fifties. As a wife's financial independence grows, says Dr. Messer, so does her power in the home. She ceases to act a secondary role and can afford to indulge her suppressed fancies, be they practical or romantic. "If she has too large a nose or a receding chin, she can afford to go to a plastic surgeon and have her nose bobbed or her chin remolded," Dr. Messer states. "Since these can be changed, she feels, by the same token, no need to throttle the desire for domestic surgery."

Similarly, the husband, feeling his financial oats, has no hesitation in trotting off to greener pastures. As a Western businessman told Dr. James A. Peterson, Chairman of the University of Southern California's Sociology Department: "I've been married fifteen years—and I've had enough. As for money, I've made my pile and can set up the wife and kids so they'll never want for anything. I'm going to travel, laugh, and play. Your job is to help my wife adjust to the fact that I'm through with her. The kids? They're old enough now so they don't need me. I can't get another chance like this. But I can always get another wife."

While financial independence is frequently the trigger, many long marriages actually break up because of the haste with which they began. Take the spur-of-the-moment or "pregnancy" marriages, with a brief courtship, during and shortly after World War II. A Michigan engineer, who just divorced his wife after 28 years, recalls: "I proposed to Ruth after knowing her only a week before I was shipped overseas. After I returned home, I found we had little in common. I always liked sports and classical music, and she found them a bore. She was more interested in clothes, bridge parties, and decorating and redecorating our home. She dressed sloppily—I'm almost fastidious—and talked too much. Even our married daughter tells me, 'Daddy, I don't know how you and Mother lived together all those years.'"

While some marriages fail because of a partner's inability to change, others break up because of radical changes in either the husband or wife. A 20-year study of 300 couples by E. Lowell Kelly, University of Michigan psychology professor, found that either partner was capable of major change in outlook, interest, and attitude—and occasionally in their whole personality. Some characteristics became stronger, others weaker, ultimately resulting in new behavior patterns.

Confirming this in another study, UCLA's Dr. Kalish reports that these new patterns can break up a marriage of seemingly compatible partners. "Now they must confront each other," he says. "They have both changed in the intervening twenty or so years. One spouse at forty suddenly begins to grow while the other remains stagnant. The wife returns to school. Her husband sticks his head in the sand of his work. Or the husband enters a new phase of job responsibility while the wife insists the household requires all her energies." Finally, the gulf widens to the point where each sets sail on a solo course through divorce.

A final and crucial factor in the increasing break-up of long-married couples is the relaxation of divorce laws by several states. New York, where adultery had been the only ground almost since colonial days, liberalized its statute in 1966. A law went into effect in 1972 which cut from two years to a year the waiting period for divorce based on separation and abandonment.

California's 1970 law stipulates two simple grounds for divorce: "irreconcilable differences" and "incurable insanity." No corroborating witnesses are necessary. Formerly the grounds were adultery, desertion, cruelty, neglect, or a felony conviction.

A new Texas "no-fault" law permits divorce on petition of either party if the marriage has become "insupportable" and there is no reasonable expectation of reconciliation.

Canada, too, has a broadened new law, which recognizes "marriage break-down" and other reasons for grounds for divorce. Previously, adultery was the sole ground. Under the law, Canadian divorce actions have tripled—many by long-married couples.

Historically, of course, the fragmentation of middle-age marriage is part of the breakdown of social customs that have been the foundation of American life. And in recent years, the breakdown has been accelerated by many factors, including the revolt of youth and the unconscious acceptance of some of their unconventional and "revolutionary" attitudes by the middle-aged.

Despite the increase in divorce at all ages, however, marriage as an institution still seems here to stay. For although we, as a nation, have only recently begun to record a million divorces per year, we are also experiencing a marriage boom—in recent years 4,000,000 Americans have exchanged "I do's" annually a figure unprecedented except for immediately after World War II.

Apparently, Americans keep trying!

How to Mend Middle-Aged Marriages

What measures can be taken to prevent middle-age divorces? Since individuals are involved, there is no overall formula. But experts recommend the following as helpful:

More time together without the children. More second honeymoons. More mutual interests as marital partners rather than just parents.

More celebrations on wedding anniversaries; sentiment is a part of all enduring relationships.

A more imaginative approach to sex to keep it from becoming an act without meaning, and a better understanding of male-female needs. Emotionally, they do not always coincide. "A wife wants to make love at the height of her self-esteem, a husband at the depths of his," says Dr. Clark E. Vincent, who is a behavioral scientist at Wake Forest University.

More awareness of life's ever-changing aspects. Couples should seek new challenges—social or educational—or reinvigorate old ones.

No bottling up of resentments. An honest quarrel clears the air, says Dr. George R. Bach, Director of the Institute for Group Psychotherapy. And honesty means avoiding hostile conversational patterns, withdrawals, insults, accusations, and stirring up old irrelevant grievances, according to psychiatrist Jurgen Ruesch of the University of California Medical Center.

More tolerance and mutual respect for each other as individuals. These are qualities, psychologists say, that can keep a couple happy even when romance ebbs.

Keep an interest in each other as individuals. For a wife, this may mean concerning herself with her husband's career, at least to some extent, and the people he works with. For the husband, it may mean participating in some of his wife's community activities. After 40, many couples discover that they have "lost touch" with each other's developing interests over the years—and they also discover that they cannot go back in time to rectify the loss.

PORTNOY'S MOTHER'S COMPLAINT
Pauline Bart

A young man begs his mother for her heart, which a betrothed of his has demanded as a gift; having torn it out of his mother's proffered breast, he races away with it; and as he stumbles, the heart falls to the ground, and he hears it question protectively, "Did you hurt yourself son?"

Jewish Folktale

Mrs. Gold is a young-looking Jewish housewife in her forties. A married daughter lives about 20 miles away. Her hyperactive brain-damaged 13-year-old son has been placed in a special school even further away. After his departure she became suicidally depressed and was admitted to a mental hospital. I asked her how her life was different now, and she answered:

It's a very lonely life, and this is when I became ill, and I think I'm facing problems now that I did not face before because I was so involved, especially having a sick child at home. I didn't think of myself at all. I was just someone that was there to take care of the needs of my family, my husband and children, especially my sick child. But now I find that I—I want something for myself, too. I'm a human being, and I'm thinking about myself.

She was dissatisfied with her marriage; their mutual concern for their son held the couple together, but when their son entered an institution this bond was loosened, although they visited him every Sunday.

My husband is primarily concerned with only one thing, and that is making a living. But there's more to marriage than just that (pause) you don't live by bread alone.

Mrs. Gold states that she is not like other women for whom divorce is simple. She is considering divorcing him if their relationship does not improve. Yet another patient whom I interviewed later told me Mrs. Gold had cried all night after her husband came to tell her he was divorcing her.

Although she believes her life was "fuller, much fuller, yes, much fuller" before her children left, she used to have crying spells:

But in the morning I would get up, and I knew that there was so much dependent on me, and I didn't want my daughter to become depressed about it or neurotic in any way, which could have easily happened because I had been that way. So I'm strong-minded and strong-willed, so I would pull myself out of it. It's just recently that I couldn't pull myself out of it. I think that if there was—if I was needed maybe I would have, but I feel that there's really no one that needs me now.

Her inability to admit anger toward her children and her perfectionist demands on herself is shown in the following remark: "it was extremely hard on me, and I think it has come out now. Very hard. I never knew I had the amount of patience. That child never heard a raised voice."

While she is proud of her daughter and likes her son-in-law, there is an element of ambivalence in her remarks.

Naturally as a mother you hate to have your daughter leave home. I mean it was a void there, but, uh, I know she's happy . . . I'm happy for my daughter because she's happy.

Since she had used her daughter as a confidante when the daughter was a teen-ager, she lost a friend as well as a child with her daughter's departure. Mrs. Gold said she didn't want to burden her daughter with her own problems because her daughter was student teaching. The closeness they had now was "different" since her daughter's life revolved around her husband and her teaching, and that's the way it should be." They phone each other everyday and see each other about once a week.

Like most depressives (Mrs. Gold is in the hospital for treatment of depression) she feels inadequate: "I don't feel like I'm very much." Between the day of her son's departure and her hospitalization she spent most of her time in bed and neglected her household, in marked contrast to her former behavior.

I was such an energetic woman. I had a big house, and I had a family. My daughter said, "Mother didn't serve eight courses. She served ten." My cooking—I took alot of pride in my cooking and in my home. And very, very clean. I think almost fanatic.

She considers herself more serious than other women and couldn't lead a "worthless existence" playing cards as other women did. She was active in fund raising for the institution her son was in, but apparently, without the maternal role—the role that gave her a sense of worth—fund raising was not enough. Formerly her son "took every minute of our lives" so that she "did none of the things normal women did—nothing."

I can pardon myself for the fact (that he was placed in a school) that I did take care of him for 12 years and he was hyperactive. It was extremely hard on me, . . . I never knew I had that amount of patience.

Like most women interviewed, Mrs. Gold is puritanical and embarrassed about sex.

I think anything that gives you pleasure or enjoyment, anything like that. It's just that I'm not that kind of woman.

Mrs. Gold's problem, psychologically and sociologically, is, perhaps most dramatically apparent in her response when I asked her to rank seven roles available to middleaged women in order of importance. She listed only one role: "Right now I think helping my children, not that they really need my help, but if they did I would really try very hard." Thus she can no longer enact the role that had given her life meaning, the only role she considered important to her. Her psychiatrist had told her, and she agreed, that a paying job would help her self-esteem. But what jobs are available for a 40-year-old woman with no special training, who has not worked for over 20 years?

Mrs. Gold has most of the elements that are considered by clinicians to make up the pre-illness personality of involutional depressives: a history of martyrdom with no payoff (and martyrs always expect a payoff at some time) to make up for the years of sacrifice, inability to handle aggressive feelings, rigidity, a need to be useful in order to feel worthwhile, obsessive compulsive super-mother, superwife behavior and generally conventional attitudes.

Why Study Mrs. Portnoy and Her Complaints

Some of my friends have asked me what I am doing studying depressed middle-aged women. The question, implying that the subject is too uninteresting and unimportant to be worth studying, is itself evidence for the unfortunate situation these women find themselves in. But a society's humanity may be measured by how it treats its women and its aged as well as by how it treats its racial and religious minorities. This is not a good society in which to grow old or to be a woman, and the combination of the two makes for a poignant situation. In addition, there are practical and theoretical reasons why such a study is important. Practically speaking, women today live longer and end their childbearing sooner than they did in the last century. They are more likely now to reach the "empty nest" stage or the postparental stage (a term used by those investigators who do not consider this life cycle stage especially difficult). Moreover, in clinical terms, depression is the most common psychiatric symptom present in adults, but, like middle age, it too, has been generally ignored by sociologists.

Problems of middle age are important theoretically for several reasons. In the first place, there is contradictory evidence on the question of whether middle age is in fact a problem for women. After a study of middle age in 35 different cultures, for example, I found that most women in most of these cultures do not think of middle age as being a particularly stressful time. This would seem, at the very least, to refute such biological determinists as Hubert Humphrey's physician adviser, who, in a celebrated exchange with Representative Patsy Mink, declared that women ought to be barred from positions of serious responsibility because of the "raging hormonal influences" that overwhelm them in menopause. Nevertheless, it is fact that many women in American society do undergo a painful period with the onset of middle age, and it is also a fact that some of these women collapse in a state of clinical depression, like Mrs. Gold.

This raises some serious questions. Why is it that one woman whose son has been "launched" says, I don't feel like I've lost a son; I feel like I've gained a den," while another mother reports that the worst thing that ever happened to her was:

When I had to break up and be by myself and be alone, and I'm just—I really feel that I'm not only not loved but not even liked sometimes by my own children . . . they could respect me. If—if they can't say good things, why should they, why should they feel better when they hurt my feelings and make me cry and then call me a crybaby or tell me that I—I ought to know better or something like that. My worst thing is that I'm alone, I'm not wanted, nobody interests themselves in me . . . nobody cares.

Role and Self

The role one has in life and one's image of himself are intimately interconnected. When people are given the "Who Are You?" test, they usually respond by naming their various roles—wife, doctor, mother, teacher, daughter and the like. As a person goes from one stage of life to another, however, or from one step in a career to another, he or she must change his self-concept because the relevant or significant others, the people with whom he interacts, change. A loss of significant others can result in what Arnold Rose call a "mutilated self." One woman put it to me this way:

I don't—I don't,—I don't feel like—I don't feel that I'm wanted. I don't feel at all that I'm wanted. I just feel like nothing. I don't feel anybody cares, and nobody's interested, and they don't care whether I do feel good or I

don't feel good. I'm pretty useless . . . I feel like I want somebody to feel for me, but nobody does.

Another woman stated that:

I don't feel like doing anything. I feel just like I'm standing still, not getting anywhere.

The traditional woman bases her self-esteem on a role, motherhood, that she must finally relinquish. Some do this with ease; some others, especially those with inflexible personalities, cannot. But the problem is not hers alone; society has provided no guidelines for her, no rites of passage. There is no bar mitzvah for menopause. The empty nest, then, may prompt the extreme feelings of worthlessness and uselessness that characterize depressives. One can think of these women as overcommitted to the maternal role and then, in middle age, suffering the unintended consequences of this commitment.

But there is more to it than that. Ideally a mother should be flexible enough to stop mothering adult children, but if her personality is rigid, as depressives' usually are, she can't and she can't expect them to stop acting like dependent children either. When the children do not act this way, she may feel resentful. But since a woman is not "allowed" to be hostile to her children, she may turn the resentment inward and become depressed.

Moreover, a woman who overplays her role as mother may consciously or unconsciously want to place her children morally in her debt. Dan Greenberg's best-selling satire, *How to Be a Jewish Mother*, refers to guilt as the mother's main method of social control. It is no accident that his second book, *How To Make Yourself Miserable*, begins with the sentence, "You, we can safely assume, are guilty." It is the "supermother" who feels she can legitimately expect her children to be more devoted to her, more considerate, bring her more satisfaction than would otherwise be the case. Furthermore, in this situation, there may even be some payoff in the depressive collapse. When that happens, once again she gets the attention, sympathy and control over her children she had before they left.

I should make clear at this point why I have been quoting so extensively from Jewish empty nest mothers, women, moreover, who had been hospitalized for clinically defined depression. The most obvious reason is that in terms of the larger study that I have done on the problem of middle-aged women cross-culturally, Jewish women in America occupy a pivotal place.

The literature on the Jewish mother is practically unanimous in painting her as "supermother" especially vulnerable to being severely affected if her children fail to meet her needs, either by not making what she considers "good" marriages, not achieving the career aspirations she has for them or even by not phoning her everyday. Not only is the traditional Jewish mother overinvolved with or over-identified with her children but the children are viewed as at the same time helpless without the mother's directives and as powerful, being able to kill the mother with "aggravation." As one depressed empty nest woman says, "My children have taken and drained me." In a sentence completion test, she filled in the blank after the words "I suffer" with "from my children."

Now, the theory governing my larger study of middle-aged women can be stated plainly enough. First, depression in middle-aged women is not due to the hormonal changes of the menopause, as is implied, for example, in the psychiatric diagnosis of "involutional melancolia." Rather, it is due to sociocultural factors that drastically reduce a woman's self-esteem. Second, depression is linked to actual or impending loss of significant role; therefore, depression in middle-aged women will be linked with maternal role loss. Third, certain roles and attitudes toward them increase the effect of loss. For example, "supermothers" will have a higher rate of depression than normal mothers, and full-time housewives will have a higher rate of depression among Jewish mothers than among Anglos or among blacks. For, as everyone knows, the stereotypical Jewish mother is almost by definition an exaggerated version of the "supermother." Moreover, again, according to the theory, one would expect to find that Jewish women would be more prone to depression than to other mental illnesses and that European-born Jewish women, being presumably more traditional, would have higher rates of depression than American-born Jewish women.

Patients

These were my suppositions; to test them out I examined the records of 533 women between the ages of 40 and 59 who had had no previous hospitalization for mental illness. The women were in hospitals, ranging from an upper-class private hospital to the two state hospitals that served people from Los Angeles County. I compared women who had been diagnosed "depressed" (using the following diagnoses: involutional depression, psychotic

depression, neurotic depression, manic-depressive depression) with women who had other functional nonorganic diagnoses.

I made every effort to overcome diagnostic biases on the part of the doctors and myself. First, the sample was drawn from five hospitals. Second,

TABLE I
Jewish Mothers are More Depressed than Mothers of Other Groups

Ethnicity	Percent Depressed	Total No.
Jews	84	122
Anglos	51	206
Blacks	22	28

The percent depressed among all non-jews was 47 percent. Further investigation at one of the five hospitals showed 67 percent (six) of Jewish women with native-born mothers and 92 percent (thirteen) of Jewish women with European-born mothers to be depressed. Although the cases are few, the findings are suggestive.

"neurotic depressives" were merged with the "involutional" and "psychotic depressives" and "manic depressives" since I suspected that patients who would be called neurotic depressed at an upper-class hospital would be called involutional depressed at a lower-middle-class hospital—a suspicion that was borne out. Third, I used a symptom check list and found that depressed patients differed significantly from those given other diagnoses for almost all symptoms.

Fourth, a case history of a woman with both depressive and paranoid features was distributed to the psychiatric residents at the teaching hospital for "blind" diagnosis. In half the cases, the woman was called Jewish and in half Presbyterian. The results showed no difference in number of stigmatic diagnoses between the "Jews" and "Presbyterians" since the most and least stigmatic diagnoses (neurotic depression and schizophrenia) were given to "Presbyterians." Fifth, 39 MMPI (personality) profiles at one hospital were obtained and given to a psychologist to diagnose "blind." He rated them on an impairment continuum. The results supported the decision to combine psychotic, involutional and neurotic depressives, because the ratio of mild and moderate to serious and very serious was the same, for all these groups.

Next, I conducted 20 intensive interviews at two hospitals to obtain information unavailable from the patients' records, using questionnaires already used on "normal" middle-aged women. I also gave them the projective biography test—a test consisting of 16 pictures showing women at different stages in their life cycle and in different roles. These interviews provided an especially rich source of information. I did not read their charts until after the interviews so as to leave my perception unaffected by psychiatrists' or social workers' evaluations.

Maternal role loss was recorded when at least one child was not living at home. I considered an overprotective or overinvolved relationship to be present when the record bore statements, such as "my whole life was my husband and my daughter" or if the woman entered the hospital following her child's engagement or marriage. Ratings of role loss, relationship with children and with husbands were made from a case history which omitted references to symptomatology, ethnicity or diagnosis, and high intercoder reliability was obtained for these variables. (Jewish coders were more likely to call a parent-child relationship unsatisfactory than non-Jewish coders. Categories were refined to eliminate this difference.) A woman was considered Jewish if she had a Jewish mother and regardless of profession of faith. The attitudes and values I am discussing need not come from religious behavior. For example, Mrs. Gold didn't attend religious services and was unsure of her belief in God. But she taught her daughter that "we just don't date Gentile boys" and considers herself very Jewish, "all the way through to the core."

You Don't Have to Be Jewish to Be a Jewish Mother

My suppositions were confirmed: Jews have the highest rate of depression, Anglos an intermediate rate and blacks the lowest rate (see Table 1). Jewish women are roughly twice as likely to be diagnosed depressed as non-Jewish women. Moreover, the very small group of Jewish women whose mothers were born in the United States had a rate of depression midway between that of Jewish women with European-born mothers on the one hand and Anglo women on the other. The low rates for black women suggest that their family structure and occupational roles tend to prevent depression. However, when I controlled the data, holding patterns of family interaction constant, the difference between Jews and non-Jews sharply diminishes (Table 2). To be sure, overprotection or overinvolvement with children is more common among Jews than among non-Jews. But it is clear that you don't have to be Jewish to be a Jewish mother. For example one divorced black woman, who had a hysterectomy, went into depression when her daughter, her only child, moved to Oregon. The depression lifted when the woman visited her and recurred when she returned to Los Angeles. Yet these results may simply reflect a greater unwillingness to hospitalize depressed black women in the Black community. Depressives are not likely to come to the attention of the police unless they attempt suicide. Therefore, if the woman or her family do not define her condition as psychiatric, she will remain at home. Only a prevalence study can fully test the hypothesis about the Black Family.

Any doubts about the validity of my inferences from the hospital charts were dispelled by the interviews.

Even though they were patients and I was an interviewer and a stranger, one Jewish woman forced me to eat candy, saying, "Don't say no to me." Another gave me unsolicited advice on

TABLE 2
Overinvolved Mothers Who Lose Their Maternal Role Are the Most Depressed Group

Condition	Percent Depressed	Total No.
Role Loss	62	369
Maternal Role Loss	63	245
Housewives with Maternal Role Loss	69	124
Middle-Class Housewives with Maternal Role Loss	74	69
Women with Maternal Role Loss Who Had Overprotective or Overinvolved Relationships with Their Children	76	72
Housewives with Maternal Role Loss Who Have Overprotective or Overinvolved Relationships with Their Children	82	44

whether I should remarry and to whom, and a third said she would make me a party when she left the hospital. Another example of extreme nurturant patterns was shown by a fourth woman who insisted on caring for another patient who had just returned from ECT (shock) while I interviewed her. She also attempted to find other women for me to interview. The vocabulary of motives invoked by the Jewish women generally attributed their illness to their children. They complained about not seeing their children often enough. Non-Jewish women were more restrained and said they wanted their children to be independent.

Two of the Jewish women had lived with their children, wanted to live with them again, and their illness was precipitated when their children forced them to live alone. However, in another study I did, even women who lived with their children were all depressed. As one such woman complained:

> Why is my daughter so cold to me? Why does she exclude me? She turns to her husband . . . and leaves me out. I don't tell her what to do, but I like to feel my thoughts were wanted.

All the mothers, when asked what they were most proud of, replied, "My children." Occasionally, after this, they mentioned their husbands. None mentioned any accomplishments of their own, except being a good mother. This was reflected also in the ranked answers to the question of what was most important to them: being a homemaker, taking part in church, club and community activities, being a companion to one's husband, helping parents, being a sexual partner, having a paying job or helping children. Needless to say, "helping children" was most frequently ranked first or second by these postnest mothers. Since it is difficult to help children who are no longer at home, women who value this behavior more than any other are in trouble. (Interestingly, "helping parents" was ranked first by only one. No woman listed "being a sexual partner" first, and three married women did not even include it in the ranking.)

Those interviewed were also given the projective biography test—16 pictures showing women in different roles at different ages. The clinical psychologist who devised the test and analyzed the protocols without knowing my hypothesis noted they were "complete mothers." One of the pictures, showing an old woman sitting in a rocking chair in front of a fireplace, got overwhelmingly negative reactions. As one put it:

And this scene I can't stand. Just sitting alone in old age by some fireplace all by herself (pause) turning into something like that. And to me this is too lonely. A person has to slow down sometime and just sit, but I would rather be active, and even if I would be elderly, I wouldn't want to live so long that I wouldn't have anything else in life but to just sit alone and you know, just in a rocking chair.

Another woman who was divorced and had both her children away from home said, "This could look very much like me, I'm sitting, dreaming, feeling so blue." When she chose that as the picture not liked, she said, "Least of all, I don't like this one at all. That's too much like I was doing—sitting and worrying and thinking." Two women even denied the aging aspects of the picture: "Here she is over here sitting in front of the fireplace, and she's got her figure back, and I suppose the baby's gone off to sleep, and she's relaxing." This woman interpreted every picture with reference to a baby.

What Is to Be Done

It is very easy to make fun of these women, to ridicule their pride in their children and concern for their well-being. But it is no mark of progress to substitute Mollie Goldberg for Stepin Fetchit as a stock comedy figure. They are as much casualties of our culture as are the children in Harlem whose IQs decline with each additional year they spend in school. In their strong commitment to and involvement with their children, they were only doing what they were told to do, what was expected of them by their families, their friends and the mass media. If they deviated from this role, they would have been ridiculed (ask any professional woman).

Moreover, what I am really talking about here is what happens to women who follow the cultural rules, who buy the American Dream, who think there is a payoff for good behavior, who believe in justice and who therefore suffer depression, a loss of meaning, when they discover that their lives have not turned out the way they expected. We even find the same syndrome in men. Men who have involutional psychosis are usually in their sixties, the retirement age. I would predict that these are men whose occupational roles were "props." Like the women who derive their identity almost exclusively from their role as mothers, there are men whose identity is completely wrapped up in their work. With retirement, then, one could expect to find symptoms of depression. And in fact, the director of admissions at the teaching hospital where I worked reported that it was not unusual for army officers to suffer involutional depression on retirement. And a 1965 study on involutional depression in Israel found loss of meaning a factor among old pioneers who believed "that the values so dear to them were now alien to them and the sense of duty and sacrifice as they knew it seemed to exist no longer. They felt different, isolated and superfluous."

But the cases of these women tell us something else that is important. Two psychoanalysts, Therese Benedek and Helene Deutsch, state that menopause is more difficult for "masculine" or "pseudomasculine" women. The former describes this woman as one whose "psychic economy was dominated—much like that of a man's—by strivings of the ego rather than by the primary emotional gratifications of motherliness." Deutsch states that "feminine, loving" women have an easier time during climacteric than do "masculine, aggressive ones." However, my data shows that it is the women who assume the traditional feminine role—who are housewives, who stay married to their husbands, who are not overtly aggressive, in short who accept the traditional norms—who respond with depression when their children leave. Even the MMPI, masculine-feminine scores for women at one hospital were one half a standard deviation more feminine than the mean.

Until recent years, a common theme of inspirational literature for women, whether on soap operas or in women's magazines, has been that they could only find "real happiness" by devoting themselves to their husbands and children and by living vicariously through them. If one's sense of worth comes from other people rather than from one's own accomplishments, it follows that when such people depart, one is left with an empty shell in place of a self. If, however, a woman's sense of worth comes from her own interests and accomplishments, she is less vulnerable to breakdown when significant others leave. This point is obscured in much of the polemical literature on the allegedly dominant American female who is considered to have "lost" her femininity. It is, after all, feminine women, the ones who play the traditional roles, not the career women, who are likely to dominate their husbands and children. This domination, however, may take more traditional female forms of subtle manipulation and the invoking of guilt. If, however, a woman does not assume the traditional female role and does not expect to have her needs for achievement or her needs for "narcissistic gratification," as psychiatrists term it, met vicariously through the accomplishments of her husband and children, then she has no need to dominate them, since her well-being does not depend on their accomplishments. It is unreasonable to expect one sex in an achievement-oriented society not to have these needs.

The Women's Liberation movement, by pointing out alternative life styles, by providing the emotional support necessary for deviating from the ascribed sex roles and by emphasizing the importance of women actualizing their own selves, fulfilling their own potentials, can help in the development of personhood, for both men and women.

Section IV

SEX IS A MANY SPLENDORED THING—SOMETIMES!
Michael J. Sporakowski

The title of this section stems from a quote by an author unknown which went something like this: "We are born with the ability to reproduce, but not with the ability to enjoy it." Certainly sex and sexual adjustment are important aspects of marriage. Books on the topic abound and bring great wealth to the authors. Counselors' offices are full of needful people who often state dissatisfaction with sex as their primary reason for being there. Masters and Johnson types abound everywhere in response to these needs today.

This section begins with some humor that parodys the "marriage manual." To complete Thoreau's idea "I lose my respect for the man who can make the mystery of sex the subject of a coarse jest, yet when you speak of it earnestly and seriously on the subject is silent," the Collier and Ellis readings examine human sexuality in greater depth. "The article by Hicks and Taylor adds a perspective based on some recent data gathered from college students." Since the length of this chapter cannot possibly allow enough to be said, several readings, as outside resources are recommended to you.

Brecher, Ruth and Edward. *An Analysis of Human Sexual Response.* Signet Paperback T 3038.

Belliveau, Fred and Lin Richter. *Understanding Human Sexual Inadequacy.* Bantam paperback QZ 5959.

Hastings, Donald. *Sexual Expression in Marriage.* Little, Brown, 1966.

Articles

1. Gerald Sussman—The Official Sex Manual
2. Jennifer S. Macleod—How To Hold A Wife: A Bridegroom's Guide
3. James Collier—The Procreation Myth
4. Albert Ellis—The Great Coital Myth
5. Mary W. Hicks and Donald Taylor—Sex on Campus, The Student's Dilemma

Name: _____ Date: _____

Student #: _____ Sex: M or F

Answer these true or false.

1. T F Sex should be avoided during pregnancy.

2. T F The most satisfying intercourse position is the male superior.

3. T F The older you become the less important the influence of sex.

4. T F Sex during menstruation is harmful.

5. T F The larger the penis the greater the female's satisfaction.

6. T F Women who enjoy sex "too much" are nymphomaniacs.

7. T F Married women frequently say they do not have enough sex, whereas their husbands usually say they have too much.

8. T F Simultaneous orgasms are needed for conception to take place.

9. T F Urination by the female after coitus will prevent conception.

10. T F Women ejaculate as do men.

11. T F The natural (normal) reason for intercourse in humans is procreation.

12. T F In light of cross-cultural data, especially when compared to more "primitive" peoples, Americans have a very high rate of intercourse frequency.

13. T F Of the animal species, man has one of the lowest rates of intercourse frequency.

14. T F Oestrous (heat) and menstruation are the common sexual tie between higher and lower animals.

15. T F The erroneous zones are the most sexually sensitive parts of the male and female body.

16. As compared to other persons your age and your sex who you interact with, would you say you have

    less_____, more_____, or about the same_____amount of knowledge about sex.

17. What have been the three most significant sources for you of knowledge about sex?

    (a)

    (b)

    (c)

18. Did you ever have a "birds and bees" talk with your parents?

Yes _____ No _____.

19. If yes, both parents _____ mom only _____ or dad only _____.

20. At about what age? _____

21. Do you feel you can communicate freely with your parents about sex? Yes _____ No _____

22. What reading materials have had the most significant influence on you regarding:

(a) Sex knowledge

(b) Your attitudes about sex

(c) Your own sexual behavior

23. Define orgasm for:

(a) females

(b) males

24. What is the relationship of orgasm to sexual adjustment?

Describe.

25. What is the relationship of sexual adjustment to marital adjustment?

THE OFFICIAL SEX MANUAL

At last—a no-holds-barred,
straight-from-the-shoulder,
pulls-no-punches,
courageously frank, daringly
intimate guide to the art
and techniques of the
actus supremus

Gerald Sussman

Introduction

The art of coginus goes back a long way. But until 1946, male and female partners had little knowledge of what they were doing. Most partners avoided coginus as much as possible, insisting they did it only in their sleep, while dreaming or thrashing about. They regarded coginus as the handiwork of Satan. While this may be true, I feel that Satan has done more harm than good. He spread his blanket of ignorance, fear and guilt over the act of coginus and many partners blindly covered themselves with it.

This book is a direct answer to Satan and his blanket. It throws off his coverlet of ignorance and replaces it with what the French call savior faire. Now, for the first time, you can enjoy the benefits of the most complete, definitive manual ever written on the art and science of coginutal techniques, the product of many, many years of experience in the field and in oral consultation. It has been written in frank, easy-to-understand language and offers you the first really new and provocative approach to coginus since Von Leml. It tells you everything you must know to become exciting, nay, an exquisite coginutal partner. This manual has been warmly endorsed by many organizations, societies, clubs and study groups.

FOREPLAY: PRELUDE TO COGINUS

Phase One:
Audiovisual-Premanipulative

Foreplay means everything you do to your partner before coginus. Foreplay is to coginus what the build-up is to the punch line of a joke. Many partners are completely unaware of foreplay and go directly to coginus itself. Of course, the laugh is on them. You will soon learn that "getting there" is three eighths to five sixths of the fun.

Foreplay is carried out in Seven Separate Phases of building coginutal excitement, although some overlapping is permitted. Phase One is called the Audiovisual-Premanipulative or the Hot Line. The Hot Line is exactly what it implies, a hot line of coginutal communication between the male and female partners. It begins with an urgent mouth-to-ear phone call by the male partner, asking his mate to meet him. When the partners meet, they exchange hot looks and words of endearment, gradually building a deeply sincere line of warmth that arouses a feeling in the chest not unlike an old-fashioned mustard plaster or a rainbow heartburn. This is followed by more hot looks and a certain little cute way of flirting.

Phase Two:
Fingernail Manipulative Play

Phase Two, Fingernail Manipulative Play, is an exploratory phase for the partners, a chance to discover the many erroneous zones and to make erroneous "friends," so to speak.

The erroneous zones are those areas of the body which are exquisitely sensitive to coginutal stimulation. They are located all over the place. The female partner is exquisitely sensitive in 187 spots, the male partner in 75. We cannot describe them all in detail. For our purposes, we will list the basic zones, the ones that are most friendly and offer the warmest welcome.

The female partner's Premium Quality erroneous zones are the scalp, chin, Adam's apple, knuckles, kneecap, heel and arch. In Fingernail Manipulative Play the male partner lightly touches these highly sensitive areas with the tips of his fingernails or, if he wishes, with a pair of soft cotton gardening gloves. His fingernails or gloves should barely touch, as if he were only tickling. The motions should be: tickle—withdraw, tickle—withdraw, tickle—withdraw.

A Little Fooling Around
The Bliss

At this point many partners stray from the phases of Foreplay and do a lot of blissing. The bliss is not recommended from a health standpoint. But when you are young and caught up in coginutal passion, you don't listen about your health. You feel as if you're strong as a horse. If blissing is your cup of tea and it gives you erroneous pleasure without any side effects, wonderful. But if you start losing your hair or get little things under your arms, you can be sure it wasn't from eating with dirty hands.

A Little More Fooling Around:
The French Bliss

This is a much more sensible way of blissing, if you must bliss at all. First make a few slices of French toast. Just dip some white bread in a batter of eggs and milk. Fry the bread in hot butter until golden brown on both sides. Then sprinkle with sugar, cinnamon, honey, jam or marmalade, or pour maple syrup over it. When you and your partner have a lot of French toast in your mouths, lean over the table and bliss. The French toast and its topping (especially good, thick orange marmalade) acts as a protective barrier or filter, stopping strange germs from entering your mouth. Do not attempt a French Bliss without a full mouth of French toast.

Phase Three: Caressa Intima

Phase Three of foreplay, Caressa Intima, marks the introduction of the basic caress or fondle, a delightful semirhythmic stroking motion carried out by the male partner's elbow, the most erroneous instrument he possesses.

After the female partner has become moderately aroused with hot looks, blisses and fingernail play, the male partner should begin a crisscross counterclockwise caressing motion with the tip of his elbow across his partner's pomerantz, a tiny, heart-shaped object located near the ankle. A well-caressed pomerantz is extremely important, for it is the only source of lubricating secretions in the entire area. It provides fluid for the proper stimulation of the female partner's heel, arch and kneecap, as well as the ankle. The pomerantz is indeed "the last lubricating station before the bridge to the vesuvious."

Phase Four: Benjie Play

Phase Four, Benjie Play, is still considered indelicate by many, but it is very popular with the younger set (it should not be confused with something called "petting").
Here are the basic techniques:

1. The erroneous zone of the benjie is the brittle. In the basic hold the male partner grips the brittle between his thumb and index finger as if it were a marble. Then he flicks the brittle in and out, as if he were "shooting the marble."

2. The male partner sits on a chair with his legs crossed, leaning over backwards as far as he can. With a long Chinese back-scratcher dipped in peanut oil, he bastes his partner's brittles every 15 minutes or so.

Phase Five: Pleasure-Pain

By now both partners will be soaring higher and higher in the clouds of coginutal excitement. As the male partner becomes aroused, his eyebrows swell and grow turgid. The female partner's teeth begin to chatter as her fervor increases. This is the time to introduce Phase Five, the Pleasure-Pain techniques.

The Lingle-Vontz
Pleasure-Pain Techniques

1. The Love Bite: Grab your partner by the flesh and give it a good bite.

2. The Nip: The nip is Japanese in origin. It is a sneaky little bite on the back.

3. The Scratch: The common house scratch for relieving itch is often felt to have erroneous overtones. I have known some partners who have scratched each other into a frenzy. They even claim to have reached an oregon. They only found fool's gold. If you scratch too much, you and your partner will more than likely end up with a rash.

4. The Knee in the Loin: A delicate move done by the female partner requiring a lot of practice. To be most effective, the knee in the loin should use the element of surprise. The two best surprise approaches for this technique are: "Look! There's a bird in the room!" and "Your shoelace is untied." They are self explanatory.

134

THE VESUVIOUS

Phase Six: Plethora Play

The female partner's vesuvious is a many-splendored thing. After you have found it, begin to explore for its most responsive part, the plethora (sometimes known as the cameo). The plethora is a tiny, football-shaped object located near the pomander tubes. It becomes erect and hard (like the male partner's vector) when it is stimulated correctly.

Now that you have found your partner's plethora, what to do with it? Don't panic. You can amuse her when she asks you if you have found her plethora by saying, "I didn't know it was missing." But get back to foreplay immediately. You are now ready for Phase Six, the stimulation of the plethora, or Plethora Play.

The most widely practiced techniques of Plethora Play are:

1. From a Standing Start: Begin with a brisk circular massage with the knuckles. Follow it up with a golf-club grip and squeeze gently.

2. From a Running Start: Begin with a rotary motion of the elbow, starting at the base of the plethora (the okris) and move to the tip (the splendina), making stops along the way for a quick hello to the cortio and the labella.

A Warning

There are many other areas of the vesuvious that have immense potential for erroneous pleasure. The giselle, for instance, which is located between the avus and the splendina, above the vestibule of the frappe, is especially receptive.

But you will note that the inner lips of the giselle will sometimes part and reveal the spatula, or Nostril of Aphrodite, a small, triangular-shaped organ that must be left alone. Don't play with your partner's spatula and don't ask us why. If you are curious and are overcome by your playful nature, you will feel sorry later. If there is a later.

Phase Seven: Vector Play

There is an old saying around the Caspian Sea that goes, "Mamoun setourias keboul haddadi," which means, "It takes two to have coginus." Female partners: You've got to do your part. Coginutal foreplay isn't just centered around your pomerantz, benjie and vesuvious. If only your partner's vector could talk, it would tell you how keenly it desires you to stimulate it. Listen closely to your partner's vector. Learn how to give it erroneous pleasure. It will help prevent tension from forming later on. Here is Phase Seven, the final step in foreplay, some good ice-breaking vector-play techniques for you to try:

1. The Eastern Grip: This is basically "shaking hands with the vector." Grasp the vector firmly and shake it.

2. The Western Grip: With your pinkie extended, place the vector in the palm of your hand, resting your thumb on the milo. With your pinkie, poke the tentacles gently, gradually increasing intensity.

3. The Continental Grip: This may feel unfamiliar at first, and requires some practice. Grip the vector at the hornis and pinch or tweak the fulcrum, bending your elbows slightly. Then throw back your head and give a wanton laugh.

THE WEDDING NIGHT

For Female Partners

Breaking the Hyphen

Most of the fear and anxiety of the wedding night centers around the breaking of the hyphen. There is a good case to be made for having it broken by a licensed physician sometime before the wedding. If you cannot afford this, there are many reputable gypsy palm readers who will do it nicely. If you can't get it done before the wedding night, for heaven's sake don't worry.

COGINUS: THE
ACTUS SUPREMUS

The Classic Position

This is the simplest, most widely used position for beginners. In this position, the female partner lies on her back, stretched out on the floor, with her legs under the bed. The male partner lies on the bed, either on his right or left side, and reads selections from Greek or Roman literature.

Cossack Style

A lusty, highly dramatic position that originated in 19th Century Russia when marauding bands of Cossacks attacked the villages of the huroks, the peasant landowners. In this position, the male partner storms into the bedroom and pulls back the bed sheets. The female partner cries aloud and runs out of the room.

Face to Face

In this position, male and female partners sit across a dinner table. The table should be set with a nice white linen tablecloth and candles. Dinner should be nothing but the best: shrimp cocktail, steak, French fries, peas and carrots, mixed green salad with French or Russian dressing, strawberry shortcake and coffee. A sparkling Albanian wine or a zinfandel should be served, and after the meal, a suitable ice and mint.

This is probably the most romantic position of all. The partners gaze adoringly at each other's handsome, well-groomed faces, and in between courses their hands are free to engage in erroneous stimulation.

On the Side (a Sergio)

A highly pleasurable position that can be used when one or both partners are a bit fatigued. The male partner lies on his side, the female partner lies on her side. In the middle is an upright sword.

From the Rear (a Postoli)

Coginus a Postoli offers an unusual variation on the regular positions and, at the same time, brings new erroneous zones into play. As the name suggests, it is done from the rear. Both partners kneel back to back. The female partner keeps her legs close together and leans forward. The male partner does the same. An exquisite fusing of the lubbocks is achieved.

Female Partner Astride

In this position, it is desirable for the female partner to use a saddle. It would also be nice if she had a horse. Then she could saddle the horse and mount it. This, of course, would put her in the astride position. Some male partners feel that since they must play a more passive role in this position, they will lose their sense of dominance and masculinity. They may even feel resentful and tell their partners to "get off their high horse and get back where they belong."

The Five Royal Variations of Sheikh Ben Hym

For a refreshing change of pace, many partners are now turning to Oriental and Middle Eastern cultures for new erroneous pleasures. And no other work on the art of coginus offers more subtle and exotic variations than the ancient and revered Arabian manual The Colored Fountains of Kohlrabi. For example, here are the legendary "Five Royal Variations of Sheikh Ben Hym":

Position One (El Shazar): In which the female partner lies on her stomach, arching her head and legs up as the male partner rides toward her on a zebra.

Position Two (El Shazam): In which the male partner lies on his stomach, arching his head and legs up as the female partner rides toward him on a zebra.

Position Three (El Onasis): In which the female partner is invited aboard the male partner's sailing vessel, where she is entertained beyond her wildest dreams. When she awakens the next day, she does not remember what happened to her after she playfully threw the rubies into the water.

Position Four (El Nekechef): In which the partners squat on a large purple handkerchief and partake of much kalouf and bouz.

Position Five (El Avek): In which the partners venture out into a heavy sandstorm and are never heard from again.

Positions for the More Advanced Partners (Flexia Extrema)

A highly stimulating position for more experienced partners has the male partner seated on a chair, legs crossed and hands clasped in back of his neck. The female partner lies on her back, legs arched slightly and hands at her sides. In this position, the female partner plays the more active role. She can move from side to side, rock up and down and rotate her melvin in a circular motion. The male partner is free to do almost anything he wishes with his hands and feet. To achieve deeper stimulation, a violin under the female's novella may help.

Flexia Extrema, continued

Another position to try is this: The female partner lies on the bed with six pillows under her neck. She brings up her legs and grasps her knees firmly, with her toes pointing downward and most of her weight on her spine. The male partner squats on his knees, preferably on a tumbling mat, with his legs spread and his palms down on the mat. He puts his head as far back through his legs as possible, pushes his body forward and tumbles over, landing on his lubbocks in a seated position. This is known as the forward roll or "tumblesauce."

OREGON

Heaven only knows how many words have been written about this ineffable state. Oregon is the culmination of all the foreplay, all the exquisitely erroneous positions of coginus we've described. It is that last burst of indefinable ecstasy at the summit of coginutal communion.

The female partner will feel herself at the threshold of oregon when the walls of her haven enlarge and his blondelle becomes taut. The male partner will feel numb and fuzzy for a few seconds as though his body has been shot through with Novocain. Suddenly the tip of his vector (the perma) will become limp. At this point, something wonderful happens to both partners as their oregon starts. They take a leap into the unknown. This is the only risky part. By now the partners are carried away in a flight of ecstasy, and when they leap (they usually leap toward each other, arms outstretched), they don't always look where they're going and sometimes crash into things and get hurt.

This advice may sound a little unrealistic, especially when you're going to be in the middle of incredible ecstasy, but try to remember: look before you leap.

AFTERGLOW

When the excrutiating ecstasy of oregon subsides, a great feeling of peace and inner contentment comes over you. The muscles of your body relax and you can unwind and feel a deep bond of friendship with your coginutal partner. This feeling is known as afterglow.

Afterglow should be accompanied by a good smoke. What if you shun tobacco? How can you enjoy afterglow? Many partners like to light up a chocolate cigarette. Others just use a thin pencil flashlight and make believe.

FOR THE
MALE PARTNER:
VECTOR CONTROL

Let's say you're young and fairly inexperienced, but your erroneous responses are very powerful. Naturally you practice the techniques we've outlined until you can do them perfectly. You start coginus and pop goes the weasel! In less than a minute you've reached a nothing-type oregon (premature congratulations). Now you're understandably vexed. "What did I do wrong?" you ask yourself. My dear sir, you did nothing wrong. You simply forgot that to prolong coginus you must build vector control. You must maintain an erect vector (vector mature) and, at the same time, exercise perfect control so that it does not congratulate prematurely.

BASIC METHOD

One of the oldest methods of vector control is biting on a towel. Close your eyes, contract every muscle in your body and bite as hard as you can, This method is simple and gives you excellent vector control for about three seconds.

MIND-OVER-MATTER
TECHNIQUE

Dr. Desmond Spitzer-Hunt has advanced the theory that improper vector control comes from a state of mind. He contends that all the male partner has to do when he feels himself getting out of control is to shift his mind from coginus to a completely different subject. In his fascinating study of vector control, Hold Your Horses, he outlines his mind-over-matter technique:

> If you feel you are at the danger point and may go out of control at any moment, shut out the image of your female partner and quickly think of Konrad Adenauer. If you are still out of control, think of Babe Ruth. That should do it. But if for some reason you have not cooled down, think of Mao Tse-tung. If that doesn't work, close your eyes, squeeze the sheets tightly and think of commercial cod fishing off the New Jersey coast. This last step should work in 92 out of 100 cases.

PROBLEMS
Matriculation

Almost everyone has matriculated at one time or another. No harm can come of it, if it is not done to excess. But continuous matriculation will lead to blindness. You may say, "All right I'll do it until I need glasses." We say, all right do it. But remember, matriculation is habit-forming. It will lead to addiction and addiction means blindness, and from there, a quick trip to the crazy house.

Impertinence

Many male partners have an occasional lessening of coginutal desire, especially after a day of mountain climbing, bicycle racing or shoveling snow. This kind of coginutal fatigue should not be confused with impertinence. Impertinence is a deep-rooted problem that goes back to your childhood. If you were ill-mannered and spoiled as a child, there is a good chance you are impertinent today.

The obvious way to cure impertinence would be to call or write as many people from your childhood as possible, apologize to them for your bad manners and promise them it will never happen again. But this is impractical in most cases. The next best method to cure impertinence is to have your ears soundly boxed and get a good talking-to. A talking-to is usually finished off by a smart rap across the face and a few medium to light fist flicks on the chin in a comradely "hang in there, fella" style. Please do not enlist the aid of a friend in a "home cure" of impertinence, however. A good talking-to can be administered only by a trained, licensed physician.

Vector Inferiority

Another so-called problem among male partners is vector inferiority, the feeling that your vector is too small to do the job properly. This is nonsense. The myth of vector inferiority was dispelled many years ago by the anthropologist Margaret Chase Itzbitzka.

In her classic work, Vector Behavior in the Lesser Antilles, Professor Itzbitzka proved scientifically that there is no such thing as vector inferiority. She chose the Lesser Antilles for her study because she heard that the male partners on these islands had a "lesser" type of vector mature, smaller in size and circumstanced at the age of publicity. She accomplished the herculean task of measuring every vector mature on the islands, discovering that the men with vector matures of only four, five and six pilasters in length were more highly regarded as coginutal partners than the nine and tenners.

CAN YOU HAVE COGINUS AFTER 30?

This is a question asked by almost everyone who reaches the change-of-life age. To dispel all your fears and anxiety, the answer is no. But, and this is a big but, you can do an awful lot of fooling around if you don't tire yourself. There is no reason why you can't caress, engage in benji, pomerantz and vector play, and even bite and scratch a little. Don't be discouraged. There are 1001 substitutes for coginus, many of them profitable and fun. My forthcoming book, tentatively titled *1001 Substitutes for Coginus,* will help you considerably.

CONTRADICTIONS
Conundrums

This is the most commonly used method to date. Conundrums are lightweight, easily portable and now come in many wash-and-wear models. Although the manufacturers say you do not have to iron them, we recommend a light touch-up to avoid puckering. A recent magazine article check-rated three brands. They are:

*ATLAS, MODEL TR 190, $1.49 PER PACK. Durability, good, although quilted lining had no special benefit. Wet strength, fair. Frequency of repair, average. Became a little softer and noisier after repeated launderings.

*PREVENTEX , MODEL DS 43, $1.29 PER PACK. Durability, nice. Wet strength, fairly good. Frequency of repair, above average. This was the only conundrum with a zip-in alpaca lining, a feature that offers some protection in winter, but can alter an otherwise good fit.

*ECONOMO, MODEL OL 67, 79c PER PACK. A BEST BUY. Durability, below average. Wet strength, so-so. Frequency of repair, not determined. Tended to crumble after repeated launderings.

Not Acceptable

APOLLO, MODEL XK 190, $7.50 PER PACK. Durability, poor. Wet strength, not too good. The "deluxe" silk lining shrank and faded after laundering. THIS CONUNDRUM WAS CONSIDERED A SHOCK HAZARD AND COULD NOT BE RECOMMENDED UNDER ANY CIRCUMSTANCES.

The Diagram

The question every female partner asks her doctor when she is thinking of getting a diagram is, "Do I have to draw you one?"

The answer is yes. You must draw your diagram in exact detail so that the finished product will be made to fit you perfectly. You do not have to draw it freehand. You can use tracing paper and a soft pencil. But make sure you get an accurate tracing of the area between the ava (sometimes called the Isle of Melnick) and the portis. This is where fermentation is most likely to take place.

The Rhythm Method

The Rhythm Method is somewhat similar to the box step, or 1-2-3-4, developed by a famous dancing master and his followers. While the master contended that the Rhythm Method could be taught, we say it comes naturally and you have to be born with it.

The Pill

We've heard rumors about this thing for a long time, but until we see it, we remain skeptical. A tiny pill that can keep spumoni away from the portis and prevent fermentation? That will be the day!

AMNESIACS

Ever since the days of the Bible, male and female partners have concocted food and drink that they hoped would provide extra stimulation and arouse greater desire for coginus. The earliest written example of amnesiacs occurs in the book of Agog, chapter IX, verse 3:

> And so it came to pass that Shadeg, the son of Goom, lay in his tent with Heshi, the daughter of Bim. And it came to pass that Heshi was comely and pleasing to his eyes and he gave her a goblet of plumence, limber and miltz and bade her partake. And it came to pass that Heshi drank of the goblet and her mouth was wet and her nostrils were open and her melvin was heavy with desire for Shadeg.

We could hardly hope to improve on Shadeg's original formula of one part plumence, one part limber and one part miltz. It's still the best all-round amnesiac in the business.

HOW TO HOLD A WIFE: A BRIDEGROOM'S GUIDE
Jennifer S. Macleod

Oh, lucky you! You are finally bridegroom to the woman of your dreams!

But don't think for a minute that you can now relax and be assured automatically of marital happiness forever. You will have to work at it. While she may have eyes only for you now, remember that she is surrounded every day by attractive young men who are all too willing to tempt her away from you. And as the years go by, you will lose some of the handsome muscularity of your youth: you will have to make up in skill and understanding what you will lack in the bloom of youth. It will be up to you to make your physical relationship so exciting, so totally satisfying to her, that she won't be tempted to stray!

Yes, boys, we are talking about SEX. Don't turn away in embarrassment. For if you are to hold that wonderful woman, you will have to practice and work hard at making her sex life as marvelous as it can be.

But how?

Here is what you need to know and do to succeed in your marriage, your greatest challenge in life—and the one that will be utterly essential to your wife's future happiness and thus your own.

1. Let's start in with the essentials. You should always be available to your wife whenever she wants you. It is of course your husbandly prerogative to say no, but you will be wise never to do so unless you are really ill, for that may tempt her to turn to other men to fulfill her essential needs. She cannot do without sex, so you as a smart husband should always be ready to provide it.

2. That means that you should never let yourself get too tired to perform. The cardinal sin for a husband—and a good way to lose the wife you love—is to fail at your duty to achieve a good erection and sustain it until your wife is fully satisfied. So never let your work or anything else get in the way of plenty of rest each day, regular but moderate exercise, and plenty of protein in your diet—and stay away from excessive alcohol.

Remember that women's sexual needs vary. Some need it more often than others, and some (lucky you if you are married to a real woman like that!) can achieve multiple orgasms in a single night of love, if you can do your part!

3. "But how about me?" you may ask. "How about my sexual needs and satisfactions?"

Now men's passion, of course, often does not equal that of women. But you have a wonderful surprise in store for you, if you concentrate your efforts on your wife's pleasure and don't worry selfishly about your own. For sooner or later you will discover the ecstasy of truly mature male coital orgasm that can be induced only by total surrender to the exquisite sensations of a woman's orgasmic contractions. This type of mature male climax will be attainable by you when you learn to inhibit the juvenile tendency to ejaculate prematurely, and await your wife's orgasm while sustaining your erection. Be glad if it is a long wait, because this will prolong and intensify her pleasure.

4. Because your juvenile sexuality is centered in your penis, you may think that the central act in intercourse is the capture of your penis by your wife's vagina. Don't make that common mistake! Always remember that the secret of the successful sex act—the one that brings about the wife's orgasm which in turn triggers the husband's ejaculation—is excitation of the wife's clitoris.

There are of course many techniques of clitoral stimulation; I need not go into them here because they are readily available in marriage manuals; they also give information that will be helpful to your wife in assisting you to your full erection. She should understand that she, too, should not be too selfish in her concentration on her own pleasure!

5. Remember that your first duty is to your wife. So if you fail to satisfy her (and yourself, too) in the above-described natural way, you should talk to a good psychiatrist who specializes in this kind of problem. She will help you if, for instance, you have not yet fully accepted the natural masculine role that will bring you the joy of selfless service to others instead of the futile envy of women's natural leadership role.

6. But you may find that sometimes you do not achieve the ejaculation that usually comes in response to your wife's orgasm, especially if your wife is one of those who have multiple orgasms. Don't worry too much about this—many husbands have the same problem. Your wife should be patient with your failures, and understand that men's passion sometimes does not match that of women. Don't be embarrassed—talk with her about it. She may be able to help with a little more foreplay to help stimulate you.

It should not be necessary, in a happy and loving marriage, for a man to resort to husbandly artifice in feigning an ejaculation that does not actually take place. But do keep in mind that her female ego does depend on her believing that she satisfies you fully and deeply, so beware of bruising her self-image by any word or action that might lead her to believe she does not completely meet your sexual needs.

7. Now for a practical matter: Assuming that you, like most modern couples, want to limit and space the growth of your family, your wife and you should decide together what method of contraception you wish to employ. Most likely, you will choose one of the fine methods available to the modern husband. Consult a qualified urologist. She will explain to you several methods, their advantages and drawbacks, and your wife and you can make the final decision.

One widely used method is the insertion of sperm-killing liquid into the urethra before intercourse. She (your doctor) will show you how. You may find it awkward and uncomfortable the first few times, but soon you will get the knack. If you are a truly considerate husband, you will do this routinely every evening as you prepare to retire, so that you will never have to keep your wife waiting while you make your preparations. A drawback of this method is that it does occasionally fail. And some wives—especially busy, successful ones for whom the time required for the abortion is a hardship—blame the husband for the slip-up, thinking that perhaps he did not take the proper precautions.

The other widely used method is of course the Capsule, a powerful formulation of various hormones that render you infertile so long as you take it without fail. There are minor undesirable side effects in some men: you may gain weight around the abdomen or buttocks, get white pigmentless patches on your face (which you may be able to conceal with beard or face-bronzer), or suffer some morning nausea. But be patient—these effects often decrease or even disappear after a few months. The one serious drawback of the Capsule is that you are several times more likely than otherwise to suffer eventually from prostate cancer or fatal blood clots. But these ailments are relatively uncommon anyway, so that many couples consider it worth the risk, especially since this is the one method that is 100 per cent effective.

So talk it over with your wife: this is one of the first, and most important, decisions for you to make together as woman and husband.

8. Now for a subject that may seem trivial: your appearance and dress. Don't overlook it—it is a vital ingredient in marital happiness.

Every woman likes to be proud of how attractive her husband is, so dress to please her. If she likes you to show off your youthful figure, by all means do so! Broad shoulders can be accentuated by turtleneck jerseys (with shoulder pads if needed), as can the well-tapered waist. Small, firm, well-shaped buttocks (very much in fashion this year) can be set off by well-cut clingy stretch pants.

And if you need the help of corsetry (as many do, especially as the years go by), today's well-constructed corsets make a good figure within the reach of almost every man. And they can be surprisingly comfortable, even for wear all day long. They can help you attract those wonderful compliments from your wife and her friends that are music to every man's ears!

One last piece of advice: the time may come—hopefully not for many years—when you can no longer provide your wife with all the sexual satisfactions that are her birthright. Your potency will decline, while her sexual appetite will increase well up into her 50s and 60s. That is the time that attractive younger men will tempt her. Build up the nonsexual as well as the sexual aspects of her life with you, do that even if she strays to others from time to time, she will happily return to you and the warm and affectionate home that you provide for her.

If and when that time comes do not nag her or make her feel guilty. Remember that she has strong sexual needs that must be met, and as long as she does not hurt any young men by deceiving them that there is hope for a permanent relationship, your home can still be a happy one. You are hers forever, and knowing and appreciating that, she will always come back to you.

If you do your job well—for husbandhood is the true career for all manly men, worthy of all your talent—you will keep your wife happy and hold her for the rest of her days. Remember that marriage, for a man, should be Life's Great Adventure. So relax—relax—relax—and enjoy it!

Name: _____ Date: _____

Student #: _____ Sex: M or F

1. T   F   More women than men participate in extramarital intercourse.

2. T   F   Neither men nor women should have sexual relations outside of marriage.

3. T   F   Men are more likely to be involved in both premarital and extramarital intercourse.

4. T   F   Extramarital sex always adds a positive dimension to marriage.

5. T   F   Extramarital intercourse is okay for men, but not women.

6. T   F   Most married people would like to have extramarital intercourse experiences.

7. T   F   Premarital sex is condoned for males because it gives them the experience they will need later on for marriage.

8. T   F   People who are involved in premarital sex are later likely to be involved in extramarital sex.

9. T   F   Swinging is practiced by emotionally disturbed persons.

10. T   F   Most people rate their sex lives very satisfactory.

11. Define:

(a) Normal sexual relations

(b) Abnormal sexual relations

12. Many people consider sex to be a problem area whether inside of or outside of marriage. What do you consider to be the major factors making it such a problem (list 5)?

(a)

(b)

(c)

(d)

(e)

Define the following:

13. Impotency

14. Frigidity

15. Adultery

16. Fornication

17. Coitus

18. Satyriasis

19. Ejaculatory incompetence

THE PROCREATION MYTH

James Collier

As humans evolved, so did sex—from its primary function of making babies to having fun

Sex is "for" making babies. Every schoolboy knows that. The idea is as ingrained in this society's consciousness as the concept of the cycle of the seasons or the inevitability of death. It is as obvious as moonrise and tide fall that sex is for reproduction. Nothing could be plainer. Man is propelled into the fevers of that splendid and ludicrous act by some basic drive wired into him by a beneficent Mother Nature bent on seeing that the species is preserved. Without the lovely fires of lust, there is no sex; without sex, there are no babies; without babies, there is no longer man. Indeed, so important is this bit of information that we call it *the* fact of life.

And since this fact is so central to our understanding of life, no wonder that it is the foundation stone on which all sexual thought has been built for ages. As the Christian Church puts it, in God's scheme, reproduction is the natural end and goal of that ineluctable moment. Therefore, any diversion from that natural course perverts God's law. All of Western society's basic strictures about abortion, birth control, masturbation, oral sex, pornography and the temptations of little girls, sheep, ducks and watermelons spring from the idea that sex is for reproduction and should not be used for any other purpose.

In the past couple of decades, a few people have suggested that perhaps we should not be quite so certain we know what God had in mind when He invented copulation: Perhaps He would not really care if we sometimes balled just for fun. Yet even if sex can be fun as well, surely its basic purpose must be conception.

As it happens, it isn't. The so-called facts of life are incorrect. On this point, our thinking is simply dead wrong. The Christian Church is wrong, most legal theory on sex is wrong; indeed, most secular sex theorists are wrong. In this article, I will try to show that for human beings, the main purpose of sex is not reproduction but something else. Conception—the making of babies—far from being the goal of copulation, is merely a rare, almost accidental by-product.

Sex, though it may not always seem so, is a ferociously complicated act. For most of man's existence, he had not had more than a vague inkling of what it is for and how it works. But the new science of ethology, new information about the labyrinthine dips and turnings of evolution and the new facts about sex and people turned up by Kinsey, Masters and Johnson, and their confreres are beginning to add up to a radically new picture of what our sex lives are all about.

The best place to begin is with the notion beloved by the Victorians that sex is not the same among human beings as it is among the other animals. People are higher beings; their sexual habits are of a quality different from those of pigs and baboons. And the old idea is correct: Human sexuality *is* different from that of the lower animals—for, unlike virtually all other forms of animal life man is endlessly preoccupied with sex. The affliction is relentless. From the point of view of any rational pig or baboon, man must seem a creature crazed with sex, a mad animal gripped by a permanent frenzy. There is no escaping it; before anything else, man is a sexual being. Consider: The statistically average human male—assuming there is such a creature—will have sexual intercourse between 1000 and 10,000 times in his life. Extrapolating from Kinsey's figures, we can put the mean somewhere around 5000. He will masturbate in adolescence and afterward some 1000 times. He is able to have an orgasm (though not ejaculation) long before he is first conscious of the experience. He is able to have an erection from the moment of birth and will do so 50,000 to 100,000 times thereafter. In fact, he may be born with an erection and die with one. Beyond this, he kisses, hugs, engages in occasional homosexuality, reads erotic books, goes to erotic movies and fantasizes endlessly about movie actresses, the girl in skintight jeans who just came into the classroom, visionary creatures invented by his own fertile imagination, boy scouts in short pants and even those aforementioned sheep, ducks and watermelons.

The sexual activity of his female consort is less direct, more subtle, but it is equally unremitting. She will have somewhat less intercourse than he. She will masturbate a good deal less—in some cases, perhaps not more than a few dozen times. She will fantasize about sex much less often. Yet, on the other hand, she will spend a considerable portion of every day appointing and anointing her body to make herself as sexually attractive as possible—

scouring her teeth with abrasives, smoothing her skin with powders, scenting the moist places of her body and fussing endlessly over the most minute details of her dress. This female obsession with appearance is unquestionably as sexual as male erection. Even when a woman chooses the low-calorie salad plate instead of the lasagna, she is being driven by her sexual nature.

It is important to understand that man's preoccupation with sex is not socially conditioned, not something that has been beaten into us from birth nor squeezed out of us by the constrictions of our puritanical society. Our concern with sex is innate, as much a part of us as the blood and bone with which we were born. In most human societies outside the so-called civilized world, every adult member of the group normally copulates at least once every 24 hours. Our own puny rates of copulation would cause gleeful amazement in cultures such as that of the Aranda of Australia, in which people often have intercourse three to five times nightly, the Thonga of Africa, in which it is not unusual for a man to make love to each of three or four wives in a single night, or the Chagga of Tanganyika, of whom one responsible authority reports that "intercourse ten times in a single night is not unusual"—although perhaps not always with orgasm. (As a matter of fact, Kinsey turned up a number of American men who regularly average 25 sex acts a week.) It is obvious that our own comparatively dismal copulatory record is not the natural human way but the result of centuries of self-imposed punitive attitudes toward sex. In nature, sex for humans is as regular as breakfast and sometimes lunch and dinner, too. Naturally, where the act is frequent, you would guess that less attention is paid to it; but this does not alter the fact that a constant, unremitting concern with sex is as basic a part of human nature as is the normal animal concern with food, air and water.

Now, lions are not always leering at lionesses on the veld, nor are their consorts constantly fussing with their fur. An endless preoccupation with sex is rare outside of the human being. No other mammal evidences it. Man's closest relations in the animal world, the great apes, are singularly unsexual creatures. This may surprise anybody who has spent any time in zoos, but it is true, nonetheless. In zoos, monkeys are prone to antics that make mothers hustle children off to the aviary; but new studies, most of them made within the past decade, clearly indicate that the behavior of captive animals is not normal behavior.

Zoologists such as George Schaller, Jane Goodall and the pioneer C. R. Carpenter, operating on the rather plausible assumption that animals in zoos do not behave the same way they do in their natural habitats, have begun to find ways of studying them in the wild. And they have consistently found that in nature, sex for many species is a far less pressing matter than it appears to be in zoos. Consider the work of Schaller, who has studied one of man's closest relatives, the mountain gorilla. By dint of patience and perseverance, Schaller was able to watch gorilla groups from very close hand—sometimes perching on a branch directly above them. In 466 hours of observation, he saw only two acts of copulation. By comparison, a similar study made on a group of Americans would reveal considerably more copulatory acts. Gorilla females are receptive to intercourse only three of four days a month and usually not at all in later stages of pregnancy or when nursing their young. Says Schaller, "Since most females are either pregnant or lactating, the . . . males in the group may on occasion spend as much as a year without sexual intercourse."

But the sex lives of human beings differ from those of other mammals in more ways than mere frequency. For example, Homo sapiens is the only known animal averse to copulation with its offspring, and he is one of very few mammals to form permanent mateships. But possibly most important of all is the mammalian process of oestrus.

All female mammals, with one exception, go through phases of sexual activity and passivity known as the oestruous cycle. (Oestrus should not be confused with menstruation, which is quite a different thing and limited to the higher primates only.) The oestrous cycle is of the utmost importance to sexuality, because it is entirely physiological—caused by the flow of various hormones alternating in sequence, which in turn are controlled by the hypothalamus, the brain's vital regulatory center. Oestrus has nothing to do with how an animal was brought up: You can produce the process in the lab with a hypodermic full of hormones.

During oestrus, the female mammal is not only willing but eager to copulate. In some species, she becomes positively nymphomaniacal during oestrus, forcing her attentions on one male after another in a way that would leave most humans gasping for relief. It all sounds rather jolly until you realize that the stretches between oestrus periods can be long, indeed. Perhaps even worse off than the poor gorilla are animals such as deer and bear, whose females come into oestrus only once a year. Even the oftmaligned cottontail rabbit is not interested in copulation six months of the year.

Few mammalian females will permit copulation when they are not in oestrus. In fact, males do not usually attempt it: Broadly speaking, mammalian males are aroused only by the physical provocation of oestrous females. Indeed, in the guinea pig and in the chinchilla, the vagina is actually covered by a flap of skin during the inactive period, making copulation physically impossible. (Exceptions occur in some primates whose females may present themselves in a copulatory position to show submissiveness in order to placate an angry dominant male or to win his favor for a bit of food.)

The oestrous cycle is a standard feature of mammalian life—so standard that one could almost use it as a definition. Almost, but not quite; because there is one species that does without it. And that species, of course, is man.

This is a fact of the utmost significance—as significant as the fact that we alone of all species make tools, have speech and can form abstract thought.

The creature we have come to call man almost certainly evolved from one of a group of jungle-dwelling apes present on earth during the Miocene era. About 13,000,000 years ago, the Miocene ended and was succeeded, according to Robert Ardrey's popular explanation, by a period of drought called the Pliocene, which lasted until 2,000,000 or so years back. With the coming of the great Pliocene drought, the forest shrank and was replaced by broad, grassy savannas. In increasing numbers, the great apes were deprived of the forest vegetation on which they had fed. Threatened with extinction, one group of beasts reacted by turning ever more to a diet of meat. Thus, there began to develop that unique creature, a carnivorous primate—man.

An ape, lacking claws, fangs and speed of foot, is poorly equipped to hunt. Indeed, even should he make a kill, he has no real means of getting at the meat inside the skin, as anybody who has tried to eat a deer whole will know. It was a question of adapt or die, and adapt he did. He evolved an erect posture that freed his hands for carrying weapons and allowed him to see over the grass, an apposable thumb for using tools and, above all, an ever-enlarging brain. And at the same time, his female began to level out her oestrous cycle. Instead of being driven periodically to intense sexual activity with long quiescent phases in between, she began to develop a pattern of steady but somewhat lower-level interest in sex. The male, too, changed,

so that instead of being sexually aroused only by an oestrous female, he was able to be excited by a whole range of stimuli associated with women, but especially by the sight of the female genitals.

Now, there is nothing automatic about evolution. No animal has an internal mechanism that it can call on to fix it up with horns or fangs to meet some change in its environment. Evolution occurs only when some animal happens to be born better suited to the environment than its fellows. Its teeth are just a mite longer, its claws a mite sharper, its pelvis a mite more suited to upright walking. It has an edge—and in the vast range of evolutionary time, even a minute edge will win out and spread through a species.

Thus do species acquire new traits. Furthermore, it's obvious that a species can acquire only traits that have some kind of survival value—a more efficient means of feeding, better protection against predators or disease, an improved method for begetting and nurturing offspring. (According to evolutionary theory, it is possible in certain circumstances for a species to acquire traits that have no survival value, but these instances are rare.)

It is clear that any trait that appears in the whole range of life is part of nature's plan. This is true of the oestrous cycle found in most mammals and it is equally true of the absence of oestrous periods in the human female. It was not philosophy nor experience that eliminated the oestrous cycle from womankind: It was the great laws of life. And this is rather odd, for the oestrous cycle is an extremely useful device—as, indeed, it must be, since it is so nearly universal among the mammals. Consider for a moment its virtues.

First and most obvious, oestrus allows copulation to occur only when the female is actually able to conceive. It is a kind of rhythm method in reverse, which prevents sex during the safe periods and is obviously a much more efficient reproductive system than the helter-skelter breeding of humans. Second, the oestrous system permits the strongest males to do most of the breeding. When all the females in the tribe are available constantly, the harem is too extensive for the jealous leader to guard successfully; but when the females come into oestrus only one or two at a time, the stronger animals can better dominate the sexual activity— for the general good of the species. Third, the oestrous system limits the amount of time the members of the group spend quarreling over their females, courting and breeding, and thus enables them to devote most of their energies to more important pursuits, such as the search for food and the care of the young.

Oestrus, then, is an effective system. But man does not use it. He has evolved in a different way. In other mammals, each act of copulation has a very high chance of leading to conception. In man, the ratio is reversed: Each act of intercourse has very nearly the minimum chance of ending in reproduction. Indeed, man has put oestrus so far behind him that it is most difficult, even with modern medical techniques, for him to tell with any real accuracy when the ripe egg is moving through the Fallopian tube and the female will be able to conceive. It is as if nature had deliberately gone out of her way to hinder man from obtaining maximum procreative efficiency. There is no way around it: The human reproductive method is extraordinarily wasteful and inefficient. And unless we are to abandon all we know about evolution, we are driven to admit that it has been designed that way by the laws of life. The plan—God's plan, if you wish—is that men should copulate at will, with no thought of reproduction.

This is not to say, of course, that sex has nothing to do with breeding. Nature is conservative: It likes to make one mechanism serve many functions when it can, like the clock on my desk that also serves as a paperweight. For man's precursors, those dimly seen apes hidden in the shadows of 10,000,000 years, sex was no doubt basically reproductive. But through those millions of years, the element of pleasure increased by infinitesimal degrees, until we can say today that reproduction is only a secondary function of sex. The original mammalian brain was merely a kind of message center driving the animal through more or less automatic responses. The human brain still performs this function, but it also has the added and humanly distinctive capability of abstract thought—similarly, with human sexuality.

After all, the human race could do enough breeding in a month to perpetuate the species. Even in the bad old days, when early man, with his stone axes and small brain, was losing some 75 per cent of his offspring before they reached maturity, one birth a year per woman was enough to bring about gradual population increase. Man never did need this surging, endless preoccupation with sex merely to perpetuate the species.

Let me make it clear that I do not mean something mystic—some mysterious drive or life force. When I say that as man evolved he abandoned the oestrous system, I am referring to physical facts having to do with hormone flow and pituitary functions. Man's glands, nerves and brain—the actual cells of his body—have been set, in ways we do not yet understand, by evolutionary processes to give him a constant sex life for a purpose other than reproduction.

What, then, is that purpose? At this stage in the study of the evolution of man's sexual patterns, we can do nothing more than make what are, we hope, shrewd guesses; but the answer, like so many other answers about the human being, almost certainly lies in his life as a carnivorous primate.

It is generally accepted that early man lived in groups of 30 to 80 men, women and children, which wandered about over a fairly large area of plain; the women and children, gathering roots, nuts, eggs and whatever else edible they came across, while the men hunted anything there was to hunt. We know that early man was eating large animals, such as the woolly mammouth, an elephantlike beast that stood nine and one half feet tall at the shoulder. It would have taken a concerted effort by a large number of men to hunt down and dispatch a beast of this size. It has been estimated that a band of this type would have needed a range of perhaps 25 miles each way, and it follows that given the exigencies of the chase, the group would often have become scattered with the women and children left hours, and perhaps even days, unprotected from the large cats with whom they shared the land. These cats—early versions of the leopard, among others—found the children of the two-legged beasts easy pickings. We have, in fact, the skull of a child who some 1,000,000 years ago died with the canine teeth of a leopard in his brain. But for an animal of any size, facing a group of men equipped with hand axes, sharply pointed sticks, perhaps even slings, was a different matter entirely. By perhaps 1,000,000 years ago, man had become the king of beasts, unconquerable by any living thing—as long as he worked, played, hunted, fought and died in groups. For the human being, the group was crucial. Outside it, there was no survival; fragmented, its members were picked off one by one. But drawn together into a rudimentary social system, the group became an all-conquering force, a power so mighty that within a sliver of universal time, it has turned forests into desert and back again and recklessly driven into extinction one species after another. The power of man in groups is awe-inspiring and the glue that has kept the group together is sex. The pleasure of sex is the basis of society. The key necessity, for the several million years of man's existence, has been to keep the men with the women and children. What, for example, was to stop the hunters, once they had made the kill, from camping there in the wilderness until they were replete? Who among us would look forward to dragging a ton of raw meat back home over 25 miles of rocky plain to a cave full of nattering women and squalling babies?

There must have been a reason for going home, and the one that comes to mind, of course, is sex. It follows that groups in which the women were most often available for sex had a survival edge—an adaptive advantage. That is to say, the longer that the women in the tribe were in oestrus, the bigger the survival factor. (By the opposite token, those men who decided to skip the trip home and have sex with each other did not reproduce, so in an evolutionary sense, homosexuality was a negative trait.) Accordingly, the oestrous cycle lengthened and lengthened at both ends, until it finally met at the middle. And if you want to have a little speculative fun with the theory, you can guess that the explanation for the tendency among many women to be more sexually inspired around menstruation—before and after—is simply that at these points lies the beginning of the now-vanished oestrous period.

And so, finally, we are faced with the inescapable fact that the primary function of sex in human lives is to provide pleasure. What does it all mean? Simply, that an ethical code based on the theory that the primary function of sex is reproduction is built on quicksand. Two thousand years of Judaeo-Christian effort to get human beings to copulate only to procreate has failed precisely because the dogmatists had the facts wrong. You can insist that the world is flat if you like—but you will never discover America if you do. Equally, as long as we continue to base our sexual philosophy on a scientific untruth, we will continue to plague ourselves with bad marriages, illegitimate children, mechanical and inept intercourse and all the other ills our unhappy ethic has brought us. Reason is strong; man is strong. But he cannot fly in the face of nature, because he is part of nature. The evidence points to a defensible, scientifically valid argument that in human beings, the purpose of sex is pleasure; and on that realization we must build our sex code for the next millennium.

THE FOLKLORE OF MARITAL RELATIONS—THE GREAT COITAL MYTH
Albert Ellis

The fact is that almost all of what we call "sexual incompatibility" in marriage is quite unnecessary and is largely created and abetted by our Great Coital Myth.

Considering the hullabaloo that is made about courtship and premarital sex relations in our public prints and productions, references are surprisingly rare to the particular form of human behavior to which courtship is supposed to lead, that is, marital copulation. References to sex organs and to coitus can occasionally be found in the mass media of our culture, almost invariably in some euphemistic form. But in the hundreds of stories that are told and enacted each week in our popular magazines, over our radio airways, and on our movie and television screens, it is almost unheard of to find any allusion to what married couples do in bed.

From other sources, however, it is not too difficult to discover (a) what, according to our folklore and sexual tabus, husbands and wives are *supposed* to do in the privacy of the marriage bed; and (b) what they *actually* do. What spouses should—or should not—do after they put out the television set and the cat, may, perhaps, best be gleaned from a perusal of our statute books. Almost every state in the Union, we learn, has a law against what is called sodomy or unnatural sex acts. Robert Veit Sherwin, in his book on *Sex and the Statutory Law,* tells us that a typical sodomy statute reads as follows: "Every person who shall carnally know, or shall have sexual intercourse in any manner with any animal or bird, or shall carnally know any male or female by the anus (rectum) or with the mouth or tongue; or who shall attempt intercourse with a dead body . . . is guilty of Sodomy."[1]

A few states which do not specifically legislate against sodomy, or define it as does the above stat-

Albert Ellis, *The American Sexual Tragedy* (New York: Lyle Stuart, Inc., 1962), pp. 75-82, 85-96. Reprinted by permission of the publisher.

ute, have other laws against unnatural sex acts. Thus, New Hampshire has a "Lascivious Acts" law which declares in effect that "whoever commits any unnatural and lascivious act with another person, is subject to a maximum term of five years, or a maximum fine of one thousand dollars or both." Vermont has a statute entitled "An Act Relating to Sexual Perverts," which states in effect "that any person participating in the act of copulating the mouth of one person with the sexual organ of another is subject to a maximum penalty of five years imprisonment."[2]

"In Georgia," Sherwin notes, "there is perhaps the most interesting distinction of all in the way of two separate statutes. The Sodomy Statute declares that sodomy is the carnal knowledge and connection against the order of nature by man with man, or, in the same unnatural manner with women. And the penalty given for said act is life at hard labor. And the cases that have followed and interpreted the statute declare further that connections *per os* and *per anum* are included in the statute's coverage. Then there is a statute entitled 'Bestiality' and it defines it as the carnal knowledge and connection against the order of nature of a man or woman in any manner with a beast, and the penalty is five to twenty years."[3]

Harriet F. Pilpel and Theodora Zavin, in their recent book, *Your Marriage and the Law*[4] summarize our legal attitudes toward marital copulation in this way: "If there is any one policy behind our laws governing sexual conduct, it seems to be that they are directed to channelling all sex relations into so-called normal intercourse in marriage. In this sense, 'normal' intercourse . . . must be the type of sexual contact that can lead to the procreation of children. . ."

Typical penalties for violating a sodomy law or for engaging in what is termed unnatural sex practices even with one's own husband or wife, Sherwin tells us, range from one to ten years imprisonment and/or a one thousand dollar fine. Some of the harsher jail penalties may be found in Arkansas (5—21 years), Connecticut (30 years), Florida (20 years), Georgia (life at hard labor), Massachusetts (20 years), Minnesota (20 years), Nebraska (20 years), Ohio (1—20 years), Rhode Island (7—20 years), and Utah (3—20 years).

In addition, Sherwin, Pilpel and Zavin, and Judge Morris Ploscowe[5] inform us, "unnatural" sex acts are often heavily penalized in civil court cases, in that divorce and annulments are frequently granted where one spouse claims that the other cruelly mistreated him or her by insisting upon par-

ticipation in oral-genital, anal, or other so-called unnatural marital acts.

In the light of these heavily censorious and legally penalizing attitudes toward certain sex practices in marriage, we might suppose that Americans would rarely engage in these acts. All the facts that have ever been gathered in this connection, however, prove the contrary. G. V. Hamilton (in *A Research in Marriage*[6]) some twenty-five years ago found that almost fifty per cent of the hundred husbands he interviewed admitted practicing fellatio, cunnilinctus, or other sex relations that are termed unnatural with their wives. Kinsey, Pomeroy, and Martin (in *Sexual Behavior in the Human Male*[7]) report that "mouth-genital contacts of some sort, with the subject as either the active or the passive member in the relationship, occur at some time in the histories of nearly sixty per cent of all males."

Since even the most liberal Americans are loathe to admit these sex practices, the figures of Hamilton and Kinsey may be taken as minimum estimates of the actual frequency of so-called perverse relations. These minimum figures would tend to show that, on the basis of this type of sex activity alone, over half our married couples deserve severe fines and/or jail sentences.

Although they do not literally expect to be arrested, literally millions of our married couples guiltily refrain from these acts because our laws and our folklore deem them iniquitous. I had, for example, a fifty-year-old patient who, for thirty years of married life, had been avoiding everything but what he called normal intercourse (and rigidly permitting himself that but once a week, no matter how often he and his wife desired it). When, after several sessions of psychotherapy, he began, for the first time in his life, really to enjoy his marital sex relations, he came to me in a near-panic state and said: "We're doing almost everything now, doctor. But isn't it really wrong? Aren't we getting to be *perverted?*"

"Perverted?" I replied. "Actually, you've been a pervert for thirty years before you came for psychotherapy; and now, when for the first time you're becoming fairly normal, you talk of being a pervert!"

I went on to explain the following facts to this patient. From the standpoint of scientific fact it is virtually impossible to label any sex act abnormal or perverted or deviant. In the last analysis, any human act becomes abnormal because the citizens of a given community unconsciously or consciously decide to view it as abnormal, and not because we have any indubitable, invariant standard of normality which we can apply to all peoples at all times in all places.[8] When we call a sex act abnormal because it is statistically rare (as in the case of incest), we must realize that society's views and laws concerning the act have often made it rare. When we call sex behavior abnormal because it is biologically inappropriate (such as homosexuality or oral-genital relations which cannot lead to reproduction), we must remember that our concepts of biological inappropriateness—such as the concept that reproduction is more valuable than sex satisfaction—are community-made, essentially biased viewpoints. When we label sex activity as abnormal because it seems to be injurious to mental or physical health (as in the case of sadism, necrophilia, or exhibitionism), we should acknowledge that exceptionally few sex acts are dangerous or health-destroying in themselves, but that many become self-destructive because society insists on viewing them as such and making them so. (Rape, for example, actually inflicts little or no harm on adult victims if they are raised to view it lightly; but if they are raised to look upon it as a heinous attack, they may actually be seriously harmed by it.) When we call sex acts abnormal because they are illegal or "immoral" (as in the case of public nudity or adulterous sex relations), then we patently are making them abnormal by social fiat rather than by any unassailable definition.

All told, then, only the rarest of sexual activities—such as sexual murder—would be universally agreed upon, by all peoples of the world, as being indubitably abnormal. And these rare acts, we invariably find, are committed by individuals who are psychotic. Sex acts committed by non-psychotics might be labeled (from the standpoint of their statistical frequency) peculiar, strange, or bizarre; but it is almost impossible to find any universal criterion by which they may be unequivocally labelled abnormal or perverted.

From a psychological standpoint, however, there is a fairly reasonable and accurate means of describing a sexual (or a nonsexual) act as abnormal, perverted, or deviant, and that is by using the criterion of fixation, fetishism, or exclusivity. Psychologically speaking, any act is abnormal or neurotic if an individual performs these acts because he has arbitrarily narrowed down a potentially wide field of action into a very limited act which he feels that he must perform if he is to be comfortable or satisfied.

Eating habits may be taken as an example. Theoretically, any average human being can eat and enjoy a good many different kinds of food. Suppose, however, a given person, who is in good physical health and has no special allergic reactions, insists on eating nothing but meat and potatoes; or suppose he only will eat once a day, at three in the morning, and will not touch a bit of food at any other time, even if he is starving; or suppose he will only eat off a particular set of blue plates, and will absolutely refuse to eat if these are not available. In any of these instances, even though we would be hardly justified in calling this individual wrong or immoral, we may justifiably call him, from a psychological standpoint, abnormal, fetishistic, neurotic, or deviant.

Similarly, with human sexuality. Although as great a psychologist as Sigmund Freud made a serious mistake by trying to distinguish between "neurotic" behavior and sexually deviated or "perverted" behavior, it has become clear in recent years that the two are actually the same, and that sexual deviants are actually emotionally disturbed, or "neurotic," individuals who are fetishistically attached to some particular type of sex activity—and who usually, though not always, became fetishistically attached to this form of behavior because of peculiarities or fixations which arose during their childhood. Sexual neuroses are essentially the same as other forms of neurosis—except that, in our antisexual society, we emotionalize them and tend to view them in a special light.

The psychological criterion of sexual "abnormality," therefore, becomes that of fetishism or exclusivity. A brief consideration of homosexual behavior may illustrate most clearly. As I have elsewhere pointed out,[9] there is nothing "abnormal" or "deviant" about homosexual activity in itself—since the human animal is biologically plurisexed, and will (if not arbitrarily hemmed in by his culture) engage spontaneously in monosexual (masturbatory), heterosexual, and homosexual acts at different times during his life. Normally, in a sexually restrictive culture like our own, he learns to give up most monosexual and homosexual activity, and to confine himself, especially after marriage, to heterosexual behavior. But the point is that he does so because he *learns* to be heterosexual, not because he is created so by nature. Even in our own culture, which is violently opposed to homosexuality, Kinsey and his associates[10] have reported that some 37 per cent of all males exhibit homosexual behavior at some time during their lives; and the probability is that the vast majority of all males at some time desire to participate in homosexual activity, but many refrain from doing so out of guilt and fear.

If, then, a male in our culture engages in some homosexual behavior, alongside of his more socially acceptable heterosexual activities, we are hardly justified in calling him abnormal from almost any standpoint—since biologically, statistically, and psychologically he is behaving in a normal fashion. But suppose this male becomes *mainly* or *exclusively* homosexual. Then, from a psychological standpoint, there is little doubt that he is fixated, neurotic, or abnormal. For unless we believe that homosexuality is innate or inborn in some individuals—which virtually no psychologist who has kept up with the recent literature now believes—it is clear that an exclusive homosexual is neurotically afraid of heterosexuality, or is fearfully fixated on a homosexual level of behavior, or is obsessed with the idea of homosexuality, or is compulsively attached to homosexual activity, or is otherwise neurotically (or perhaps psychotically) attached to his exclusive homosexual activity. If he merely prefers homosexual to heterosexual relations (as a man may prefer blondes to brunettes), that is one thing; but if he simply cannot, under any circumstances, engage in any kind of heterosexual behavior, then he is unquestionably emotionally disturbed, and hence "abnormal" or "deviant."

Most educated individuals have little difficulty in seeing that exclusive homosexuals in our culture are psychologically disturbed or deviant, but they are loath to admit that heterosexuality, too, can also be neurotic. The fact is, however, that what is scientific sauce for the goose should also be sauce for the gander, and that exclusive heterosexuality can be just as fetishistic as exclusive homosexuality. This does not mean that all individuals in our culture who are exclusively heterosexual are neurotic—though it might be maintained, with some justification, that such individuals are afflicted with a social rather than an individual neurosis, in that their social upbringing arbitrarily induces them to abhor one perfectly natural mode of sex activity. Assuming, though, that exclusive heterosexuals are not necessarily neurotic, the fact remains that *some* of them are—namely, those heterosexuals who are distinctly *afraid* of homosexuality, who are compulsively heterosexual, and who under no circumstances (even, say, if marooned on a desert island with only other males for a long period of time) could permit themselves to engage in homosexual activity.

Similarly, for other sex activities. If a human being, from time to time enjoys unusual sex participations, such as being beaten while he is having sex relations, or copulation with animals, or having intercourse with members of the other sex who are dressed in some special way, we may justifiably call him odd, or peculiar, or statistically unusual. But we may not, from a psychological (or biological) standpoint, justifiably call him abnormal, perverted, or deviant. If, however, this same man *mainly* or *only* enjoys sex relations of some special sort, then we may, psychologically speaking, call him fixated, neurotic, or abnormal. By the same token, if a man can *only* enjoy one special mode of statistically prevalent sex relations, such as having intercourse in one single face-to-face position, or having it only when the moon is out and an orchestra is playing sweet music in the background; then we can justifiably call him neurotic or abnormal—since it is clear that out of many possible forms of pleasurable sex relations, he has arbitrarily and fetishistically selected a single one, and ruled out all others.

It may be asked whether, if certain sex acts, such as bestiality or necrophilia, are not to be considered as being perverted as long as they are not an individual's main or exclusive form of sexual response, they are nonetheless to be considered undesirable. The answer, in regard to some of these acts, is obviously yes. There is nothing, for example, necessarily neurotic or perverted about an individual's robbing a bank or picking a fistfight with his fellow citizens—at least, in some instances. Yet, we would not ordinarily encourage such acts. Similarly, my own prejudices lead me to believe that such acts as rape and sexual assault should definitely be discouraged, although I should rarely consider a rapist as a pervert. Several kinds of sex behavior may well be considered dangerous or antisocial, and consequently banned by a given society. But these types of activity should not be confused with neurotic or perverted sex acts—which, I insist, should scientifically be conceived of as sex relations which have been fetishistically and arbitrarily singled out by an individual for his main or exclusive practice.

My patient, then, who had been for many years fearfully avoiding all kinds of sex relations except what he thought was the normal, face-to-face, position in intercourse, and who in addition had been restricting himself to copulate but once a week throughout his married life, was psychologically neurotic or abnormal; and he only began to become unneurotic and nondeviant when he began to extend the range and frequency of his sex acts. When I told him that he had actually been abnormal or perverted for many years he was, as I had intended him to be, quite shocked. Since then, he has come to see that I was right; that he is now, for the first time in his married life, becoming psychologically normal or nonperverted.

To return to the conflict between our sex statutes concerning what they interpret as unnatural sex practices and our actual participation in such practices: the situation becomes even more ridiculous when we note that many modern sex manuals are specifically recommending the very acts that they call unnatural and that are still criminally punishable in virtually all our states. Thus, the very latest edition of Hannah and Abraham Stone's authoritative and widely sold book, *A Marriage Manual*,[11] states: "I do not think that we can consider any particular method of sexual union as normal or abnormal. . . Variety in the sexual approach is much to be desired for marital sexual satisfaction. . . There is nothing perverse or degrading, I would say, in any sex practice which is undertaken for the purpose of promoting a more harmonious sexual adjustment between a husband and wife in marriage." Presumably, for recommendations like this, the Stones and many other writers of modern sex manuals should be arrested and jailed for inciting to the commission of a felony in most of the states of the Union!

Another great American myth, which goes hand in hand with that of the vaginal orgasm, is that, in spite of the fact that they truly love each other, many couples are naturally sexually incompatible, and that therefore they cannot get along in marriage. Actually, if these couples thought about it instead of *just* believing this myth, it would be most difficult, and in some ways almost impossible, for them to be sexually incompatible.

Sexual incompatibility exists, usually, when a husband desires a greater frequency or a different mode of sex relations than does his wife, or when a wife desires sex relations more often or differently than does her husband. Perhaps ninety-five per cent of all such incompatibility exists because, in our culture, we make a fetich of one particular form of sex play—namely, penile-vaginal coitus— and neglect most other sex activities.

Consider, by way of illustration, the case of Mr. Jennings, as presented by his wife. "My husband," she said to me when she came to ask about getting a divorce, "is simply—well, impossible. It's not that

I'm sexually cold myself; in fact, I believe that I'm perfectly normal. But he just seems to be insatiable. He *always* seems to want intercourse." ("Jennings" is a pseudonym, of course.)

"How many times a week do you actually have sex relations?" I asked. "Oh, about two or three times a week. That's quite enough for me: plenty, in fact. But he could have it, apparently, every night—maybe two or three times a night. And I, of course, I could never do *that*."

I was skeptical; not that she couldn't or at least shouldn't have coitus with her husband two or three times a night, when she was satisfied with two or three times a week, but that she couldn't and quite easily, have *sex relations* with him quite as often as he wanted. I explained to her, as I have to do to so many of my patients, that coitus and sex relations are by no means synonymous, and that the former is only one of the many possible ways of engaging in the latter. I showed her how, quite easily, she could have noncoital sex relations with her husband, especially employing manual manipulation, several times a night, if that is what he desired.

At first, she presented the usual objections: "But is that *right*, doctor? Isn't that just like—well, *masturbation?*"

In the first place, I replied, it is not like masturbation, in that *two* partners are being involved. But even more important, I added, masturbation, whether solitary or mutual, is a perfectly natural mode of sex activity, and is not to be sneered at or moralized about by any intelligent person. Both the normal male and female animal are (whether we like it or not) designed so that they require *some* form of phallic (clitoral or penile) friction in order to achieve satisfactory orgasm. *What* form this friction takes is essentially irrelevant; and derogatorily to designate one mode of friction as mutual masturbation while, at the same time, approvingly to designate another mode as natural or normal intercourse is ridiculous.

I continued, in this wise, to tell Mrs. Jennings (perhaps fifteen years belatedly) the facts of married love; and, fortunately, she listened attentively and was willing to learn. The upshot was that she stopped considering herself a martyr to her husband's "inordinate" sex demands, and began to satisfy him, in one way or another, every time he desired to have sex relations. He too, at first, was inclined to be somewhat disturbed about having noncoital sex relations, up to and including orgasm, with his wife; but a single session with me calmed his qualms, and gave him a new, realistic outlook on marital sex activities. In the end—as I had predicted to Mrs. Jennings might well be the case—it turned out that five or six climaxes a week, and not two or three a day, were quite sufficient for Mr. Jennings. It was just that, having fewer than the number of orgasms he normally required, he and his wife both imagined that he was almost insatiable—just as a man who consumes fifteen hundred calories of food a day, instead of his needed twenty-five hundred, will be hungry virtually all the time, and will get the illusion that he could regularly consume thirty-five hundred calories daily. It also turned out—as I had also predicted it might—that in the course of satisfying her husband noncoitally when she did not feel like having intercourse with him, Mrs. Jennings not infrequently became sexually aroused herself and came to desire more orgasms than she ordinarily thought herself capable of desiring. All together, the Jennings now have a marriage that is quite sexually, as well as otherwise, compatible.

On the other side of the fence, consider the case of Mrs. Robin . . . She came to me with this problem.[12] "It's not that I don't get aroused when my husband makes passes at me. I always do. But then, when we have intercourse, nothing happens, and I'm just as aroused at the end as I was in the beginning. The next day I'm all tense and can hardly do anything. Naturally, when he wants intercourse again, I start making excuses, saying that I'm tired, or pretending that I'm still menstruating. He's not stupid, of course, and I'm sure he often knows what I'm doing and feels hurt. But how can I help it?"

After further questioning had elicited the information that Mrs. Robin began masturbating at the age of thirteen, the interview proceeded as follows:

Counselor: Do you obtain a satisfactory orgasm through masturbation?

Mrs. Robin: Oh, yes, always.

Counselor: And about how long does it take you to do so—how many minutes of active manipulation of the clitoris?

Mrs. Robin: Oh, about fifteen to twenty minutes.

Counselor: Ever less than fifteen minutes?

Mrs. Robin: No, I don't think so.

Counselor: And when you have intercourse with your husband, does he ever manipulate your clitoris before actual entry?

Mrs. Robin: Yes, he usually does. He knows all about that, having read a book on it.

Counselor: And how long does he manipulate your clitoris?

Mrs. Robin: Oh, about four or five minutes I would say.

Counselor: Ever any longer than five minutes?

Mrs. Robin: No, I don't think so. No, I'd say never more than that.

Counselor: Why not?

Mrs. Robin: Well—I—well, he just seems to think that's long enough.

Counselor: And have you ever talked to him about it—ever let him know that it isn't long enough?

Mrs. Robin: I—uh—no, no we never have talked about it. I—uh—I guess we're—uh—we're ashamed to talk about things like that.

Counselor: Well, if, as you say, it never takes you yourself less than fifteen minutes of active manipulation to give yourself an orgasm—and you, you know, are a better judge of your own sensations than anyone else can possibly be—how do you expect your husband to help you achieve a climax in no more than five minutes? You should tell your husband what your sex requirements are so that he can act accordingly. You cannot expect him to be a mindreader or to figure them out for himself.

Mrs. Robin quickly got the idea. From that very night on, her sex problem with her husband began to be worked through and now they are fully sexually compatible.

The fact is that since women, in our culture, have for many centuries been sexually subservient to men, and have not been *supposed* to enjoy sex relations a cult of coitus has arisen whose main premises are: (1) that the only proper and manly form of sex relations is penile-vaginal copulation; (2) that whenever the husband is sexually desirous, it is his right to beg, cajole, or demand coital relations with his wife and that, to keep him happy, she must acquiesce just about as frequently as he desires; (3) that the wife must obtain her sex satisfaction, including orgasm, through the same type of vaginal-penile intercourse that satisfies her husband; (4) that if the wife wishes to have intercourse more than her husband, that is just too bad for her; and (5) that, all told, the perfect union is one where husband and wife naturally and automatically desire intercourse exactly the same number of times per week or month, and where serious discrepancies exist in their desires, sexual incompatibility is inevitable.

This, we say, is the Great Coital Myth of past and contemporary American (and Western European) culture. Actually, the facts, as revealed by modern psychosexual research, are these:

1. Although coitus is *one* of the most satisfying of human sex experiences, it is not necessarily *the* most satisfying experience for all men and women. In psychosexual research with average

males, as well as in clinical contact with disturbed ones, it is continually found that, in spite of their being instilled in our culture with prejudices against sex practices that are called unnatural, almost all males can be brought to satisfying orgasms by several different kinds of sexual activity, especially by coitus, manual manipulation of the penis, and oral-genital relations. In my clinical practice, I invariably find that those males who have the idea that they can only be satisfied through coitus are literally guilty or afraid of being satisfied in other ways; and that when their fear or guilt is removed through education or psychotherapy, they find noncoital sex relations as satisfying, or almost as satisfying, as coitus. One of the main reasons why men exaggerate the importance of coitus is because they are raised to believe that this is the only "manly" method of sex relations. When they rid themselves of this arbitrary notion, their coital fetiches usually vanish, and they become much more labile as far as the range of their sex satisfactions are concerned. Men who are released from believing in the sacredness of coitus frequently find that they derive more satisfaction from some forms of noncoital relations than they do from sexual intercourse.

2. Women, to even a greater degree than men, may often be fully satisfied by noncoital relations. Many women, in fact, find it difficult or impossible to achieve orgasm during intercourse, even when there has been considerable previous sex play, but find it easy to achieve orgasm through noncoital manipulation alone. Women who do enjoy coitus, and who sometimes or often receive orgasm in the course of it, usually do not need it for orgasmic relief, but may obtain full climax by manual, oral, or other manipulation of the clitoris, vulva, and/or introitus (entrance to the vagina). Although, in our culture, a good many women feel that they must have intercourse for full orgasmic release, this is often actually untrue: since, when they are released (through proper sex education or psychotherapy) from the idea that they must have intercourse to have full orgasm, they usually begin to have perfectly satisfactory climaxes in noncoital relations. There are many women who certainly seem to have the most pleasurable forms of sex activity when they have intercourse; but is as yet unclear whether their needs in this connection are largely physiological or psychological. One of my patients who at first swore that no sen-

sation could possibly equal that which she obtained through coitus, was surprised to find, when she experimented without prejudice, that her husband's manipulating the inside of her vagina with his fingers gave her the most powerful orgasm she had ever experienced; and several of my patients who also swore by coitus at first were later willing to admit that, when they let themselves go sexually and surrendered their prejudices against noncoital relations, their husbands' manual or oral manipulation of their clitorises gave them a more intense and satisfying sensation than coitus ever had.

3. Although there is nothing to be lost, and often much to be gained, by a husband and wife's trying to adjust themselves sexually so that they each achieve an orgasm during intercourse, and often achieve it simultaneously, there is danger in their convincing themselves that mutual orgasm in intercourse is the only or even necessarily the best mode of sex satisfaction on all occasions. Orgasm is orgasm, however and whenever achieved, and may be thoroughly enjoyable on a nonsimultaneous basis. A husband may legitimately give his wife an orgasm before or after he has one himself—or without ever having one himself. Similarly, a wife may help her husband to achieve a climax before, or entirely apart from her own climax(es). In many marriages, the achievement of simultaneous orgasm in intercourse will seldom or never occur; and still the spouses may have a truly satisfying and perfectly compatible sex life.

4. There are some reasons to believe that many females, when fully released from sexual inhibitions and tabus, are biologically more sexually adequate than the average male. Sexually released women, very often, may have climaxes that are more frequent, more intense, and more lasting than those had by equally released men. Consequently, no man should in any way feel ashamed of the fact that he cannot fully satisfy his mate solely by means of penile-vaginal intercourse. It may well be only the rare male who thus can satisfy a sexually released, reasonably highly-sexed female. In the event that a given husband cannot satisfy his wife by means of coitus, he can, and certainly should, satisfy her by some other means. Similarly, if a wife cannot satisfy her husband by means of coitus, or if for some reason she does not frequently enjoy coitus, she should satisfy him in some noncoital manner.

5. Considerable more realism about marital sex relations is desirable in modern marriage. Although husbands and wives should normally not engage in coitus when both do not desire it, there is no reason whatever why they should not sexually satisfy each other in one or more non-coital ways when they do not themselves desire to be satisfied. Every wife who loves her husband does numerous things she does not enjoy doing in order to help him and keep their marriage a going partnership: for example, cooking, washing dishes, shopping, and housecleaning. To add to these chores another ten or fifteen minutes of manipulating her husband's genitals, even when she is not sexually aroused herself, is certainly more important to his, and therefore to her own, happiness than many of the other non-pleasant jobs she performs. Moreover, if she does overcome her inertia and attempts to satisfy her husband sexually whenever he wants to be satisfied, the chances are, that in the process, she herself will often become sexually aroused, and will find considerably more pleasure in sex acts than she would otherwise find.

By the same token, although it is true that most men lose their sexual desire to satisfy their wives after they themselves have had a climax, and although it is true that it is not easy for all males to hold off their climaxes until their wives are ready for their final orgasm, there is nothing too onerous about a man's giving his wife two or three more orgasms, if she desires them, after he has had his first and/or last for the evening. Marriage involves all kinds of not too pleasant duties and responsibilities; and unless a man sufficiently loves his wife and has enough interest in satisfying her no matter what may be the number of orgasms she requires per day or week, he has no business marrying her in the first place. The sexual responsibilities of marriage are no more troublesome than many of its other responsibilities, and it is often more important that they be maturely and realistically acknowledged and fulfilled.

6. Naturally, there are exceptions to every rule. Some males or females, for example, seem to be almost continually aroused sexually, and would want an enormous amount of sex relations from their mates. Other men and women insist that their spouses satisfy them sexually in some particular way—such as through intercourse or through oral or anal relations—which the spouse is either incapable of performing or finds highly distasteful In such cases, where the sex demands of one spouse become a real imposition on the goodwill of the other, a psychologist or marriage counselor should be consulted to determine whether the imposed-upon or imposing mate is acting in an unreasonable or emotionally disturbed manner; and, with the help of professional assistance, some adjustment usually may be made. If it cannot be, then divorce or separation may be necessary, or one of the partners (or both) may have to compromise seriously with his or her sexual needs in order for the marriage to continue on a peaceable basis. My own marriage counseling experience shows, however, that true sexual incompatibility is quite rare in marriage, and that most of what is called sexual incompatibility is actually the result of sex ignorance and arbitrary bias, often accompanied by lack of love and emotional disturbance.[13]

7. There are various techniques of prolonging coitus, such as those outlined in Edwin Hirsch's *The Power to Love* and *Modern Sex Life*[14] and in G. Lombard Kelly's *Sexual Feeling in Married Men and Women.*[15] There are also various emotional and physiological reasons why some males suffer from premature ejaculation, and many cases of this type of sex disturbance may be cured or alleviated by proper psychological or medical treatment. The average male in our culture, however, as Kinsey and his associates have shown in *Sexual Behavior in the Human Male,*[16] takes less than five minutes of active copulation to reach a climax; and many women simply cannot be brought to their climaxes in less than ten minutes of coitus, while many other women apparently can never, or at best can rarely, reach a climax solely through coitus. The obvious solution, therefore, to the problem of the relatively short-timed climax of many men and the relatively long-timed climax of many women is to have some of the husbands of the long-timed women resort to extra-coital methods of bringing their wives to orgasm. In the case of those women (who are probably relatively few) who require actual intromission for sexual satisfaction, husbands who are not sufficiently potent to meet this requirement by means of penile-vaginal intercourse may still effectively do so in many instances by using their fingers to massage the inside of the wife's vagina (while, preferably, using the fingers of the other hand to massage the clitoris). The chances are that those women who cannot, under any circumstances, be satisfied with manipulation of the clitoris, vulva, and/or vagina, but who specifically re-

quire penile-vaginal coitus, are fetichistically attached to the idea of coitus, and should undergo some form of psychotherapy or counseling in order to release themselves from their fetichistic attachments. Similarly any men who cannot be sexually satisfied with any other form of sex activity but coitus are probably fetichistically attached to this idea, and should undergo psychotherapy to help them overcome their fetich.

Because of the discrepancies existing between the Great American Coital Myth and the actual facts of human sexuality, many sexually incompatible marriages do, in fact, exist, and do give rise, every year, to literally hundreds of thousands of divorces, annulments, separations, desertions, twin beds, twin bedrooms, and widespread marital starvation in the midst of plenty. Not only are innumerable wives and husbands sexually starved because, as a result of the ignorance encouraged by this Great Coital Myth, their mates do not know how to satisfy them, but—even greater tragicomedy!—countless other mates are sexually frustrated because, although they and their spouses refuse to employ them because they consider these techniques unnatural, immature, or unmanly.

(It may be parenthetically noted, as well, that in the area of premarital and extramarital relations, where noncoital sex relations are particularly desirable because they eliminate virtually all possibility of pregnancy or disease, numberless males and females refuse to employ these techniques, and instead insist on either coitus or abstinence: because, like their married confreres and consoeurs, they consider petting to climax to be immature, unmanly, or perverted. Among all the modern moralists who attempt to prevent young people from having premarital copulation, only one current writer—Alex Comfort in *Sexual Behavior in Society*[17]—seems to go to the logical conclusion of actually advocating premarital petting, up to and including orgasm, as an intelligent and logical substitute for coitus.)

The fact is, that almost all of what we call sexual incompatibility in marriage is quite unnecessary, and is actually created and abetted by our Great Coital Myth. Likewise, probably the great majority of the literally millions of instances where wives are "frigid" and husbands "impotent," and where spouses are distressed by their mate's or their own desires for extracoital sex play, are directly or indirectly traceable to ideas and attitudes stemming from this Great Coital Myth. Marital sex relations, in these United States, are officially and unoffi-

cially conceived of as coital sex relations; and anything over, under, or around this limited sex technique just does not count—or counts so much as to make the spouses liable to being jailed.

It is not clear, from the anthropological literature, how unique the worship of the Great Coital Myth is to Western Civilization. Many other peoples of the world permit and encourage extra-coital sex relations. Clellan S. Ford and Frank A. Beach, for example, tell us that manual stimulation of the female genitalia by the male is commonly prevalent in several societies, including the Aranda, Aymara, Azande, Chamorro, Crow, Dahomeans, Hopi, Koryak, Ponca, Siriono, and the Trobrianders. Manual stimulation of the male genitals by women normally occurs among the Alorese, Aranda, Crow, Hopi, Siriono, Tikopia, Trobrianders, and Wogeo. Oral stimulation of the genitals is also encouraged by several peoples, particularly among the Trobriand Islanders and the Alorese, Aranda, Kusaians, Marquesans, Ponapeans, and Trukese.[18]

It is not clear from anthropological reports, however, which societies encourage extra-coital sex play (a) merely as preliminaries to coitus and/or (b) as orgasm-producing techniques in their own right. It would appear that in most instances the former type of permissiveness, and not the latter, exists; and that almost none of the peoples of this globe frankly and openly, abet noncoital sex relations up to and including orgasm. The human male, in almost all past and present societies, seems to have dominated the sex scene to the extent of foisting *his* desired practices on the human female, and he seems to have done so largely by promulgating the tenets of the Great Coital Myth. As idiotic as we Americans are in this connection, we at least appear to be typical rather than unique.

NOTES

1. Robert Veit Sherwin, *Sex and the Statutory Law*. New York: Oceana Publications, 1949, p. 36.

2. *Ibid.*, p. 36-37.

3. *Ibid.*, p. 37.

4. Harriet F. Pilpel and Theodora Zavin, *Your Marriage and the Law*. New York: Rinehart, 1952.

5. Morris Ploscowe, *Sex and the Law*. New York: Prentice-Hall, 1951.

6. G.V. Hamilton, *A Research in Marriage*. New York: Boni, 1929.

7. Alfred C. Kinsey, Wardell B. Pomeroy, and Clyde E. Martin, *Sexual Behavior in the Human Male*. Philadelphia: Saunders, 1948.

8. Albert Ellis, "What Is Normal Sex Behavior?" *Complex*, 1952, 8, 41-51.

9. ———, "On the Cure of Homosexuality," *Internat. J. Sexology*, 1952, 5, 135-38.

10. Alfred C. Kinsey and others, *op. cit.*

11. Hannah Stone and Abraham Stone, *A Marriage Manual.* New York: Simon & Schuster, 1952.

12. Albert Ellis, "Marriage Counseling With Couples Indicating Sexual Incompatibility," *Marriage and Family Living,* 1953, 15, 53-59.

13. ———, *ibid.*

14. Edwin Hirsch, *The Power to Love.* New York: Knopf, 1952. Edwin Hirsch, *Modern Sex Life.* New York: Permabooks, 1949.

15. G. Lombard Kelly, *op. cit.*

16. Alfred C. Kinsey and others, *op, cit.*

17. Alex Comfort, *Sexual Behavior in Society.* New York: Viking, 1950.

18. Clellan S. Ford and Frank A. Beach, *Patterns of Sexual Behavior.* New York: Harpers, 1951.

SEX ON CAMPUS: THE STUDENTS' DILEMMA

Mary W. Hicks and Donald Taylor

The current trend toward permissiveness, though generally acknowledged, is not fully accepted even by the college population we studied. American attitudes are still highly ambivalent about sex in general and premarital sex in particular.

Current data suggest that changes in both sexual attitudes and behavior are prevalent on college campuses. More college students are having intercourse and having it more often than 25 years ago; more are having intercourse in a relationship that is not directed toward marriage even though they are emotionally involved with their partners; more females enjoy their first intercourse experience and have a greater number of partners; and more males have their first sexual experience with a female with whom they are emotionally involved. The amount of guilt experienced today is probably much less than it has been in the past. Indeed, on college campuses, one finds a great deal of talk about sex, a great deal of sexual activity, and practically no one complaining of any cultural prohibitions over his going to bed as often as he wishes or with as many partners as he wishes.

In order to get the students' perspective about sex in their lives, several classes, involving over 100 students, in sociology and family life (at Virginia Polytechnic Institute and State University, and Southern Illinois University at Edwardsville), were asked to respond to the questions: "What are your sexual problems?" and "What are the sexual problems of college students in general?" One option, of course, was to say there was no problem—few students took this option. In actuality, the amount of accord in their responses was impressive and a pattern emerged which is discussed here. All comments quoted were taken from their papers.

The student is confronted almost immediately with a need for a personal decision about his own sexual activity. What kind? How much? What partners? The pressure for action is extraordinary. On the campus, as elsewhere, there is a general preoccupation with sex—a preoccupation which has made sexual experimentation more justifiable and acceptable than ever before. Even more insidiously, perhaps, it has begun to imply that those who don't experiment are the deviants. A freshman girl meets someone and by date three (if not before) the question of sex comes up. She may not even have decided yet whether she likes him when the question hits and demands an immediate decision about sexual standards and behavior. A freshman boy meets someone, and after date one (very often) the other fellows ask him what he "got." He may not even know her last name when the question hits!

THE CHALLENGE OF CHOOSING

Choice—a new and disconcerting idea for many college students. It is now legitimate to choose a standard; one need not live by the standards he learned at home. The freedom to choose a sexual standard is according to Ira Reiss, the significant characteristic of the present. "Although we may prefer one of the choices to the other we consider all of them in the range we ought to tolerate. Young people have made the choice legitimate." The personal freedom to choose the most appropriate standard certainly carries with it important

Reprinted by permission of Mary W. Hicks. Originally published in *Sexual Behavior,* March, 1973.

positive results for the individual and some problems are eased. Ironically, though, the college student may now not suffer from the absence of choice, but from an excess of it! For some the burden of choice is heavier than the burden of repression.

Needless to say, most parents have not abandoned the bastions and turned over the right to choose any sexual standard to their own college student. A great many claim fervently that young people cannot have this choice, because any alternative to chastity is wrong. Data support the assumption that parents are more restrictive when their own children are confronted with the possibility of choice. At this time parents' own feelings about whether premarital sex is acceptable is likely to be that it is *not*. Nevertheless, the college situation presents a choice about sexual activity and demands that students make it.

Traditionally, in our society, all sexual behavior was expected to occur in marriage. All other activity was a violation of the norm. This has not meant, of course, that all sexual behavior conformed to the norm. There has been violation, and in abundance, it would seem. What it has meant is that even though increasingly ineffective in deterring premarital sex, the traditional code was focal in sexual decision making. For example, the pros and cons of premarital sex, so often listed in books on sex and marriage, are based generally on traditional assumptions about the effect of premarital sex on the marital relationship. Reasons to refrain are, therefore: premarital sex sabotages family life, premarital sex leads to subsequent adultery, premarital sex leads to unhappiness in marriage, and premarital sex is sex without love—a central requisite for marriage in America. Reasons to engage are, therefore: premarital sex leads to improve marital selection, premarital sex leads to improved sexual relations in marriage, and premarital sex leads to greater sexual competence in later married life. At the same time, as Ira Reiss has demonstrated in his theory of sexual permissiveness, certain violations from the traditional code have gained in acceptance among youth. "Permissiveness with affection" is a violation that is more acceptable than is "permissiveness without affection." It might be assumed that the traditional links between sex and marriage are more intact in a "sex with affection" relationship than they are in a "sex without affection" relationship. Thus, in some ways, sex with affection is not a "real" violation of the traditional code since it involves relative commitment and fidelity. Many sociologists would claim this is consistent with the prevailing American marriage model which, too, involves only relative commitment and fidelity.

Individual decisions to engage in, or refrain from, premarital sexual activity have been, therefore, based on the general rule that premarital sexual intercourse was wrong (for girls particularly) since it was detrimental to the marital relationship. The choice that the student had was either to live by the traditional code—or to violate it. But, even in violation, the individual understood the role of sex and the expected nature of the sexual choice. For example, if he could demonstrate that sexual activity strengthened an engagement relationship, then this was considered a violation in the spirit of the law, if not the letter. Or, if he could demonstrate that sex involved commitment to marry then this was also considered a legitimate violation. In this way the student established his code of behavior on the basis of the traditional code—whether he behaved in perfect conformity to it or not. As an example, a female freshman reported her way of adhering to the traditional code. By defining "marriage" idiosyncratically, she does not violate the prohibition of sex outside marriage:

> The biggest question concerning sex that I ask myself is, what is premarital sex anyway? What is marriage, and does a license really "marry" two people? I can only answer this problem for myself and set down my own guidelines. Moral standards are very personal and individual, therefore I cannot judge anybody else's sexual behavior. Behavior that I consider premarital may not seem so to someone else and conversely. My personal ideas about what is right sexually vary in degrees, but my basic concepts are stable. I have thought out my "morals" and feel comfortable with them. The conclusion that I have drawn for myself is that the term "marriage" is not definitely and exactly defined. Each person must define the term and decide whether or not a piece of paper and a few choice words really unites two people in "Holy Matrimony."

SEX FOR ITS OWN SAKE

On the other hand, when any choice is legitimate, sexual activity is not pre-anything because marriage is not in the picture. This separation of sexual activity from marriage makes sex "an end in and of itself." For some, no doubt, the idea of "sex as an end in and of itself" carries with it the notion of unbridled hedonism. Others, no doubt, might approve such a notion. However, most students do not see sex for its own sake as identical either with hedonistic pleasures or simply egocentric fun. They feel their sexual behavior is a particularly significant aspect of their being; and many believe that freedom of choice will help them develop responsibility, integrity, and self-awareness, as well as the ability to relate intimately and meaningfully.

What "moral" guidelines do students use when sex and marriage are separated? When sex is an end in and of itself? Students' comments about their decision-making dilemma indicate that they often formulate their rules on the basis of an equal and mutual exchange. Sexual transactions can legitimately include exchanges of pure physical gratification or love and affection as well as intangibles—prestige, power, or the privilege of belonging to an exclusive clique. Fundamental to the transaction, though, is the belief that each person must get something and be satisfied with the exchange. A senior female said:

> I feel that sex is a pleasurable experience if both parties that engage in the act have a true understanding of the act itself, if they both realize the other's feelings about it, and if each individual is sure of his or her feeling or attitude before allowing intercourse to take place.... No one should be used by another person for the sole purpose of his enjoyment. Sex is an act that should be enjoyed by both partakers.

Notions about bargaining and exchange have long been a part of sexual interaction. A prostitute is paid—clearly a bargaining transaction, money in exchange for a sexual service. A "wedding gift" of virginity carries with it the idea of exchange—virginity, for marriage and security. In each of these bargains the acknowledged fair exchange value grows out of traditional views about sex and marriage. Traditional rules no longer apply; the unique feature of the present situation is that there are *no* rules. As a result, there is no agreement about what is to be exchanged at what level. Sexual transactions, or bargains, become enormously complicated by the fact that each student not only must decide for himself what he considers a complementary exchange, but also must mesh this decision with that of another individual. This is difficult when some see sex as nothing but a fun outlet—if sex impulses do not hurt another they need never be denied; when others see sex "as meant only to be enjoyed in marriage"; and when myriad others define a "fair exchange" to suit their values, mood, individual needs, etc. An engaged male senior reflected on the resulting predicament:

> There are three different groups among college students today—those who will, those who won't, and those who are afraid. The problem comes in trying to determine who belongs to which group and matching them up.

Students must now generate their own rules to govern sexual transaction, and very often the rules governing complementary exchanges do include those things which enhance and improve relationships—i.e., honesty and integrity, responsibility and communication, and mutuality of feeling and expression. Ideally, there is less usury and gamemanship. However, it is important to note that the new rules provide no more than a set of alternative strategies to meet the problems of actual face-to-face interaction.

In this respect a female junior noted the mutuality of experience, "his pleasure, her pleasure" was important in her rules of barter and exchange:

> I believe that the sexual union between a man and a woman is a beautiful and stimulating experience. There is no comparison of the feelings I possess when lying in my lover's arms after being physically and mentally satisfied. I enjoy sexual relations and don't feel that I have to be in love with a man to have sex with him. I am not sexually satisfied every time I have sex. I can be satisfied mentally (depending on who my partner is) by just knowing that I have satisfied him. Although I would prefer the physical aspect as well.

For a female senior, a fair exchange involved an emotional component and sharing, while an unfair exchange involved exploitation:

> It's great to admit that I have sexual needs. I pick and choose, but carefully. There are men who want to grab you, screw you and leave. I avoid them like the plague. Other men, less visible, put themselves into the relationship. They don't exploit. They share.

The exchange couldn't be any simpler than it is for one male junior:

> Bra-less, liberated women are running through the countryside, shouting that they want sex just as much as a man. And as their cries grow louder and louder, more and more men are devoting their free time to satisfying the women's demand. No problem.

THE STRUGGLE FOR DECISION

Over and over again, the theme of value conflict between parents and peers and the struggle for "choice" is found in comments by college students:

> I feel the greatest problem concerning sex for me is conflicting ideas. I have a hard time trying to determine what I want to do, what others think I should do, and what I was taught to do.
>
> My personal attitudes toward sex are founded primarily on physical and emotional needs. Physically the need or desire for sexual pleasure. Emotionally the need to be accepted, wanted, loved, etc. But, as most people, my parents raised me to the idea that sex is only right for

married persons. No matter how I evaluate this myself, my parental views still have some bearing on my feelings.

Other attitudes that affect my own attitudes come in the way of peer pressure. This could be seen in the good roommate who knows you don't have a date for Friday, so he gets you one with the so called "dirty baby." Well, when you get in he wants to know everything that happened. If it didn't, there's something wrong with you. In situations involving peer pressure you can find yourself not only unable to decide your own views of sex but often times unable to even select your own sex partners (*a male senior*).

In general, the conflict for myself, and I think for many, comes from my peers. I have values now that have been derived from my church and my parents and these values are constantly being attacked by my peers. I don't really mind this, but it produces a conflict within myself as to what I should do. If I had intercourse, I feel I would be hurting my parents. So now I am in the process of trying to rationalize any behavior I may take in the future. This could be true of a lot of college students (*a male junior*).

Problems of college students:

1. Conflicts, between sexual opinion of peers and those of parents.
2. Influence of friends often causes feelings of non-acceptance if you are not in agreement with their sexual code.
3. Widespread openness about sex forces college students into sex before they really have a chance to think and discover their own thoughts.
4. The pressures of college often cause sex to provide an "out" from the worry, fatigue, and fast pace (*an engaged female junior*).

For me, the main problem would be mainly adjusting to college life, the great numbers of students and the morals of these students. I am rather conservative so it is difficult for me to even accept some of the ideas and standards that some students have set. Therefore, it is basically a fear (*a female freshman*).

For myself my biggest problem regarding sex is feeling conflict between my own beliefs of what is right or wrong opposed to what my parents feel is right or wrong. . . . However, I again see my values as a reflection of my parents (*a female junior*).

One of the problems of college students exists as a value judgment of morality vs. immorality. Until college, parental influence is very high. If a person has been brought up with the idea that sex is wrong outside of marriage, he might find a conflict of values when he reaches college. After reaching college, a student is more on his own and usually doesn't have his parents to tell him what and what not to do. Peer groups, which were influential earlier in life also, become even more influential. But most of all, at the college age a person usually starts making up his own mind and taking stands on various issues. He will usually make up his mind about the morality and immorality of sex and be satisfied with his decision. But sometimes problems arise when he still clings to his parents' values and yet cannot uphold them. Then he has guilt feelings which can lead to an unsatisfactory sex life (*a female junior*).

OTHER FACTORS

Choosing sexual standards is further complicated by several other forces. One, the double standard which continues to flourish, despite protestations to the contrary, on the campus. Few have shed the constrictions and distrust engendered by the double standard. Fathers still warn their daughters. "Be careful because boys are after only one thing," while they are winking at their sons and saying, "Do anything you want, but be careful you don't get caught!" Males and females alike believe "nice girls don't do it," and are inhibiting feelings and behavior.

An even more injurious outgrowth of the double standard, apparently, is the general lack of trust engendered between the sexes. It complicates communication and hampers sexual transactions at every level of relationship. Because of the double standard, many girls view any sexual transaction with suspicion since they believe that all males are naturally self-seeking:

My own major problem with sex is that I am always very much afraid of being exploited so it is hard for me to be comfortable about physical contact with a guy (*a junior*).

Many males seem to expect sex as a payment for a movie and, if you're lucky, a hamburger and coke. Most of my female peers, I feel, have been raised to believe that a girl's sexual desires are dirty and should be suppressed. Boys seem to be taught that it is manly and, therefore, desirable to "make it" with a girl. The problem arises when the boy is taught that "those girls" are not the type to marry. The girl, trying desperately to suppress her sexual needs, meets a boy who wants to prove his masculinity by "making out" with a girl—any girl. Finally, the girl gives in. After one, maybe two or three sessions in bed she finds not only that that particular boy doesn't want her, but also that anyone who has communicated with him shares his opinion. The dilemma is now irreversible—the girl's name is slandered publicly and her self-respect is destroyed (*an engaged junior*).

Another problem I have is that for some reason, it bothers me *very* much to think that the man I love will have had past experience. I have to force myself to accept the fact that few men will have saved *themselves* for one girl. Again, though, I know if I did have intercourse I would feel *horrible* and would feel I had lost something so very important to me for whatever reason (*a sophomore*).

My own major problem with sex is that I am always very much afraid of being exploited, so it is hard for me to be comfortable about physical contact with a guy (*a junior*).

I think a basic problem is that often guys and girls don't understand each other as far as sex is concerned. They have differing viewpoints which may cause conflict if the guy feels like the girl owes him something because he took her out and the girl feels that she doesn't owe him anything (*a junior*).

One of the most outstanding problems I have noticed is that women have formulated the idea that sex is to be enjoyed only by the man. The couples have not learned to communicate their feelings and desires to one another (*a senior*).

Sometimes lost in the general furor over the double standard's emphasis on the inferiority and suppression of women is the fact that men, too, suffer its consequences. The idea of men supposedly "driven" by their intense sexuality imposes hardships on the males who seem, somehow, to have escaped this inheritance. They claim to be pressured into sexual activity which they do not want and which they do not enjoy. Their choices are onerous too. Here is what one male senior wrote:

> Also during this time the student is in contact with many other individuals with whom he or she would not ordinarily come into contact. The effect of the group situation causes the individual to go further in his or her sexual relations. Also, typically, with boys at this age they can be pushed by friends into sexual relations that they would not have had. In some cases, it is almost expected of you to have sexual intercourse and you can be ridiculed if you don't try and exploit girls.

Often enough, too, misinformation and an utter lack of knowledge tend to increase the difficulty of decision making. In spite of the fact that sexual knowledge can be bought at any bookstore and how-to-do-it books are rolling off the presses, there is still ignorance about many aspects of sex and sexuality. Part of this problem, since parents have refused to deal with sexual issues, is lack of any kind of information or previous experience from past generations to use as guides. One student reported:

> Because I am a nurse and student I am frequently approached by other students with such questions as:
> Can I get pregnant if I swallow it?
> When can a woman get pregnant?
> How long do sperm live?
> Can I have sex during my period?
> How do I know if I have "the clap"?
> How do I know if I'm pregnant?
> Where can I get birth control pills?
> Does it hurt the first time?
> I am surprised that students have such little basic knowledge about sex. When I ask what information sources they have for their questions, the answer is usually "books or friends." Most have had little said to them by parents in the form of "facts," rather negative values on sex have been stressed.
> A female junior commented:
> Misconceptions, fears, guilt, and incredible to humorous ignorance run right down the lines of sexual experience from teenagers to graduate students. The crucial thing about sexual ignorance is that it can, in some cases, lead to serious problems that could have been relieved or prevented if brought into the open.

THE OUTSIDERS LOOKING IN

And there is the forgotten, silent minority: those who, for one reason or another cannot get a date and do not express their sexuality in any interactional way at all! Overlooked, frequently, in the myth of the campus orgy and the concern over wild parties and sexual excesses are those who do not have the interpersonal skills or the confidence to date—much less act out their sexual selves. They are separated from the others by a wall of fear, bad skin, fat, or feelings of inferiority. The problems of not being able to get a date or not knowing how to get involved in a heterosexual relationship are more widespread and damaging than is generally credited. Their dilemma is based on the fact that they have no choice:

> The only complaint I have about my sex life is lack of sex life! It seems to be an unwritten law in our society that a male is not allowed to date a member of the opposite sex who is not a perfect 36-24-36. Consequently, at the age of 19 I have had few dates, because until this year I had this terrible complex that I was fat. I didn't suddenly lose the "baby fat" but I am slowly losing the complex. I realize that there are other overweight people in the world and they get along. Until this year I had a terrible time talking to boys, and I am years behind in the feminine art of flirting (*a sophomore female*).

> I have never really learned how to play the dating games according to how it should ideally be played. Somewhere along the line, sex and girls have become the same term for me. So to avoid bad situations in which I would not know how to play the game correctly, I have not played the game very much. I guess I can't read girl's expectations very well or get them confused with mine. When I straighten out my morals as to sex, then I feel that I will be able to play the game a lot better. Of course I will be older then, too (*a male junior*).

> After working 11 p.m. to 7 a.m., 40-48 hours a week, then carrying 16 hours of school work, I don't even know how to pronounce let alone spell the WORD [sex] (*a senior male*).

THOSE WITHOUT DOUBTS

As might be expected, there are students on campus who have few doubts about their sexuality or their sexual behavior. There are certainly those who consider their present life adequate whether it includes sex or not. This group embraces those who are voluntarily chaste, those who have chosen to delay their sexual activity, and those who enjoy intercourse and are sexual because they want to be.

These people handle their sexual lives privately and without its being an apparent problem to themselves or others.

> I have been enjoying sex with my fiance' for almost three years now, and it gets better every time. He is the more adventurous person, and is the first one to suggest something new. I do not feel a need to engage in sexual intercourse because it is expected of me by him. He expects me to engage in it only when I truly want to (*a female junior engaged for two years*).

> I am dating steadily and have been for two years and seven months. We have plans for marriage in the future. Virginity is of utmost importance to both of us and we have discussed sexual matters often.

> The problem I can think of is that of preserving our virginity for the rest of our single life. There have been times when one of us has "wanted" to have intercourse, but so far at that same moment the other person has had the "sense" (conscious sense) to keep us from doing what we both don't want to do deep inside. I just hope that this will continue to hold true because I feel it is a vital part of our relationship (*a female freshman going steady*).

And there is the fringe of exponents of the Playboy philosophy:

> Yeah, I've tried the 187 positions described in the manual. Perhaps I am exaggerating when I say 187 because some of the positions are practically impossible—after training for gymnastics, I might make all of them. How do I feel about these experiences? No feeling really. It's sort of a physical readiness program. It's more fun than jogging. I'm ready to settle for less activity (*a male senior*).

> I can't say I've specialized in positions, but I could brag about the number of partners I've had. How do I feel about these experiences? Well I believe sex has to be something more than physical. What I have been doing is more exciting than masturbation but it's about the same level. I'm not knocking it but I hope to find something more when I get married (*a male junior*).

CONCLUSION

Internal and external pressures collide in the life of the college students to make sex particularly troublesome for them. They find themselves in an atmosphere where they can freely engage in sexual relations, those students who do so are part of an accepted pattern even though the activity itself is disapproved by some members of the college community as well as the larger community. They are confronted with the need to evaluate their own sexual standard and behavior and to decide how they want to integrate them into their personalities. Since free sexual activity has most often been taboo in their growing up experiences, they are ill prepared to make these decisions. Yet one cannot help but be impressed by their efforts to use sexual behavior constructively—to increase integrity and commitment, and to value human beings more.

Bibliography

1. Reiss, I. The Social Context of Premarital Permissiveness (New York: Holt Rinehart, and Winston, 1967).

2. Bell, R. Premarital Sex in a Changing Society (Englewood Cliffs, N.J.: Prentice-Hall, 1966).

3. Reiss, I. Premarital Sex Codes: The Old and the New; in Grummon, D. and Barclay, A. (eds.): Sexuality, A Search for Perspective (New York: Van Nostrand Reinhold Company, 1971), p. 195.

Section V

SURVIVAL OF THE FIT
Michael J. Sporakowski

The importance of parenting and the choices exercised within this role affect the lives of a number of people. The old idea of parent-child interaction has been much modified to include reciprocal interactions and those initiated by the child. More and more we see the need for education for parenthood as we finally realize that biological parenthood does not necessarily mean readiness for the many other facets of the parenting relationship. This section provides a number of readings which will hopefully cause the reader to think about parenthood and to examine the pros and the cons involved in its many aspects. An emphasis is given to the very early parenting experience of the sharing of childbirth. The final article deals with a topic many young parents find difficult to deal with in their young children, sex.

Articles

Name: _____   Date: _____

Student #: _____   Sex: M or F

1. T   F   Fathers should not be allowed in the delivery room.

2. T   F   Anyone can give birth easily if they use "natural childbirth."

3. T   F   *If female,* I would want the father of my children to be present at their births. *If male,* I would want to be present at the birth of my children.

4. T   F   Bottle feeding is superior to breast feeding.

5. T   F   Childbirth can be an orgasmic experience.

6. T   F   It is generally better for the mother and baby, for the mother to be "asleep" at the time of birth.

7. T   F   Complicated deliveries (births) requiring a physician's help occur in about 25% of all cases.

8. T   F   "Natural childbirth" mothers tend to feel more positive about the birth experience than do mothers who have gone the more conventional route.

9. (a) List three reasons why people want to become parents.

   (b) List three reasons why people would reject parenthood.

10. (a) List three advantages of having "husband coached childbirth."

    (b) List three disadvantages of husbands participating in the birth process.

11. Do you want to become a parent at some time in your life?

       Yes _____   No _____
            Go to 12   Go to 13

12. If yes, list your reasons.

13. If no, list your reasons.

14. As compared to your peers how well prepared for parenthood do you believe yourself to be?

      Very well _____ About average _____ Poorly _____

15. What things or sources have contributed to your preparedness for parenthood?

16. What aspects of parenthood do you feel best prepared for?

17. What aspects of parenthood do you feel least prepared for?

HUSBAND-COACHED NATURAL CHILDBIRTH
Karen Wullenweber Hurley

A man in blue-green surgical cap and coat emerges from the delivery room. In one hand he holds a camera; with the other hand he guides his wife who carries the baby that *they* have just brought into the world.

Several people in the corridor do double takes as the couple passes by. Mothers after childbirth are supposed to be too weak and sore to move—and most of them are heavily doped anyway. As for the father, he's supposed to sweat it out in the waiting room, not the *delivery* room. And what's he doing with a camera?

This is a "husband-coached natural childbirth" couple and they have just given birth to their child *together*. The wife was unwilling to submit to what she considered the "depersonalizing" methods of hospital obstetrics where having a baby is much like having a tumor removed. She chose to give birth naturally (without medication) so that she could be awake and aware and active during the entire event. The husband likewise refused to play the role of pacing the waiting room floor with a pocketful of cigars. He chose to be with his wife from labor to birth in order to share this experience with her and to help her in any way possible. He took his camera along to record those first moments of their child's life (his "Daddy picture") and the smile on his wife's face telling of the great joy of her childbirth experience. Neither husband nor wife was content to sit by while someone else "delivered" their baby.

"Delivery" is a bad word around natural childbirth couples such as this one. To them it connotes the many traditional obstetrical practices which make it impossible for both mother and father to share in the joyous experience of the birth of their child because the mother is under sedation and the father is absent from her side. More and more parents across the country are coming to realize what a rich experience childbirth can be for both of them. One mother explains her feelings in this way: "I had an easy time delivering the first baby; I had a spinal. But it seemed to me after the baby was born that I had missed something—something that I didn't experience which I wish I had.

"With a spinal," she continues, "I saw my baby being delivered, but it was like it was happening to someone else because I couldn't feel anything. And I didn't like this. I wanted to *feel* that my son was born. I told my husband right afterwards that

when I got pregnant again I wanted a natural childbirth." She did get pregnant again and she did have natural childbirth, but only after talking her doctor into it and convincing the hospital to let her husband into the delivery room.

Fortunately for couples who want to enjoy the experience of childbirth, an increasing number of hospitals, especially along the East and West coasts, are becoming more "family-centered." Many are instituting classes in natural childbirth, allowing fathers into the delivery room, and developing facilities which will permit mothers and babies (and fathers, too) to spend more time together while they are in the hospital.

In addition to hospital efforts in this direction, there are numerous groups of interested parents around the country attempting to promote natural childbirth and husband-coached childbirth by sponsoring series of weekly classes to teach the techniques of natural childbirth to anyone who wants to learn. (Information concerning this movement can be obtained from the International Childbirth Education Association, 1310 North 26th Street, Milwaukee, Wisconsin).

One of the first questions raised by the uninitiated is what exactly does "natural" childbirth mean? Janet Fortin, a teacher at one of the natural childbirth classes that I visited and a natural childbirth mother herself, explains first of all what it is not: "A lot of people think of natural childbirth simply as unmedicated childbirth—that we just choose to endure all the pain." This is not the case at all.

"Natural" childbirth means "educated" childbirth, she insisted. By preparing mentally and physically, by learning to breathe correctly and to relax completely, the natural childbirth mother *minimizes* discomfort and *maximizes* the pleasure and excitement of giving birth to her child.

Fear of pain is one thing that convinces most mothers to have their children with the aid of some medication or anesthetic (general or local). But this fear is really unwarranted, experienced natural childbirth mothers testify, as long as you have properly prepared yourself. "Of course there is some discomfort with natural childbirth," one mother admits; but she quickly adds, "You cer-

Reprinted from December, 1968, issue of *St. Anthony Messenger,* 1615 Republic St., Cincinnati, Oh. 45210. Reprinted with the permission of the author and publisher.

tainly feel a lot more discomfort at other times of your life than during childbirth."

Ignorance of what natural childbirth is all about is another reason why mothers decide upon a medicated delivery. This is where husband-coached natural childbirth classes come in. I visited one such class in Cincinnati which was part of an eight-week series. Mothers-to-be, assisted by their husband-coaches, were practicing childbirth exercises on portable mats while I talked with Carol Ulrich, a nurse and one of the instructors.

These exercises, Carol explains, build up the muscles used in childbirth and should be done every day, at least during the last six to eight weeks of pregnancy. A husband is very important in bolstering his wife's enthusiasm, which tends to wane as she becomes larger and larger. And there are some exercises which the husband must help with.

Referring to the exercise being practiced in the background, Carol says: "This exercise to spread the legs apart is very important because this is exactly what is required during childbirth. It is somewhat painful to begin with, but the same muscles which are being strained in this exercise are strained in childbirth. This straining is what is associated with birth pains. That pain in particular can be completely eliminated by strengthening these muscles ahead of time through exercise.

"It's like touching your toes," she insists. "If you gradually work up to it, you can touch your toes with no pain at all. But if you are forced to do it all at once without any warming up, it is a very painful thing for most people. This is the same thing with childbirth; warming up these muscles can eliminate this kind of pain."

If so much of the pain of childbirth can be eliminated through the proper education and training, then why are so many women afraid to have a baby?

"It's traditional for one thing," Carol explains, "It's part of our religious tradition. We have always thought that to have children in pain was one of the results of the sin of Adam. Therefore, women are conditioned to expect pain."

What about all the grueling tales told by grandmothers who gave birth without medication of any kind? Was this just a problem of psychological conditioning?

"Only partly," she responds. "It is not enough to just give birth naturally and expect that there will be no pain involved. It takes *training*." It seems that the "know-how" of childbirth is not instinctual in humans as it is in animals. It is something that we must learn—just as we have to learn

to swim, while every other animal when thrown into the water swims instinctively."

It was by observing animal births that Dr. Robert Bradley developed many of his natural childbirth ideas and techniques. (Dr. Bradley is now one of the foremost promoters of natural childbirth and the author of the book *Husband-Coached Childbirth*.) He noticed that animals did not seem to experience pain or anxiety in giving birth, but remained calm and peaceful throughout. Therefore he adapted their body positions, patterns of breathing, times for pushing and times for relaxing and recommends these for human childbirth. By learning these techniques from the animals, whose instinctual "know-how" is not overshadowed by conscious and unconscious fears and anxieties, mothers can be freed for a more *human* childbirth experience than our culture provides for at the moment.

But can every mother give birth naturally? What about complications?

Natural childbirth instructors say that practically everyone can give birth naturally—if they really want to. Obviously, the woman's physician must be consulted, but breach births, transverse babies and other such complications provide no insurmountable obstacle.

Where cesarean section is judged necessary by the doctor, natural childbirth would be impossible. But some C-section mothers decide to go through with the husband-coached natural classes anyway because they feel that the childbirth exercises contribute to their general good health in pregnancy. They feel that the attitudes toward childbirth which are promoted in these classes better equip them to more fully enjoy the birth of their baby, even though natural childbirth is impossible.

Dr. Bradley claims to have assisted well over 9,000 mothers in giving birth to their children naturally. In the course of his job as birth-coach to these mothers, he realized that a peculiar thing was happening in his relationship with these women. They reached out to him for moral support in addition to the technical coaching that he might offer them. After the baby was born, it was he that the jubilant mother shared her joy with and many times showered with kisses.

The light finally dawned, Bradley says. A woman should be sharing these intimate moments of her life with the person with whom she is most intimately involved—her husband. The idea of making the husband an integral part of the childbirth experience took shape.

As the ideas of Dr. Bradley have become increasingly popular in the United States, delivery room doors across the country are beginning to open to dads. Yet what can a husband do in a delivery room? Won't he be in the way? And what about the germs?

Room is no problem. With a natural childbirth fewer people are required in the delivery room than with a medicated childbirth. The stool at the head of the delivery table where the anesthesiologist would normally sit becomes the "Daddy stool." And in the labor room, far from being in the way, he is able to free hospital personnel for other things by getting his wife ice chips when she wants them and by doing other simple things to make her more comfortable—like adjusting her pillows.

Germs are no problem either, Dr. Bradley says. Babies are usually born with a natural immunity to the bacteria in their home environment. The usual precaution about germs in the delivery room is not that the parents themselves might infect their own baby, but that their baby might carry bacteria back to the nursery to other babies not so immune. Therefore, if a baby is to stay in the mother's room (The latest trend in many hospitals), instead of going back to the nursery as is customary, both father and mother can hold and touch their baby right after birth. And the natural childbirth mother can nurse her baby right on the delivery table. (This is one of the plus factors of natural childbirth for the baby, supporters say, citing psychological findings that it is important for a child to be cuddled and held right after birth.)

One father, whose doctor charged him $50 extra for husband-coached childbirth, jokingly bemoaned the fact that he had to pay extra only to be put to work in the labor and delivery rooms. This father will testify that there are many things husbands can do.

First of all, there is the simple matter of moral support. In the first stage of labor the role of the mother is rather passive; she imitates sleep while she allows her uterine muscles to work involuntarily. It is important for her to relax and not interfere with their working—which would cause pain and discomfort. The husband helps his wife relax. Dr. Bradley recommends that the husband help his wife relax by talking to her quietly as he does in making love to her. "Play the lover role, then," Bradley insists, "during the climax to your act of love—the birth of your baby."

At this time he also helps his wife to assume a position most comfortable and most conducive to complete relaxation. The good husband-coach has observed his pregnant wife during her deepest slumber to discover her most comfortable sleeping position. In the labor room he helps her to assume that position so as to be as comfortable and relaxed as possible.

The husband-coach also helps with his wife's breathing. They have practiced this together before. By placing his hand on her abdomen he can tell if she is breathing properly. If not, he gently reminds her.

In the delivery room the father might be called upon to crank up the delivery table so that his wife can assume a position she prefers. During the final stages of the birth process, when his wife is actively pushing with her abdomen muscles to assist the baby's entry into the world, he will be busy supporting her with pillows in a semi-sitting position during her contractions and helping her to relax in the in-between times.

These are all things that the doctor or nurse would have to do were the husband-coach not on the scene. He may not be as professionally trained as they, but this matters little to his wife. He is the person she has come to depend on throughout her pregnancy; he is the one she has learned to work with efficiently and confidently.

"The hardest thing was going through the transition (from first-stage labor to second-stage)," says Jane Hissett, a natural childbirth mother who was relating her experience to a group of couples at the childbirth class. "I forgot what to do but Bob (her husband) remembered that I was supposed to take deep breaths and not pant."

"When she started to push hard," Bob Hissett recollects, "I helped her by supporting her with pillows."

Doctors and nurses express amazement at the smooth functioning of natural childbirth couples like Jane and Bob. They are even more amazed when mothers-to-be joke with their husbands in the resting periods between contractions. One doctor said he felt like an intruder into a private world where two people were completely concentrating on each other and the wonderful thing that was about to happen to them—the birth of their baby.

Another natural childbirth mother confessed to the class that she had wavered at the end and went through with natural childbirth only because of the moral support of her husband. After the birth she was grateful to him for the needed encouragement and describes their experience in this way: "It was like New Year's Eve. My husband and I were carrying on like we were the only two people in the world that ever had a child.

"But it all went so fast," she says. "You just want to relive it a thousand and one times. It was so glorious—I can't begin to tell you how great it was. I was so charged up—I was screaming, 'It's a girl! It's a girl!' I'm still charged up. I love to tell the story over and over again."

This mother was not unusual. Deborah Tanzer, writing on natural childbirth in the October *Psychology Today,* reported that women with husbands at their side during delivery tended to use the following words to describe their feelings about themselves: queenly, receptive, victorious, trusting, joyous, blissful, rapturous, supreme, in ecstasy, integrated.

Enthusiasm in abundance is the mark of every husband-coached natural childbirth couple I have talked with. Each person they meet is a potential listener to the marvelous tale they have to tell.

"After it is all over and you get back to your room, you just feel like you are flying," says one natural childbirth mother.

"I just can't tell you how pleased I am," says Jane Hissett. But she does point out one "disadvantage" to letting her husband in on the action. "When I got home from the hospital everyone already knew the entire story; my husband had told everybody. And I couldn't find anyone to tell. The Avon lady came to the door and *I* got her," she says with relief.

Her husband Bob jokes about the biggest plus factor of husband-coached natural childbirth as far as he is concerned: "Usually when you go to a party and all the women begin talking about pregnancy and childbirth, you and the rest of the guys with drinks in hand head for another room. When we get there I can now say to the guys, 'Well, when my wife was on the delivery table...' "

A favorite topic for jest among natural childbirth couples is the reaction of some hospital personnel to natural childbirth. One mother tells of the nurse who asked her what kind of medication she was to receive. When she said "None" the nurse stared as if to say, "Really, are you one of that kind of nuts?"

When asked exactly what kind of people really do choose natural childbirth, a group of instructors responded in various ways.

Many of them are educated women; some are LaLeche League girls already interested in breast-feeding their babies.

More important than their educational status,

one instructor pointed out, is the fact that "these are girls who want to enjoy every minute of the birth and life of their children while they have them."

A natural childbirth mother might be "anyone that is really sensitive to life," says a three-time childbirth mother.

Are there any tie-ins between religious attitudes and attitudes toward natural childbirth?

"That depends," says nurse Carol Ulrich. "If your religion is geared toward love and you take your religion as a religion of love, I would think so. You would have to be somewhat religious to really appreciate the values of natural childbirth."

"You would have to believe in God," conjectures Karen Crew, a natural childbirth mother and one of the class instructors.

"They say there are no atheists in a fox hole," states Sheila Ferguson, another instructor. "And I think you can also say that there are no atheists in a delivery room."

These women are all members of the Husband-Coached Natural Childbirth Association in Cincinnati, which typifies many other such groups around the country. The Cincinnati association got under way less than a year ago. Already it has graduated three classes of natural childbirth couples.

The goals of this organization are very much tied up with the personal goals of individual members.

"We want to help mothers and fathers discover that childbirth is a beautiful experience," says Karen Crew in explaining her involvement in the group.

"We feel that natural childbirth can do a lot for a woman," says Emily Froehlich, who was the original impetus in getting the association off the ground. "Women in this society need to feel that they can accomplish this. There are so many women torn between being a wife and mother and having a career. They ask, 'Is being a housewife enough?' Well, this is one thing that they *can* do and they can do well."

Does this swing toward natural childbirth, then, represent a drive to keep women out of the career world and in the home by convincing them to be content with their lot as wife and mother?

Sheila Ferguson rejects this as an accurate representation of what they hope to promote. She says: "I think that the women who come to us could very well be career women and probably many of them will pursue careers outside the home as soon as their children are a little older."

"Dr. Bradley's philosophy of children," interjects Emily, "is to have them, love them, and let them be. A woman has a responsibility to herself to utilize her talents where she feels indicated. If she pursues a part-time career when her children are in school, she may well be able to be a better mother because of an increase in her self-esteem."

"I think that you can work both—having children and having a career," Sheila added. "And having children ultimately makes you better able to involve yourself in a career. In having natural childbirth and breastfeeding your baby, you have to actively give of yourself. In any organization or job that you are in, the more you can give of yourself, the better you will be in that position. And so with this background of giving to your children, you are going to be better able to give to other people too."

Perhaps the best insight into the why and wherefore of natural childbirth was offered by Janet Fortin in explaining what she felt the Husband-Coached Natural Childbirth Association was trying to do: "We are just trying to bring families closer together by telling them and showing them how they can be together during labor and childbirth."

Bob and Jane Hissett agreed wholeheartedly that husband-coached natural childbirth had indeed brought their family closer together. "Afterwards I felt such a tremendous love for Bob," says Jane. "We really shared something together and he really showed me how much he loved me by going through this with me and wanting to be there. I don't think that we could be any closer than we are now—unless we have another one!"

FATHERS' PRESENCE IN DELIVERY ROOMS
Robert A. Bradley, M.D.

As a result of the increasing number of programs of psychological and physical preparation for childbirth, there is a steady rise in incidence of unmedicated conscious deliveries. The mother experiences such a joyful exuberance at this moment (so aptly described by the late Grantly Dick-Read, M.D.[1]), that there has been a great demand for the presence of fathers in delivery rooms to share in this important event.

Hospital regulations have for many years entirely excluded husbands from the delivery rooms. In view of the past percentage of medicated uncooperative patients, these rules appeared purposeful and husbands were relieved not to have to be associated with their "sick and suffering" loved ones. However, in light of the newer trends towards patients demanding and getting conscious, natural, spontaneous deliveries, the practice of excluding the father of the infant should be reviewed and reconsidered.

Articles are appearing in an increasing number of lay magazines that stress the psychological importance of maintaining the home environment throughout the progress of labor with emphasis on the husband's presence. A new popular song, "The Green Leaves of Summer," has included this concept in its lyrics: "It was so good to be young then, to be close to the earth and to stand by your wife at the moment of birth." Husbands have sued hospitals for the privilege of being with their wives; indeed, one devoted husband has even chained himself to his wife to ensure his presence, because "I love her and she needs me." Laboring mothers have taken unnecessary risks by delaying the trip to the hospital until delivery is imminent, in order to be with their husbands. In an attempt to cooperate with this growing demand, sympathetic doctors are compromising their obstetrical judgment unnecessarily by doing home deliveries.

This problem is becoming progressively acute. A report on the private practice of obstetrics at Porter Hospital in Denver, Colorado, is timely, therefore, where for the past eight years, in over 4,000 deliveries, the author has always included husbands throughout labor and delivery as very essential members of the "birth team."

Antenatal education and preparation of both the husband and wife, delineating their respective roles in achieving conscious delivery, is a *sine qua non* for the presence of husbands in delivery rooms. Equally important is the husband's desire to be there. This does not mean that every man who looks squeamish at the first mention of the idea should immediately be excluded. Burdened with old wives tales of yesterday, probably 75 per cent

Reprinted from *Psychosomatics*, Vol. III, No. 6, November-December 1962, by permission of the author and publisher.

of our husbands have looked skeptical originally. But after careful explanation of "why" and "what," we have had well over 95 per cent with their wives, and these without exception were enthusiastic afterward, and "wouldn't have missed it for the world."

Assuming the premise propounded by psychologists, psychiatrists, anthropologists, and others, that husbands should have an active rather than passive role in the birth of their children, we would like to itemize some of the pros and cons from the standpoint of the obstetrician.

Indications

(1) *Husbands like it*—Emotionally they reap a rich harvest that is obvious in their professed delight afterwards. The manifestations of tenderness and joy exchanged between husband and wife immediately at birth are heart-warming. They seem to contribute to the solidity of family ties. The mother's delighted "When can we have another one?", addressed to her husband at birth, replaces the accusatory "Never again, *you* have the next one," of post-anesthetic blues.

(2) *Wives like it*—In a recent lay woman's magazine a series of articles entitled appropriately "Cruelty in Maternity Wards" (*Ladies Home Journal,* December 1958), the indignant letters from mothers included the repeated plea, "If I could only have had my husband with me." Our patients have been unanimous in their gratitude.

(3) *Husbands are needed*—Husbands are essential as trained assistants in the conduct of conscious cooperative deliveries. We are convinced that without the careful guidance of trained husbands, our statistics on unanesthetized births could not exist (93 per cent of vaginal deliveries). Many times we have requested the husband to "take over" the coaching and have seen a frightened uncooperative patient change immediately to a calm cooperative one; the familiar voice of a loved husband works wonders. We whimsically tell our prenatal classes, "We do not *deliver* babies, we train husbands how to teach their wives to give birth to babies."

(4) *Husbands save doctors' and nurses' time*—An attentive husband, carefully coaching his wife throughout the course of labor, means less frequent visits required by the attending physician and nurse. Husbands cheerfully run errands (ice chips, cold cloth on brow, etc.) otherwise required of nurses. The husband and wife take mutual pride in self-accomplishment.

The few hours devoted by the physician in group prenatal instruction is well compensated for, also, by the remarkable shortening of all stages of labor (primiparas: average first stage, 8 1/2 hours, second stage, 1/2 hour; multiparas: average first stage, 5 1/2 hours, second stage, 12 minutes).

(5) *Fewer rectal and vaginal examinations for the patient*—These distressing examinations can be kept to a minimum as conscious cooperative patients can recognize the various stages of labor previously so carefully described in parents' classes. They learn to rely on the subjective manifestations of labor and cervical dilatations, and are amazingly accurate in their interpretations. This greatly reduces the need for repeated examinations. In experienced patients we are gaily dismissed from the labor room by our patient's "Goodbye, we'll let you know when it's time!"

(6) *Second stage labor and delivery*—Most comfortable part. We asked experienced unmedicated patients, if gas anesthetics were to be given for ten minutes to relieve pain completely, which ten minutes would they choose in the course of labor. Not one ever said second stage or birth; always transition stage, just prior to pushing.

In the later periods of the first stage, some patients find relaxation difficult. Doing nothing (relaxing) takes considerable self-control during the height of uterine activity. However, doing something (bearing down with the contractions) all patients find simple and easy. This, combined with the partially empty uterus slowing down the force and frequency of contractions, makes the second stage more manageable.

Some hospitals allow husbands in labor rooms during the uncomfortable period, then exclude them from the delivery rooms where the most comfortable part of labor and the joy of seeing the baby take place. This appears illogical to us.

(7) *Baby's first picture*—In the total absence of anesthesia or anesthetic machines, husbands are permitted to use flash cameras and record for the baby book the first meeting between baby and mother. No words can adequately describe the exuberant, joyful expression on an unmedicated mother's face at her first glimpse of the baby. This glorious moment of her life, as she is handed her child, should be preserved in the baby's book as a constant reminder to the child of the mother's happiness at his arrival. How often have psychological deviations of personality been based on a feeling of rejection, after overhearing mother condemn the horror of the individual's birth? These beautiful

"Daddy Pictures" speak eloquently, for all time, reassuring the child that he was "wanted," and his arrival welcomed joyously by both parents. The role of photographer we feel is another psychological asset for both the husband and child. For the former it adds to his feeling of usefulness, and for the child it proves in later years that Daddy was interested enough to be there and proud enough to preserve the event.

(8) *The paucity of postpartum psychoses*—One of the most striking aspects of husband and wife training together during pregnancy, and the husband's active role as a teacher and coach during actual labor and delivery, is the decreased incidence of emotional illness associated with childbirth. We have had many patients take the course and give birth by these principles, who had postpartum psychosis with previous unprepared deliveries, but who were completely well adjusted following their trained births. In our eight years we have seen only three postpartum psychoses, and these were in known and previously recognized psychotics. This incidence is far below the average as listed by Dr. Carl L. Kline.[2] In discussing the problem, he states "One of the most frequently expressed sources of resentment (of a wife towards her husband) is passivity on the part of the husband." We feel the *active* role we assign husbands may reduce the incidence.

(9) *Reassurance to the inexperienced*—Probably no aspect of our method is as convincing to the anxious new pregnant woman as the reassurance that her husband is invited to be with her throughout the course of labor and delivery, and that our reason for this invitation is simply that we know he will enjoy the experience. Copies of "Daddy Pictures" presented to us by proud fathers are passed around for inspection at our first prenatal class; they are convincing in themselves that husbands shouldn't miss this happy event. The change from anxiety to calm self-assurance is remarkable as husband and wife train together in preparation for the shared event.

(10) *Shortening of hospital stay*—The guidance and coaching of a husband, resulting in unmedicated mothers, also produces the benefit of lessening the need for prolonged hospitalization.

Healthy mothers, capable and eager to walk from the delivery room with their husbands at their sides and babies in their arms, can see no reason for being "hospitalized" after giving birth. They repeatedly point out they are not *sick!*

We feel the benefits of "rooming-in" are multiple and justifiable, but the expense prohibitive.

Our patients are instructed to have the assistance of another woman at home for the first two weeks to help with the household chores. They are told they must stay in the hospital two hours after the birth (the fourth stage of labor), but in the absence of complications or medications, may go home whenever they wish.

An added factor of safety is the reduction of postpartum hemorrhage by immediate breast feeding in 85 per cent of our mothers. This is primarily possibly due to the activity of seven local chapters of the "La Leche League," wherein both husband and wife have received prenatal instruction in their roles relative to breast feeding. They are further reassured of continuous availability of advice during the postpartum by experienced officers of this nationwide organization.

This not only releases many hospital beds for others, but adds the psychological benefits of home environment, demand feeding, and "T.L.C." of the infant, and reduction of cross infections of baby and mother from exposure to others.

As Dr. Thaddeus L. Montgomery has stressed,[3,4] "The hospital is a good place to deliver a baby but a poor place to board it."

(11) *Better public relations for hospitals*—The trend of public criticism against impersonal cold attitudes of hospital personnel and procedures ("I was treated like a goat") has not been evident in our group. On the contrary, the hospital administrator has received many warm-hearted letters from husbands expressing gratitude and pleasure with the management of their cases and the privilege of being with their wives.

Possible Objections

(1) *Husbands get in the way*—In our experience this is not true. They remain seated at the head of the delivery table on the stool formerly occupied by an anesthetist. They have been instructed not to leave this honorary seat, and do not present an obstacle to the functioning of the attending nurses.

(2) *They will get sick or faint*—This has not happened. The outmoded misconception that the birth of a baby is a nauseating event to behold is probably best dispelled by hundreds of photographic documents appearing in magazine articles on natural childbirth, and our own collection of prints. These are used for teaching purposes at our classes, followed by a careful rehearsal of the entire course of labor, including a visit to the delivery room in advance, to familiarize the husband with all aspects. He is prepared for the appearance of his

wife's face during the act of pushing with contractions in second stage. He is a useful coach in breath control and guides his wife by performing with her. His most valuable asset is a sense of humor, and many jovial comments pass between wife and husband during the uterine rest periods, which add an atmosphere of confident wholesome joy to the entire event.

We take note of the value of husbands, also, by seeing that they are given food trays with their wives regularly during labor. Sometimes a faint feeling is a simple hypoglycemia from having been ignored and unfed! The husband also shares the complimentary glass of iced orange juice, which is given to the patient immediately on delivery to compensate for the unpleasant drying effect of the mouth breathing and to restore depleted blood sugar. In patients trained for natural childbirth, nausea and vomiting is practically unheard of.

Husbands are invited to see everything their wives see, and literally have their "heads together" in the delivery room. This does not include the perineum, except in cases where the husband is medically trained. Unless a patient is a contortionist she cannot see her own perineum, and husbands are invited to share their wives experience in seeing the *baby* at its birth.

(3) *Husbands are "dirty" and will contaminate the delivery room*—This has not proven to be the case. The husbands are attired in the same fashion as the doctor and attending nurses (gown, cap, and mask). They remain seated on the absent anesthetist's stool and do not interfere with "sterile" technique.

Hospitals that allow husbands in delivery rooms do not have a higher incidence of infections; in many cases, it is lower.

(4) *Husbands will be critical of the case and increase the likelihood of malpractice suits*—On the contrary, we feel there is less likelihood of criticism when the husband is included. Phantasies of mismanagement are more likely when the patient is "hidden" from the husband, especially with the emotional turmoil this produces in the worried imagination of a distraught separated husband.

(5) *What if there are unforeseen "complications"?*—Complications of any conceivable nature can be handled by the obstetrician far more efficiently with a calm cooperative patient. The presence of the husband is, in our opinion, the greatest factor available to maintain cooperation and self-control.

Complications are exceedingly rare to begin with (96.4 per cent of vaginal deliveries are spontaneous births). However, when they occur, completely honest explanations are made to the parents at the time, and their assistance elicited. Their clear understanding of the problem at the time is followed by appreciation of the obstetrician's assistance. A forceps bruise on a baby will be far better accepted by a husband who, by his presence, clearly saw the lack of progress necessitating the forceps, than by a bewildered, doubtful husband who, by his absence, imagines all sorts of mismanagement. Gratitude for helping his wife is far better than bitter resentment for imagined wrongs.

(6) *What if the baby were deformed?*—For this exceedingly rare occurrence we have no way of "keeping it from" the parents, as all are assured during pregnancy the privilege of seeing their baby at birth.

In the absence of anesthetic depression of the mother we feel there is no contra-indication to complete honesty to both parents at birth. They will have to know the facts eventually, and we can see no advantage in giving the parents an erroneous conception that their baby is all right and then shocking them later with the truth. This would result in greater emotional stress over a longer interval.

In our opinion it would be a crime to deprive thousands of the joy of seeing their normal babies at birth in order to postpone the inevitable stress of the exceedingly few with abnormal infants.

Discussion

Incident to the progressive interest of laymen and the increase in prenatal education programs stressing shared concepts of parenthood, the role of a father in pregnancy and childbirth is changing.

Yesterday's concept of a father was a distraught anxious chain-smoker, pacing nervously for hours in the waiting room, hearing with guilty anguish the distant screams of pain from his beloved wife, and realizing in his misery that his act of love brought on this horror from which, mercifully, he is excluded. This was a useless, pitiful status of manhood and as such has been subject to ridicule. Could the rising divorce rate and high percentage of postpartum frigidity problems, psychoses, etc., be related to such a degrading role of the father in the family?

This passive bewildered clown today becomes a proud useful companion, who by his presence elicits peaceful cooperation from his beloved wife in the ennobling act of bearing his child. (In trained mothers, attendants are impressed by the absence of evidence of discomfort; hence, the numerous articles by natural childbirth mothers referring to "painless childbirth.")

Two people working together can happily share an experience that will further strengthen the bonds of matrimony.

The deliberate inclusion of the father in the delivery room as an essential member of the birth team is reviewed in the light of newer trends.

This has been based on the experience gained in eight years of private practice of obstetrics in a metropolitan area. The essential prerequisite of thorough prenatal emotional and physical training of the husband, as well as the wife, in their respective roles in achieving conscious spontaneous delivery is stressed.

It is demonstrated that such a policy is: (1) an exhilarating experience for the parents, (2) an advantageous procedure for the hospital, and (3) a useful practice for the obstetrician.

Acknowledgment

The author gratefully acknowledges the willing assistance given by the staff of Porter Hospital, Denver, Colorado; the former administrator, Mr. Harley E. Rice, the present administrator, Mr. Olof T. Moline, and Dr. Adrian D. Baer, Chief of Physical Medicine.

Bibliography

1. Dick-Read, G. *Childbirth Without Fear.* New York: Harper and Brothers, 1944.
2. Kline, C.L.*Amer. J. Obst. & Gynec.*, 69:748-757, 1955.
3. Montgomery, T.L. *Amer. J. Obst. & Gynec.*, 76:706, 1958.
4. ———. *Amer. J. Obst. & Gynec.*, 81:890-901, 1961.

NATURAL CHILDBIRTH: PAIN OR PEAK EXPERIENCE?

Deborah Tanzer

"Then I don't remember anything. I don't remember asking him what I had. The next thing I knew my husband has come to visit me. I asked him what I had. I said "oh" and fell back asleep, except when my husband tried to leave. The whole thing was not too great for a while."

"Like an orgasm . . . a different kind . . . the wonderful free feeling . . . Joy, a wild joy. I had known it, but it was very special . . . seeing a real honest-to-goodness baby. He looked like a porcelain eskimo, and all kinds of colors—blue, green, red and shiny. And having Bill there . . . great!"

"Like an orgasm." "Not too great for a while." Thus, two women recalled their experience in childbirth one month after the event. The differences of tone and language, the contrast between the liveliness and accuracy of one statement and the dullness and deprivation of the other are obvious. The mother of the "porcelain eskimo" had delivered her baby using the natural-childbirth method: the other had no special psychological or physiological preparation.

In terms of the so-called "third force" or humanistic psychology (neither Freudian nor behavioristic) we could easily conclude that the first mother had a "peak experience." Abraham Maslow of Brandeis University describes a peak experience as transcendent ecstasy, too blissful a state to be described as happiness. (See Psychology Today, July.)

Was this mother's experience the result of natural childbirth? Why did she stress the presence of her husband Bill? To answer these questions, I undertook a controlled study of pregnant women, some of whom had elected to deliver their babies by the common method, others by natural childbirth.

Natural Childbirth may be defined as a method of delivery based on complete or substantial elimination of sedation in labor and delivery, the conscious participation of the mother during the entire birth process, and the preparatory education during pregnancy.

By contrast, in the course of traditional childbirth, analgesic and amnesic agents commonly are administered during labor. Usually this sedation consists of a combination of demerol and scopolamine, sometimes with the addition of a barbiturate such as seconal. Typically, the baby emerges while the woman is unconscious, under a general anesthesia such as ether or nitrous oxide. "Low" forceps are often routinely used to assist in the delivery. Several hours after the baby's birth, the woman awakes—usually in a "recovery room."

The dangers of sedation in childbirth are known. Anesthesia causes 10 percent of maternal deaths in childbirth. The agents used can have dangerous depressant effects on the fetal respiratory system. They may lengthen labor and delivery, especially if they interfere with the expulsive efforts of the mother. But sedation continues to be used, mainly because it relieves the woman's suffering.

Pain in childbirth is a complex matter, and many of its strictly physiological aspects need further investigation. So, too, do its psychological aspects, for delivery and labor are truly a psycho-physiological area. But even more broadly, the entire nature of pregnancy and childbirth are dramatically in need of investigation as psychological experience.

Unfortunately, most studies of pregnancy are inadequate. Much of the literature concerns fairly narrow investigations of single factors. Even worse, most of the studies treat pregnancy as an illness or pathology, both implicitly (through their tone and diction) and explicitly (by investigating such factors as conflicts, anxieties, hostilities and fears.) Psychological studies of childbirth itself have most often attempted to correlate psychological characteristics with obstetric complications and abnormalities. Almost nowhere are pregnancy and childbirth treated as healthy phenomena.

Certainly the typical childbirth resembles an illness. The woman enters a hospital (the locus of anxiety, sickness and treatment), is handled as a passive patient and often not told what is being "done" to her. She is given anesthesia (as for an operation) in order to remove something from her body. Her very presence as a psychic being often is treated as an interference, or at best, superfluous. She experiences the unpleasant effects of medication and recovers from what has had the character of a surgical operation.

The best studies conclude that—despite genuine obstetric advances—the psychological needs of pregnant and parturient women have been almost blatantly neglected. Such studies refer to a crisis resembling psycho-pathology. They go on to insist on the need for environmental support of the mother during pregnancy and her active participation in childbirth. Natural childbirth claims to provide precisely these benefits.

There are two major forms of natural childbirth in the world today. They are the Read Method, practiced primarily in Anglo-Saxon countries, and the Psychoprophylactic Method, until recently practiced almost exclusively in the Soviet Union and France. At present both forms and various mixtures of them are practiced in this country.

The principle behind the Read Method is that pain in childbirth is neither natural or inevitable, but rather a product of civilization and culture. It is culturally transmitted *fear* of childbirth that is the origin of the pain of childbirth. Fear leads to tension; tension tightens those very uterine muscles that should be relaxed and open. It is this resistance that causes pain.

The principles presumed to underlie the Psycho-prophylactic method—popularized in the West by French obstetrician Fernand Lamaze—are complex and not universally accepted as its actual basis of operation. In general, Pavlovian theories of physiology give the method its central thrust, especially regarding the question of pain. Labor pain is considered "conditioned" in character and hence not inevitable. For this reason it is considered preventable.

Natural childbirth is said to "work." Many claims have been made: anxiety during pregnancy and pain during labor and delivery are reduced; a woman's feelings about herself are improved, as are both her feelings toward and actual relations with her husband and her baby; the act of childbirth itself is much more positive, to the ultimate benefit of both individual and species. But conflicting claims have been made about psychologically harmful effects to mother and child, and to husband as well. Because of these important claims and criticism, attempts at evaluation of natural childbirth are needed.

Yet it is precisely the psychological questions involved that have been made almost completely neglected. Implicit in the few studies of natural childbirth that have been made, however, is a feeling that the psychological variables are intangible and hence not amenable to analysis or experimental treatment. I disagreed.

My experiment sought to answer several questions: What sort of woman chooses natural childbirth? What is the effect of natural-childbirth training on both pregnancy and childbirth? What is the effect of the natural-childbirth *experience* in the *post partum* period? What are the implications of natural childbirth and of childbirth generally for psychology and psycho-physiology?

The study began with 41 women. Five of these had premature deliveries and so were not followed through the complete program, but their records were retained for some of the early sections. Of the remaining 36 women, 22 were in the natural-childbirth group (18 of these were pregnant for the first time; four had previous deliveries). They all used the Psychoprophylactic Method. In the control group were 14 women who used the common method of delivery (10 of these were first pregnancies; four previous deliveries).

We studied the women in three different sessions. The first was a two-hour session at the start of the seventh month of pregnancy. Soon afterward the training program for those using the natural childbirth method began. The second session lasted one hour and was scheduled two weeks before the expected due date. The third session, again two hours, took place one month after delivery.

The women (almost all highly cooperative) were told that little systematic research had been done on the psychological aspects of pregnancy and that our study would explore this area. The division between the natural and common methods of childbirth was not stressed; we mentioned it simply as one factor of interest. We assured them that, while we would ask highly personal questions, their replies would be anonymous and confidential.

Comprehensive records were gathered at the initial interview. The tests included basic information, medical and "autonomic perception" questionnaires, pulse and temperature recordings, and inventory of attitudes toward pregnancy, anxiety scales, the Maslow Security-Insecurity Inventory and self- and husband-rating scales. When the women returned for a second interview, we repeated some of the tests. In the third session, some earlier tests were again given, as well as new ones probing *post-partum* reactions to the self, the husband, the baby and to childbirth itself. In addition, we wrote out each woman's complete qualitative, narrative description of the entire labor and delivery. Finally, medical information was obtained from obstetricians and hospitals.

We distinguished between "choosers" and "non-choosers" among the women. The choosers all independently had wanted natural childbirth; often they selected their doctors on this basis. The non-choosers were women with no interest in natural childbirth, women who were undecided about the question, and women who had not considered natural childbirth before their doctors suggested it.

Comparisons of many psychological and physiological characteristics yielded by the testing data disclosed no significant differences between choosers and non-choosers. Throughout this study "significance" was determined by standard statistical test. Contrary to a common assumption, it is not a certain "type" of woman who chooses natural childbirth.

Women who took the natural-childbirth course and used the learned procedures during labor and delivery are referred to as "takers." When we compared takers with non-takers the control group, we discovered no significant difference between their scores on physiological measures indicative of sympathetic nervous system activity and interpreted anxiety. The only significant score change was in attitudes toward pregnancy. The non-takers' attitudes remained the same, but those of the takers improved. Further, no significant differences existed between choosing takers and non-choosing takers on this item. Apparently, taking the natural-childbirth course positively affects attitudes toward pregnancy, and it is the course itself and not any "type" of woman within that is responsible for the improved attitudes.

A Birth Index Score was prepared for each woman, consisting of the degree of pain reported and a rating of the birth experience as positive or negative. We compared these scores for women with husbands present at labor only, at delivery and labor, and at neither. No significant differences existed among these three groups. But in the experience of rapture or near-mystical bliss—those feelings commonly associated with a peak experience—sharp differences became apparent (see illustration below). Of the seven reported peak experiences, six

Peak Experiences in Childbirth

	Husband at delivery	Husband at labor	Husband at neither
Experienced rapture	6	1	0
No rapture	5	14	10

PEAK EXPERIENCES IN CHILDBIRTH. Only women whose husbands were at their side during labor or delivery reported rapture or near-mystical bliss during childbirth. Husbands seem to be included in, perhaps even necessary for, peak experience in childbirth.

were by women whose husbands had been with them in the delivery room. The seventh had planned to have her husband with her but had to have a Caesarean section. She was conscious throughout the surgery.

While not all women with husbands present at normal delivery had such feelings, all women who did report these feelings had their husbands present. Analysis showed that four of the women peakers had chosen natural childbirth before our group formed, and three were non-choosing takers. Again, the women experiencing rapture were not of a type that predictably would choose natural childbirth. Husbands would seem to be included in, perhaps even necessary for, the peak experience in natural childbirth.

Other results support this conclusion. We asked the women which of 17 intrinsic, higher or "B-value" words might characterize the way the world had seemed to them during the birth of their babies. (see illustration on next page.) When we compared those whose husbands had been with them at delivery with those whose husbands were absent, a striking difference emerged. Women whose husbands were present scored significantly higher than the others.

Another word list tested how the women themselves had felt—as opposed to how they perceived the external world—during labor and delivery. (see list, bottom right). The positive scores, representing high self-actualization—typical of the person whose basic emotional needs are gratified—were again found more often in those women whose husbands were with them at delivery.

Qualitative analysis of descriptions written by the women a month after the birth strikingly showed that husbands of the natural-childbirth women were perceived and responded to much more positively than were the husbands of the group used as a control.

Natural-childbirth husbands were overwhelmingly seen as strong, competent and helpful during childbirth, especially in providing emotional support and encouragement. They were often "in charge and could be leaned on."

"Roy was there, holding up my back," one woman reported. "He was marvelous. He said a nurse was also doing it, but to me it was all Roy."

Control group husbands, on the other hand, were usually described by their wives as incompetent, weak, helpless or impotent, nervous, in the way and needing themselves to be "taken care of."

Statements from the control group largely reported the contact with their husbands as consisting of him "telling me what I had." A typical description ran:

"... and the next thing I knew, it was four in the afternoon and Carl was slapping my face, and he told me I'd had a boy."

We also studied the effect on labor and delivery of taking the natural-childbirth course and using its procedures. Takers experienced a significantly higher ratio of positive to negative emotions. It would seem that for those using natural-childbirth delivery was a more positive event. Of course, the events were recollected subjectively after the birth and may not have "really" occured. But the beliefs exist, and the memories and "meanings" will become incorporated and affect future views of childbirth by these women and those they influence.

The study offers valuable information on pain-relief, a topic bruited about with more heat than light by both advocates and critics of natural childbirth (see illustration on next page). On a five-point scale of recollected pain, takers reported significantly less pain than non-takers. The voluntary choice of natural childbirth was not a factor in pain reduction. Within the group of takers, choosers and non-choosers were distributed alike on the pain scale, as were first-time mothers and mothers of other children. At this point, we could conclude that natural-childbirth training reduces pain. Women who took the course generally received less medication.

How the World Seemed
B-Value Words

Truth
Goodness
Beauty
Connectedness
Aliveness
Uniqueness
Perfection
Inevitability
Completeness
Justice
Order
Simplicity
Richness
Effortlessness
Playfulness
Self-sufficiency

INTRINSIC VALUES. Women whose husbands were present at delivery agreed that these words accurately described the world as it seemed to them at the time.

Women's Feelings About Themselves

Queenly
Receptive
Victorious
Trusting
Joyous
Blissful
Rapturous
Supreme
In Ectasy
Integrated

SELF-ACTUALIZATION. Women with husbands at their side during delivery tended to use these words to describe feelings.

While the breathing techniques learned in this course helped eliminate or reduce the pain for many, some—mostly cases with obstetrical complications—were not helped at all. Several women asked for partial sedation. They were given usually demerol—some wanted midway to "give-up" and be completely anesthetized. None did give up, and among the natural-childbirth group only cases with severe complications were given a general anesthetic. All the rest reported being ultimately glad they had remained awake.

Pain in Childbirth

	High Pain	Low Pain
Choosing takers	8	5
Non-choosing takers	6	3
Takers of course	14	8
Non-takers of course	13	1
Good menstrual history	8	9
Poor menstrual history	14	0

PAIN IN CHILDBIRTH. Natural childbirth appears to reduce pain in labor and delivery with good menstrual histories. Takers generally required less medication.

A dramatic change occurred in the late stages of labor, when a large number of takers reported feeling markedly better, physically and emotionally. We examined many statements and concluded that the greatest rewards of natural childbirth seem to lie during this stage, when women could begin their pushing activity—after full cervical dilation—to help propel the baby into the world.

Since it was in late labor and delivery that strong positive feelings began to emerge, we isolated the specific features of this stage. Consciousness, various perceptions and interpersonal relations in the delivery room, activity, pushing and often the presence and participation of the husband turned out to be the ingredients responsible for this effect. One woman whose husband was present said:

> "From that point on, I'd deliver a baby every day of the week, it was so exciting. I almost had a change of personality at that point. Before, I'd been sleepy and in pain and concerned for myself. At this point we were joking, and Bill put on all the gear for the delivery room, and we talked in between contractions. And they brought the stretcher and I got onto the stretcher myself. And the pushing was very exhilarating."

The finding that natural childbirth reduces pain must be qualified. In our study, we found that pain in childbirth and a poor menstrual history were clearly related (see illustration on this page). A poor menstrual history was indicated by a composite index based on irregularity, severity of cramps, irritability and depression. (The kind of menstrual history—good or bad—had no relation to choosing the natural-childbirth course, corroborating by gynecological function that the chooser type does not exist.)

There are three possible reasons for this high correlation. First, anatomical and physiological conditions responsible for poor menstrual history may also contribute to impairment or abnormality of the reproductive system, resulting in a difficult childbirth. Second, the anxiety surrounding past menstrual difficulties may condition attitudes and responses that bring about pain in childbirth. Finally, certain psychological conflicts surrounding the reproductive system—including impending motherhood—could create the anxiety that caused both the earlier menstrual problems and the childbirth pain. Apparently taking the course is likely to reduce pain in childbirth for women with a relatively good menstrual history. Pain reduction thus appeared to be a joint product of taking the natural-childbirth course and previous menstrual history.

But even the woman with poor menstrual history and pain may experience the positive heightened subjective emotions. Both the statistics and the narrative clearly demonstrated that a woman can experience extremely high pain and yet report positive emotions and the rapture of a peak experience. These are benefits from natural childbirth itself, especially from the husband's presence at delivery. And the husband is allowed to enter the delivery room only if his wife has taken the course.

Our prescription for childbirth would read: For positive emotions, take the course. For pain reduction, have a good menstrual history and take the course. For rapture, have your husband present.

In describing the period after birth, women in the natural-childbirth group expressed feelings of physical well-being and positive emotions, unlike most in the control group. In addition, women in the natural-childbirth group seemed to view their bodies more positively, as indicated by their statements about defecation and their interest in the placenta.

In an attempt to discover whether the natural-childbirth course produced potentially lasting personality or self-image changes, we had takers and non-takers repeat the Self-Ideal Differential Scale one month after delivery. A significant difference in change from the initial session emerged between the two groups. Among the natural-childbirth group, the gap between self and ideal self narrowed far more than did the gap for the control group. The self-concept scores improved similarly.

Analysis showed this change was the result of small movements on a number of items, rather than large changes on a single component, supporting the idea that the general view of the self is improved after natural childbirth. This change in self-image was not dependent upon choosing or nonchoosing, upon rapture or the lack of it or upon the degree of pain or the husband's presence. The critical variable was taking the course.

Sometimes the change in self-concept—and in feelings toward the husband could be pinpointed.

"I felt a little self-conscious about my husband seeing me in this very awkward position, legs up in the air," one woman in the natural childbirth group told us. "All traces of femininity had flown out the window. But at this point Dr. R. said, 'Come here, Jeff, here's your baby's head. It's the size of a quarter.' He showed him. At this point I lost all sense of pride, this foolish thing about childbirth. I felt no more about him seeing me in this position when the doctor pointed him (the baby) out. I'd thought before, seeing pictures of women, whether I'd feel very comfortable, but I'd thought this

was wonderful. I could have been giving birth to an elephant, I couldn't have cared less. That stupid feeling evaporated."

Qualitative analysis of the personal narratives strongly supported our statistical conclusions on the nature of the birth experience. Narrative descriptions showed the experience to be vastly different for the two groups of women. For almost all in the natural-childbirth groups it was a highly positive event, while for the women in the control group it was almost uniformly negative. The natural-childbirth group described joy, excitement, feelings of continuity and positive first contacts with their babies. The control group described negative emotions, a gap in continuity, and fearful and unpleasant memories of the anesthetized period as well as of anesthesia itself.

A mother who took the course and used the natural method had this to say:

"I was pushing all the way into the delivery room, and it was really the most wonderful thing in the world to watch the baby being born. It was just fantastic. And to push with all my might to get him out, and to see him, his little body."

A contrasting experience from the control group read:

"The next thing was about 8:20 a.m., and the doctor had my husband leave, and I remember being wheeled into the delivery room. The doctor gave me a shot, and the next thing, he held up the baby, and put her on my stomach. And I remember yelling, "Take her away!""

In describing labor, the natural-childbirth group stressed activity work, concentration, confidence, coping; the control group stressed passivity, helplessness, suffering, screaming, pain. Thus we hear from a taker:

"The ride all the way to the hospital was very nice because somehow being in the car, breathing, and being with my husband, I was very much in control."

A non-taker said:

"I was lost. No medication till then. I was screaming and everything. I wasn't really hysterical . . . I was screaming purposely, because I was hoping one of the doctors would give me medication. It was horrible. I kept thinking I was dying, wishing I was dead."

When we evaluated the findings of our study, we found the place of the husband in childbirth particularly interesting. Several of the husbands at the session after delivery were eager to be interviewed themselves. They had an intense interest in the whole process of childbearing.

This notion of male identification with childbirth finds historical and anthropological support.

In cultures such as the Caribs of South America, the Ainus of Japan and the Basques of the Pyrenees, it is the husband who takes to bed, fully attended and catered to, as if he were giving birth. Among the Shoshone Indians of North America strong notions exist pointing to an "identification" between father and newborn. In our own culture, studies have shown a high incidence of pregnancy-stimulating gastro-intestinal symptoms in men with pregnant wives.

All this, as well as certain psychoanalytic formulations, support the idea that the male is psychologically involved in childbirth to an extent that has not been realized. Our observations confirm this.

It is important to note that male interest, gratification and participation in childbirth need not involve demasculinization, as is often thought. Indeed, quite the opposite was seen to be the case. It was the natural-childbirth husbands who were seen as possessing the traditional elements of masculinity. It was the control husbands who were more often seen as weak, which produced feelings of superiority and condescension in their wives.

Our major finding, that natural childbirth seems to provide many psychological benefits, has broader implications. Childbirth is a major part of our biological inheritance. Most female humans give birth at some time, and childbirth is each person's introduction to life. Further, childbirth is the initial episode in the relationship between mother and child. Perhaps it influences that relationship, as well as the separate lives of both. A more positive and rewarding method of childbirth obviously is desirable.

Beyond this, there are specific mental-health implications, in terms of mother-child relations and the psychology of women generally. From the organismic or truly psychosomatic viewpoint, an approach that did not arbitrarily separate a woman's psychological and reproductive functioning would seem desirable. As a by-product many academic questions concerning the relation of mind and body and their possible reciprocal influence could be clarified if natural childbirth were more widely used. Finally, the humanistic psychology of health and growth, of peak experiences and self-actualization, would welcome a method that enabled a woman to feel competence, worth and dignity in place of experiencing herself as a passive disoriented object or an animal, present at the event only in body. For these reasons alone, natural childbirth would seem to have much to recommend it.

Natural childbirth should not be used by women or couples who do not want it. But where it is desired, it should be more easily available. There is still much prejudice and passion, much institutional opposition to what might mean revolutionary changes in practice. Many doctors are themselves uninformed or misinformed about the process. With further investigation along the lines of this study, perhaps our approach to all the psychological aspects of childbirth will become more solidly grounded in fact.

Name: _____ Date: _____

Student #: _____ Sex: M or F

1. T   F   Men are better prepared to be parents than women.

2. T   F   Fathers have a greater direct impact on their children than mothers during the child's first five years of life.

3. T   F   Mothers tend to be more stern disciplinarians than fathers.

4. T   F   Mothers place more positive value on children than do fathers.

5. T   F   Child abuse is more likely among lower income groups.

6. T   F   Men are more frequently child abusers than women.

7. T   F   Children's problems are frequently reflections of their parents'.

8. T   F   Family sex education should come from the parent of the opposite sex of the child.

9. T   F   Parenthood of young children is less traumatic than of teenagers.

10. T   F   Parenthood is the most rewarding time of the individual's life cycle.

11. Recently a pilot program for parenthood has been launched in a number of high schools around the country. What do you think would be the *five* (5) most important topics or areas covered in such a program?

   a.

   b.

   c.

   d.

   e.

   "We all wanted babies, but did any of us want children?"

12. In retrospect, how well prepared do you think your parents were for parenthood?

   Very well _____ About average _____ Poorly _____

13. How good a job of parenting do you think they did?

   Outstanding _____ Average _____ Poor _____

If I were to become a parent:

14. I would want to have _____ children.

15. I would want _____ boys.

16. I would want _____ girls.

17. I would want my first child to be a: boy_____; girl _____; it makes no difference _____.

18. If I could not become a biological parent, I would adopt. Yes _____ No _____

19. Briefly discuss the relationship of parenthood to marital adjustment, listing at least three (a) pros and three (b) cons.

WE ALL WANTED BABIES—BUT DID ANY OF US WANT CHILDREN?

Eda T. LeShan

My daughter and I were having lunch in a drugstore crowded with young mothers and their children. Four of the young women were very pregnant, and after my daughter had listened to them screaming at their nursery school age children for about fifteen minutes without letup, she asked a very perceptive and logical question, "If they hate their kids so much, why are they having more?"

A Dutch emigre, mother of four and grandmother of seven, asked me the same question recently when we were discussing the young families she was observing the suburban community she had come to live in. "They complain so much—they have so many children, and they don't seem at all glad to have them. Is this an American trait?" Whether one could call it a trait or not, it does seem to me that in the last ten years I have met more young families with four to six children, usually one to two years apart, who seem to feel overwhelmed—after the fact. Millions of American couples are having larger families and enjoying it; we all know about them. What we don't talk about as often is the parents who are in serious conflict.

In an article in the *New York Times Magazine,* Dr. Francis Bauer, a psychiatrist, wrote of "The Plight of the Brand-New Parent." He reported on a study undertaken at the University of Michigan which had revealed some interesting facts:

> . . . Basically . . . many young parents are troubled because they are unable to reconcile their true, inner feelings with the way they think they ought to feel. . .
> . . . conflicts arise from an overemphasis on fulfilling the needs of the newborn. Ever since Sigmund Freud focused attention on the importance of early childhood . . . it has been open season on new mothers. . . It is not surprising that when the new mother leaves the hospital with her baby in one arm and three volumes on child care under the other, her thick smile often fails to mask her underlying sense of panic. She is in many instances terrified at the prospect of motherhood and has grave misgivings about proving equal to what has become the most formidable challenge of modern society—raising a healthy happy infant.

Most of us mothers who grew up twenty or thirty years ago, played with dolls and had lovely dreams of marrying a handsome prince and having several beautiful and charming children. This kind of fantasy has probably been true for most children over many generations. But our growing-up time was different and special in some ways. Many of us belong to the first generation to be told that dreams do come true and that we would live happily ever after. It was an era of hope, of increasing prosperity, of a sense of power about man's ability to conquer disease, poverty, unhappiness. The increasing power of mass media added fuel to a climate of "life can be beautiful." Advertisements teased up with easy answers and over-simplified solutions to complex problems: Use the right deodorant and you will meet a rich and handsome man; buy the right set of sterling silver and the domestic scene will be forever blissful; feed your babies the only baby food guaranteed to be fortified with every vitamin and mineral and your baby will never be sick or cranky or funny looking. Neither our parents nor the movies we saw nor the magazines we read ever suggested that life was more complicated, that happiness was a fortuitous by-product of living, not an end in itself. In truth, we had the least realistic preparation for the hardest job of all.

We knew about the joys and pleasures of marriage and parenthood, but no one ever really told us about the displeasures, the serious responsibilities, the plain drudgery.

I think most of us carry into marriage not only our childlike illusions, but we bring to it as well the demand that it has to be wonderful, because it's supposed to be. Of course the biggest illusion of all is that we are going to do the job of parenthood so well: it will all be fun and always deeply satisfying.

When we bring our babies home, we do feel proud and happy, and to the degree that our natural instincts are still permitted to operate, there is a strange and marvelous sense of having found one's destiny. But before we can really relax and let ourselves feel, we begin to get scared. First of all we get scared because we find we don't enjoy a baby every minute of the day and night. We feel uneasy because we begin to realize the utter helplessness of this baby, and the fact that we will belong to him and to his needs for a long, long time. Occasionally there is the feeling that we have unwittingly accepted life imprisonment! No man or woman I ever knew loved to spend half of every night feeding and walking and changing a baby. The large majority of perfectly decent, civilized adults simply do not enjoy a steady diet of having to wake from a deep sleep, move around in cold dark rooms—especially while one's spouse snores peacefully—and know that even after the baby is clean, and fed and happy, this whole operation is coming up again in a few hours, when, unbelievable, it will still be earlier than you ever got up before!

Discussing this with friends recently, one mother said, "My memory of those first few weeks is of a sense of utter chaos and of my being completely incompetent. I wasn't, but I felt that I was. Everytime I made the formula I was sure something would go wrong, and I was absolutely certain I would never get the baby's clothes washed and dried in time. I could not imagine there was any possibility that I would ever again have time for such activities as reading a book, really talking to my husband or going to a movie. Shopping becomes a nightmare of anxiety—I couldn't leave the baby carriage outside the store and of course the baby was too young to sit in the shopping cart. The whole business was so traumatizing that I can't remember what I finally did do!"

As parents, we all know and remember the joys and satisfactions: the attention we received, the pride in seeing other people's reactions to the baby, wheeling a carriage down the street, feeling this warm, tiny body snuggled against one, feeling that one has participated in this great miracle of life. With an easy, relaxed baby, it can be fun most of the time—but even under the best of circumstances it just has to be a nuisance sometimes. The isolation for the mother who now may lose contact with a job or with friends, being alone with a baby who certainly isn't much of a conversationalist, having to do the same routine things over and over again—all this is not completely compensated for because babies happen to be absolutely adorable. But we get frightened the very first time we think, "Why didn't we take a trip instead? Now I'm a prisoner forever—this baby owns my body and soul—I'm finished, all washed up!"

Wives feel trapped, husbands feel betrayed and neglected. Lack of sleep makes tempers short, and love which thrives on privacy is thwarted—and then that baby starts crying again! Nothing could be more normal. Life is never easy or fun all the time. Parenthood has wonderful attributes which hardly need explanation; it offers a special kind of fulfillment, it brings with it a keener sense of being alive, a renewed and reawakened sense of wonder at life and at growth, and it is of course an affirmation of love—it makes the meaning of marriage more tangible and real. But even little babies can be big

burdens, and why shouldn't we hate and resent them once in a while? Most of us feel overwhelmed with guilt if we are not delighted every single second.

We begin to come closer to a sane view of life and love when we begin to accept parenthood as a worthwhile but often difficult and trying job. I remember what a father told me, with a sheepish smile, when his four-month-old son started howling for the eighth time during a dinner party, "It's a funny thing, I never used to notice how many people murdered their babies but when I read a newspaper now, that's all I seem to notice! Has there been a sudden epidemic of cases of infanticide, or do I just notice it more now?" If most of us were really honest with ourselves and each other, we would admit that there were moments—! One of the best-kept secrets is that almost every mother alive, at some time or other, has screamed at, shaken or even at times hit her baby. We work so hard to maintain the myth that changing diapers, worrying about fevers, cleaning up vomit and listening to crying are the most popular activities and the greatest privileges obtainable.

Another mother told me, "One day our very colicky and cranky three-month-old daughter just cried so much and made me feel so incompetent and helpless and miserable that I shook her hard and dumped her into the crib, ran out of the room, and sobbed and sobbed until my husband arrived home, found us both bawling, put his arms around us and said, "there, there" until we both stopped gulping hysterically and calmed down." That is as much part of the reality of becoming a parent as the blissful, wide-eyed wonder that one also feels the first time the baby smiles, rolls over, or says "Dadda."

People used to have children because (among other reasons) they needed them: for farming the land, for settling new territories, for developing commerce on the seas—for keeping the human race going, in fact. Infant mortality was so high and death from childhood diseases so common that every living breathing child was a precious and necessary economic asset. Obviously things are quite the reverse now—we are made to feel guilty if we support the population explosion! While only four or five years ago birth control or population control were rarely if ever discussed publicly—a complete change has taken place. Magazines, newspapers—even politicians—are now discussing a real and grave concern: overpopulation. Margaret Mead, in *Redbook* magazine, stated openly and clearly "Why Americans Must Limit Their Families":

188

... At the present rate of increase the population of the United States, now at some 189 million, is likely to reach 351 million in the year 2000 ... Continuing at the same rate, the United States alone will pass the billion mark in 2050 A.D.

Whatever else all this may mean, one thing is sure: it does play a role in how we feel about children. Children are an economic drain on parents to such an extent that in all likelihood all those children who are brought into the world intentionally must have been conceived for reasons completely different from those past civilizations. Even in earlier times the desire to have children was of course based on motives other than economic, but it makes a difference when society no longer needs so many children for survival. When we have children for emotional reasons, for love only, then our expectations are of an entirely dissimilar nature. This experience has to be more satisfying and rewarding, or we feel cheated.

To have children for reasons of emotional gratification and fulfillment and for fun may be perfectly reasonable, if we accept what this means. There will be no rewards for good behavior; children will not appreciate our selfless devotion and behave angelically just because we try so hard. We must not look forward to a time when our children will be an economic or a social asset; it will be a long, long drain on our resources of every kind. It can't be fun all the time; being human, children get sick, are often a nuisance, will have at least the normal range of problems that are simply part of growing up. We never get what we bargained for; there is no use in having prior claims and expectations, because these demands are a distortion of life and an impossibility. It is as foolish to say, "I will have a sweet, quiet child." as it is to say, "My child will look like his father."

To have children is no way to solve problems, whether it be a shaky marriage, a wish to quit working at a dull or tiring job, the next "right thing to do," a way to please one's parents, or a way to postpone the "menopause blues" when we don't quite know what to do with ourselves and feel less and less needed by our growing children. Most of us had mixed reasons for and mixed feelings about becoming parents; but all things considered, we will get on with the job at hand far more successfully if at the outset we try to gain some clarity on what we have been feeling and expecting.

Accepting reality—with its joys as well as its problems—makes it easier for us to plan, lest from the very beginning parenthood become the be-all and end-all for us; if it does, then our demands for satisfaction from it are just too awesome a burden for any child to carry. To keep one's sanity while raising an infant, one has to maintain a sense of proportion and perspective. That baby is not going to stay helpless and dependent forever, and he's not going to need us one hundred percent of the time, so we had better tend other gardens as well, such as seeing that our marriage is given time and attention, that we make opportunities for adult-centered activities, keeping us with friends and our interests. Both husband and wife have a stake in the maintenance of a life apart from child-raising, and both must work at finding those outlets and opportunities that can keep their own communication and contact alive. One thing that we have to afford—it is as vital as the baby's regular visits to the doctor—it is a long list of really reliable baby-sitters. Some of us may be lucky enough to have a number of volunteers, like grandparents, on our list, but it should also include several other older people who might be available when we need them. Such a list tends to make one feel less trapped—that there is, after all, an escape clause! Getting away for one afternoon a week to do something adult and refreshing and enriching is a necessity, not a luxury. Some women whine that it can't be done. It can. There is just no excuse for much of the self-pity we are sometimes inclined to wallow in.

Already with a tiny baby, parents feel the impact of the experts: the pediatrician; Dr. Spock; the lady in the park who's had seven children; the vaguely remembered pitfalls described in the psychology courses one took at college; the more than generous advice of grandparents. This is the time when one should begin thinking about how to make decisions, what "common sense" is; how to be discriminating and at the same time open-minded in learning to care for a child. Common sense is really the way in which we learn to combine information, experience, intuition and spontaneity. We never succeed completely, but there is simply no such thing as a perfect score where human relationships are concerned.

With all the realities of infant care that we may have been unprepared for, this is as nothing compared to our surprise at what children are like! They begin by saying, "No," and we have the first inkling of the battles for power that lie ahead. We feel undermined, attacked; panic and anger set in. Then they begin to get into everything, nothing is sacred, and we have to change our entire household arrangements. Right after absolutely refusing to do what we tell them, they cling to us, won't let us out of their sight, and we find that we can't even go to the bathroom alone any more!

We begin to feel the pressure on us from grandparents and experts to toilet-train; we are instructed on how to encourage good eating habits; when to pick up a crying child, when not to. No two theories are very much alike, and none of the instructions seem to have much practical applicability to the crises we are facing. Nightmares may keep us sleepless, clinging, and shyness embarrass us; as well as talking back, biting, selfishness with toys, aggressiveness with other children—this is just the beginning! At least they are still cute when all this starts. But they are no longer so cute when some of the most exasperating and frightening things begin to happen—lying, stealing, starting fires, not learning fast enough—and then, to add insult to injury, the final straw: they begin to show an intense dislike for us from time to time. A mother recently said, "Sometimes I just look at Marian; who is this fresh, sloppy, unpleasant child? Can she really be that adorable baby I had twelve years ago?"

THE PROBLEM OF PARENTAL LOVE
Snell and Gail Putney

Thou art young, and desirest child and marriage.
   But I ask thee:
Art thou a man entitled to desire a child?
Art thou the victorious one, the self-conqueror,
   the ruler of thy
passions, the master of thy virtues? Thus do I ask thee.
Or doth the animal speak in thy wish, and
   necessity? Or isolation?
Or discord in thee? FRIEDRICH NIETZSCHE

. . .out of some forty families I have been able
   to observe,
I know hardly four in which the parents do not
   act in such a way
that nothing would be more desirable for the child than
to escape their influence. ANDRE GIDE

A certain amount of love for one's young is probably inevitable, but there is little profit for either parent or child in encouraging or glorifying it. That such a statement may seem irresponsible, if not downright immoral, indicates the degree to which love has become a sacred cow in American culture. Most Americans are only too aware that their interaction with their children is not what they might wish, but they fail to perceive the source and meaning of most of their difficulties. Uncritical adulation of parental love blinds them.

Love is probably the emotion most talked about and extolled by Americans and probably also the least understood. In large measure this is because love seems a natural human emotion that requires no explanation. It is taken for granted that love for one's spouse and children is a universal element in human experience, something that men of all places and ages have felt in common. Affection and warmth are universal, to be sure, but not love in the middle-class sense of the word. What seems to be a natural emotional response is largely a conventional response.

The range of human emotional potential is broad, and that set of responses which is accorded the highest value in one society may not be highly regarded in another. Thus, filial piety was considered the finest emotion in traditional Chinese society, patriotism was the transcendent emotion in ancient Sparta, the Puritans extolled the fear of God above all else, and the modern Americans exalt love.

As it would have seemed sacrilege to the Puritan to suggest that man approach God in any attitude but fear, so it seems sacrilege to the modern American to suggest that the parent approach his child with anything but love. In America, love is regarded not only as man's finest feeling but also as a prime mover. The American tends to assume that whatever is not done for money is surely done for love, and when he says that he would not do something "for love or money" he means that he would not do it at all.

Americans differentiate many levels and types of love, for much the same reason that the Arabian nomads had a thousand words for "sword." But the underlying psychological mechanism of love is essentially the same, whether the love in question be called puppy love, mature love, romantic love, platonic love, parental love, or any other relationship that involves adoration of one person by another.

What happens, in essence, is that one person projects some part of himself which he values highly onto someone else, where he adores it. He then begins to act as if this person were an extension of himself. Longing to enjoy the misplaced part of himself, he clings to the person on whom he has projected it, he is possessive and jealous, he delights in the loved one's presence, but feels anxious and incomplete when this person is absent. Stated thus baldly, love may sound neither very admirable nor enjoyable. But this is nevertheless the kind of feeling the American has in mind when he says "I love you."

There are many parallels between romantic love, the subject of the last chapter, and parental love. In the same way that the American learns to consider certain attributes appropriate and desirable for one sex but unacceptable for the other, so he learns to consider certain qualities endearing in children but inappropriate for adults. Children can be affectionate, warm, and dependent in ways that most adults do not permit themselves to be. Children can feel free to do outrageous things such as rolling in the mud or being rude to visiting relatives. And children can loaf and play, free from responsibility.

The capacity and the desire to behave like a child are not lost by the adult; they are supplemented by, and ultimately subordinated to the adult self image, but they remain as latent potential. Often the adult has a rigid and narrow conception of maturity that excludes his childlike potential. Yet the proper adult has his impish side still, and refusing to recognize it does not obliterate it. The adult who has sexualized and alienated his desire to cuddle and be cuddled may be stiffly aloof most of the time, but his desire remains. And the adult who bristles with independence has merely alienated a strong desire to be dependent on others. These and other alienated characteristics are customarily projected onto children, in whom such desires and behaviors are deemed appropriate.

Some adults are so concerned with holding their childlike potential at a distance that they are uncomfortable with the children on whom they project it. These are the adults who confess that they simply do not enjoy children. But most adults find their childlike potential amusing, charming, and *lovable* when projected onto children—particularly when the children involved are their own. The desire to experience vicariously and to indulge projected childlike facets of the self is one of the basic ingredients of parental love.

The desire to re-create the self through one's child is another important factor in parental love. Recoiling from the thought of his own death, the parent seeks to cheat the grave by creating himself anew in his offspring. While he is about it, he hopes to make some improvements. He hangs on the child his own unrealized potential and sees not the child but the projected image of the person he would like to be. The loving parent has clothed his child with a great deal of himself and he clings to the child possessively.

Often, as in romantic love, the desire to repossess projected aspects of the self is interpreted as a desire to unite physically with the person on whom they are projected. Such a desire is usually given a sexual interpretation. However, incestuous desire is highly tabu in American culture, as is sexual interest in children. The effect of these tabus is to drive from consciousness the sexualization of love for the child. It is then experienced via projection, and the parent may become preoccupied with curbing what seems to him the child's precocious sexual interest, or with protecting his child from sexual interest he attributes to the child's playmates or to sex perverts. (This is not to deny that the latter two groups—or the child himself—have sexual interests. It is rather to note that they are often targets for the projected sexual interests which the parent is unwilling to admit are his own.)

The American father is generally more inhibited in fondling his children than is the mother. He is also more prone to assuming that his interest in physical contact with them is sexual in nature. He is likely to practice a studied avoidance of physical contact with any child past puberty, the age at which (in American mythology) the child is transformed from a sexless creature to a sexual one. And in the case of a male child, the father's fear of homosexuality is added to the fear of incestuous desire. He is terrified at the thought of being physically attracted to a young boy and is likely to be awkward and inhibited in any physical contact he has with his son. Thus, parental love (that is, the parent's emotional involvement with qualities he has projected onto his child) is likely to have suppressed sexual undertones. This means that love can actually inhibit the expression of physical warmth between parent and child, particularly between a father and his adolescent son.

Love is essentially a neurotic response. A neurosis is an internal, nonorganic barrier to need fulfillment, and love arises in the parent because of his incapacity to satisfy his need for an accurate and acceptable self-image. When he has induced comparable problems in his child, the child will reciprocate this love.

The adjusted American experiences tension and conflict in parenthood and is concerned about it. If his home contains few books it will still be likely to have a cross-indexed volume on how to raise children. Yet the underlying source of much of the conflict escapes recognition because it is a normal neurosis. Holding love to be of all emotions the most elevated, the American blinds himself to the deleterious effects that love has on his relations with his family—indeed, he struggles to overcome these effects by loving them more.

What Does The Lamb Say?

There is the common case of the devoted mother who is preoccupied with a small daughter whom she deeply loves. The mother lives a restricted life. Taking the toddler anywhere is an exhausting experience for both, and when visitors come the child manages to preempt most of her mother's attention. As this mother sees it, the needs of her baby leave little time for doing things with other people, or for herself. She recognizes that not all women are so monopolized by their children, but views this as evidence that other mothers are less conscientious than she. She insists that a child needs its mother's full attention and that she loves her baby so much she is glad to devote her life to her child. The latter is true enough.

Chronically uncertain about her capacity to succeed at anything, this woman worried during pregnancy about whether she could be a good mother. From the time she came home from the hospital (apprehensive about being on her own with the baby), she has been preoccupied with trying to prove that she is an adequate parent. Motherhood has come to dominate her self-image—significantly, she usually refers to herself as "Mommy."

Devoting herself to her baby, this mother begins to identify with the child and to hang all manner of projections on her. She is convinced that her daughter will be pretty and talented (she has always thought of herself as plain and inept). She resolves to make certain that her daughter develops her potential. Having projected so much of herself onto her daughter, she finds the child's presence indispensable—but she is not clinging to the child,

only to her projections. She wants to be with her daughter continuously to enjoy vicariously, to encourage, and to protect the alienated facets of herself with which she has endowed her daughter.

There is another element in the relationship, also deriving from the mother's self-doubts. By spending most of her time talking baby talk and playing with her baby, this woman is able to escape from adult interaction. She retreats into a pseudo-childhood, with the comforting rationalization that her actions are those of a loving mother. In the process her doubts about her capacity to function as an adult are aggravated. The little girl, meanwhile, is prevented from experimenting with her own childhood.

In spite of this mother's devotion, the child's needs are often left unsatisfied. They are ignored by the mother, who insists that the child satisfy needs which the mother projects onto her. Picture the mother, the child, and the father as they go for a drive in the country. The mother is delighted to get out (hers is a confining life) but from the time the car rolls down the driveway she devotes herself to "making the ride fun for the baby." Her own desires to see and to enjoy are projected onto the child, whom she holds up to the window.

Before long the little girl begins to squirm and says "night-night," her signal that she is sleepy. The mother ignores the request (*she* is not tired) and burbles, "See the cow? Isn't that a pretty cow?" The child is not looking. With still greater animation the fond parent tries to rekindle interest. "See the little lamb! What does the lamb say?"

"Go night-night!"

Only when the exhausted baby is tense and fussing does the mother decide to put her on the back seat for a nap. By this time, however, the child is no longer relaxed enough to sleep. The mother struggles to quiet her, but a howling baby, a frantic mother, and a profane father return from the ride.

Boys Will Be Boys

Parental love also interferes with the child's struggle to grow up. Here is the mother who worries about having sent her only son to camp. She is certain that he will lose his clothes, forget to brush his teeth, be neglected by the counselors, and become homesick. For the sake of argument, let us grant that her predictions are essentially correct. But if her son is less able to take care of himself than other boys are, it is because he has never had a chance to learn. He is accustomed to his mother's loving care.

The key to this mother's love is the projection of her own irresponsible, dependent qualities onto her son. In accordance with major aspects of her self-image, she takes pride in being a responsible, orderly, and self-sacrificing adult. But an alienated part of her would like to be demanding and selfish, to strew things about, and to let others worry about the consequences of her actions.

This woman was raised to believe that children—particularly boys—have a right to be and to do such things, and she projects her alienated desire to be dependent and undisciplined onto her son. When she indulges him she is indulging the aspects of herself which she has hung on him. In effect, she encourages him to be irresponsible and demanding, and, in time, her projections are a good fit. When her husband complains about the boy's behavior she defends the child, contending that his actions "only prove that he is all boy."

Because she cherishes the childlike facets of herself which she experiences through her son, and because she allows herself no other or more direct enjoyment of these aspects of herself, she has no wish to see him grow up. When her husband declares that it is time the boy learned to assume responsibility, she answers, "Children grow up too soon, why crowd him?" She loves her son as she has created him—demanding, irresponsible, and careless.

Typically, the more a child is loved the less he is enjoyed. The loved child has little chance to learn to amuse himself or to develop independence. He learns only to expect the continuous attention of his loving parent and he becomes a demanding child. His demands, when added to those that the parent projects onto him, amount to a staggering total. However much the parent may welcome an opportunity to indulge his projected childlike nature, there is another side to his feelings: resentment.

Yet this emotion is unacceptable to the loving parent and he (or she) recoils from it. Commonly, such a parent denies that the resentment exists, while simultaneously becoming a doormat for the child as a means of atoning for it. The wear and tear endured while serving as a doormat increase the resentment, and a vicious circle is set spinning.

The parent is likely to try to conceal his resentment from himself by projecting it. The mother who encourages her child to be demanding and careless is likely to be certain that all those who have contact with her son are annoyed by his demands and his carelessness. Such projections may fit, but it is nevertheless her own resentment against which she sputters and fumes—and from which she attempts to shield the boy. If her husband openly resents the child, she will have a convenient place to hang her own resentment and the child will become a focal point for marital conflict.

Some Go Wrong

The American parent expects his child to be a source of emotional satisfaction and hopes to find his relationship to his child a deeply meaningful experience. He assumes that such hopes and expectations are natural, and if he finds that he does not love his child he is disturbed. The resentment a new father feels when his wife is suddenly monopolized by an infant and the guilt the new father feels about his resentment are familiar. But we are here concerned with a more complex pattern, in which a father who was once devoted to his small son comes to reject the boy as he grows older and to be concerned about his inability to love him.

Frequently such a father is seeking immortality and vicarious fulfillment of his own undeveloped capacities through his son. It is easy to see almost any potential in a tiny child, and a father's projections on his infant son can take any direction he fancies. Thus, the father may be tremendously attached to his small son. But inevitably as the boy grows older he develops a self of his own—and not precisely the self that his father had in mind. The father demands that the son succeed where he himself has failed and develop qualities which the father has allowed to remain latent. When the son does not, the father is disappointed.

When it becomes abundantly clear that projections do not fit the person on whom they are hung, love cools abruptly. The husband who finds that his wife does not fit his image of the ideal woman (a composite image of cherished qualities he has alienated from himself) may begin to look ardently at women who are unfamiliar enough to seem to fit his projections. Similarly, the father who perceives that his fond hopes are not being realized in his son may begin to make invidious comparisons between his son and other boys who are distant enough to seem sterling lads.

Because the father believes that he *should* love his son, he is disturbed when he finds that he does not. He feels that there must be either something wrong with himself or something unlovable about the boy. The latter is the more palatable possibility to the father, and so he finds fault with his son. He can always find shortcomings in the boy to explain why the latter is unlovable. For one, there is the fact that the boy is turning out poorly (that is, he is no improvement on his father).

He is likely to find his son demanding and ungrateful. He tries to give his son opportunities that he himself did not have as a child (wanting to participate vicariously in an idealized childhood). But losing sight of his motivation, he assumes that these are things he does for the boy and he expects gratitude. Because things the father would like if he were a child again do not necessarily appeal to his son, the boy is not always grateful for his "advantages." The father points out that his son takes things for granted (being accustomed to having them showered upon him), does not appreciate things (not having particularly wanted them), or asks for something more (having his own ideas of what he wants in *his* childhood).

The conflicts between this father and son are in large measure a result of the father's attempts to love his child and to rationalize his failure to do so. The father alternates between trying to make his son fit the image he is prepared to love and, failing in this, trying to prove that the boy is simply not lovable.

The Little Tin God

The expectation that the child will love the parent is one of the covert motives which lead the adjusted American to want children. Insecure and longing for approval, the parent hopes that he can raise someone to love and admire him. The ancient commandment "Honor thy father and thy mother" has been subtly altered in American culture to "Love thy father and thy mother."

The child is aware of his dependence on his parent for physical and emotional sustenance, and, perceiving his parent as the bringer of satisfactions and the righter of wrongs, he values him. But he also perceives the parent as the imposer of restrictions and punishments, and he fears and resents him. The inherent nature of the relationship between parent and child leads to ambivalent emotions. However, the American child soon learns that he is expected to conceal his fear and anger responses and to reciprocate his parent's love.

There is an element of love in the child's feeling for the parent, and it is similar to all other forms of love. The child finds in his parent qualities which he believes are not in himself and which he longs to make a part of himself. Insofar as this results in the child taking the parent as a model, this is a functional emotion. If the child is given assurance that in time he can develop capacities similar to those he admires in his father (or mother), hero worship of the parent can contribute to the child's development of a viable self-image. *But this development requires that the child become aware of his own latent potential.*

The parent who seeks indirect self-acceptance through the child's love is more likely to encourage the hero worship for its own sake than to turn it toward the child's development. This may be the only hero worship he has ever received and he may unconsciously exploit it.

Such a parent is likely to overwhelm his child, playing off the child's puny efforts against his own, engaging in games with him (in the name of being a "pal" to his son) but excelling without teaching. By continuously displaying his skill in comparison to the child's he squeezes the last drop of adoration from him but at the expense of the child's self-confidence.

When the parent plays God in a small universe, he expects his child to worship him. But a child who seems to do so actually worships his own unrecognized potential. Projecting his own latent strength and skills onto his parent, he sees himself as weak and bungling. He then cries out for the parent to accept him, for he cannot accept himself.

Yet the parent who creates such a needful child is singularly unlikely to grant the approval his child seeks. The child tries desperately to be "perfect," for he thinks that perfection would bring the coveted acceptance from the parent. But small steps in the learning process are all that he is likely to achieve in a short space of time, and these small improvements are likely to elicit from such a parent only impatient remarks about how slowly the child is progressing. (After all, this parent would feel threatened by any real success on the part of the child.) Long before the child has approached even a small measure of perfection, he is likely to quit in tearful shame. Pinning his hopes for acceptance on intense but spasmodic efforts to acquire some skill, then retreating in shame and self-doubt may become a pattern for the child. Repeated in various areas of activity, the pattern leads to an overwhelming sense of failure and personal inadequacy. The future course of the child's life is sadly predictable.

A variant of this kind of parent worship occurs when one parent holds the other up as a model. An occasional mother may hold up her husband to her son as the epitome of all that is manly, hiding his imperfections. She may feel that the father has too little contact with the son for the latter to be able to see his father's best qualities, and so she makes a point of qualities which she would like to see the boy emulate. (These are likely to be qualities which she has projected onto her husband.) But whatever the mother's motives, the effect is pernicious. The son will either try to protect his tenuous self-acceptance by refusing to accept his father as a model, or will lose sight of his own potential and worship his father from a vast psychological distance.

Because the parent is inevitably stronger and more skillful than the small child, such a parent-worshipping relationship may continue its neurotic course for a number of years. The child may never feel capable of achieving the same level of skill as his father and may languish in the parental shadow all his life. The sons of famous fathers are often caught up in this pattern. Their family (and outsiders) may expect them to repeat their father's achievements, but a lifelong sense of being inferior to the father may leave such sons incapable of developing their own potential.

More frequently, the time comes when the adolescent boy begins to feel that his childhood image of his father was false, or at least inflated. The father appears as a fraud and the son feels cheated. But although the boy may experience a sense of loss when he becomes aware that his view of his father has been exaggerated, he does not necessarily acquire thereby an awareness of his own latent capacities. He may simply come to feel that his father, too, is a bungling incompetent.

The child who sees his parent less as a hero and more as a human being can take his parent as a model. As a small child he is less likely to adore his father, but as an adolescent he is less likely to scorn him. And he is very likely to become aware of his own potential at an early age.

The Child Beyond Love

Undeniably, the human infant needs more than food, drink, and sanitation. A child seems to require a considerable amount of physical handling and comforting. Simply being in bodily contact with its mother seems to be important to the small child. In cultures where infants are carried most of the time next to their mothers' bodies it is rare to hear a baby cry. Experiments on human babies are generally frowned upon, but monkey babies have been raised in experimental situations with a surrogate mother made of wire and terry cloth (and a feeding bottle). These monkeys show extreme anxiety when deprived of physical contact with

their "mother." Clinging to the source of physical satisfaction seems to characterize small primates.

This is presumably the need long since noted by the advocates of "tender, loving care." But the infant's need is more for tender, frequent handling than for the kind of emotional involvement most American parents have in mind when they talk about loving their children. For all their concern about their children, Americans exercise an amazing restraint on bodily contact with them. In striking contrast is the relation between parents and children in many "underdeveloped" cultures. In a survey conducted in a rural region of Mexico, people were asked to indicate their favorite and most frequent pastimes. Far and away the most frequent answer to both questions was "playing with my children." And this did not mean organizing ball games or hand-craft activities; this meant tossing and tussling and physical fondling.

Too often, the American parent communicates to his child at a tender age the idea that he should not press himself on others too demonstratively, and the child turns his impulse to touch and fondle others into more aggressive contact. The tabu on fondling is reinforced shortly by the kindergarten teacher who bears down on the matter of "keeping your hands to yourself." The final product is an individual who is almost incapable of expressing warmth physically. Thus one inhibited generation inhibits the next.

And thus the American parent is likely to find it difficult to give his children the fondling they need simply because he (or she) has never learned to express physical warmth. Moreover, the love relationship itself may inhibit warm physical contact between parent and child, for it is likely to aggravate the parent's buried fears that his desire to handle the child may have a sexual basis.

The child's love for the parent and the parent's love for the child are generally stultifying to the child and disappointing to the parent. Moreover, love is ever one side of a basic ambivalence. To love one's child is also to resent him. Yet, being creatures of their culture, adjusted Americans assume that the only alternatives to loving a child are rejection and indifference. Happily this is not the case. Indeed, rejection and indifference most often derive from an unsatisfying attempt at loving a child.

Interest in children can be founded in love (although the parent who loves his child may scarcely know what the child under the projections is like). But interest in a child can also be founded in a healthy self-interest. Being a good parent is an important part of the self-image of most adults, and children provide the opportunity to explore and enjoy this potentiality of the self.

This motivation can lead the parent to a variety of behaviors, some constructive, some destructive. If he insists that his child achieve and behave so that he, the parent, will appear to be a splendid parent in the eyes of the community, the result will be continuous and destructive interference with the life of the child. But the same motivation can lead to a richly rewarding relation between parent and child if the former conceives being a good parent as a matter of helping the child discover his capacities and develop a viable self-image. Seeking to develop his own capacity for being an effective parent, he will discover that shaping a child can be fascinating. As the sculptor draws out and enhances the beauty inherent in his medium, so the parent can elicit and encourage the inherent qualities of his child. Leading a child to self-discovery is a creative art. It is also a delightful activity.

The parent who has learned to live his own life fully makes an incalculable contribution to the development of his child. Because the child imitates his parents' neurotic and healthful patterns alike, it is a fortunate child who has the opportunity to take as a model a parent who effectively satisfies his own needs. Moreover, the parent who has achieved insight into his own neuroses will be able to give dignity to his child's problems.

The relationship between parent and child will inevitably have tempestuous moments, if only because of the controls which the parent must impose for the child's safety. But on balance the relationship can be warm, accepting, and rewarding for all concerned, if the complexities of love are not added. The parent who does not love/resent his child can establish a pattern of mutual need satisfaction with him. In his parental role he finds self-acceptance through acting on capacities he values; the child in turn discovers and accepts himself through interaction with his parent. Such relationships are rare between American parents and children but not uncommon between a boy and his favorite uncle.

It must be underscored that interaction based on mutually rewarding behaviors is not an exalted stage of parental love. It is founded on an entirely different basis: on habits of mutual need satisfaction and self-acceptance. Such a relationship is not love and lacks love's detrimental effects.

WHAT'S SO BAD ABOUT BEING A MOTHER?
Lee Salk, Ph.D.

Through all of human history and in every variety of culture, the achievement of motherhood has always been equated with the highest good. But there is a tendency today, especially among the more militant of the Women's Liberation groups, to downgrade motherhood as a social and political artifact invented by that oppressor, man, in order to keep women in bondage. It is hard for me to believe that very many women hold such a simple-minded view.

Motherhood represents a complexity of interlocking patterns and drives, all directed toward (1) the propagation of the species, (2) the protection of offspring during its critical early development, and (3) the fulfillment of the mother herself. These patterns and drives are not arbitrary cultural whims-of-the-moment. They have emerged through aeons of evolution and they are undoubtedly crucial to the survival not only of the human race, but of those values we have traditionally prized as uniquely human.

If motherhood is bondage, it is a beautiful bondage (I watch the beauty of it every day of my professional life); and any woman who gives it up ought to examine seriously what she is "liberating" herself from. The deep and delicate interplay of mother and child, full of nuances and subtleties, is a wonder to behold—and, without it, both would be cheaters of their birthright. The child thus cheated is much more likely, when he or she grows up, to make war, not love.

There is an important distinction to be made here: While the drive toward motherhood is primarily biological in nature, the human expression of it is social. Biology cannot be abolished or denied by social edict, but it can certainly be distorted. When it is, not only are the individual mother and child in trouble, but so is the entire society, if not the species itself. Today, at a time when we are all concerned with our survival, we are at the same time witnessing widespread (and, in large measure, laudable) attempts to eliminate role differences between male and female. Where these attempts deal with economic issues, such as equal pay for equal work, I vote Yes, resoundingly. But where they seek to induce women to put down their most basic human feelings, I begin to get more than a little apprehensive.

There is much shrill vocalizing about how degrading and enslaving are the tasks of motherhood. And indeed some of its responsibilities, even when carried out with love and tenderness, can become tedious. But what role in life (a husband's job not excepted) does not include some frustration and drudgery?

It is too bad that so many women have children because it has been set for them as a social goal rather than through a sense of emotionally gratifying fulfillment. These are the women most likely to turn their children over to someone else to care for as soon as possible after birth. Many women do this through social pressures. A woman may prefer to care for her own, but if she "doesn't have to" financially, then to do so is to lose status among her friends. This holds, of course, only among the affluent.

Now, suddenly, those less favored economically are demanding this dubious benefit of affluence. At many of the Women's Lib parades last month, the poor, too, carried placards insisting on free 24-hour-a-day child-care centers. This is fine for mothers who must work and have no safe place to leave the children. What I deplore is the all too prevalent attitude that it is desirable for mothers to get rid of the kids and go to work, whether they have to or not—the feeling that the very fact of staying home to care for little children in itself renders the mother underprivileged. Perhaps what needs altering is our social attitude toward motherhood rather than our techniques of baby care. Valuing motherhood in its true light might discourage many who would otherwise be inclined to "farm out" their children—especially newborn infants.

Animal studies are fascinating in this regard. When a lamb or a kid is separated from its mother immediately after birth and kept away for perhaps no more than an hour, the mother seems to lose her capacity to differentiate her own young from others. She may even reject her offspring altogether. But if the two stay together and the mother has a chance to lick her newborn, she will then be able to identify it in a large flock even after a long period of separation.

These observations and similar ones suggest that a critical period exists for the establishment of a bond between a mother and her newborn. If this interval passes without the necessary contact, the bond is weak, the newborn loses the benefit of this vital interchange, and its chances for survival to full maturity are lowered. The mother loses something too: She is less inclined to protect her young from predators and will fail to provide the sensory stimulation through touching, hearing, licking, and visual experience that is also necessary for later learning.

Is there some human insight to be gleaned here about the current estrangement of the generations? One must always be cautious about extrapolating animal data to human behavior. Nevertheless, some striking studies have been made of human infants cared for in foundling homes. These children were well cared for physically. They were cleaned and fed and received adequate medical attention. But they were not handled or played with or otherwise stimulated—and the mortality rate among them was inordinately high during the first year of life. They were highly susceptible to infection, appeared depressed and lethargic, showed little interest in their surroundings, and didn't look anyone in the eye. They would rock back and forth for hours examining their own fingers and bodies as if they had given up on the outside world. These children are often described as "good" babies because they play by themselves, make no demands on anyone, and don't cry. They have, in effect, withdrawn from the world of people, and have probably been permanently damaged.

My personal observation of hundreds of mothers with their newborn children convinces me that the animal studies are not altogether inapplicable here. There is mutual need for nearness and stimulation. There is undoubtedly a very intricate set of biochemical changes that release built-in evolutionary behavior patterns. The mother is highly sensitive to certain events, particularly the presence of her baby. (This raises questions about the wisdom of the common practice of separating mothers from their babies right after delivery in most hospitals.) She feels a powerful, instinctive desire to touch her baby to hold and talk to him. As the child grows older, the mother almost always smiles back with great pleasure whenever her baby smiles, and soon the baby learns from her responses.

No matter how qualified and competent a nursemaid is, the response of the biological mother, under most circumstances, is deeper, warmer, and surer.

In the early weeks and months of life, an infant needs someone who is alertly sensitive to his cues and ever ready to respond. If this need is met, he is likely to develop a sense of trust in others rather than to turn inward for his satisfactions. Love, care, handling, responsive faces, a conviction that the environment reacts when he acts—all these required to give the child a feeling that people are worth relating to. The natural biological tendencies of the mother, if they are not interfered with will effortlessly provide this kind of satisfaction for the baby.

The infant's capacity for receiving information from the environment is enormous. All his senses are alive and receiving on many frequencies—sight, hearing, taste, smell, touch, movement. The early stimulation of this sensory apparatus in the baby's nervous system will, later in life, give him tremendous capacity for learning. If, on the other hand, this apparatus remains largely unused, the child's later chances are considerably diminished. And this applies not merely to the kind of learning that takes place in the classroom, but to all the situations of life. Babies who have been exposed to more varied sensory experiences are less inclined to be fearful and anxious. They are not so easily overwhelmed by changing circumstances and can deal successfully with greater amounts of stress compared to infants who have experienced little change, or had little to look at, or listen to, or feel.

All this back-and-forth trading of a whole spectrum of experience cannot be substituted for in any other way or made up for later in life. To bring it off, the mother must be willing to follow her own nature. If she turns her back on it, she throws away one of the profoundest and most meaningful facets of all human experience. But in that case the baby loses even more—his capacity to love and trust other human beings. Anyone who disdains the job of mothering as unrewarding scutwork simply doesn't know what life is about.

Though I have so far emphasized the need of the newborn for this intensive brand of mothering, it serves the child well all through his early years. He learns mostly by imitation. This offers the parents an excellent opportunity to instill the habits and patterns of behavior that help socialize a child;

and, if they care about this aspect of upbringing, it also helps them teach, through example, their own ways. All sorts of behavior, including language and cultural attitudes, are readily adopted from the adults who take care of a child. Leaving him with someone whose manner, attitudes, and background are different from yours encourages the child to be like that other person, no matter how strongly you may urge the child to be like you.

I don't mean to imply by all I have said so far that a mother must constantly sit and interact with her baby, or should never leave him with anyone else. On the contrary, it is important for a mother to be free of the child at times and be able to divert her interest to other things. But it is vital for the early months at least that she undertake the primary responsibility of caring for her child.

When she does leave her child with someone else, that person should be carefully chosen. Most people take more pains in choosing a repairman to fix the car or television set than in selecting a caretaker for their children.

The ideal caretaker should be concerned with the child's emotional as well as his physical needs. Many baby nurses, unfortunately, consider that they are doing a good job as long as the child is kept neat, clean, quiet, and away from his parents. While this may not result in any instantly discernible damage, it may well prevent the child from developing his full potential. I recognize, of course, that a child of any age, even a small baby, can form a strong tie with someone other than his biological mother—as witness the frequent success of parents with adopted children. But there must be some kind of mutually satisfying relationship very early in life for emotional development to take place, and this is most likely to occur between a baby and his mother, or that rare surrogate parent who feels like a mother.

Mothering is more than the act of giving birth. It is the continuing care of the baby in a way that answers his physical and emotional needs while giving pleasure to both mother and child. This is not likely to happen when social and cultural influences are allowed to interfere, or when other people are allowed to modify or distort a mother's natural tendencies.

It is hard to overemphasize the importance of a woman's role as a mother. It has served humankind well throughout the millennia of history. Few things are more worth fighting to protect than a woman's right to motherhood. And hardly anything is more degrading to the female than the notion that this role can be casually handed over to someone else.

This does not mean that I think motherhood is the be-all and end-all for a woman. She can be a complete human being without giving up her most precious natural resource. Nor do I think that every woman ought to be encouraged to become a mother.

A perfectly normal and fulfilled woman may want to dedicate herself to other things. One's time in life is limited, and no one can handle too many high-priority responsibilities simultaneously. The woman who does not want to take time out to be an effective mother, especially during the child's early years, should not feel compelled to do so. Nor should she be the object of any contempt for making this choice.

At a time when overpopulation appears to be a threat anyway, it may be well to encourage any woman who sees motherhood as a tedious and uninteresting enterprise to do herself and the world a good turn by seeking some other means of personal fulfillment.

I AM CURIOUS (TODDLER)
Virginia E. Pomeranz, M.D. with Dodi Schultz

Sex is seldom a problem for small children—but it often is for their parents. For a good deal of what your children do—and say—in this area is going to surprise you. I say that with assurance, because I am sure you will not remember that you in all likelihood did and said the very same sort of things when you were small.

For instance, take the taboo subject: masturbation. The fact is that small children do masturbate. Practically all of them, at one time or another. Many begin as early as the age of six months; some have been known to start as early as two or three months. The timing depends upon when the individual infant happens to discover that the activity gives him or her pleasure.

A boy may begin when his hands innocently—and naturally—explore his own body. A girl may find her clitoris in the same way. Or a sense of pleasure may occur while they're being bathed, or from the rubbing of their clothing. In any case, once they discover the sensation, they might seek it deliberately.

Many adults are extremely uptight about any discussion of this subject because of the sea of misleading information that has been disseminated in the past—and is unfortunately still being disseminated. Despite what you may have been told to the contrary, masturbation will *not* cause memory loss, visual impairment, mental illness, future sexual problems, acne, or anything else. It is in no sense a perversion; nor is it a "bad habit" of which a child should be "broken." It is a normal human fact.

The mother of one of my patients once received an illuminating insight about masturbation. "Jimmy," she asked her four-year-old exasperatedly one day, "must you play with yourself so much?" Jimmy looked at her thoughtfully and answered, "Mommy, you're just saying that because you don't have one!" It took her a moment to recover, at which point she suggested, "Well, I would rather you do it privately."

Which is, of course, the answer. It *is* a private matter, like using the bathroom. Not "dirty" or shameful" but private.

If a child is excessive in his actions, there *is* something wrong—but not with the child. Experts in this field have found that children do masturbate a great deal more when they are bored, tired, or unhappy; it is, after all, a pleasant activity, otherwise the child would not persist. I suggest, if this is happening, that you look for reasons for the child's boredom, fatigue, or unhappiness and make some effort to provide the child with some other interests.

Gender awareness also may prove a disconcerting development. It typically dawns on a child about the age of two or three that there are two different sorts of people in this world. That thought frequently leads to intense curiosity about the *other* one, one's *own* classification having been ascertained.

Reprinted by permission of *Family Health Magazine.* From the October, 1973 issue, pp. 24, 25, 55.

This curiosity is often directed at a sibling (or playmate, if there is no sibling) of the opposite sex, and frequently takes the form of wanting to watch the other child urinate. Should this be permitted? you might wonder. I don't think you will have any choice. Children generally manage to arrange these things between themselves. Once their curiosity has been satisfied, and they've witnessed the event two or three times, they are not going to insist upon hanging around and watching every time the other child makes a visit to the bathroom or changes clothes.

But you may, at this point, be assaulted with a few queries, mainly centering about the obvious anatomical difference and beginning with "Why?" Certainly the earliest "Why doesn't *she* have—" and "Why don't I have—" questions can and should be answered as simply as possible: "Because you're a boy and she's a girl" (or vice versa, if that happens to be the case).

Psychologists worry a lot about the child's going on to theorize that her penis was stolen (if the child is a girl) or that his penis may be subsequently lost (if it's a boy)—thus creating considerable anxiety. I haven't found that this is generally true. However, a child may well press you further for an answer. I think you can probably get away with something along the lines of "It's just one of several differences between boys and girls. These differences don't really mean much now, but when you grow up they will. Girls grow up to be women, and they can also be mommies. Boys grow up to be men, and they can also be daddies. You'll see, when you grow up."

Questions about the origin of babies are also something you are certainly going to be confronted with if you have one child—or more than one—and are expecting another. A youngest child may not become interested in this topic until a bit later, unless there is a pregnant friend or neighbor in evidence. But whenever a child gets around to asking questions about pregnancy, always listen carefully to the child's question and answer what has been asked. Also remember, children repeat questions to which they have already received answers. Not instantly, but perhaps days, weeks, or months later. Therefore, be consistent; the child repeating a question may have forgotten the answer, or he may be looking for confirmation.

Here follow some common questions—your child may phrase them somewhat differently—and my suggested answers, which of course must be modified to respond to the particular query your child has posed. Though I have arbitrarily orga-nized them into a hypothetical "conversation," they are not in fact likely to be posed all on the same occasion, and certainly not necessarily in the same order. Typically, a child will ponder the answer to one or two questions, then return—either on the same day or at some later date—and pursue the subject further. (Or start the questioning all over again!)

Q. "Why are you (or why is Mommy) beginning to get so fat?"

A. "Because there's a baby growing inside of me (or her)."

Q. "Where inside you (or her)?"

A. "In a special place called the uterus, that mommies have." (Don't say it's in the stomach, or belly, or any other part of the body that the child might be aware that he or she possesses.)

Q. "Is it a boy or a girl?"

A. Answer truthfully. And if you don't know say so. If by chance you have, for another purpose, had embryonic cell sampling done, and you know what the baby's sex will be, say so.

Q. "How big is it?"

A. "When it is ready to be born, it will be about" (visually demonstrate a length or height of about nineteen or twenty inches—the average height of a newborn). "Right now, it's still growing and it's only about *this* long."

Q. "How will it get out?"

A. "When it is time for it to be born, it will start to push its way out, and the doctor will help."

Q. "And then *where* does it come out?" (Whether the child says so or not, the belly button and the anus are prime possibilities in his or her mind.)

A. "From a special place mommies have, called a vagina. Not the same places urine or bowel movements come from" (or whatever you call those functions, in your particular family).

Q. (And here is the really sticky one.) "How did it get there?"

A. "The mommies have a tiny, tiny seed that joins with another tiny seed from the daddy, and when that happens the two seeds together make a baby."

Q. "How come mommies can have babies and daddies can't?"

A. "Because that's what makes them daddies and not mommies. Mommies are the ones where the babies grow."

200

Q. "Will I ever have babies?"

A. Obviously, the answer depends on the sex of the child. If a girl: "Yes, you will be able to; you'll have that special place for a baby to grow." If a boy: "No, you will not be able to. Boys grow up to be daddies, but not mommies."

Q. "Can I watch the baby come out?"

A. "No I'm afraid you can't. I (or Mommy) will be going to the hospital when that happens, so the doctor can help me (or her) and the baby, and nobody else is allowed to get in the way, because it's very important." (Or if the father is planning to be present at the birth "—and they don't allow children to be there, because all the grownups will be very busy, and children might get in the way.")

Q. "Do you have to wait until you are grown-up before you can have a baby?"

A. "Yes—little boys and girls do not have the seeds to make a baby. That will happen to you only when you are more grown-up."

Q. "Do people have to be married to have a baby?"

A. (As I've said, I do not think you should lie. Ever.) "No, but it's better that way, because then the baby has a family, both a mommy and a daddy, to take care of him or her."

Q. "Did it hurt you (or Mommy) a lot when I was born?"

A. "Why do you ask that?" (If you haven't discussed this, it's well to get the child's information source—and how much "hurt" was reportedly involved—before you answer.) Then, if you are the father of the child, I'd suggest referring the question to the mother. If you are the mother, an appropriate answer might be, "No, not really. When a baby is born he pushes hard to get out. The mother, to, has to work. Sometimes it's pretty hard work, but I wouldn't call it hurting. I was so glad to have you, I soon forgot about the work anyway."

Most experts in child care agree that after infancy it is not a good idea to parade around nude in your child's presence—especially, though not only, a child of the opposite sex. There are basically two reasons.

One concerns the parent of the *same* sex. The body of an adult is vastly different from that of a small child. These differences may be frightening to a youngster since he or she often tends to compare his own body with others'; the comparing of bodies is best done with other children of the same age and stage of development.

A second reason is that viewing the nude body of a parent of the opposite sex can create confusion in the child's attitudes to the opposite sex when achieving sexual maturity.

I do not mean, of course, that you should go into panic if your child happens to glimpse you in the nude. Simply behave naturally and continue whatever you are doing. The body revelation in such a situation is an incidental event and completely acceptable—unless in overreacting *you* make it otherwise.

Section VI

PLANNING—FAMILY AND OTHERWISE
Michael J. Sporakowski

A concern of many people in many ways is birth control. Whether this be contraception or abortion, family spacing or inducing fertility, the topic is in the forefront of much of today's world. This section first provides some information on techniques to birth control, then delves into the choice of parenthood in a reading by Barnard.

Articles

1. Michael J. Sporakowski—Planning: Family and Otherwise

2. Charles Barnard—Sperm Banks: The New Idea in Planning Parenthood

Rip Off #13
Section VI

Name: _____ Date: _____

Student #: _____ Sex: M or F

1. T F Birth control materials and information should be available to anyone who wants them.

2. T F Lack of B.C. information and materials prevents premarital sex.

3. T F Birth control should be used only in spacing children, not preventing them completely.

4. T F The typical, natural result of intercourse is conception.

5. T F Birth control should be taught in the schools.

6. T F Parenthood is the responsibility of all married people.

7. T F The poor have large families because they value children more than the middle class.

8. T F Birth control measures should be used only by persons who have had at least one child.

9. T F Use of effective contraceptives generally increases sexual enjoyment.

10. T F Easy availability of birth control measures increases promiscuity.

11. T F Douching is a highly effective method of contraception.

12. T F A woman on the "Pill" risks blood clotting problems more than the women who has been or is pregnant.

13. T F I.U.D.s are more effective as a form of B.C. than "the pill."

14. T F Nonprescribed birth control methods are always less effective than those obtained with a physician's prescription.

15. T F Condoms and chemical jellies and creams, besides having B.C. effects, also tend to reduce V.D. infections.

16 T F Women cannot be on the B.C. pill for more than 2 years according to FDA rules.

17. T F I.U.D.s must be inserted before each intercourse experience.

18. T F Side effects associated with condoms are: nausea, breast tenderness, weight gain, and "freckling."

19. T F Salpingectomy refers to blocking the cervix for B.C. purposes.

20. T F Diaphragms must be refit from time to time, especially after weight gains and after the birth of a baby.

21. T F Sterilization should be available to anyone who wants it—married, unmarried, parent or not, etc.

205

22. T F I, personally, would consider using sterilization as a form of birth control.

23. T F Sterilization should only be considered by couples with three or more children.

24. T F Sterilization is immoral.

25. T F Sterilization procedures are easily reversed.

26. T F I would (or do) use sterilization as my method of choice in contraception.

27. T F Sterilization decreases one's sex drive.

28. T F Sterilization and castration are the same thing.

29. List five birth control methods requiring a physician's prescription and/or consultation.

30. List five birth control methods that can be obtained or used without a medical consultation or supervision of a physician.

List the five most frequent reasons given for family planning.

31.

32.

33.

34.

35.

List the five most frequent reasons birth control methods fail.

36.

37.

38.

39.

40.

PLANNING: FAMILY AND OTHERWISE
Michael J. Sporakowski

Contraception is nothing new. It has been around in both idea and fact for thousands of years. Historically we can trace the use of contraceptives back at least to 2700 B.C. where there is evidence in a Chinese book about the use of an oral contraceptive. The recipe (prescription?) for it went something like this: Take some quicksilver (mercury, for those of you who have not survived Chemistry 113) and fry it for a day in oil (mineral, Quaker State, or whale?). Then take a piece of the quicksilver about the size of a nickel and swallow it—preferably on an empty stomach. The taker will never become pregnant (and will probably be buried two days hence).

Other evidence of oral contraceptives can be found in the histories, especially medical, of most old civilizations. Concoctions like a mix of willow leaves and rust in water, sulphate solutions, lead, arsenic, iodine and strychnine all have from one time to another been used as contraceptives.

Douching and fumigating are methods from writings as far back as 1850 B.C. The Romans, Japanese, and English all have historical evidence of the use of the sheath or condom—whether it be made from fish bladders, animal intestine or leather.

Biblically we find Onan using coitus interruptus, or withdrawal, in the years way back.

All sorts of fruits, oils, and naturally occurring substances have been used. Mixtures of honey and fruit pulp were used to clog the cervix; salts and oils acted as spermaticides, and blocking action was provided by wool and pitch, grass, chopped rags, leaves, or even sponges. People tended to use what was available once they figured out how conception took place. If you didn't have crocodile fat to mix with honey, then elephant fat would do.

Rhythm as a method of contraception also is very old. Frequently it was tied to taboos about when intercourse could take place and under what conditions. Breast feeding seems to have been used although its effectiveness frequently was based on taboos against intercourse with lactating females.

In a sense, then, at least with regard to contraception, nothing is new; we just have different, perhaps more refined methods. For example, camel herders in the Middle East have been said to have used intra-uterine devices to prevent their charges from untimely conception. Pebbles were blown with reeds into each of the camel's uteri—apparently they have two each, so you better be sure to be safe—and conception was inhibited. Today we use plastics, nylon and metals to do the same thing but with humans.

Let's now take a brief overview look at some of the more typically used contraceptive methods of this day and age. Basically they will be divided into nonprescriptive and prescriptive categories as a matter of convenience. Nonprescriptive here means folk methods or methods not requiring a physician's consultation, examination, fitting, or continued supervision.

Nonprescriptive Methods

In the drugstore, frequently near the toothpastes lie a variety of gels, creames, and powders that have sperm killing, clogging, or smelling good abilities which are purported to be contraceptives. They come in tubes, aerosol cans, sealed foil wrappers and pre-filled "one shot" containers.

Brand names like "Delfen," "Emko," "Ortho-Gynol," "Koromex" and "Contra Creme" to name but a few, fill the shelves. Basically all of them are inserted into the vagina and either immobilize or kill the sperm, clog the cervix so no sperm pass through it, cleanse the vagina, or perhaps, some combination of all three.

The *douches*—the ones used as spermaticides—are inserted soon after intercourse, and by their flushing and sperm killing actions theoretically provide contraception. Some estimates have stated the douching needs to take place within 90 seconds after ejaculation to be effective, otherwise some sperm have already entered the uterus and may be well on their way to the conception staging area and not effected by the douche. The douche material may also force some of the ejaculate to the cervix or into the uterus thus fostering conception.

Douching, although used for contraception, may also be used for birth control to try and determine the sex of the child-to-be. If Y carrying sperm cause conception the baby will be a boy; if X, a girl results. Acidic douching tends to immobilize Y carrying sperm, while basic (chemically) tends to immobilize X carrying sperm. Thus, with method, madness, and luck Landrum Shettles (Rorvik, 1970) says that 85% accuracy can be achieved in choosing the sex of your child.

Most women, though, are more familiar with douching as a hygienic method. Since they have been often taught that sex is dirty or at least messy, or that the genitalia are unclean they feel the need to douche—or perhaps their mothers or fathers told them they did. Frequent douching may upset the vagina's natural balance—since it, like most other bodily organs and systems, tends to be self cleaning under normal conditions. So a word to the wise here, unless you feel that douching is the only method of birth control for you, use it infrequently for hygenic reasons—unless your physician is consulted and advises to the contrary.

At this time it might be wise to point out that there are strawberry, raspberry, and lemon-lime douche products available, but that they probably have limited contraceptive value, even though they may make you think you smell good and are clean. Also, the genital deodorants: some are great for killing roaches, keeping cats away, or quashing fish odors, but they aren't contraceptives, and may cause irritations of the genital area. Perhaps some good old soap and water would help you feel clean.

The *jellies,* gels, *creams,* cremes, *foams* and *suppositories* are also in this chemical category. Unfortunately, we do not have charts saying which is most effective and when, although some have been tested and reported with regards to their spermaticidal effectiveness in the medical literature. In general, these chemicals are inserted before coitus. The suppositories take longer to be effective because they need to melt (and do, at body temperature). These methods are spermaticidal and/or clogging in action. When used as directed, they can be quite effective—some moreso than others. There is a tendency towards messiness, for "what goes in must come out" in some form. Some women, and perhaps their male partners, will find these chemicals irritating. Other brands may be tried, but if the irritation persists, see a physician—it may or may not be the method that's causing the problem.

Generally speaking these chemicals are fairly inexpensive, probably running in cost from two to four dollars per month for the "average" couple. One caution here, if the couple has more than one intercourse experience they should insert additional foam, cream or whatever to be maximally effective. This may be more "messy" or costly, but will be more contraceptively effective. An additional caution, not all things in aerosol cans or tubes are contraceptives. "Crest" may fight cavities, but its contraceptive potential is doubtful. Also, all suppositories are not for killing sperm; if you use this method and are unsure of brands ask your druggist or physician.

Probably the most widely known and used form of contraception in the U.S. is the *condom*— sheath, safety, rubber, skin, or whatever you call it. This membrane fits over the penis and is a physical barrier which ideally prevents sperm from ever entering the female. It is also used in water fights, if balloons aren't available; fit over automobile exhausts to cause a bang; left in parking lots and shrubbery areas to keep grounds-keepers employed, and nice old ladies upset; and as an adjunct in helping induce fertility with artificial insemination. The latter use is very important where collection of ejaculate is desired and masturbation considered immoral or undesirable.

Condoms are more obviously available today in magazine and newspaper ads as well as on the open shelf in drugstores. The shy no longer have to hand the little old lady or sweet young thing behind the counter a note, since in these days of self service, they can pick them out themselves. In many states they are available in restrooms and other functional spots in vending machines that say "For protection from Veneral Disease only."

Since most are made of latex, they come in one basic size, although shapes vary. Some have nipple or reserve ends; some are dry, others lubricated; some rolled, others flat; some—most in fact—in sealed foil. Some come in colors—red, blue, green and black—most are just neutral. Some are extra thin to enhance sensitivity, others have special creams for lubrication to enhance sensitivity. Some fit basically the whole erect penis, others just the tip, while others have all sorts of do-dads on the end and may be called "French ticklers." Some are made of animal skin or intestine.

Depending on the quantities you buy them in, they probably will run from 15 or 20 cents each for the "plains" to two or three dollars (or more) each, for the "fancys."

Cost is not necessarily a measure of effectiveness. Generally, condoms should not be used more than once, even though some people will cleanse them and reuse them several times. Timing is a vital concern here in that some males will only feel they need to wear the condom just before and at the moment of ejaculation, even though some seminal fluid *may* leak from the penis prior to ejaculation. Too, the couple that prolongs coitus may find that the condom comes off in the vagina as the male loses the erection, and thus a concentrated amount of ejaculate may be in the vagina.

Nevertheless, condoms, when used appropriately, can be an effective contraceptive. And as was mentioned earlier they may help prevent the spread of V.D. Now and then you will hear the reason for not using a condom as follows: "They don't let me feel very well." This is unlikely, but something that must be dealt with—especially if the sexual partner requires the male to wear three at one time.

Brand names frequently reflect virility, god like-ness, or something. Examples are: Trojans, Sheiks, XXXX, Naturalamb skins, Sultan, Ramses, Fether-lite, Spartans, Swan Vials, Tuxedo Skins, Silver-Tex, and Super Thin Vikings. Probably the best place to buy them is a drug store that has a fair amount of turn over, for although most are sealed in foil, they do have a shelf life expectancy, and although historic relics are interesting, they may not work so well. Too, condoms carried in wallets for several weeks probably are more likely to be damaged than those stored in more desirable places.

Another method which might be used that has both a barrier and chemical action is the *sponge and foam*. The sponge aspect probably goes back over 4,000 years in history. Over the years a sperm-aticidal liquid or powder has been added as an improvement. The chemical aspect works once it is placed on a moistened sponge which is then placed into the vagina. The sponge should be placed before intercourse occurs and removed about six hours after the intercourse experience. Materials for this method may be purchased at many drug-stores. Cost is about the same as for chemical foams and creams. A brand name here is Durafoam powder or liquid. This is a relatively infrequently used method, perhaps because of the messiness and drainage and perhaps because it is not as highly rated for contraceptive effectiveness as other methods.

Two other nonprescriptive methods that do not involve dollar-type costs are abstinence and coitus interruptus (also known as withdrawal, coitus reservatus and "Oh Damn"). Abstinence, or re-fraining from intercourse, should be obvious as to how it works as a contraceptive. It may require a great deal of self control, or conversely, a lack of interest. It is the crux of the rhythm method, which will be commented upon later.

Withdrawal is based on the idea that the male will have sufficient control to withdraw from the female just prior to ejaculating, therefore not allowing sperm to enter the vagina. This reasoning may be fallacious in that in many, perhaps most, males, some seminal fluid may escape from the penis before ejaculation. If the reproductive plumbing has even the slightest leak, the risk factor is increased. Some couples seem to pride them-selves on testing limits such as these to see just how far they can go. Like abstinence, we must not only weigh inexpensiveness in dollars, but assess what the impact costs the couple and its individuals emotionally. Back in the early 1800's the Oneida Community made very effective use of this method for about 20 years.

Prescriptive Methods

The first method under this category is rhythm—sometimes called Vatican roulette, safe period, periodic continence, or "Oh Damn II." It is included under this heading because it is optimally used by "the average couple" only under close medical supervision. (The latter referring to maxi-mal knowledge and understanding of the method, testing and temperature taking, and calculating times as accurately as possible. In reality, rhythm is often used to help subfertile couples achieve preg-nancy.)

The basic idea behind rhythm is that if you can accurately predict when ovulation takes place, and if you will abstain from sexual contact 24 to 48 hours before and 48 to 72 hours after the time of ovulation, conception is *unlikely*. A volume could be written about the problems of irregular cycles, multiple ovulations, abstaining, etc. but suffice it to say, many couples are not sufficiently motivated to use rhythm effectively and/or do not have the knowledge about reproduction to be effectively in control on an objective basis. As one jokingly often hears, "people who use rhythm are called parents." Nevertheless, under the best conditions, which probably means adequate instruction and medical supervision, rhythm can be effective.

Dollar costs might come from supplies such as calendar charts, themometers, or testing tapes. Per-haps several dollars would be an approximation of initial costs for using rhythm.

For many the most well known prescriptive method is *"The Pill"* or oral contraceptive. There are many on the market and since these hormones do affect the female's physiological functioning they require a prescription. The good physician will do a pap smear, pelvic exam and medical his-tory on patients that are being seen for the first time. Often, the physician will require routine 6, 8, or 12 month check ups before continuing the pill. Basically the pill is effective because it inhibits or surpresses ovulation and because it tends to keep the mucous secretion of the cervical canal hostile to sperm activity. This is accomplished by artificially mimicking pregnancy: Follicle Stimulating Hormone and Lutenizing Hormone are not secreted and thus ovulation is inhibited.

Today most pill regimens are based on 28 days: 21 days on the pill, 7 off. Some packaging includes 28 pills for the women who find taking a pill everyday helpful as far as regular scheduling goes. The last seven pills are usually of a different color, and placebolike.

Brand names frequently prescribed today are: Demulen, Ovulen Orval, Norlestrin, and Provest. Two types of "pills" have been available: sequentials and combinations. Cost per month for pills is about two dollars.

Contraindications for use of the pill include previous history of: cancer, retinal thrombosis, thromboembolism, thrombolphlebitis, pulmonary embolism, "stroke", heart disease or defect, severe endocrine disorder or recurrent jaundice of pregnancy. Women who have or have had the following may take the pill, but should only do so under close medical supervision: high blood pressure, asthma, migraine headaches, variocose veins, diabetes, psychiatric disturbances and epilepsy.

Some people will probably be frightened off by the above lists, but it must be remembered that the pill is hormonal in nature and can have a variety of effects and side effects. Nevertheless it is probably, over large groups of users, *the* most effective method—for those who can and will use it.

Side effects sometimes noted with the pill are: nausea (morning or evening sickness) in the early months of use; spotting (breakthrough bleeding before the normal menstrual period time); weight gain due to water retention; increase in breast size; tenderness or secretions; reduced, or in some cases increased cramping; reduced or in some cases increased acne problems; less fear or concern about pregnancy; and, especially for women on the pill for several years, a greater likelihood of vaginal infections due to a lessening of the acidity of the vaginal environment.

The pill is probably the most researched contraceptive we have today. Nevertheless we often see headlines such as "THE PILL LINKED WITH CANCER." Most of these studies prove things like: if you are a beagle and are taking the pill, you are likely to develop breast cancer (something female beagles are likely to develop anyway); or, if you are a rat and on human size doses of the pill, you are more likely than nonusers to develop uterine cancer. Yes, we need to continue the research, and to be cautious, so check with your physician, and

if he or she doesn't have good reasons why he or she prescribes the pill or does not, go to someone else. Too, blood clotting problems have been linked to the pill, but the data looks something like this (based on a 1966 English study): at age 20-34: death rate of non-pill users, 0.2 per 100,000; for pill users, 1.5 per 100,000; for women who were or had been pregnant, 22.8 per 100,000. As the age increased, so did the risk of death for all categories. It would appear that pregnancy was associated with a greater likelihood of death during the years studied than was use of the pill. But nonpregnancy status, and nonuse of the pill was even less hazardous. Many questions still need to be researched about many aspects of contraception, including those associated with the pill.

Intrauterine devices are another very much talked about and used method of contraception today. They are usually made of plastic or nylon or metal, or perhaps a combination of materials. A physician fits and inserts the I.U.D. in an office procedure. I.U.D.s seem to work by causing an environment in the uterus which will not allow implantation of a fertilized egg or by causing the fertilized egg to be sloughed off very early. Another theory is that the I.U.D. causes the egg to pass too rapidly through the Fallopian tube for fertilization to take place. The former reasons seem to be more likely as to the "Why?" of its working.

Cost of the I.U.D. is often ridiculous—probably less than a dime—but having it inserted and the prior exam will often run $25 to $50.

Many women experience increased cramping or heavier flow the first cycles on the I.U.D. Some will actually find that it is expelled. For this reason most I.U.Ds. have beads or a thread attached to them so that the woman can check with her fingers to see if it is in place, since it is unlikely that she can feel it in place in the uterus. For those who expel I.U.D.s, reinsertion and retainment tends to be successful for most. Nonetheless, some women are unable to tolerate the I.U.D. bodily.

Chief advantages of the I.U.D. are its inexpensiveness over time, and the fact that it is coitally independent (does not need to be used or taken just before or just after intercourse). Regular Pap tests and pelvic exams should be done as with any other method. Removal or reinsertion requires the physician's help. From time to time pregnancies do occur with the I.U.D. in place. Generally it is left there and expelled during the birth process. For these women, perhaps a better method of contraception could be found.

Another prescriptive method in wide use prior

to the advent of the pill is the *diaphragm* with jelly or cream. This is a rubber domed hemispherical device which is fitted to the posterior one third of the vagina. With proper fitting it provides a physical barrier so that sperm do not enter the uterus. The use of contraceptive cream on the edge of the diaphragm and in the center provides additional protection. This method requires fitting by a physician, and may require refitting if weight changes significantly, or the woman has a baby.

The diaphragm is inserted before intercourse and left in place 4 to 6 hours afterwards. Initial cost will vary from $15 to $40. When the diaphragm does not work, its lack of effectiveness can frequently be attributed to displacement during intercourse. The diaphragm, like most contraceptives, requires regular, knowledgeable use. One story about a diaphragm pregnancy went something like this: Mrs. Smith went to her doctor to have something done about her having too many babies. He fit her with a diaphragm and said, "Be sure to use this every night, and you won't have any more babies unless you want to." Four months later Mrs. Smith was back cursing the diaphragm and Dr. Jones because she was pregnant again. Yes, she had used it every night, but the nurse found out that Mrs. Smith's husband worked nights, and so when they did have intercourse it was more likely to be during the day.

A method similar to the diaphragm, but not widely used in this country is the cervical cap. It is smaller than the diaphragm, and fits tightly over the cervix. Researchers in fertility have used it in artificial insemination cases where the vagina was so acidic that it killed off all the sperm. By having the male use a condom during intercourse, ejaculate was collected and placed in the cervical cap, which was then placed on the cervix there bypassing the "lethal" vagina and often overcoming infertility.

Basically, these are the most frequently used contraceptives in the U.S. today. In what studies we have the effectiveness ratings usually show the pill to be most effective over large groups and over time while the I.U.D. is next most effective. Condoms, diaphragms, and spermaticides are all about next equally effective, then rhythm, coitus interruptus and douching. Nevertheless, this is an individual matter and many factors need to be considered before a choice is made.

Calderone (1966) stated three contraceptive axioms:

1. Any method of birth control is better than no method.

2. The most effective method is the one which the couple will use consistently.

3. Acceptability is the most critical factor in the effectiveness of a contraceptive method. (p. 152)

In considering the contraceptive choice one must look at frequent reasons for contraceptive failure: lack of information, cost, irregular use, refusal to accept responsibility for use, guilt or shame, and a communications failure. There are personal, couple, family, religious and economic factors to be reckoned with, and thus effectiveness ratings over groups of people may not be accurate for individuals.

As people exercise a choice in parenthood and as new methods are developed contraception and family planning will take on new meaning.

Two other forms of birth control need to be aired here: sterilization and abortion. Basically when we speak of *sterilization* we need to categorize as to male sterilization—or vasectomy—and female sterilization—or tubal ligation. Other procedures bring about sterile conditions, for example castration or hysterectomy, but are not generally used as means of achieving sterilization.

Vasectomy, or taking a section of each of the two vas deferens tubes, may be an office-type procedure. This method has increased considerably in "popularity" during the past ten years. A typical schema for the actual doing of the procedure has the male go to the office or clinic where it is done, so that he can rest over the weekend, and return to work the following Monday. The procedure involves a local anesthetic, an incision in the scrotal wall of each testis, and a cutting or sectioning and tieing off of the ends of the tubes. Usually the physician will advise the patient that he or his partner use some additional method of birth control for four weeks to as much as six months after operation, as some sperm may still be in the tubes connected to the urethra or, in less than one per cent of the cases, the operation may not have been a success and sperm are still transversing a "normal path." (Guttmacher, 1969) Several checks of sperm count are usually made during the first six months after the operation. If after that period no sperm are included in the ejaculate, it is assumed that the procedure has been 100% effective. With this method hormones and sperm are still produced, but the sperm do not follow their normal path and are resorbed into the body system.

In considering the use of vasectomy it is important to view what this procedure will mean to the male and the couple. Since, for all practical purposes, this method should be considered permanent, the emotional stability, self concept, and sex role of the patient must be considered. Some clinics which do vasectomy frequently have claimed as high as a 90% success rate of rejoining the tubes, but such places are rare. Even so, 10% of the cases could not be successfully rejoined and thus at least 10% remained sterile. Individuals and couples choosing this method should recognize its permanence.

Another "side effect" of vasectomy involves the male's feeling about his sexual virility. Some feel "great, I don't have to worry about causing pregnancy." Others feel as though they have lost their manhood and develop impotence or low feelings of self-worth.

Many hospitalization plans will now pay part or all of the cost for both male and female sterilizations. If cost is a consideration, this should be investigated. At the present time, costs vary from about $50-150 for vasectomies, higher if you choose the hospital in-patient route.

The female sterilization procedure, traditional form, tends to be expensive and may require 3-5 days of hospitalization. Frequently it was done after the birth of the "last child." Since the woman was already in the hospital, and access to the reproductive structures was easier through the vagina at this time, the procedure was performed within a day or two of the birth. This usually extended the recovery period by about two days beyond the typical stay for childbirth. If not done soon after childbirth, the incisions are made in the abdomen. Very simply speaking, the Fallopian tubes are cut, a section of each removed, and the ends bent back and tied off or cauterized. Eggs and hormones are still produced, but the eggs are resorbed into the body system since they do not travel the tubes to the uterus. As with vasectomy, we have a situation where the reproductive cell is produced but its typical movement is detoured. After several days, the cell disintegrates and is resorbed.

More recently a procedure known as laparoscopic sterilization (or belly button surgery) has been developed for the female. This usually requires at most a one day hospital stay or, in some clinics, is done on an outpatient basis. Two small incisions are made in the abdomen, one in the navel area—thus the name belly button surgery—and a tube containing a light and mirror is inserted (the incisions are about an inch long each). Through the second incision a cauterizing instrument is inserted, and the skilled surgeon then cuts and cauterizes each Fallopian tube. Some physicians feel this is a less effective method than the sectioning and tieing method mentioned above, but as yet no large scale comparisions have been made. The method tends to be less expensive in terms of both time and money. The laparoscope procedure typically involves one or less days of hospitalization and a cost of $150-$500; the tubal ligation typically the higher end of those figures for surgeons fee plus two to five days of hospital and related costs. (As with anything, costs and time vary from place to place, and condition to condition.)

Less mention is made in the professional literature about emotional effects of sterilization upon the female. Perhaps the procedure is less a threat to the sex identity of the female than the male, and perhaps more females feel a sense of relief since they are the ones who bear the children, and now have decided to terminate this function.

With greater concern for self and environment, sterilization is becoming a more frequent form of birth prevention. Physicians and hospitals are more willing to perform the operations, and now even single people are choosing this option and finding places where they can have it done. Since the procedures should still be thought of as permanent, the couple and individuals involved should make every effort to thoroughly think this decision through.

The last method of birth control to be mentioned here is *abortion*. It should be obvious that this is not a contraceptive, and thus a clamor about morality often rises. From this author's point of view, abortion is not a method of choice in family planning, but when other methods fail it is an alternative some will consider. Today abortion is more available legally than ten years ago. Thus its risks to the female who is pregnant, from a medical point of view have decreased.

Generally speaking there are four techniques of abortion: 1. Vacuum aspiration; 2. Dilatation and Curettage; 3. Saline injection; and 4. Hysterotomy. Up to twelve weeks into the pregnancy vacuum aspiration and D and C are usually used. D and C involves dilating the cervix, inserting a curette into the uterus, and scraping the uterine wall. The tissue is removed with a forceps. This procedure is also used to help treat infertility, and often used in treating menopausal or postmenopausal women for uterine problems. Usually this procedure means several days in the hospital due to the use of general anesthesia, although local anesthetics like a cervical block are increasingly being used.

Vacuum aspiration involves sucking the contents

of the uterus out by means of a sterile tube with a vacuum sump. The procedure usually takes 3 to 5 minutes and frequently no anesthesia is used. This procedure is often an out-patient or clinic method requiring little or no hospital stay. D and C's will probably cost $400 to $600, vacuum aspirations $300 or less. Costs will vary with length of hospitalization, surgeons charges, insurance coverage, and procedure used. For the medically indigent, low cost or free abortions are often made available.

The 12-16 week period of the pregnancy may see the use of a combination of D and C and vacuum aspiration. At this time the uterus tilts and makes removal of all the fetal tissue more difficult, and the likelihood of puncturing the uterine lining greater. Some physicians recommend waiting until 16 weeks and then using saline injection or "salting out."

Saline injection is a method of inducing miscarriage. A needle is inserted through the abdominal wall and into the uterine cavity. Amniotic fluid (several ounces) is withdrawn and replaced with an equal quantity of salt solution. This kills the fetus and prevents release of placental hormones. Labor is followed by miscarriage, or birthing of a dead fetus. This procedure usually involves a several day hospital stay and a cost of $700 to $800.

Hysterotomy is a procedure used after 20 weeks if saline injection or D and C are for some reason not possible. This involves removal of the fetus via an abdominal incision. This is major surgery and requires a more lengthy hospital stay, and usually costs around $1,000. Unlike hysterectomy where the uterus is removed, hysterotomy does not usually affect the woman's ability to bear children in the future.

In 1970/71, according to The Population Council (1971), over 60% of the legal abortions performed in the U. S. were done with vacuum aspiration. Saline induction was the next most frequently used method, then D and C, and, least used was hysterotomy and hysterectomy.

An important part of the abortion process is counseling, since for most people this decision can potentially involve moral and highly emotional aspects of the individual and her interpersonal relationships. One source for such counseling is the Clergy Consultation Service which functions in both referral and counseling modalities. State and local phone contact numbers are usually available in local phone directories.

New developments in contraception as of this writing were: injections that last one, three, six or as much as 12 months (for the female) and prevent ovulation—and also menstrual periods; hormone packages placed in the uterus with minute dosages released over time which prevent ovulation or implantation; and, skin implants of hormones working on the timed release principle. I.U.D.s of a variety of sizes and shapes, often employing metals such as copper are being tested. "Morning after pills"—D.E.S. (diethylstilbestrol)—have been administered after intercourse experiences, and are available for "emergency use," such as after rape. Dangers of these "pills"—also available as shots—in terms of side effects are not yet conclusively shown. This method has not been F.D.A. approved for other than emergency use.

"Male shots," valves in the vas deferens or fallopian tubes, etc. are possibles of the future. More importantly, low dosage "mini pills" taken every day with no stopping for a menstrual period have recently been marketed. Early studies show, though, a slightly higher pregnancy risk than "The Pill." As our understanding of conception increases and our technology for coping with it improves more "perfect" contraceptives will evolve.

We have looked at a variety of methods of preventing and controlling conception. All can be effective, but effectiveness tends to vary with users and their knowledge, goals and motivation. Armed with some beginning knowledge, the choice should be one which not only produces the desired conception result, but also allows the persons involved to feel good about themselves and their relationships, and deal more effectively with the world in which they live.

References

Calderone, M. *Manual of Contraceptive Practice*, Baltimore: Williams and Williams, 1966.

Guttmacher, A. *Birth Control and Love.* Toronto: Macmillan, 1969.

Rorik, D.M. *Your Baby's Sex: Now You Can Choose.* New York: Dodd, Mead and Company, 1970.

The Population Council. *The Population Council Annual Report 1971.*

Name: _____ Date: _____

Student #: _____ Sex: M or F

Where do you stand on abortion?

1. T F   I think abortion should be a private matter between a woman and her physician.

2. T F   If I were in the situation where I was involved in an unwanted pregnancy, I would find abortion a plausible alternative (for myself or my partner).

3. T F   Abortions should be available to married women only.

4. T F   If abortions were widely available the birth rate would go down to zero.

5. T F   Abortion is a cop out and evidence of gross irresponsibility.

6. List three positive reasons for abortion.

7. List three negative reasons against abortion.

8. Although we theoretically have more and better methods of birth control available today, there is evidence that out-of-wedlock pregnancy and birth is occurring more frequently than ever. List 3 or more reasons as to why you think this is.

9. T F   Abortion will make you sterile.

10. T F   Most abortions in the U.S. are done illegally.

11. T F   Married women, today, have more abortions than do single women.

12. T F   Doctors must perform abortions if their patients ask for them.

13. T F   Another name for miscarriage is spontaneous abortion.

Artificial insemination is a fairly effective method of helping overcome infertility in some couples.

14. T F   If I wanted to become a parent and my partner and I were having difficulty achieving pregnancy, I would try A.I. if I (or my partner) was the donor.

15. T F   If I (or my partner) was sterile (sub-fertile), I would probably use A.I. with a donor's semen to achieve pregnancy.

16. T F   A.I. is immoral (adultery).

17. T F Uterine and ovarian transplants are legitimate aids in overcoming infertility.

18. T F If I (or my male partner) was vasectomized, I would have several semen samples deposited in a sperm bank for possible future use.

SPERM BANKS
THE NEW IDEA IN PLANNING PARENTHOOD
Charles Barnard

Freezing and storing male sperm is a unique answer for many couples faced with dilemmas about birth control. When should you consider it? If your husband's low sperm count makes pregnancy difficult for you.... Or if some situation exists that threatens to make him sterile.... If you opt for vasectomy but may want babies in the future!

Jack Freye is not the kind of man who goes in for fads or gimmicks. Friends used to kid him about being a Teddy Roosevelt conservative. He is 30, has been married for six years, and is the father of three girls. He is an actuary for a large insurance company.

Jack's wife, Paula, is 29. She is bright and sophisticated but has no particular interest in women's lib and has never picketed or demonstrated against anything in her life. Her high school yearbook says she wanted to be the first lady veterinarian in Wisconsin. Somewhere along the years she gave up that ambition, and now she plays the flute in a local orchestra.

So what are Jack and Paula doing in the reception room of a sperm bank?

"I don't care who sees us here," says Jack. "I think it is a very sensible and responsible thing to do. We already have our three children—"

"But you never did get your boy," Paula teases him.

"Doesn't matter. We both agree that three more people is all we should add to the world population." So Jack is scheduled for a vasectomy the following week. The couple are at the sperm bank on the advice of Jack's physician, who had suggested what an increasing number of doctors are suggesting to husbands before they undergo vasectomy: have some sperm frozen, just in case husband and wife change their minds about more children. The procedure, like vasectomy itself, is quick, easy, and relatively inexpensive. It doesn't guarantee future pregnancies, but the odds are much better than the odds on reversing the vasectomy itself.

The Freyes' situation is certainly not what you would call typical of American couples today, but it *is* typical of those who are taking the opportunity offered by the relatively new availability of sperm-banking facilities. These banks are opening up all over the country, and their principal stimulus is vasectomy.

Vasectomy is the cutting of the male vas deferens to block the passage of sperm. Most doctors tell their patients to regard the operation as something that cannot be undone later. Despite this, the number of vasectomies performed in the United States has been increasing at an astronomical rate. There were only about 40,000 such operations in the country in 1960, but there were an estimated 500,000 to 750,000 in 1970, and preliminary figures for last year showed a continued increase. Latest figures show that vasectomies have been performed on a million and a half men whose wives are in the childbearing years. Some experts in the birth-control field have estimated that there will be five million vasectomies annually by 1975, and most of them base their predictions on the growth of sperm banking.

"With the emergence of the frozen-sperm banks, we now have—in effect—reversible vasectomy," says John Rague, executive director of the Association for Voluntary Sterilization.

When this becomes widely understood, say the sperm bankers, not even the proponents of vasectomy dare estimate how many of these quick, relatively easy operations will be performed each year. As one sperm banker puts it: "If you think the Pill created an explosion, vasectomy will be Vesuvius!"

What sperm banking simply means, to those couples who feel it is right for them on personal, religious, psychological, and financial grounds, is a form of permanent birth control with an escape clause—a kind of built-in insurance against the unexpected.

But why would the Freyes or other such couples ever change their minds about the limit they've put on their families? One of the most common concerns is that something might happen to the children they already have, leaving the couple without a family while they are still young enough to want to try again. There is always the possibility that the wife might die and the husband remarry and wish to start a family with his second wife. Divorce could create the same situation. Many other reasons are given. The Freyes, like many couples, are concerned that vasectomy might have a bad psychological effect on the man. "Perhaps I was being a little selfish," says Paula, "but I didn't want to go through a tube-tying operation, which is much more serious than a vasectomy. And I knew I couldn't take the Pill indefinitely. Vasectomy seemed the best solution to both of us. But Jack's a male, king of beasts and all that. I didn't want to silence his roar."

Although prevasectomy insurance is one of the most common reasons for using the facilities of a sperm bank, there are other—perhaps less controversial—reasons why a man might seek such services.

Oligospermia—the medical term for low sperm count—is a common cause of infertility in males. The condition itself may not be altered, but by concentrating sperm from many ejaculations, a frozen product can be created that has a better statistical chance of producing pregnancy through artificial insemination. As word spreads through the medical profession about this particular sperm-bank service, more and more males who had long ago given up on their own fertility are now hopeful.

Athletes engaged in rough, body-contact sports like football or hockey are already among the hundreds of males who have put sperm away for future use. Knowing that testicular damage could possibly render them sterile, a number of far-sighted quarterbacks and goalies have taken the precaution of putting some potential babies on ice.

As the use of atomic materials grows in U.S. science and industry, sperm-bank operators believe they will acquire a whole new group of customers—those who fear that prolonged exposure to even low levels of radiation might cause genetic changes in reproductive organs.

Another type of sperm-bank depositor is the man who faces involuntary sterilization through surgery or who is undergoing radiation or chemotherapy treatments. One surgeon recently advised a young male patient to put sperm on deposit in the Genetic Laboratories' bank in Minneapolis, prior to castration for cancer of the testes. "It not only gave the man hope that he might someday become a father," says the doctor, "but it was also a way in which I could convincingly reassure him that *I* thought he would lick cancer."

What are the odds that this young man—and all the other thousands who now have their future hopes in deep freeze—will achieve the expected results? Will frozen sperm really work? How long can it be kept without deterioration? Are there any risks to the unborn? Can mistakes be made?

Despite words of caution recently published by the American Public Health Association to the effect that the viability of human sperm stored over a "protracted" period of time is not yet established, Dr. Jerome K. Sherman of the University of Arkansas department of anatomy says, "I can attest to the retention of the fertilizing capacity of human semen samples stored in my laboratory for at least ten years."

There is also evidence that frozen sperm has been used as successfully as the bull sperm that has been employed in animal husbandry with outstanding results for 25 years. Over five million calves are born each year from frozen sperm. In the 19 years since the first human baby conceived with frozen sperm was born in 1953, there have been over 400 similar births. Only two minor defects have been noted in this closely watched group of children, a percentage which, although derived from a small sample, is actually lower than that of the general population.

Typical of the companies now operating the sperm banks that have been made possible by these scientific advances are Genetic Laboratories in Minneapolis and Idant in New York City. The two differ somewhat in their procedures, fees, and policies, but the basic service provided is the same. Idant (the name is derived from the Greek *idios,* meaning *own, personal*) occupies basement space in a large, modern office building in the heart of Manhattan.

At both Genetic Laboratories and Idant, each of the prospective clients is interviewed by a technician who explains the process, answers question, and, without being too nosy, tries to determine the man's reasons for wanting to deposit his sperm in a bank.

Single men are just as welcome as married. In some offices, they represent almost 40 percent of the clients to date.

"Some of the young, single men think they may be banking better quality sperm in their twenties than they will be producing later in life," says Genetic Laboratories' Dr. Robert Ersek. "This makes a lot of sense to me, but much as I'd like to tell them they are right, there is really no medical evidence to support it. The age of the mother has a lot to do with the health of the child, but the age of the father or his sperm seems to have nothing to do with it."

Many men come to the sperm banks with their wives. "Wives tend to be more interested in semen storage than their husbands," Idant's Dr. Jerome Silbert states. Howard Rowe at Genetic Labs says 30 percent of the telephone inquiries he receives are from women.

"They feel they can't stay on the Pill indefinitely," says Rowe, "and they also know that a vasectomy is a much simpler procedure for their husbands than a tube-tying operation would be for themselves. No wonder they are interested in anything that will make a vasectomy seem more acceptable."

What kind of procedure is involved in banking sperm?

Most banks work about the same way. Semen samples are best taken after three or four days' abstinence from sex; three or more specimens may be taken over a period of a week or more in order to have sufficient quantity and concentration of sperm to fill from 36 to 42 small containers for freezing. Private rooms are provided for clients.

"But some men just can't produce sperm under stress," says Howard Rowe. "Some even take their wives into the room with them. It might be easier to do it at home, but we want the sample taken here, not brought from the outside. When sperm is produced on the premises, I know when it comes out of that room who it came from and that it is fresh."

Elaborate precautions are taken to assure that sperm samples are correctly identified—by name, by number, by blood-serum samples and other means. Genetic Labs seals the sperm in small glass ampules, with the name of the donor etched into the glass. Idant uses plastic straws about the size of a ball-point-pen refill. These are stored, in turn, within aluminum tubes similar to those in which expensive cigars are sold.

The inventory of living human cells is kept in stainless-steel tanks that are as big as kitchen refrigerators, insulated like thermos bottles, and filled with liquid nitrogen. All a depositor's samples are never kept in one place. The client's sperm may be divided among several storage tanks on the remote possibility that one might rupture or otherwise fail, and protection can go as far as elaborate electronic safety devices that automatically dial the telephone numbers of five staff members at any time of day, night, weekend, or holiday if the level of liquid nitrogen falls to a critical point within the storage tanks. Some banks send part of a man's sperm to a distant city for storage, just in case something goes wrong at the main bank.

Fees vary. Minneapolis' Genetic Labs charges $55 per deposit of semen (three usually required), and this $165 includes the first year's storage. Thereafter, the cost is $15 per year. Idant charges a flat $80 for collection of samples and the first six months of storage. Thereafter, their charge is $18 per year.

From the outset, both sperm banks have been acutely conscious of public reaction to what they were doing. Before he opened his service to the public, Dr. Ersek was afraid of what he calls "the hilarious quality in the term 'sperm bank.'" He now says, frankly, "We feared and expected criticism from racial groups, the Catholic Church, and others. But we got none."

Dr. Ersek, a young physician who had studied experimental surgery at the University of Minnesota, began several years ago to freeze sperm, in a tentative way, for private patients—simply because the animal-husbandry department of the university got tired of telling people the department couldn't take the responsibility for freezing and storing human sperm. Eventually, under the pressure of demand, Dr. Ersek went into business openly, and now his Genetic Laboratories and the New York facility, Idant, are about to offer stock in their companies. "I simply made up my mind that we had a service the public was entitled to and which should not be kept secret," Dr. Ersek explains.

Dr. Silbert of Idant reports a couple of crank telephone calls, but no more. Despite the occasional criticism, and despite signs of a mounting concern among social scientists about the vasectomy explosion, the sperm-bank business shows all the signs of becoming a highly profitable enterprise. From its small, noncommercial beginnings at a few university hospitals in Iowa, California, and Illinois, human-sperm freezing is suddenly a growth industry. Within a few months, almost every major city in the United States will have a sperm bank, and most of them will be geared for volume business.

Dr. Silbert guesses that half of the doctors who performed vasectomies in the past year were unaware that their patients could have banked sperm (even by air) prior to the sterilization surgery. Now that the word about sperm banks is spreading through professional channels, Silbert believes all doctors will make patients aware of the option.

Many, of course, will not take it, for religious or private reasons. Indeed, some experts have basic doubts about the procedure.

Dr. Aquiles Sobrero, director of the Margaret Sanger Research Bureau in New York, is one who looks with real apprehension on the whole development of sperm banks. "Any man who thinks he might want to change his mind about his future fertility," says Dr. Sobrero, "is not a good candidate for vasectomy. A man should make up his mind he wants no more children and stick with that decision even if something happens to his present family."

There are also those who have nothing in particular against sperm freezing but have real doubts about the motives that lie behind many vasectomies. Mrs. Shirley J. Southwick, staff supervisor at the Family Service Organization in Worcester, Massachusetts, recently wrote in *The New York Times:* "Marriage counselors have growing doubts that vasectomies are always benign. Family service agencies across the country are reporting cases in which the operation has compounded sexual difficulties, increased anxieties and tensions, and helped break up marriages." Mrs. Southwick feels that, to the extent sperm banks may make vasectomy an even more attractive procedure, more caution should be taken in screening the people who ask for the operation. "If people have concern about their future fertility to the extent that they feel they must bank sperm," she says, "then perhaps they should reexamine their reasons for the vasectomy itself."

But sperm banker Ersek replies that it is psychologically absurd to try to separate sterilization from castration in a man's mind, no matter how well adjusted or clearly motivated he may be. "Knowing that they still retain the capacity to sire children by means of frozen sperm can be an important psychological boost for many men who otherwise have every good reason to have a vasectomy."

Dr. Silbert adds: "One obviously shouldn't choose vasectomy as a means of solving life's problems. It is simply a very effective form of contraception."

Section VII

DOLLARS AND SENSE
Mary W. Hicks

Although financial adjustment is often excluded as a significant factor in marital relationships, in broad cultural context, economics are as basic to the family as biology. While research shows no consistent relationship between size of income and marital adjustment, Landis and Landis report that their research shows that it takes couples longer to work out problems revolving around spending and controlling the family income than problems in any other area except sex relations.*

Why should spending and controlling the income be problems in marriage? Our society emphasizes money and material possessions, yet there is no unanimity concerning who should control money in marriage or what is worth buying. These issues are complicated by the psychological aspects of money which have been recognized from time immemorial. The expression "Money makes the mare go," illustrates the importance attached by the folk mind. That money is a motivating force is indicated by the expression, "I wouldn't do that for love or money." The Biblical reference, "Money is the root of all evil," suggests that monetary motivations are held to be morally and ethically wrong. Money is equated with security, love, deprivation, control and achievement, so that problems of domination, submission, insecurity, inferiority feelings, and many others are frequently created or exaggerated by the circumstances surrounding the control and use of the family money.

Family discord is frequently attributable to failure to agree on money matters, so almost all married couples find that they must compromise in order to achieve a good working relationship in the area of family finance. When couples differ greatly on how the money should be used or controlled, the resultant feeling of frustrated irritation sometimes affects their behavior in a variety of ways. The husband or wife may become overly critical of the mate's actions in other matters since it is often easier to be generally critical than to debate the subject of economic values. Either one may engage in behavior the other does not approve, such as going out in the evening or drinking too much. Or, either one may become surly, moody, and hard to live with, behaving in general like a worried or irritable person. Thus, any discussion of marriage must include an analysis of the part finances play in the relationship.

Articles

1. Michael J. Sporakowski—The Money World: $$, Cents, and Nonesense.

* Landis, Judson and Landis, Mary, Building a Successful Marriage, Englewood Cliffs, New Jersey, 1968, p. 358.

Name:_____ Date:_____

Student #:_____ Sex: M or F

1. Amount of income, use of income, and control of income are three factors involved in family economic adjustment. Which do you think cause the most difficulties? Why? Which the least? Why?

Rank the following in terms of largest (1) to smallest (5) proportion of a typical family budget—average expenditures.

2. _____ transportation

3. _____ food

4. _____ medical care

5. _____ housing-shelter only

6. _____ clothing

Matching

7. _____ Primarily savings   A.   Term life

8. _____ Savings and Protection   B.   Endowment

9. _____ Primarily protection   C.   Straight life

What are the three biggest purchases you expect to make in your llife?

10.

11.

12.

13. Do you have a credit card? Yes_____ No_____

14. If yes, how many?_____

15. Would you like to have a credit card? Yes_____ No_____

16. Why, or why not? _____

17. How much life insurance should be carried by a man? a woman?

18. What conditions would make this amount vary?

19. To raise a typical middle class child from birth to age 18 costs about_____

20. T   F   At present interest rates, if you buy a house for $30,000 today and pay it off as agreed, over twenty-five years, the total cost would be about $35,000.

21. T   F   Most people know why they manage their resources the way they do.

22. T   F   The key to family financial management lies in the concept of value more than in amount of income.

23. T   F   Family financial conflict is a form of discord unforeseeable before marriage.

24. T   F   Basic personality needs may influence management practices more than having a knowledge of such practices and skills.

Assume that you are married and your take-home pay is $550 per month. Make a budget for two. Include specific amounts for all of the following that you consider necessary in a family budget.

25. Rent and utilities $ _____

26. Groceries $ _____

27. Clothing $ _____

28. Furnishings for the home $ _____

29. Insurance (life, sickness, car, home) $ _____

30. Recreation $ _____

31. Gifts to charity and friends $ _____

32. Taxes $ _____

33. Transportation $ _____

34. Auto expenses, gasoline, payment, repairs $ _____

35. Savings and investments $ _____

36. Miscellaneous, cleaning, laundry, dues, haircuts $ _____

37. Medical and dental $ _____

38. Smoking, drinking $ _____

39. Others, specify $ _____

40. Suppose someone gave you $250—no strings attached—how would you spend it?

41. What if someone gave you $5,000?

THE MONEY WORLD: $$, CENTS AND NONSENSE

Michael J. Sporakowski

Marriage counselors have frequently commented on how money and sex problems are the two complaints most likely to be presented by persons seeking their services. Frequently these "presenting problems" are seen as symptomatic of other sub-surface difficulties, usually lack of positive communication and lack of adequate information. For many people the topics of sex and money were rarely discussed at home. Thus they became, like parenthood and death, areas the individuals were supposed to know something about and be able to deal with as though they had inborn, instinctive problem-solving capacities for these tasks.

It is not unusual for parents to say "Johnny doesn't know how to use his money wisely." We probably have seen many instances where Johnny has had few experiences in handling money or coping with money management tasks over time. From simple budgeting tasks to long form income tax returns, few of us have had much experience before age 16 or 18 in handling financial matters. How many people do you know who can't write a check properly, balance a check book within $5, or compute true annual interest rates? Yet most of us have to handle our funds reasonably if we are to survive. What if Johnny (above) marries Sally who is equally inept, inexperienced or ignorant? Do they avoid bankruptcy, sponging off their parents, going on welfare?

Hopefully this section will help you examine some of the financial and economic tasks young marrieds and young families are likely to have to cope with. Many books have been written that offer more detail. Some are listed in the reference section and can provide you with additional depth and breadth.

PLANNING

Two *cannot* live as cheaply as one! (But they might be able to live less expensively than two did separately.) To do this requires some communication, discussion of attitudes and values, and some pooling of resources.

Budgeting is one of those nine letter words that has a great deal of four letter word potential for some people. It frightens, offends, belittles and generally deals a lot of blows to many of our fragile egos. Why? Because of its unkown quality; because it implies structure, inflexibility, and fore-thought; and, because of its "you should know how to do it and follow by it" quality.

To budget is to estimate, to plan. Income versus outgo needs to be "balanced." But like all plans, budgets are subject to change. The water pump on the car goes out, an unexpected medical emergency occurs or a particularly good buy on carpeting happens unexpectedly and "bam!" there goes the budget. Or does it? Well it all depends on what you've anticipated, saved for, had insurance for, or built into your plans. Some factors that go into those plans are: (1) actual money available; (2) regular, planned expenditures for basic needs; (3) anticipated changes in income/outgo; (4) expectations of each individual for economic life style; and, (5) plans for emergencies. Of course not all people are in a position to deal with all of these factors at all times; and the factor titles may mean different things to different people. For example, "plans for emergencies" may mean a "rainy day" savings account to one couple or sending wife and kids to live with her folks temporarily. "Actual money available" could mean all income after regular pay-check deductions or cash on hand after the monthly bills have been accounted for. This is where communication comes in: whose money is it? His, hers, theirs, or? All too often statements like "she always runs out of her food money before the end of the month" reflect a potential for major marital conflict that is only superficially related to money.

Many guides for budgeting exist giving proportions and percentages of income spent on given items. These are usually based on someone's "average family or couple" and thus should be used only as examples of what might be. Things like chronic medical conditions, unusual food requirements or special transportation problems may play havoc with the prescribed proportions of the USDA budget for young families. Nonetheless, such data may be helpful in initial planning. Later, previous experience as baseline data will prove most useful, although using the period you stock the pantry for the first time as a typical week for food expenditures is a wee bit unrealistic. Some "typical couple," percentage expenditures as part of a routine budget, over time, would probably look something like this (based on income before taxes): food—18-20%; shelter—14-18%; income taxes—10-15%; utilities—5-7%; medical care—4-6%; transportation—12-16%. Other items would include: insurance—car, dwelling, medical, life; clothing; additional taxes, including social security;

recreation; savings; contributions and gifts; personal care items; and so forth.

Generally your budget/plan should be based on goals—current, near future, and long range—estimates of income and expenses, and actual data. One reason many plans do not work out is related to the inability of a given couple or family to discuss and set goals. Planning ahead is a way of life that may be unique to many people. Still, a setting of general as well as specific financial goals for the next 1, 5, 10, and 25 years can be not only productive in terms of dollars and cents, but also in terms of potentially improved communications. Too, it may aid youngsters in their gaining of realism related to the day-to-day financial world we all live in.

One last thought on plans. Record keeping may not only be a way of improved coping with income tax time, but also be an asset in resolving insurance claims and helping to determine where financial wastage occurs. As a task you may never have the courage to do again, try keeping a record of every cent of income and outgo you have for six months. Not only is this enlightening in terms of monetary flow, it also gives a fair amount of insight into attitudes, values, and emotional states as they relate to significant events.

CHILDREN

Family planning has often been related to contraception and population control. It also has significance in terms of the financial status of the family. "The experts" tell us that today it will cost the "average middle-class family" anywhere from $30,000 to $150,000 to raise each of its children from conception to age 18. If you throw in four years of college, add in another $10,000 to $30,000. Obviously, having children and raising them *a la mode* can be expensive.

For starters, the couple experiencing pregnancy will probably have to ante up $200 to $400 in advance for the obstetrician. If this is the first child, there will probably be some initial expenditures to fix up a room, obtain basic clothing and supplies, etc. The costs of a working wife not working, temporarily or for a longer period need to be acknowledged. The hospital stay for the birth will probably run $400 to $700 in addition to the obstetrician's fee, assuming things go "normally."

As the child grows, things like utilities, housing, and transportation need to be calculated, as well as food, clothing, schooling, medical care, and other more obvious items. These comments are not meant to say "don't have kids, they cost too much." Their intent is to convey the message that planning is essential in many areas if anticipated outcomes are to be achieved successfully.

CREDIT AND BORROWING

One of the major financial developmental tasks we find ourselves having to cope with is in the area of borrowing. Two of the largest purchases we make during our lifetimes are houses and cars. Rarely does anyone pay cash for either. Yet by not being able to make major purchases for cash we may end up paying more than double the value of the item. For example, if you borrowed $30,000 to buy a home and were to pay it off regularly over 25 years at a 9% interest rate the total repayment would be $75,528.00 based on monthly payments of $251.76. (And this would not include taxes, insurance, etc.) Shopping around for a better rate or term is important. That same $30,000 loan @ 9% over ten years would "only" cost you a total of $45,603.60. At 8% for 25 years you would pay back $69,465.00, while at 10% the figure would be $81,786.00. Rather than astound you with more figures like these, let me just say that when you borrow, you pay for it. On the other hand, such borrowing does have some tax advantages and may be the only way to survive let alone get ahead. Unfortunately, many of us only get a short sighted view—"a dollar down, a dollar a week"—of the costs, either by choice or design. Recent consumer oriented legislation requires that we be given "truth in lending statements" which indicate the actual interest rate as well as totals to be repaid. Yet many people either do not read these statements, cannot understand them, or do not care. Whatever the case, we all end up paying more than the selling price of the items.

On a somewhat more mundane, everyday level, we find ourselves being charged from 12%-18% on many credit card accounts or "revolving charge accounts." One card uses a slogan something like "think of it as money," and perhaps that would not be such a bad idea if we really knew how to deal with our money. But for many of us that card purchase just delays our financial reality by 25 or 60 days. Some of us even get into a game called "credit card roulette" where we play one piece of plastic against another to delay even longer our day of financial reckoning. (If I sound like a preacher here it is with some good reason. As a member of a credit committee—the group that decides who gets loans—at a Credit Union, as well as a counselor, I have seen many persons in great financial need who got there partly because of "easy credit" and a value system which was based on much gross ignorance and/or lack of the ability to delay gratification.)

It may be of interest here to note that consumer credit is only of fairly recent advent. If you were to go back as few as 75 years in this country you would find it rare if an individual or family were able to borrow. Only businesses tended to use credit, and then considerably more judiciously than today. But consumer credit has become a moneymaker. It is said that many large retailers, for example Sears, make more money on credit charges than on actual profits from item sales. So is it any wonder that every time you make a purchase the clerk asks if you would like to "charge it" or apply for a charge account?

What about charges for use? Generally, on credit card or "revolving charge" accounts there are at least three methods of computing the interest cost to you. Probably the most expensive is calculated on the "previous balance." This means you pay based on what was, without regard to partial payments you've made. A second method is based on the average daily balance. The third method, usually the least expensive, is based on the actual unpaid balance. Many of these cards and accounts will not charge anything in the way of interest if you pay within a specified time (usually 25 days) of the billing date. But watch out! Sometimes there is a discrepancy between the billing date and the date mailed, or worse yet, the zip coders route your payment via Mars and it takes 10 days to make a normal one day trip.

When it comes to loans, the unpaid balance method usually is advantageous to you especially if you can pay off sooner than expected. Many "coupon book loans"—e.g. car loans over a specified time—may charge you a penalty rate if you pay off sooner than agreed. So it is important not only to know the interest rate, term, and amount to be repaid, but also any special provisions about prepayment, late payment, etc. Some loans are written with a balloon clause—regular "low" payments for x months and then a "bigee" for the last one, e.g., $50 monthly for 35 months and $200 for month 36. Another type includes the interest in the amount actually borrowed—you borrow $1,000 but actually have use of only $850 because the other $150 is the interest you'll pay. Even though we have more consumer protection today than in the past, borrowing and credit can be a complicated matter for the average person.

We have talked about rates and methods of calculation related to credit, but how about obtaining it? What makes you a good or bad credit risk? Credit bureaus exist to help lenders assess you as a credit risk. They may also serve, in some areas, as collection agencies (bill collectors). Do not confuse them with credit unions which are in the savings and lending business.

The credit bureau rates you as a credit risk (or provides information to the potential lender so that he can rate you). This is done for a fee. Credit bureaus are not governmental agencies. They are in the information-for-pay business. When asked to rate you as to your credit worthiness the following things *may* be taken into consideration: previous credit record; length of residence; length of employment; current salary; marital status; credit references; place and type of employment; ownership of home; and, your current monthly obligations. A credit report may be a simple, "he's paying as agreed" or as complex as "you'd better take a look at this file. It's full of judgments against your applicant, and pending court cases." In any case, the credit bureau is a conveyor of information. In some instances, though, misinformation is passed on due to clerical errors. Frequently these errors are related to name similarity. If you are having trouble obtaining credit and your record is good, it may be that some information is inaccurate. You can ask to see your file, and if materials are not yours, untrue or you feel misleading, have them removed or updated, or have a statement of "your side" included. Most credit bureaus are happy to correct inaccurate files, but in some cases you might have to seek legal assistance.

Where you borrow may be influenced by things like your credit rating, the amount you need, the availability of funds, and other factors such as confidentiality and speed of the loans availability. Small loan companys will often make funds available on "your signature only," especially for amounts under $1,500. Their interest charges, though, are usually higher than a bank's or credit union's, and their repayment schedule may be less flexable and more likely to include prepayment penalties.

Savings and loans usually loan only for mortgage or remodeling purposes, not cars, boats, or travel. Credit Unions may have limits, for example $5,000, on the maximum amount of a loan. Shopping around for terms and conditions favorable to you as a consumer is vital if you are to play the credit and borrowing game with any amount of success. Get the details, ask the questions, and consider your needs and potentials so that decisions can be made wisely.

INSURANCE

One of the most overwhelming areas of family financial functioning tends to be the area of insurance. For many of us the first reaction we have to the term insurance is to think of life insurance. Yet there are many other kinds we may find ourselves having to purchase: homeowner's or renter's; automobile; and health. Generally speaking we purchase insurance as a type of protection against the unknown or to help in a time of specific need. Policies vary all over the place as to what they cover, how they cover it, under what conditions and how they will pay off. Let us look first at life insurance.

Probably a better name for life insurance would be death insurance or survivor's insurance. But in our culture we seem to want to avoid this topic so we use the euphemism. Whatever the case may be, this type of insurance is aimed at providing funds to help those who survive have some money to live on. Life insurance comes in basically three types with an unbelievable amount of variations (riders) that can be added. Probably the form that offers the most protection for the dollar, at least initially, is *term life insurance*. Basically this type of policy says "You pay X $$ for Y period of time. If the insured dies, the company will pay the beneficiaries Z $$." If the insured does not die, there is no pay-off from the company. As the age of the insured increases, generally in 5 year increments, the amount paid for the insurance (the premium) increases since the risk to the company is greater. Another form of term insurance is called level premium or decreasing term—sometimes also referred to as mortgage insurance. In this type of policy the premium stays the same but the amount paid in the event of death decreases over time. For example, at age 30, $50 for decreasing term might buy $15,000 of protection, whereas at age 40 it only offers $10,000 of protection. The name mortgage insurance comes from this type of insurance's parallel to the decreasing amount of a mortgage loan, and the situation where some lenders require their borrowers to add this kind of life insurance to their coverage or show that they already are covered by a sufficient amount of protection. Term insurance may be a good starting point for the young adult(s) moving into a marriage or family situation since it offers the most protection for the least dollar cost. Too, if you buy the appro-

priate kinds with convertability clauses, you may insure your future insurability.

A *second* kind of life insurance is called *straight life, whole life* or *ordinary life*. It provides protection and savings. Two terms need to be introduced here: cash value and face value. *Cash value* refers to what the policy is worth if you terminate it (cash it in) before the insured dies or when it is paid up. With straight life policies, the longer you hold them and pay on them, the greater the cash value of the policy. Most policies have little or no cash value until they are two or more years old. *Face value* refers to the amount the company will pay in the event of the death of the insured. Generally this amount will be paid whether the policy has been in force one day or twenty years.

Whole life policies are paid on until the person dies or reaches some age the insurance company actuaries say most people won't. A variation is a form called 65-life. This form compresses payment of premiums into the time period up to age 65 and thus may be an asset to the retiree. At age 65 payment of premiums ceases although coverage continues. An advantage of ordinary life insurance is that it provides protection early in the life of the insured and an accumulation of savings as it matures. Persons who have minimum need for life insurance protection—no dependents, or spouse—may choose to cash this type of policy in as they retire.

The *third* type of life insurance you are likely to run into is *endowment*. Basically this is a savings plan with a minimum of protection built in. Some grandparents buy a single premium endowment policy for grandchildren soon after their birth so that after a specified time, let's say 15 or 20 years, the policy can be cashed in and used for college expenses. For most young couples or families where the income level is little more than subsistence this type of life insurance is probably a poor investment since it offers minimal protection for the money spent.

Innumerable riders can be attached to life insurance policies. Some of the more common are described as follows. *Accidental death benefit*. This means that in the event of accidental death the policy would pay off double or triple the face value. *Waiver of premium due to disability*. If the insured becomes disabled and is not able to meet the premiums the insurance company will make the payments. *Additional purchase benefit*. At certain intervals, e.g., every 5 years, or upon significant events, e.g., the birth of a child or marriage, the insured may increase his or her insurance without a medical exam. Depending on the stage of your life cycle some of these may be more or less valuable to you. Their value must be weighed against their additional cost. The latter can be determined by calling various agents and comparison shopping.

Several other comments on life insurance. In the event of death, the beneficiaries will probably have some settlement options available, unless the insured spelled them out prior to his or her demise. They may be a "lump sum settlement," i.e., the face value of the policy all at once; or X number of dollars per month for the beneficiary's lifetime; or perhaps Y number of dollars for the next Z years. Needs of the survivors should be considered, both short and long term, in deciding upon the form of settlement.

Generally speaking group policies offer less expensive premiums than policies taken out individually. Thus you may find that $10,000 of term insurance taken out as an employee of ATCO Foundry is somewhat cheaper to buy than $10,000 of term insurance as John Doe, self-employed. Professional organizations, travel clubs, ad nauseum may all be groups you can get better life insurance rates through. Be careful though in that some group policies are written in such a way that when you leave the group you are no longer eligible for the insurance or must pay premiums at a much higher rate.

Many insurance salespersons will try to sell you a package deal; a combination of several types of policies covering various family members. This may be a good deal *if* you need the coverage they suggest and can afford it. But, it has been my experience, as well as the experience of many others that such packages frequently provide considerably more coverage than is needed or can be afforded. In the past the primary "bread winner" was who you insured. Today with both parents frequently working it may be that equal or more equally distributed life insurance coverage is needed for all the bread winners. Some consideration should probably also be given to insurance for the children. The primary people who need to be insured are those who if they die would leave the survivors in financial straits—probably the parents. As such, life insurance on the kids should probably be to cover burial expenses. The only type of life insurance that would probably be helpful for college expenses of the child, with the child as the insured, is endowment, and that is probably too expensive for most families. Unfortunately for many families, many policies have been sold "on the kids" when the protection should have covered the parents.

These have been just a few of the basics on life insurance. As you decide a need for it occurs or a need to increase what you have seems evident, check around. Do some reading. Consumer oriented publications often offer up-to-date materials that are understandable and useful. Ask several companies or salespersons for their rates and do some comparing. Cheapest is not always best, but the more expensive policies had better offer better benefits or service if you buy from the companies that offer them.

Homeowner's or *renter's insurance* is another type most of us will find ourselves faced with buying. Basically both cover contents and some liability, with homeowner's covering the dwelling as well. There are usually several policies available of each kind. As you pay more, the coverage becomes more extensive. For example, under some policies only a minimum of coverage is provided for smoke damage, whereas others will cover repainting, cleaning, etc. Things usually covered under this type of policy include: fire damage; effects of storms; burglary—if forcible entry is shown; and water damage due to bursting pipes. What is covered and how is spelled out in the policy—be sure to read it, even the fine print.

Homeowner's policies usually have some kind of deductible clause which says the company will pay after the first $50 or $100 of loss. It is wise to inventory your belongings, including sales tags, receipts or estimates of values. Insurance companies will often have a form for such an inventory. Do the busy work and keep it in a safe, fireproof place, updating as needed if you want to save yourself claim headaches. Some items like jewelry, silver, coin collections, etc., may require a special rider and additional premium if they are to be covered beyond a certain value, often $500. In some instances you may need a certified appraisal before you can add such coverages. Silver tableware is a good example of an item where additional coverage may be required to reach an adequate replacement value. On today's market an eight place setting of silver easily tops the $1,000 mark. Too, with inflation continuing at its present rate, policies need to be updated from time to time or put on an automatically increasing system of upgrading coverage. For example, a house costing $35,000 five years ago would probably require $50,000 to replace it today. This is an area where an agent can be of unmeasurable assistance. Assessing what was, what is, and what might be is very important in purchasing this type of coverage.

Health or *medical insurance* is a third major expenditure in terms of a family's insurance program. Usually this refers to hospitalization and major medical policies, but may also include income protection due to disability plans, cancer protection, daily benefits policies or dental plans. Frequently employers pick up part or all of the hospitalization and major medical premiums for the employee and, possibly, his or her family. Adequacy of coverage varies from plan to plan, geographic area to geographic area. Like most other insurance, you can buy the stripped down model or the more expensive chrome or gold plated ones. Things such as private vs. semiprivate rooms are variables as are length of hospital stay, services performed, and proportion deductible (the amount the policy will actually pay).

Most hospitalization policies will cover maternity benefits as part of their scheme. There is an important note here. Usually a policy must be in force at least 10 months before such coverage is actually provided. Of recent advent is coverage on the "other side of the coin." Many medical insurers will now cover voluntary sterilization. (They've found it's cheaper to pay for one tubal ligation or laparscopic sterilization than three or more children.)

Major medical usually runs something like this: payment will be made at the rate of 80% of the actual amount billed above and beyond the first $100 you pay in a given year. The percentage rate and the deductible amount (what you pay first) vary from policy to policy. You may have options on larger or small percentages or deductibles for more or less cost. Some people who have to pay for their own medical insurance choose not to purchase hospitalization, but buy major medical with a deductible that will protect them only from a medical catastrophy because this is cheaper. In a sense medical insurance is a form of prepayment, since most of us will require some of these services at some time. For many families the child bearing, childrearing, and retirement years are when this coverage is most essential. If your place of employment does not provide this kind of coverage you will probably find it available on an individual basis but at higher rates.

What is covered and how varies considerably across policies and plans. Check out your specific policy and check with the insurer to be sure you know the inside information. Even then you may still find yourself paying for some services you hadn't expected to. Costs often not covered are things like: office visits; drugs and other medications; dental treatment except under hospital emergency conditions resulting, for example, from an automobile accident; and, some types of lab tests. Sometimes these can be picked up as part of the major medical coverage, or under additional policies. In other instances there is just no way around it, you pay.

Specialized health policies like cancer protection frequently are advertized in the "Sunday supplement" and usually are coverage above and beyond the typical hospitalization policies. The "$40 a day extra benefits" type policies may be helpful if you can afford them or as a substitution for more expensive, more comprehensive plans— but "what you see is what you get," and they may not be adequate for your needs.

Some folks have access to Health Maintenance Organizations (HMO'S) which may provide better overall medical care and may be an option of choice. We have much rhetoric about national health insurance but little has been really done beyond Medicare and Medicaid which serve special population segments. Until something better comes along we would be wise to check into what is available locally and make some decisions based on that knowledge, our particular needs, and what we can afford.

The final major expenditure in *insurance* that most of us will make is on our *automobiles*. Once again the options available to us may be more than we care to cope with, for much like the vehicles they cover, the basic models can have added to them an almost infinite array of accessories. Most states will require evidence of some basic policy before you can be licensed to drive. But look at just some of the things that are covered or may be added: bodily injury/property damage; rental reimbursement; loss of earnings; collision; comprehensive; property protection; personal injury; medical payments; combination physical damage; emergency road service; uninsured motor vehicle; death/disability; or underinsured motorist.

In addition to the usual comments about what you need and what you can afford you should probably consider things like: is the car worth less than the cost of the collision insurance; how much do you drive and for what purposes; and, if you have two or more cars, can one be insured differently and/or less expensively than the other(s) because of its use?

Rates do vary from company to company and some will give you better deals depending on how they rate you based upon: age; driving records; and, how many cars you have insured with them. Investigation and comparison in this area will undoubtably pay dividends.

A wide variety of other types of insurance exist that families may choose to buy. As the kids go to school, accident and travel policies may be made available that could be wise additions. Too, many of us are already paying into or covered by insurance programs like workman's compensation or Social Security. A useful task for many of us might be to list the coverages we have, with whom, for how much, and where they are so that as situations occur where claims may need to be made we would know where to start.

The following are some general guidelines you will probably find helpful as you move into purchasing insurance coverage:

1. Shop around; compare not only on prices, but service, policies for filing claims, availability of agents, and special policy provisions.

2. Check to see if group as well as individual rates are available and how one versus the other *may* benefit you.

3. Generally the "name" companies are better bets in our highly mobile society, but others *may* offer as good or better deals. Ratings of companies can be found at the state insurance commissioner's office as well as in publications like *Consumers Report* from time to time. Check out the company so that you'll have some idea as to whether or not they'll be around, literally as well as figuratively, if you need to file a claim.

4. If you have an option as to when you pay premiums—monthly, quarterly, semiannually, or annually—check to see if you will save money by paying less frequently. If yes and you can budget adequately it may be to your advantage to pay on an annual or semiannual basis. On the other hand, some people can deal better with $10 a month kind of payments as opposed to $100 once a year.

5. You may find that stock companies offer you a better or worse deal than mutual companies. In mutual companies you own a piece of "the rock" and if they make money you get dividends in return. With stock companies, the money made is usually distributed first to the stockholders—and owning a policy doesn't necessarily mean you own stock too. Again, do some investigating.

6. Buy what you need and allow for options for future needs where possible. Too much insurance can be as much a financial drain as too little. But what is "too" depends on you and your situation.

A wide variety of topics related to family economic functioning have not yet been discussed in this section. What I would like to do is cover five more—buying versus renting; savings; taxes; transportation; and, "routine expenditures."

Probably most of us would be thinking of housing in response to the *"buying versus renting"* statement above. Yet in today's relatively affluent society which seems to be very "thing" oriented the discussion needs to cover additional areas too. In years past we may not have had much of a choice. Either you could afford something or you couldn't. If you couldn't buy or build a house yourself or with family help, you frequently moved in with relatives or had a job where housing was part of the deal.

With today's cost of single family housing going even higher, more and more people are choosing apartment, town house, or condominium living as options that are affordable. With regard to buying or renting, there are some advantages and disadvantages to consider. If you choose to buy a house some of the advantages would include: tax advantages associated with interest payments on the mortgage; the building of equity as the loan is paid off and as property values increase; and a personal/family sense of pride in ownership. Disadvantages involve things like: large interest payments (previously discussed under credit and borrowing); maintenance costs; property taxes and insurance; and resale ability in the event of a move.

Renting has its pros and cons too. Pros: little or no maintenance; property taxes paid by the owner (but included as part of the rent); no large investment or downpayment required (although a security deposit may be needed); and, no resale problems (although a lease may require moves only at certain times). Cons include: money for rent is never seen again (no investment); you may have little control over decor; there is probably less privacy in a rental unit than an owned one; you may be subject to the whims of the owners regarding "inspections," the upkeep the owner provides, etc.; and, especially in a multiple dwelling unit, you may have little control over who your neighbors are.

When we apply the renting versus buying schema to other areas we find some additional things to be considered. With regard to automobiles, the amount spent on renting or leasing may be minimally different from buying, but, if you use the car for business the rental costs may be a tax write off, and in rentals you usually get a new car every 2 years or 50,000 miles. Too, the down payment is not needed in renting. On the other hand, someone who buys a car, maintains it well and drives it reasonably may be able to resell it later for a reasonable amount.

Rental stores today provide a tremendous range of things one can rent or lease at fairly reasonable costs. Baby furniture, concrete mixers, punch sets, lawn mowers, tools, and so forth may well be things your family needs only temporarily, yet cannot afford to buy—and perhaps doesn't want to because of limited use or storage problems. Renting may be the most functional alternative in such instances, although there are those among us of the "thing orientation" who will have to purchase everything no matter how rarely we will use it.

Many articles and books on family economics have a section on *savings* and investments. My personal and academic knowledge of the latter is minimal, and my affective response to them especially in the current depressed economic times is negative so I will focus on savings here. We often hear slogans like "save first, not last." The idea might be an excellent one, but I wonder how many people are really able to do it or are motivated in such a way? Like any other slogan it is appealing but many times less than possible. Many experts will even go so far as to say "save 10% of your gross income" as an ideal. Once again a nice intention but I wonder how many families would be able to survive with that kind of schema—on a day-to-day basis.

Savings can be very specifically goal directed, such as for a down payment on a home or to buy a car, or more generally goal directed such as for a "nest egg" or "rainy day fund." We can probably say that saving with a goal in mind is more likely to be regular and effective. Too, if we can have it taken from our pay checks before we see them, many of us are more likely to be better savers.

Although many of us have had savings in a piggy bank or a sugar bowl or in a sock under the mattress, we realized that such modes drew no interest and their value didn't increase, unless of course we saved gold or silver coins. Most saving that draws interest is done at banks, credit unions, and savings and loan-type associations. Back when banking began in this country savings accounts drew little if

any interest—they offered safety and a place to hold your money. Back in the 1940's banks were paying interest in the 2-4% range. Today, depending on the type of account or certificate and the kind of place you save, interest rates offered range from approximately 5 to 7 3/4%.

Once you decide how much you can save, then decisions have to be made on where and under what conditions. A basic passbook savings account usually lets you deposit or withdraw "on demand" and will probably pay in the vicinity of 4 1/2-5 1/4% interest. Sometimes there are regulations as to the amount withdrawn or deposited, or the number of times in a given period that withdrawals can be made. Interest can be computed in a variety of ways, and may be paid daily, weekly, monthly, quarterly, semiannually, or annually. This can mean $$ to you so be sure to check on it, since there might be more or less advantageous times to deposit or withdraw.

Other types of savings involve accounts and certificates that have specified time periods indicated on them. For example, a 90 day certificate will probably pay a better rate of interest than a passbook account, but less than a 1 year or 5 year certificate. The disadvantage of these time dated accounts and certificates is that they allow withdrawals only at stated intervals. If you need the money earlier, you forfeit a substantial amount of the interest. One way around this may be to borrow money from the institution based on your savings as collateral at a lower rate than normal. You probably won't lose quite as much as if you had to cash the certificate in prematurely.

Shop around for savings institutions like for anything else. They do vary in what they pay and how they pay it even though there is some regulation of interest rates. Too, some will offer special promotions and gifts that might, if they are useful to you, make one institution a better deal than another. Most savings institutions carry insurance that will cover accounts up to $40,000. This means that should the institution have difficulties, the insurer will make good on the account. Such insurance came into being after the great stock market fall and bank closings around the time of "the great depression." Nevertheless, some institutions are not appropriately chartered and may not be insured. Those that are prominently display signs to that effect or will be more than happy to tell you so.

The two biggest negatives about savings accounts are the results of inflation and preferred tax treatment of stock dividends. With inflation topping the 10% rate off and on recently a savings account earning 5 1/2% interest is losing ground quickly. On the other hand, at least at the moment of this writing, a 5 1/2% increase is considerably higher than the money many people are losing on stocks. Yet in times of a growing stock market, stocks turn a much better rate of growth than do savings accounts. With regard to the second negative, based on the current tax regulations (1975), the first $200 of stock dividends earned by a married couple are tax exempt. No such exemption is presently available to the persons who earn interest on savings accounts.

Savings can be a way to accumulate money towards larger investments or purchases, a way to establish an estate, a way of setting up a fund to fall back on in emergencies, or a way to help accomplish long range goals like education or for retirement. How much we save, where, and how we use the savings are all variables requiring objective as well as subjective input from the families and larger community in which we live.

Although funerals have a large impact on family financial functioning, my emphasis in the statement "the only sure things in life are death and *taxes*" will be on the latter variable. Taxes take up a large part of our income. The most obvious, initially, are income taxes—federal, state, and in many places local. Social security is a tax. Then we have sales taxes of various percentages, personal property taxes, property taxes, excise taxes, and taxes on automobile use. At every turn one governmental agency or another extracts a percentage. In the past, we often had heard how terrible the tax rate was in counties characterized as socialistic, but if we accurately figure out how much of our actual dollar goes for one kind of tax or another I would venture to say that the rate is over 50%. My point here is not political or anti-tax but that if we are to be at all realistic in our family's economic dealings we need to know what we actually have to cope with.

As in other economic areas, planning plays a vital role in our dealing with taxes. The federal government deals with this whether we like it or not by withholding monies from our regular paychecks. Can you imagine what would happen if it didn't, and we all had to pay our federal income tax on April 15? Another kind of preplanning is seen in escrow accounts related to house payments. Property taxes usually are a considerable sum so that many lending agencies offer the possibility of

escrow accounts which, incidently, rarely pay interest, but accumulate money to be payed at a later date. If you need to borrow to pay your taxes you in essence cause yourself additional "taxation" because of the interest you will have to pay.

In relation to some specifics about taxes, it is very important to keep accurate records and receipts. Many things can reduce your income taxes but you may be required to show evidence of them. Interest is not taxable, so that a large mortgage *may* be a tax advantage. Taxes paid are *usually* not taxable, so that the money spent on property taxes (as well as others) may not be taxable. Some of the others include taxes on gasoline and personal property taxes. Specific details on what taxes can or cannot be "written off" is available from the taxing agencies.

Planning ahead and prepaying taxes may save you some money. For example, payment of property taxes for two years instead of one may well put you in a lower tax bracket, where this is possible. There are many other examples of how we could save on taxes, but rather than attempt that epic task let me just say learn as much as you can about the regulations that govern your situation and use them to your maximum benefit. There are many "special cases" written into tax laws so it is well worth your time and effort to see which you can qualify for.

"It's the nickels and dimes that kill you." With inflation being what it is, the principle of that statement is as valid as ever but the coin value probably needs to be incremented by a factor of 100. One of the most costly areas of our daily expenses is *transportation*. With the emphasis we have in this country on having a car (or a car for each adult for that matter) is it any wonder that transportation often costs the "average family" 10-15% of its budget? There are lots of different estimates around, but in 1975 the cost per mile for driving a car probably came out to be between 25 and 30 cents. (This would include gas, oil, maintenance, car payments, depreciation, insurance, etc.) That figure is a theoretical average and could be considerably higher or lower for a variety of reasons. *But* it probably reflects an average cost that most of us either did not recognize or did not want to recognize. If you think about it, that means if you drive 10 miles a day to work and back you spend $12.50 to $15.00 a week. Then add in shopping trips, chauffering, church trips, and so forth and you see why car pooling and mass transportation are becoming necessities for many if not all of us. And, chances are, with gasoline and car prices continuing to increase, the budget expenditures for transportation will become even greater, both in actual and percentage outlay, if we continue to rely on the automobile as heavily as we do today.

"ROUTINE" EXPENDITURES

Day-to-day living costs are an area many of us overlook in discussing family financial functioning. Nevertheless they are frequently the source of conflict. How we deal with them involves our monetary system as well as values and attitudes, needs, and communications.

One type of daily task to cope with is how to handle money—literally. Do we deal in cash only? Credit cards? Checking accounts? or? The popular press has frequently reported the coming of the "cashless society" or the "checkless" one. Computerization has had its impact on the transfer of funds. Yet on a very basic level we need to decide on how much cash we carry, for what things we'll write checks, and when to pay bills. Cash can be misplaced, lost, or stolen. But so can checks. Thus you may have problems getting checks cashed especially if you don't have an account locally or are not a regular customer. Too, checks cost money in most instances and how many or few you write may make a difference, as well as how much you need to have on deposit. Free checking may be available but be sure to understand the conditions it is based upon.

Another aspect of checking accounts and cash is "whose?" Is the checking account in both names or only one? Do you have separate accounts? Or who carries the cash and/or pays the bills? All of these questions have importance not only in relation to economic transactions but also to the self-concepts of those involved and the marital and family adjustments they make. Some wives who are not employed for pay feel that the family's money is really their husband's. Others feel quite the opposite. Too, especially where both persons are remuneratively employed, I've seen some very bitter conflicts over whose money is used to pay what and when. Many of us see our personal worth as related to our dollars and cents value, and thus what seems to be a simple conflict over a budget for Sue and Joe may well turn into a "knock down, drag out" related to the kids, sex, "You don't love me any more," or a variety of other things. Obviously this area calls for a discussion of feelings and attitudes, as well as behaviors and the gathering and sharing of information.

Food is one of those "routines" that seems to be taking an ever increasing proportion of our income. Even though it still may be a "good buy," it is an area which many feel needs to be part of the juggling act when it comes down to economizing. One of the difficulties comes from the fact that most food stores sell more than food. For example, a $50 food bill may include $10 worth of soap, waxes, health care items, magazines, beer, and pencils. The merchandisers are as aware of the convenience aspect of "one stop shopping" as are consumers, so many other items are offered for sale at food stores. Also a problem for many of us is impulse shopping. Attractive items are conveniently placed "on sale" where you enter or check out. It is very easy to pick them up as part of the food bill even though you *may* well be paying a higher price than at the store across the street.

Comparative shopping is a good idea *if* food stores are close enough together so as to not cause you to waste a lot of travel—time, gas, or mileage. On the other hand, in my college classes we have on several occasions gone to different food stores with the same shopping list and come out with overall expenditures that were nearly identical. So if you find the same type result perhaps convenience, selection, or other personal factors will be important in your "where to shop decision."

The question of buying in quantity also relates to your food purchases. *If* you can purchase items at a good price, and *if* they store well, and *if* you have the room or facilities to store, quantity buying may be an asset—especially if it is of items you will use. Freezers are economical only where the use rate is high, and some experts indicate this means at least five or six people in the family. Otherwise the cost of the freezer and its cost of operation probably can only be justified on convenience grounds.

With more and more people turning to their own gardens, we need to examine things like canning, freezing, and storage carefully to see how really functional they are from economic, convenience, and personal gratification viewpoints.

Utility bills—phone, electricity, water, garbage, etc.—are regular expenditures that may vary from month to month depending on amount of use. Of particular note here would be the bills associated with heating or cooling our places of shelter. Suppliers of fuel or electricity may have "equal" or "time" payment plans which help to blunt the effects of heavy use months. Many people who have "all electric homes" found themselves with winter bills in the $150 to $200 (or more) range which drastically affected budgets. To help deal with this you may find it possible to be on an "equal payment plan" which allows you to pay X dollars a month for 11 months and then either receive a credit or make up the difference in the 12th month. Some utilities may still give a discount for prompt payment of bills. But more likely is the situation where a penalty is assessed for late payment, or service discontinued. Once again planning is a vital aspect of family financial functioning.

One final comment on the "routines." Many of us will undertake regular donations or contributions to our church, the United Fund, or other such organizations. Often some sort of check off system is available or a regular monthly or weekly payment may be decided upon. Still another method might involve lump sum payments. The latter might be especially advantageous for tax purposes depending on when you make the payment. Records and receipts will be of help here when tax time rolls around.

SOME CLOSING THOUGHTS

There are many factors involved in adequate family financial functioning. We have examined some, but only briefly. For further depth in both information and understanding consult the reference list at the end of this section. Too, find out who in your community can be of help. For example, the Internal Revenue Service can answer your tax questions free, where a commercial agency will cost you. It is likely that for most of us with relatively noncomplex tax situations the thing to do is do your own. Banks and savings institutions frequently offer financial advice and counseling to their customers free of charge, although in some areas, like estate planning, a charge may be a part of the deal. Extension agents, consumer agencies, Better Business Bureaus, and many governmental offices can also offer a variety of aids to better dealing with various aspects of the system.

You need to exercise your initiative in financial dealings. Some stores will not haggle about prices, but many will, especially if you know where the buys are and the basic costs and profit margins. Yet many of us don't do or won't do such homework, and so the sticker price is the price we pay.

Being able to assess our needs, having adequate information with regards to prices or processes, and being able to communicate about our attitudes and values will help all of us better cope with the financial aspects of family living. Establishing sound patterns of decision making and functioning early will foster better marital and family adjustments as relationships are established and mature.

References

1. Bailard, T.E., Biehl, D.L. and Kaiser, R.W. *Personal Money Management.* Science Research Associates, 1973.

2. Cohen, J.B. and Hanson, A.W. *Personal Finance: Principles and Case Problems.* Irwin, 1972.

3. Consumer Reports (Editors). *The Consumers Union Report on Life Insurance.* Mount Vernon, N.Y. 1972.

4. Consumer Reports (Editors). *The 1975 Buying Guide Issue: Consumer Reports.* Mount Vernon, N.Y., 1974. Also, other yearly reports.

5. Duvall, E.M. *Family Development.* Lippincott (4th ed.) 1971.

6. Garman, E.T. and Eckert, S.W. *The Consumer's World: Money Management and Issues.* McGraw-Hill, 1974.

7. Lasser, J.K. Tax Institute. *J.K. Lasser's Managing Your Family Finances.* Doubleday, 1968.

8. Porter, S. *Sylvia Porter's Money Book.* Doubleday, 1975.

9. Smith, C. and Pratt, R. *The Time-Life Book of Family Finance.* Time-Life Books, 1969.

In addition the following periodicals may prove helpful:

Changing Times
Consumer Finance News
Consumer Reports

Name: _____   Date: _____

Student #: _____   Sex: M or F

1. List proposals you think might make the marriage relationship a more meaningful one in the future. Include any changes in the laws you think might be appropriate.

2. What marriage form do you think will be the dominant form by 1980? Why?

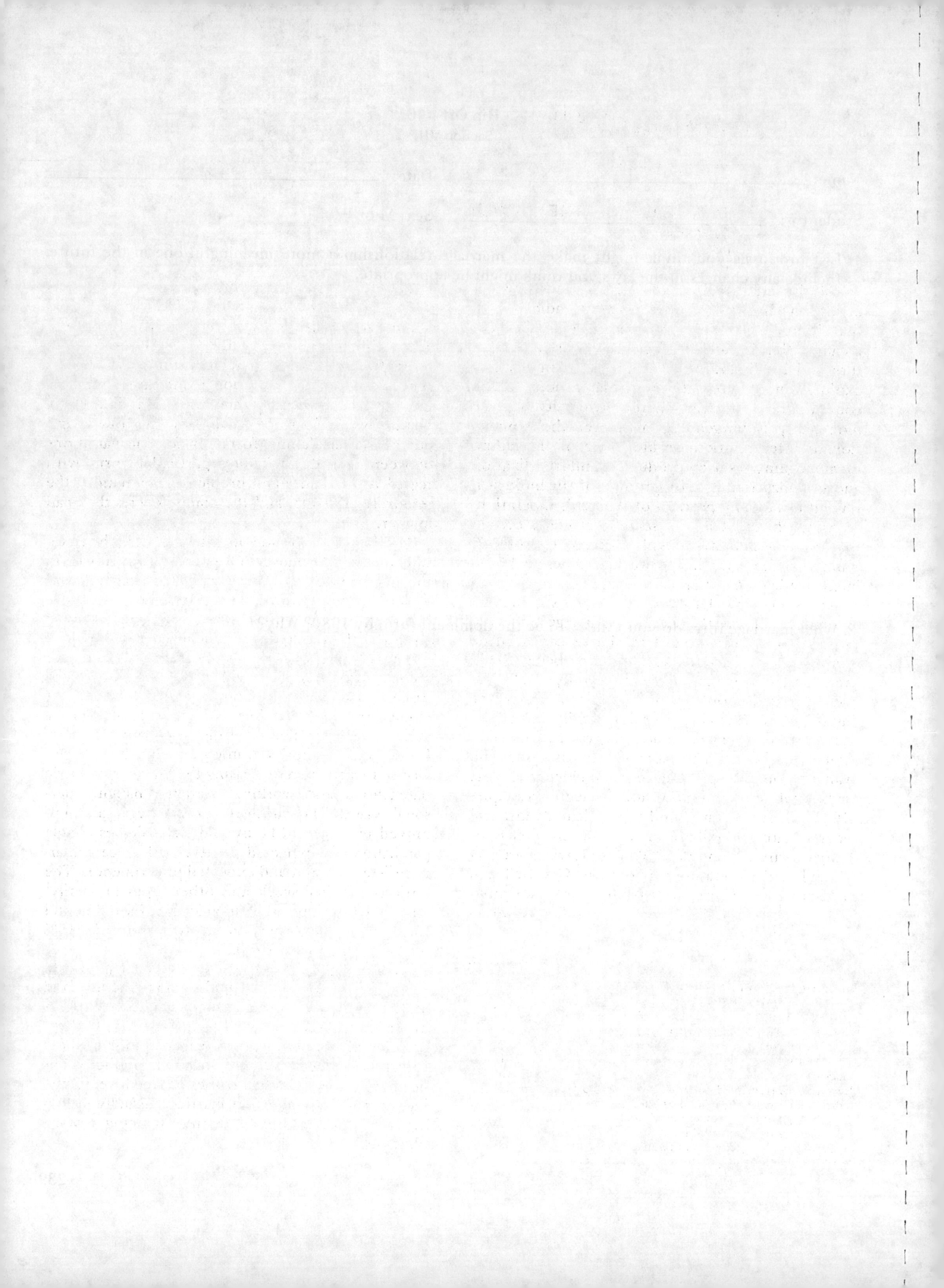

Section VIII

THE FUTURE OF THE FAMILY
Mary W. Hicks

Will the family survive as a primary social system in the twenty-first century? Every indication is that it will—but the form that it will take, the meaning that it has for its members, its role structure and its durability over time is unknown. The exploration of alternatives and alterations to the contemporary nuclear family with its surface monogamy is burgeoning. Whatever the explanation or interpretation—as indicative of the failure of monogamy, as a by-product of industrialization and urbanization, as a by-product of the biological revolution, as a by-product of Women's Liberation, or as the birth of a new society—it seems certain that these explorations will continue to flourish. Family change has been and continues to be an inextricable part of human history.

As a society we have moved and are still moving a long way from the kind of marriage our forefathers knew and believed in. There can be little doubt that the cozy fireside, and the obedient children, and the loving, close-knit family circle is a myth that exists only in our nostalgia. Yet, in the past, the traditional one-career family, a nuclear unit created by a first marriage, was the marriage model for the majority. Accurate statistics are unavailable on the prevalence or incidence of the traditional nuclear family and its legitimate spin-offs, i.e., one-parent families, nuclear dyads, and second career families; or on the incidence of "experimental" families. The following are research-based estimates provided by Cogswell and Sussman[1] of the percent distribution of the United States population living in various family structures:

Family Type	% Distribution
Nuclear Family (with children)	
Single work	30
Dual work	14
Nuclear Dyad (without children)	
Single work	4
Dual work	11
Single-Parent	13
Reconstitued (remarried nuclear)	15
Other traditional: e.g., middle or aded couple, three-generation, nuclear dyad, and bilateral or extended kin	5
"Experimental" marriages and families	8

These authors believe that if there were a census in 1972 of all the families in the United States and if these were classified according to structures similar to those described in the above classification, estimations would be that approximately 30 percent would be the traditional one-career, nuclear unit created by a first marriage. This is a static picture which does not account for the flow in and out of various family forms or for the variations between individuals in any particular form with regard to the issues and problems they handle, the resources available, and the competencies they can muster.

The long term trend appears to be that the traditional form will maintain a plurality but not be in the majority. By 1980, according to Cogswell and Sussman, there will be a continued and steady increase in the incidence of dual-work families and a leveling off of single-parent structures at between 16 and 20 percent. Dual-work, single-parent, and reconstituted families will make up the major variants from the traditional form. Reasons for these trends have been delineated by many authors. They include the increased opportunities for women in the economic structure, human service systems which are easing the burdens of single parenthood and working women, changing personal values and motives for marriage, and improved medical and household technologies. Single parenthood is expected to level off since remarriage is a common and expected phenomenon. The options for dual work and other types of family-like relationships are increasing. Experimental forms are not expected to involve more than 15% of the population in 1980.

Even though it is likely that only a relatively small percentage of the population will be involved at any one time in experimentation, it seems appropriate to describe briefly what is meant by "experimental" family forms. A reasoned look at these forms is in order because so much publicity has been given to sensational stories of free love, swinging, communes and group marriages usually implying that the traditional family is racing toward oblivion.

The typology of "experimental" family forms presented grows out of the limited research currently available, and focuses primarily on the roles and structure comprising each family type. This typology puts forth the cast of players rather than the drama itself, giving virtually no attention to the relationships and dynamics involved in the forms presented.

Experimental Forms

Experimental group marriage families (These are considered "experimental families" since procreation and rearing of children are involved).

A: Common residence or compound of households composed usually of three or more monogamous couples who practice sexual exclusivity but where members have ready access to one another for social interactions, sharing of resources, common facilities, and socialization of children. Some communes take this form.

B: Similar to A, but sexual swapping within the group is practiced.

C: Mixture of formerly married couples and singles; or composed of all singles with or without sexual swapping.

D: Multilateral marriage similar to B, but usually involving fewer than six members; most frequently two-family monogamous couples and some times only three persons.

Experimental "marriages." (Some of these forms of alliances may involve the procreation of children and their socialization; for example A and D. Most focus on the needs for identity, intimacy, and interaction of adult members.)

A: Nonrelated adults sharing a common household involving a division of labor with or without sexual accessibility.

B: Heterosexual cohabitation where there is a de facto marriage without recourse to legal requirements.

C: Homosexual unions involving same sex pairings in a single household sharing roles, intimacies, experiences, resources. In some instances more than two members may form a colony or commune.

D: Affiliated family usually involving unrelated members of different generations; for example, an aged woman and a single female parent and offspring, with a division of labor appropriate to needs and capabilities of participants.

Experiments with "traditional marriages."

A: Androgynous marriage in which prevalent role allocation based on sex is nullified and replaced by nonsex differentiated allocation, norms governing competence, needs, and expectations. The traditional form of the marital dyad with sexual exclusivity is maintained.

B: Open marriage similar to Form A but stressing multiple outside relationships, "expanded monogamy," equal freedom and identity for each partner, individual growth and increased psychic space, and development of trust.

The fears that the institution of marriage will be radically changed in the near future seem unfounded—the nature of the change is evolutionary rather than revolutionary. Yet, the growing interest in restructuring the traditional monogamous conjugal relationship is pervasive. Increasingly individuals are seeking an authentic and mutually actualizing relationship. Many couples are becoming frustrated because they have rejected the more traditional definition of a successful marriage and yet are having difficulty achieving the mutually actualizing relationship they are striving to achieve. It appears that a successful marriage continues to be difficult to achieve.

The following proposals have been offered by Dave Olsen, in discussing the evolutionary nature of change in the institution of marriage, as guidelines that might help make marriage a more meaningful and vital relationship. [2]

1. Individuals should not be encouraged to marry at an early age but should wait until they have matured emotionally and have established themselves in their chosen profession.

2. All individuals should not be encouraged or pressured into marriage.

3. Individuals and couples should be encouraged to experiment with a variety of life styles in order to choose the style which is most appropriate for them.

4. Couples should be encouraged to openly and honestly relate rather than play the traditional dating-mating game.

5. Couples should not get married until they have established a meaningful relationship and resolved their major difficulties; for marriage will only create, rather than eliminate, problems.

6. The decision of parenthood should be a joint decision which should follow, rather than precede (as it does in about one-third of the cases), marriage.

7. Couples should not have children until they have established a strong and viable marriage relationship.

8. Couples should be creative and flexible in how they work out their changing roles and mutual responsibilities, not only during their inital phases of marriage, but throughout their marriage relationship.

Individuals would have greater freedom to develop in these ways if they were given societal support rather than implicit and explicit restrictions and constraints. There are a few specific ways in which legal and legislative reform would facilitate these opportunities.

1. Marriage laws should be made more stringent in order to encourage individuals to take this major decision more seriously. Presently it is easier in most states to obtain a marriage license than a license to drive a car.

2. No-fault divorce laws should be developed while still providing for adequate support for children. California and Florida have already taken constructive steps in this direction.

3. Premarital, marital, and divorce counseling should be offered to all individuals regardless of their ability to pay.

4. Tax laws should be changed so as not to unduly discriminate against any particular life style.

5. Sex laws which prohibit any form of sexual behavior between consenting individuals should be changed to allow for individual freedom and development.

In conclusion, it seems we cannot predict what will happen to the traditional family form in the future, its prevalence, dominance and influence. We do know, however, that in a pluralistic society varied forms will continue to exist. These emerging styles have been both responsive to societal change and the cause of change. While some may feel that these attempts at change are the cause of society's problems, these behaviors might more appropriately be seen as a solution to problems in marriage and also in society. As Otto stated in his book *The Family in Search of a Future.*[3]

"What will destroy us is not change, but our inability to change—both as individuals and as a social system. It is only by welcoming innovation, experimentation and change that a society based on man's capacity to love man can come into being."

NOTES

1. Cogswell, Betty E. and Sussman, Marvin B. Changing Family and Marriage Forms: "Complications for Human Service Systems," *The Family Coordinator,* Vol. 21, No. 4, October 1972, p. 507.

2. Olsen, David, "Marriage of the Future: Revolutionary or Evolutionary Change?" *The Family Coordinator,* Vol. 21, No. 4, October 1972, pp. 391-392.

3. Otto, Herbert, *The Family in Search of a Future,* New York: Appleton Century & Crofts, 1972, p. 9.

Appendix I

A REPORT OF INITIAL RIP OFF DATA
Dennis Hinkle and Michael J. Sporakowski

The following summaries of Rip Off data are presented here to aid the teacher and student using these materials see what others who have used this text have answered. We hope that additional data can be gathered in this manner and appended to future editions or printings to make these questionnaires more useful in the classroom.

The data report responses of approximately 275 persons. In many cases the "N" is somewhat or considerably lower since not all people answered all questions. As is often typical of questionnaires, part responses may yield less than the whole. In one instance we had 252 persons say they were female and 21 say male. We assume that the two who didn't respond, did not respond by oversight rather than lack of knowledge.

The data are presented in a manner which characterizes responses by sex of the respondent. #'s in ( ) = % of males or females who responded in that manner. %'s are rounded to nearest whole #.

RIP OFF #1

	Males	Females
Curriculum		
Family Development	1 (7)	104 (49)
Home Economics	1 (7)	18 (9)
Behavioral Sciences	7 (47)	31 (15)
Natural Sciences	4 (27)	8 (4)
Arts	0 (0)	18 (9)
Engineering	1 (7)	0 (0)
Education	1 (7)	32 (15)
Academic Standing		
Freshmen	0 (0)	5 (2)
Sophomores	6 (29)	106 (43)
Juniors	6 (29)	96 (39)
Seniors	9 (43)	40 (16)
Age		
18, 19	4 (20)	86 (34)
20, 21	14 (70)	148 (60)
22, 23	2 (10)	14 (6)
Race		
Black	1 (5)	1 (0)
White	19 (95)	245 (100)
Religious Member		
Yes	19 (95)	245 (100)
No	1 (1)	1 (0)

	Males	Females
Religious Affiliation		
Protestant	15 (83)	161 (67)
Catholic	3 (17)	56 (23)
Jewish	0 (0)	0 (0)
Other	0 (0)	25 (10)
Church Attendance		
Never	3 (14)	31 (12)
Less than monthly	9 (43)	104 (42)
Once or twice a month	5 (24)	31 (12)
Three or four times a month	2 (10)	40 (16)
At least once a week	2 (10)	44 (18)
Age at first date		
12 or under	2 (10)	6 (2)
13, 14	6 (29)	87 (35)
15, 16	12 (57)	134 (53)
17, 18	1 (5)	25 (10)
Age dating regularly		
12 or under	0 (0)	1 (0)
13, 14	2 (10)	24 (10)
15, 16	11 (53)	144 (58)
17 or above	8 (38)	78 (32)
Number of people dated		
Less than 10	5 (24)	58 (23)
10-20	7 (33)	110 (44)
21-40	8 (38)	64 (25)
More than 40	1 (5)	20 (8)
Proportion time gone steady		
Never	1 (5)	35 (14)
Less than 1/4	5 (24)	77 (31)
1/4-1/2	7 (33)	80 (32)
Over 1/2	8 (38)	60 (24)
Home		
Country	3 (14)	28 (11)
Small town	6 (29)	72 (29)
City	12 (57)	151 (60)
Sexual Attitudes		
Very liberal	4 (19)	28 (11)
Somewhat liberal	9 (43)	104 (41)
Moderate	6 (27)	70 (28)
Somewhat conservative	2 (10)	42 (17)
Very conservative	0 (0)	8 (3)
Marital Status		
Single	9 (45)	134 (54)
Going Steady	3 (15)	60 (24)
Engaged	4 (20)	41 (16)
Married	4 (20)	15 (6)
Parents' Marital Status		
Married	15 (75)	222 (89)
Divorced or separated	3 (15)	15 (6)
Widow (ed)	1 (5)	7 (3)
Remarried	1 (5)	6 (2)
Parents' Marital Happiness		
Very happy	3 (16)	98 (40)
More than average	6 (32)	56 (23)

	Males	Females
Parent's Marital Happiness		
Average	7 (37)	69 (28)
Less than average	2 (11)	17 (7)
Very unhappy	1 (5)	6 (2)

RIP OFF #2

	Males	Females
All persons should be encouraged to marry		
Yes	3 (14)	21 (9)
No	18 (86)	218 (91)

RIP OFF #3

	Males	Females
1. "Which sex?"		
1. Male	1 (5)	7 (3)
Female	1 (5)	79 (32)
No difference	18 (90)	163 (67)
2. M	1 (5)	7 (3)
F	11 (52)	135 (54)
ND	9 (43)	110 (44)
3. M	8 (38)	145 (59)
F	1 (5)	2 (1)
ND	12 (57)	101 (41)
4. M	3 (14)	45 (18)
F	6 (29)	11 (4)
ND	12 (57)	195 (78)
5. M	9 (43)	94 (38)
F	0 (0)	14 (6)
ND	12 (57)	143 (57)
6. M	0 (0)	3 (1)
F	16 (76)	202 (81)
ND	5 (24)	46 (18)
7. M	0 (0)	3 (1)
F	12 (57)	145 (58)
ND	9 (43)	104 (41)
8. M	10 (48)	99 (40)
F	0 (0)	17 (7)
ND	11 (52)	132 (53)
9. M	0 (0)	3 (1)
F	10 (48)	150 (60)
ND	11 (52)	90 (39)
10. M	1 (5)	6 (2)
F	11 (52)	123 (49)
ND	9 (43)	123 (49)
11. M	8 (38)	58 (23)
F	1 (5)	20 (8)
ND	12 (57)	172 (69)
12. M	3 (14)	39 (16)
F	0 (0)	1 (0)
ND	18 (86)	209 (84)
13. M	8 (40)	66 (26)
F	2 (10)	14 (6)
ND	10 (50)	170 (68)
14. M	1 (5)	3 (1)
F	7 (33)	92 (37)
ND	13 (62)	153 (62)

		Males	Females
15.	M	5 (24)	19 (8)
	F	5 (24)	52 (21)
	ND	11 (52)	181 (72)
16.	M	15 (71)	167 (67)
	F	1 (5)	6 (2)
	ND	5 (24)	75 (30)
17.	M	2 (10)	16 (6)
	F	12 (60)	146 (58)
	ND	6 (30)	88 (35)
18.	M	6 (32)	49 (21)
	F	3 (16)	13 (6)
	ND	10 (53)	169 (73)
19.	M	2 (10)	3 (1)
	F	4 (19)	68 (27)
	ND	15 (71)	178 (72)
20.	M	4 (19)	45 (18)
	F	2 (10)	4 (2)
	ND	15 (72)	198 (80)

5. "I have found that . . ."

		Males	Females
1.	Yes	5 (24)	93 (39)
	No	16 (76)	148 (61)
2.	Yes	6 (32)	79 (32)
	No	13 (68)	164 (68)
3.	Yes	1 (5)	77 (33)
	No	20 (95)	158 (67)
4.	Yes	2 (10)	21 (9)
	No	18 (90)	224 (91)
5.	Yes	16 (80)	229 (95)
	No	4 (20)	12 (5)
6.	Yes	9 (45)	13 (5)
	No	11 (55)	227 (95)

RIP OFF #4

	SA	MA	U	MD	SD

1. When you are really in love, you just aren't interested in anyone else.

	SA	MA	U	MD	SD
Males	3 / 14.3	6 / 28.6	1 / 4.8	5 / 23.8	6 / 28.6
Females	55 / 21.8	61 / 24.2	20 / 7.9	76 / 30.2	40 / 15.9

2. Love doesn't make sense. It just is.

	SA	MA	U	MD	SD
Males	1 / 5.0	3 / 15.0	1 / 5.0	2 / 10.0	13 / 65.0
Females	11 / 4.4	40 / 16.0	44 / 17.6	67 / 26.8	88 / 35.2

3. When you fall head-over-heals-in-love, it's sure to be the real thing.

	SA	MA	U	MD	SD
Males	0 / 0	0 / 0	3 / 15.0	3 / 15.0	14 / 70.0
Females	3 / 1.2	8 / 3.2	32 / 12.6	82 / 32.4	128 / 50.6

4. Love isn't anything you can really study: it is too highly emotional to be subject to scientific observation.

	SA	MA	U	MD	SD
Males	2 / 9.5	7 / 33.3	4 / 19.0	5 / 23.8	3 / 14.3

	SA	MA	U	MD	SD
Females	40	68	57	49	33
	16.2	27.5	23.1	19.8	13.4

5. To be in love with someone without marriage is a tragedy.

	SA	MA	U	MD	SD
Males	0	1	1	5	14
	0	4.8	4.8	23.8	66.7
Females	3	14	24	57	155
	1.2	5.5	9.5	22.5	61.3

6. When love hits, you know it.

	SA	MA	U	MD	SD
Males	1	7	4	6	3
	4.8	33.3	19.0	28.6	14.3
Females	38	75	54	65	18
	15.2	30.0	21.6	25.0	7.2

7. Common interests are really unimportant; as long as each of you is truly in love you will adjust.

	SA	MA	U	MD	SD
Males	0	2	2	12	5
	0	9.5	9.5	57.1	23.8
Females	3	15	9	73	152
	1.2	6.0	3.6	29.0	60.3

8. It doesn't matter if you marry after you have known your partner for only a short time as long as you know you are in love.

	SA	MA	U	MD	SD
Males	0	2	2	9	8
	0	9.5	9.5	42.9	38.1
Females	9	27	26	89	100
	3.6	10.8	10.4	35.5	39.8

9. As long as two people love each other, the religious differences they have really do not matter.

	SA	MA	U	MD	SD
Males	3	4	2	7	5
	14.3	19.0	9.5	33.3	23.8
Females	21	44	43	87	57
	8.3	17.5	17.1	34.5	22.6

10. You can love someone even though you do not like any of that person's friends.

	SA	MA	U	MD	SD
Males	5	9	2	3	2
	23.8	42.9	9.5	14.3	9.5
Females	25	73	42	83	29
	9.9	29.0	16.7	32.9	11.5

11. When you are in love, you are usually in a daze.

	SA	MA	U	MD	SD
Males	0	2	2	7	10
	0	9.5	9.5	33.3	47.6
Females	4	20	14	84	128
	1.6	8.0	5.6	33.6	51.2

12. Love at first sight is often the deepest and most enduring type of love.

	SA	MA	U	MD	SD
Males	0	0	3	5	13
	0	0	14.3	23.8	61.9
Females	2	6	40	72	132
	0.8	2.4	15.9	28.6	52.4

13. Usually there are only one or two people in the world whom you could really love and could really be happy with.

	SA	MA	U	MD	SD
Males	0	1	1	8	11
	0	4.8	4.8	38.1	52.4
Females	6	14	38	78	118
	2.4	5.5	15.0	30.7	46.5

	SA	MA	U	MD	SD

14. Regardless of other factors, if you truly love another person, that is enough to marry that person.

Males	0	6	3	4	8
	0	28.6	14.3	19.0	38.1
Females	3	17	25	89	117
	1.2	6.8	10.0	35.5	46.6

15. It is necessary to be in love with the one you marry to be happy.

Males	10	3	2	3	3
	47.6	14.3	9.5	14.3	14.3
Females	90	69	36	47	8
	36.0	27.6	14.4	18.8	3.2

16. When you are separated from the love partner, the rest of the world seems dull and unsatisfying.

Males	3	4	1	8	5
	14.3	19.0	4.8	38.1	23.8
Females	23	62	37	84	46
	9.1	24.6	14.7	33.3	18.3

17. Parents should not advise their children whom to date; they have forgotten what it is like to be in love.

Males	1	4	4	8	4
	4.8	19.0	19.0	38.1	19.0
Females	13	35	43	106	52
	5.2	14.1	17.3	42.6	20.9

18. Love is regarded as a primary motive for marriage, which is good.

Males	6	9	2	2	2
	28.6	42.9	9.5	9.5	9.5
Females	56	91	38	48	18
	22.3	36.3	15.1	19.1	7.2

19. When you love a person, you think of marrying that person.

Males	5	6	3	6	1
	23.8	28.6	14.3	28.6	4.8
Females	53	124	25	38	12
	21.0	49.2	9.9	15.1	4.8

20. Somewhere there is an ideal mate for most people. The problem is just finding that one.

Males	6	3	5	3	4
	28.6	14.3	23.8	14.3	19.0
Females	49	84	48	39	34
	19.3	33.1	18.9	15.4	13.4

21. Jealousy usually varies directly with love; that is, the more in love you are, the greater the tendency for you to become jealous.

Males	1	3	1	6	10
	4.8	14.3	4.8	28.6	47.6
Females	12	33	25	78	105
	4.7	13.0	9.9	30.8	41.5

22. Love is best described as an exciting thing rather than a calm thing.

Males	6	8	1	5	1
	28.6	38.1	4.8	23.8	4.8
Females	50	94	42	49	16
	19.9	37.5	16.7	19.5	6.4

23. There are probably only a few people that any one person can fall in love with.

Males	0	5	3	9	4
	0	23.8	14.3	42.9	19.0
Females	14	28	49	94	68
	5.5	11.1	19.4	37.2	26.9

	SA	MA	U	MD	SD
24. When you are in love, your judgment is usually not too clear.					
Males	1 4.8	6 28.6	1 4.8	7 33.3	6 28.6
Females	15 6.0	33 13.2	21 8.4	88 35.2	93 37.2
25. Love often comes but once in a lifetime.					
Males	1 4.8	2 9.5	3 14.3	8 38.1	7 33.3
Females	5 2.0	23 9.2	25 10.0	97 38.6	101 40.2
26. You can't make yourself love someone; it just comes or it doesn't.					
Males	7 33.3	8 38.1	2 9.5	2 9.5	2 9.5
Females	60 24.0	70 28.0	46 18.4	56 22.4	18 7.2
27. Differences in social class and religion are of small importance in selecting a marriage partner as compared with love.					
Males	3 14.3	7 33.3	1 4.8	4 19.0	6 28.6
Females	18 7.1	33 13.1	29 11.5	102 40.5	70 27.8
28. Day dreaming usually comes along with being in love.					
Males	0 0	8 38.1	4 19.0	2 9.5	7 33.3
Females	22 8.8	83 33.1	40 15.9	51 20.3	55 21.9
29. When you are in love, you don't have to ask yourself a bunch of questions about love; you will just know that you are in love.					
Males	2 9.5	5 23.8	4 19.0	5 23.8	5 23.8
Females	23 9.1	56 22.2	44 17.5	73 29.0	56 22.2

*Norms** for Attitudes Towards Love Scale previously published (Knox, D.H. and M.J. Sporakowski: "Attitudes of College Students Toward Love." *Journal of Marriage and the Family*, 30 (4), Nov. 1968, 638-642).

Males	Mean ($\overline{x}$) 94.45	S.D. 13.86
Females	Mean ($\overline{x}$) 98.86	S.D. 13.81
Engaged (all)	$\overline{x}$ = 101.07	S.D. = 16.00
Not engaged (all)	$\overline{x}$ = 93.24	S.D. = 13.18
Freshmen (all)	$\overline{x}$ = 88.25	S.D. = 14.03
Sophomores (all)	$\overline{x}$ = 93.89	S.D. = 11.94
Juniors (all)	$\overline{x}$ = 97.35	S.D. = 14.67
Seniors (all)	$\overline{x}$ = 99.55	S.D. = 13.29

*The lower the score the "more romantic" the responses.

RIP OFF #5

		Males	Females
1.	T	11 (52)	92 (37)
	F	10 (48)	157 (63)
2.	T	11 (52)	139 (57)
	F	10 (48)	107 (43)

		Males	Females
3.	T	3 (15)	81 (33)
	F	17 (85)	165 (67)
4.	T	7 (33)	136 (55)
	F	14 (67)	110 (45)
5.	T	1 (5)	24 (10)
	F	20 (95)	226 (90)
6.	T	0 (0)	14 (5)
	F	21 (100)	234 (95)
7.	T	19 (100)	250 (100)
	F	0 (0)	0 (0)
8.	T	8 (38)	117 (48)
	F	13 (62)	126 (52)
9.	T	7 (35)	81 (37)
	F	13 (65)	138 (63)
10.	T	13 (65)	132 (54)
	F	7 (35)	112 (46)
11.	T	7 (33)	132 (53)
	F	14 (67)	119 (47)

RIP OFF #6

		Males	Females
1.	Yes	10 (48)	135 (55)
	No	11 (52)	112 (45)
2.	More	16 (76)	220 (89)
	Less	2 (10)	7 (3)
	Same	3 (14)	20 (8)
3.	Yes	11 (58)	162 (68)
	No	8 (42)	77 (32)
4.	Yes	14 (67)	188 (77)
	No	7 (33)	57 (23)
5.	Yes	5 (25)	17 (7)
	No	15 (75)	228 (93)
6.	Type 1		
	0-1	21 (100)	249 (98)
	2 or more	0 (0)	5 (2)
	Type 2		
	0-1	20 (95)	237 (93)
	2 or more	1 (5)	17 (7)
	Type 3		
	0-1	21 (100)	251 (99)
	2 or more	0 (0)	3 (1)
	Type 4		
	0	6 (29)	179 (71)
	1,2	10 (48)	60 (24)
	3-6	5 (23)	13 (4)
	9	0 (0)	2 (1)

RIP OFF #7

		Males	Females
2 (a)	Yes	5 (28)	13 (72)
	No	83 (36)	149 (64)

	Males	Females
Choice 1	Communications	Communications
Choice 2	Doing things together	Affection
Choice 3	Money	Doing things together
Choice 10	Recreation	Recreation
Choice 11	Spouse's jobs	In-laws
Choice 12	Conventionality	Conventionality

1 = most important   12 = least important

Only the three highest and three lowest are reported at this time. Too much overlap occurred in categories 4-9.

5. "Experience parenthood crisis"

	Males	Females
Mothers	18 (95)	203 (97)
Fathers	1 (5)	7 (3)

RIP OFF #9

		Males	Females
1.	1. T	1 (6)	7 (3)
	F	16 (94)	217 (97)
	2. T	1 (6)	28 (13)
	F	15 (94)	189 (87)
	3. T	5 (30)	20 (9)
	F	12 (70)	200 (91)
	4. T	3 (18)	1 (0)
	F	14 (82)	222 (100)
	5. T	2 (12)	5 (2)
	F	15 (88)	218 (98)
	6. T	2 (12)	21 (9)
	F	15 (88)	202 (91)
	7. T	1 (6)	22 (10)
	F	15 (94)	193 (90)
	8. T	0 (0)	4 (2)
	F	17 (100)	220 (98)
	9. T	0 (0)	0 (0)
	F	17 (100)	224 (100)
	10. T	1 (6)	24 (11)
	F	16 (94)	192 (89)
	11. T	4 (24)	17 (8)
	F	13 (76)	203 (92)
	12. T	6 (40)	66 (31)
	F	9 (60)	146 (69)
	13. T	3 (18)	18 (8)
	F	14 (82)	201 (92)
	14. T	4 (25)	74 (35)
	F	12 (75)	136 (65)
	15. T	7 (41)	109 (50)
	F	10 (59)	108 (50)
2 (a)	less	1 (6)	17 (8)
	more	8 (50)	50 (22)
	same	7 (44)	157 (70)
2 (c)	yes	6 (35)	119 (54)
	no	11 (65)	102 (46)
	both	2 (33)	25 (20)
	mom only	3 (50)	95 (77)
	dad only	1 (17)	4 (3)

		Males	Females
Communicate freely?			
yes		8 (47)	68 (52)
no		9 (53)	145 (68)

RIP OFF #10

		Males	Females
1.	T	0 (0)	12 (6)
	F	16 (100)	202 (94)
2.	T	5 (29)	138 (64)
	F	12 (71)	79 (36)
3.	T	15 (83)	163 (75)
	F	3 (17)	53 (25)
4.	T	0 (0)	2 (1)
	F	17 (100)	217 (99)
5.	T	0 (0)	1 (0)
	F	17 (100)	217 (100)
6.	T	5 (31)	61 (29)
	F	11 (69)	151 (71)
7.	T	11 (65)	92 (43)
	F	6 (35)	123 (57)
8.	T	3 (20)	80 (37)
	F	12 (80)	138 (63)
9.	T	1 (6)	27 (13)
	F	16 (94)	187 (87)
10.	T	7 (44)	49 (23)
	F	9 (56)	164 (77)

RIP OFF #11

			Males	Females
1.	1.	T	0 (0)	12 (6)
		F	16 (100)	208 (94)
	2.	T	0 (0)	14 (6)
		F	17 (100)	204 (94)
	3.	T	14 (82)	193 (90)
		F	3 (18)	21 (10)
	4.	T	1 (6)	15 (7)
		F	16 (94)	200 (93)
	5.	T	8 (50)	92 (48)
		F	8 (50)	99 (52)
	6.	T	1 (7)	5 (2)
		F	14 (93)	214 (98)
	7.	T	8 (62)	103 (54)
		F	5 (38)	89 (46)
	8.	T	11 (73)	164 (76)
		F	4 (27)	52 (24)
	4 (a)	yes	16 (94)	190 (94)
		no	1 (6)	13 (6)
	5 (a)	Very well	7 (41)	68 (32)
		About average	10 (59)	134 (62)
		Poorly	0 (0)	13 (6)

RIP OFF #12

			Males	Females
1.	1.	T	2 (12)	2 (1)
		F	15 (88)	216 (99)
	2.	T	0 (0)	8 (4)
		F	17 (100)	209 (96)
	3.	T	6 (35)	44 (20)
		F	11 (65)	172 (80)
	4.	T	7 (39)	86 (41)
		F	11 (61)	126 (59)
	5.	T	9 (53)	147 (67)
		F	8 (47)	71 (33)
	6.	T	7 (39)	57 (27)
		F	11 (61)	156 (73)
	7.	T	16 (94)	206 (95)
		F	1 (6)	11 (5)
	8.	T	0 (0)	8 (4)
		F	17 (100)	202 (96)
	9.	T	8 (44)	76 (35)
		F	10 (56)	139 (65)
	10.	T	6 (40)	60 (30)
		F	9 (60)	139 (70)
3 (a)		Very well	6 (33)	73 (34)
		About average	9 (50)	127 (59)
		Poorly	3 (17)	16 (7)
3 (b)		Outstanding	7 (44)	115 (54)
		Average	9 (56)	100 (46)
		Poor	0 (0)	1 (0)
4 (a)		None	4 (19)	52 (21)
		1-3	15 (72)	159 (64)
		4 or more	2 (10)	38 (15)
(b)		0	5 (24)	64 (25)
		1-3	16 (76)	187 (74)
		4 or more	0 (0)	3 (1)
(c)		0	9 (43)	68 (27)
		1-3	12 (57)	185 (73)
		4 or more	0 (0)	1 (0)
4 (d)		boy	9 (53)	130 (66)
		girl	3 (18)	26 (13)
		makes no difference	5 (29)	42 (21)
(e)		yes	15 (94)	188 (96)
		no	1 (6)	8 (4)

RIP OFF #13

			Males	Females
1.	1.	T	13 (87)	204 (97)
		F	2 (13)	6 (3)
	2.	T	0 (0)	4 (2)
		F	16 (100)	207 (98)
	3.	T	1 (6)	5 (2)
		F	15 (94)	206 (98)
	4.	T	3 (19)	35 (17)
		F	13 (81)	175 (83)
	5.	T	15 (94)	204 (98)
		F	1 (6)	5 (2)

		Males	Females
		Males	**Females**
6.	T	2 (13)	8 (4)
	F	14 (87)	203 (96)
7.	T	1 (6)	2 (1)
	F	15 (94)	207 (99)
8.	T	0 (0)	1 (0)
	F	16 (100)	210 (100)
9.	T	10 (63)	161 (77)
	F	6 (37)	48 (23)
10.	T	3 (19)	53 (26)
	F	13 (81)	154 (74)
11.	T	0 (0)	4 (2)
	F	16 (100)	204 (98)
12.	T	8 (50)	94 (47)
	F	8 (50)	108 (53)
13.	T	8 (50)	94 (47)
	F	8 (50)	108 (53)
14.	T	0 (0)	10 (5)
	F	16 (100)	200 (95)
15.	T	6 (40)	119 (57)
	F	9 (60)	89 (43)
16.	T	10 (71)	163 (78)
	F	4 (29)	45 (22)
17.	T	3 (21)	24 (12)
	F	11 (79)	179 (88)
18.	T	3 (20)	17 (8)
	F	12 (80)	191 (92)
19.	T	0 (0)	7 (3)
	F	16 (100)	200 (97)
20.	T	3 (30)	27 (18)
	F	7 (70)	122 (82)
21.	T	16 (100)	198 (96)
	F	0 (0)	9 (4)
22.	T	13 (81)	180 (88)
	F	3 (19)	24 (12)
23.	T	7 (44)	93 (44)
	F	9 (56)	117 (56)
24.	T	2 (13)	9 (4)
	F	14 (87)	201 (96)
25.	T	0 (0)	1 (0)
	F	16 (100)	207 (100)
26.	T	1 (6)	5 (2)
	F	15 (94)	200 (98)
27.	T	5 (31)	31 (15)
	F	11 (69)	176 (85)
28.	T	1 (6)	4 (2)
	F	15 (94)	205 (98)
29.	T	3 (19)	15 (7)
	F	13 (81)	192 (93)

RIP OFF #14

			Males	Females
1.	1.	T	13 (81)	164 (79)
		F	3 (19)	43 (21)
	2.	T	14 (88)	158 (79)
		F	2 (12)	42 (21)

			Males	Females
	3.	T	0 (0)	1 (0)
		F	16 (100)	207 (100)
	4.	T	0 (0)	14 (7)
		F	16 (100)	192 (93)
	5.	T	1 (7)	14 (7)
		F	14 (93)	189 (93)
4.	1.	T	1 (7)	4 (2)
		F	15 (93)	204 (98)
	2.	T	10 (71)	80 (40)
		F	4 (29)	119 (60)
	3.	T	4 (31)	64 (34)
		F	9 (69)	126 (66)
	4.	T	0 (0)	9 (4)
		F	15 (100)	196 (96)
5.	1.	T	14 (93)	175 (87)
		F	1 (7)	27 (13)
	2.	T	4 (29)	48 (24)
		F	10 (71)	151 (76)
	3.	T	2 (13)	7 (4)
		F	14 (87)	188 (96)
	4.	T	8 (57)	116 (65)
		F	6 (43)	62 (35)
	5.	T	11 (69)	149 (76)
		F	5 (31)	48 (24)

RIP OFF #15

		Males	Females
2.	Transportation		
	1	0 (0)	1 (1)
	2	1 (6)	21 (13)
	3	4 (25)	62 (38)
	4	8 (50)	39 (24)
	5	3 (19)	42 (26)
	Food		
	1	6 (38)	41 (25)
	2	9 (56)	107 (64)
	3	0 (0)	14 (8)
	4	0 (0)	5 (3)
	5	1 (6)	0 (0)
	Medical Care		
	1	0 (0)	2 (1)
	2	1 (6)	9 (5)
	3	3 (19)	23 (14)
	4	5 (31)	58 (35)
	5	7 (44)	75 (45)
	Housing		
	1	10 (63)	121 (72)
	2	2 (13)	28 (17)
	3	3 (19)	8 (5)
	4	0 (0)	3 (2)
	5	1 (6)	8 (5)
	Clothing		
	1	0 (0)	3 (2)
	2	3 (19)	6 (4)
	3	6 (38)	56 (33)
	4	3 (19)	63 (38)
	5	4 (25)	40 (24)

257

			Males	Females
3.	1.	Savings		
		1 = Term	2 (15)	19 (15)
		2 = Endowment* correct	7 (54)	69 (56)
		3 = Straight life	4 (31)	35 (28)
	2.	Savings and Protection		
		1	4 (31)	54 (43)
		2	4 (31)	38 (30)
		3* correct	5 (38)	34 (27)
	3.	Protection		
		1* correct	7 (54)	51 (41)
		2	2 (15)	18 (14)
		3	4 (31)	57 (45)
5.	a.	yes	5 (33)	43 (26)
		no	10 (67)	123 (74)
	b.	1	2 (40)	25 (54)
		2, 3	2 (40)	14 (30)
		4 or more	1 (20)	7 (15)
7.		less than $10,000	2 (15)	20 (15)
		$10,000-30,000	6 (46)	52 (38)
		more than $30,000	5 (39)	63 (47)
8.	1.	T interest rates	2 (14)	43 (29)
		F	12 (86)	109 (71)
	2.	T manage resources	2 (13)	32 (20)
		F	14 (87)	126 (80)
	3.	T key to management	13 (87)	142 (92)
		F	2 (13)	12 (8)
	4.	T financial conflict	7 (47)	61 (40)
		F	8 (53)	90 (60)
	5.	T personality needs	11 (85)	137 (89)
		F	2 (15)	17 (11)